Intellectual Property and Media Law Companion

For Rosa, Isaac, Matthew, Joseph and Inigo. χάρις ὑμῖν καὶ εἰρήνη.

In memory of my parents. αιωνία η μνήμη.

Ed

For my Mum and Dad

and

my brother Ste

and

my children, Tom and Matty.

Alasdair

Thank you to my wife, Sarah, for her unerring faith in me.

Thank you to my co-authors, particularly Ed for taking this over the line.

Jeffrey

Intellectual Property and Media Law Companion

Ed Baden-Powell

BA (Hons), MA (Oxon), Solicitor

Alasdair Bleakley

Bsc (Hons), Solicitor

Jeffrey Eneberi

Bsc (Hons), MBA, Solicitor

Fourth edition (2010)

Foreword to the *Companion* series
The Right Honourable Lord Woolf
former Lord Chief Justice

Preface to this *Companion*
Paddy Grafton Green
Senior Partner, Michael Simkins LLP

Advisory Editors
Gerald Montagu and Mark Weston

Bloomsbury Professional

Fourth edition first published in Great Britain 2010 by

Bloomsbury Professional
Maxwelton House
41-43 Boltro Road
Haywards Heath
West Sussex
RH16 1BJ

Tel: 01444 416 119

This publication is sold with the understanding that neither the publisher, nor the authors, nor the advisory editors are engaged in rendering legal, accounting or other professional services. If legal advice is required, the services of a competent professional person should be sought.

Third edition (1999) published by Blackstone Press Limited
Second edition (1998) published by Blackstone Press Limited
First edition (1997) published by Central Law Training Limited

British Library Cataloguing in Publication Data
Baden-Powell, Ed
Bleakley, Alasdair
Eneberi, Jeffrey
Intellectual Property and Media Law Companion 2010
1 Law – Great Britain   2 Law and legislation – Great Britain
1 Title   II Baden-Powell, Ed
346.4108 21

Library of Congress Cataloguing in Publication Data
Data available

ISBN 978 1 84766 042 8

Typeset (other than the index and tables) by Ed Baden-Powell
Index and tables typeset by Phoenix Photosetting, Chatham, Kent

Printed and bound in Great Britain by CPI Anthony Rowe, Chippenham, Wiltshire

Preface

Intellectual property has never been more significant.

It underpins not only our creative and technical industries but increasingly business at large. Companies and consumers alike have come to appreciate the premium value of content, brands and ideas. These are central to the media industries, which are undergoing radical change with the emergence and continuing evolution of digital platforms. Understanding what is protected from unauthorised use (and what is not) is critical.

So it has never been more important – whether for senior executives, junior staff, legal practitioners or those who are new to the creative and technical industries – to get a clear grasp of the basic legal principles. These form the basis of the commercial practices not only within this sector but more generally within the commercial market, especially where intellectual property is the actual asset that is traded or generates the value of the business.

The word 'intellectual' can be off-putting: it can suggest that intellectual property is a difficult topic. And in many ways it is – but this companion does an admirable job in keeping things simple. By explaining the building blocks in the first chapter, it puts the media industries in sharp focus in the remaining chapters and is invaluable in understanding the wider picture.

Despite many years working in the media industries, I find it is a constant challenge keeping on top of legal, technical and commercial developments, especially with the rapid changes in technology. There is an ever-growing plethora of online resources, but it is still as hard as ever to find a single, concise and understandable overview.

In the words of that well-known song, we all need a bridge over troubled water. And this book provides exactly that.

Paddy Grafton Green

Senior Partner, Michael Simkins LLP

Foreword to the *Companions*

I am wholly in favour of the *Companions*. Legal text books are not often to the fore when it comes to presenting legal information in an attractive, readily understandable and digestible form. However, this is exactly what the *Companion* series achieves. The law is becoming ever more complex, and there is undoubtedly a need to find new methods of communicating it to those who need to know, whether they be members of the public, law students, practitioners or for that matter judges. They will all find that it is a great advantage to have access to a *Companion*.

This is why the first volume in the series, the *Legal Practice Companion* ('**LPC**') has proved to be a success. It is now in its fifteenth edition, having been first published in 1995. The *Intellectual Property and Media Law Companion* is a worthy successor to the first volume, *LPC*.

Some of the subjects which are now dealt with by the *Companions* are not ones with which I am particularly familiar, and so I was able to find out for myself in practice whether they work. I can assure the potential reader that they do work as far as I am concerned, and that they are very user-friendly. The very clear method of presentation both provides an overview of the subject and a step-by-step guide. I feel confident that they will translate well to multimedia formats since their present style will be very familiar to regular users of information technology.

My enthusiasm for the *Companion* series is in part because they complement the reforms which I recommended for civil procedure and which I hope will make our Civil Justice System an appropriate one for this 21st century. I am very conscious that a weakness of the reforms is that in general they were confined to procedural law and left substantive law intact and in a state which means that in the majority of areas it is impenetrable to those to whom it is unfamiliar. This creates a real impediment to access to justice. The virtue of the *Companions* is that they provide a clear path through what is so often a jungle. While the *Companions* will usually provide all that the reader requires, when this is not the case, they will be a solid base from which to embark on a more detailed investigation of the tangled undergrowth of the law.

LPC was the start, and the other *Companions* followed. They have deserved to achieve the success that they have done, and I believe that they will continue to succeed in meeting that need. I congratulate the team on their initiative and on what they are achieving, and I look forward to the continued growth of the *Companion* series.

The Right Honourable Lord Woolf

former *Lord Chief Justice*

Introduction

Welcome to the *Intellectual Property and Media Law Companion*!

Intellectual property ('***IP***') is widely misunderstood – not just by the general public, but even by legal practitioners and media executives. IP can seem impenetrable at first, with its inescapable jargon and involved processes.

In this book we aim to sever that Gordian knot. It provides a guide to English law and practice in this area, and refers to certain aspects of international practice where relevant to UK industries. It sets out the context, general 'feel' and basic concepts.

It is intended to provide a basic overview for a legal practitioner, trainee or student, as well as for a non-lawyer who has some background knowledge but would like some help in understanding this area of law and practice.

For legal practitioners, it is intended to aid detailed research using primary sources, before more considered advice is given based on that research.

The book is not comprehensive – there are numerous specialist works on particular topics that serve that purpose. The demands of converting complex material into digestible points have forced us to focus on the points that strike us as generally most relevant.

Meeting the needs of practitioners, trainees, students and non-lawyers has required an original approach. This book is based on the format which has already proven so successful in the *Legal Practice Companion*.

In this book:

1.   Legal principles are set out clearly, and related practice areas are linked.

2.   Procedures are broken down into steps or flowcharts, so that they can be followed easily.

3.   Any significant new changes and developments are flagged up.

We hope that this book will become a valued tool – a trusty companion for the legal practitioner, trainee or student and non-lawyer alike – all of whom will, we hope, keep a copy within close reach.

About the authors

Ed Baden-Powell

Ed Baden-Powell is a partner at Michael Simkins LLP, specialising in intellectual property and commercial contracts. He acts for a number of leading rights-owners, sports bodies and entertainers, and advises on a broad range of contracts within the media and sports industries, including live events, acquisitions and joint ventures. Ed was formerly part of the award-winning band D-Influence, which recorded four albums and toured worldwide. As co-founder of his own production company, Ed has produced several international hits.

Alasdair Bleakley

Alasdair Bleakley is a senior solicitor at Addleshaw Goddard LLP, advising on intellectual property and commercial law. He acts for a wide range of clients in the retail, brands and financial services sectors. Alasdair has co-written each of the editions of the Intellectual Property and Media Law Companion. He is also published in the national press, Trade Mark World and Copyright World.

Jeffrey Eneberi

Jeffrey Eneberi is currently Senior Legal Counsel with one of the largest energy companies in the world. With his initial training in the City, he specialises in IP and has built up particular expertise in the renewable energy sector and also transactions in the Far East, namely, China and Japan. With a degree in Genetics and an MBA from London Business School, he has developed a passion for taking complicated matters and translating them into clear, simple messages.

Acknowledgements

First and foremost ...

This book is based on the style and format of the successful *Legal Practice Companion*, written by Gerald Montagu and Mark Weston, both of whom are the advisory editors of this book. We cannot thank them enough for their encouragement and guidance.

Our thanks go to all at Bloomsbury Professional and, in particular, to Sarah Thomas, Caroline Holme, Jane Bradford and Jubriel Hanid.

Behind the scenes ...

Ed is extremely grateful for the invaluable support and patience of his partners and colleagues at Michael Simkins LLP, particularly Paddy Grafton Green, Euan Lawson, Nigel Bennett, Jonathan Blair, Catherine Fehler, Nicola McCormick and Jon Baker for their comments and suggestions. Ed also thanks Rico Calleja for his regular updates on new developments.

Al thanks all those at Addleshaw Goddard LLP who have supported him while contributing to this edition, particularly Tim Carter, Rachel Tregear, Robert Steadman, James Whittaker, Janet Edwards and Kier Dawson. Thanks too to Fran for help when the final deadline loomed.

Jeff thanks his wife, Sarah, for her unerring love and support during this project and his sister, Annie, and his parents for the grounding and the nudge to take this project on.

There are too many others to mention – not least the rest of our long-suffering families, friends and colleagues who had to put up with our extra-curricular labours. Our thanks go out to all of them, and to all others who have commented on this book in its various guises. Needless to say, any mistakes and infelicities that remain are entirely our own.

Last but not least ...

We are very grateful to Marcus Anselm and Kerry Sharp for their contributions to the original versions of this book, without which this edition would never have been published.

The law ...

This book only covers English law. We have tried to reflect changes in the law right up until going to press, although the law is generally stated as at 1 January 2010, except where otherwise indicated.

Ed Baden-Powell, Alasdair Bleakley and Jeffrey Eneberi

London, 7 February 2010

'The idea existed before any of the machinery which made manifest the idea ... The whole difference between construction and creation is exactly this: that a thing constructed can only be loved after it is constructed; but a thing created is loved before it exists ...'

G K Chesterton

Appreciations and Criticisms of the Works of Charles Dickens, 1911

Contents

I Intellectual Property

2 Content Clearance

Ed Baden-Powell

3   Music Industry

Ed Baden-Powell

4   Film and Television

Ed Baden-Powell

5   Marketing

Index

A guide to boxes and conventions

I   Boxes

> **Legal points** and principles

> ➤   Square boxes contain information on a specific area of law or legal principle.

> **Practice points** and principles

> ➤   Round boxes contain information that is useful in practice.

II   Legislative citations

➤   At the time of going to press, certain legislation covered in this book awaits an order from a Minister before it comes into force.

     ◆   This is dependent on the drafting and approval of secondary legislation and/or regulatory codes.

> *Where legislation is not yet in force, this is indicated by putting the whole description in italics.*

III   Bullet conventions

➤   A main point will be made using a first level of bullet (eg: this arrow bullet).

     ◆   A sub-point may then be made about something related to that main point (eg: this diamond bullet is a sub-point to the arrow bullet above).

     ◆   When reading at a 'high level', the sub-points can be ignored without impairing the conceptual integrity of the text at the higher level (ie: in this example, you can read just the arrow bullets for an overview, ignoring the diamond bullets).

➤   It is therefore possible to read the next main point (ie: this arrow bullet), missing out the sub-points in between (ie: the diamond bullets above).

Table of abbreviations

Primary legislation

United Kingdom

A–B

C

CA 2003	Communications Act 2003
CA 2006	Companies Act 2006
CCA	Contempt of Court Act 1981
CDPA	Copyright, Designs and Patents Act 1988
CJIA 2008	Criminal Justice and Immigration Act 2008

D

DA 1996	Defamation Act 1996

E–G

H

HRA	Human Rights Act 1998

I–K

L

LA 2003	Licensing Act 2003

M–N

O

OPA 1959	Obscene Publications Act 1959

P

PA 1977	Patents Act 1977
POA 1986	Public Order Act 1986

Q

R

RDA	Registered Designs Act 1949
RRHA 2006	Racial and Religious Hatred Act 2006

S

SCA 1981	Supreme Court Act 1981

T

TMA	Trade Marks Act 1994

U

V

VRA 1984	Video Recordings Act 1984

W–Z

European Union

A

AVMS Directive	Audio-Visual Media Services Directive (89/552/EC)

B

C

CDR 2002	EC Community Design Regulation (6/2002/EC)
Comparative Advertising Directive	Directive 2006/114/EC
CTMR 09	Regulation 207/09/EC
CTMR 95	Regulation 2868/95/EC

D

Database Directive	Directive 96/9/EC

E

E-commerce Directive

> Directive 2000/31/EC

EU Treaty   Treaty on the Functioning of the European Union

F–H

I

Information Society Directive

> Directive 2001/29/EC

J–Z

International

A–D

E

ECHR   European Convention on Human Rights

EPC   European Patent Convention 1973

F–O

P

PCT   Patent Co-operation Treaty 1970

Q–T

U

UCC   Universal Copyright Convention 1952

V–Z

Table of abbreviations

Secondary legislation, rules and codes

United Kingdom

A

B

BPMMR	Business Protection from Misleading Marketing Regulations 2008

C

CAP Code	British Code of Advertising, Sales Promotion and Direct Marketing
CDR 2005	Community Design Regulations 2005
CEAEBR 2003	Conduct of Employment Agencies and Employment Businesses Regulations 2003
CPR	Civil Procedure Rules 1998
CPUTR	Consumer Protection from Unfair Trading Regulations 2008
CRRR 1996	Copyright and Related Rights Regulations 1996

D

DR(S)R 1989	Design Right (Semiconductor) Regulations 1989

E

ECDR 2007	Electronic Commerce Directive (Racial and Religious Hatred Act 2006) Regulations 2007
ECDR 2010	Electronic Commerce Directive (Hatred against Persons on Religious Grounds or the Grounds of Sexual Orientation) Regulations 2010
ECR	Electronic Commerce (EC Directive) Regulations 2002

F–Q

R

Radio Code	Radio Advertising Standards Code
RDO 2006	Regulatory Reform (Registered Designs) Order 2006
RDR 2001	Registered Design Regulations 2001
RDR 2006	Registered Designs Rules 2006

S

T

TV Code	TV Advertising Standards Code

U

V

VR(L)R	Video Recordings (Labelling) Regulations 1985

W–Z

Table of abbreviations

Territories, countries, courts,
authorities and organisations

A

AIM	Association of Independent Music
ASA	Advertising Standards Authority
ASBOF	Advertising Standards Board of Finance
ATVOD	Association for Television On-Demand

B

BASBOF	Broadcast Advertising Standards Board of Finance
BASCA	British Academy of Songwriters, Composers and Authors
BBC	British Broadcasting Corporation
BBFC	British Board of Film Classification
BCAP	Broadcast Committee of Advertising Practice
BECTU	Broadcasting, Entertainment, Cinematograph and Theatre Union
BPI	British Phonographic Industry

C

CAP	Committee of Advertising Practice

D

DCMS	Department for Culture, Media and Sport
DGGB	Directors Guild of Great Britain
DPP	Director of Public Prosecutions

E

ECJ	European Court of Justice
EEA	European Economic Area
EEUPC	European and EU Patents Court
EPO	European Patent Office
EU	European Union

F

FAC	Featured Artists Coalition
FRAPA	Format Recognition and Protection Association

G

GEMA	*Gesellschaft für musikalische Aufführungs- und mechanische Vervielfältigungsrechte* (German music publishing collecting society)

H

HMRC	HM Revenue & Customs

I

ICO	Information Commissioner's Office
IMCB	Independent Mobile Classification Body
ISFE	Interactive Software Federation of Europe
IWF	Internet Watch Foundation

J–L

M

MCPS	Mechanical-Copyright Protection Society
MMF	Music Managers Forum
MPA	Music Publishers Association
MU	Musicians' Union

N

NICAM	Netherlands Institute for the Classification of Audiovisual Media

O

Ofcom	Office of Communications
OFT	Office of Fair Trading
OHIM	Office for Harmonization in the Internal Market

P

PACT	Producers Alliance for Cinema and Television
PCC	Patents County Court *or* Press Complaints Commission
PG	Production Guild of Great Britain
PMA	Production Managers Association
PPL	Phonographic Performance Limited
PRS	Performing Right Society

Q

R

RACC	Radio Advertising Clearance Centre

S

S4C	Sianel Pedwar Cymru
SACEM	*Société des Auteurs, Compositeurs et Éditeurs de Musique* (French music publishing collecting society)
STIM	*Svenska Tonsättares Internationella Musikbyrå* (Swedish music publishing collecting society)

T

U

UK	United Kingdom
UK IPO	UK Intellectual Property Office
US / USA	United States of America
VPL	Video Performance Limited

V

VSC	Video Standards Council

W

WGGB	Writers' Guild of Great Britain

X–Z

Table of authorities

Cases

PAGE

PAGE

PAGE

M

PAGE

PAGE

S

PAGE

Table of authorities

Legislation: Statutes

Legislation: Statutory Instruments

1 Intellectual Property

This Chapter examines:

A   Copyright

*References in this Section are to the Copyright, Designs and Patents Act 1988 ('**CDPA**'), unless otherwise stated.*

I	Generally
II	Existence, ownership and infringement
III	International considerations
IV	Exploiting copyright
V	Digital Britain

I   Generally

➤ Copyright is a property right that 'subsists' (ie: exists) in certain types of work (*s 1(1)*):

   ◆ literary, dramatic, musical and artistic works, *and*

   ◆ sound recordings, *and*

   ◆ films, *and*

   ◆ broadcasts, *and*

   ◆ typographical arrangements of published editions.

➤ A work attracts copyright protection as soon as it is recorded in some permanent form (*s 3(2)*), eg: in writing or via an electronic medium.

   ◆ NB: there is no formality required in the UK for a copyright work to be protected (eg: there is no need to register the work). The work must, however, meet the criteria for protection examined in this Section.

➤ Copyright protects the **expression** of an idea, not the idea itself (*Football League Ltd v Littlewoods Pools Ltd* [1959] Ch 637).

   ◆ Eg: the author of the novel *The Da Vinci Code* was held not to have infringed copyright despite copying thematic material from a work of non-fiction, *The Holy Blood and The Holy Grail*, as the novel did not reproduce any of the text and no part of the 'theme' of the non-fiction book could be protected by copyright (*Baigent and Leigh v The Random House Group Ltd* [2007] EWCA Civ 247).

➤ Several copyrights can co-exist in creative material. Eg: a song consists of:

   a) copyright in the music itself (ie: a musical work), *and*

   b) copyright in the lyrics (ie: a literary work).

   ◆ If the song is recorded, a further copyright work is created (ie: a sound recording), so each copy of the whole work that is marketed (eg: a CD or download) involves the commercial exploitation of multiple copyrights.

   ▪ Each copyright owner will expect to be remunerated, and the implications for the main content industries are examined in Chapters 3 and 4.

II   Existence, ownership and infringement

➤   Before using a copyright work, there are 8 steps to consider:

Steps	
1	Is the work capable of copyright protection?
2	Is the work in a 'fixed' form?
3	Does the work qualify for UK copyright protection?
4	Is the work still protected by copyright?
5	Who is the owner of the copyright?
6	Will copyright be infringed?
7	Are there any defences?
8	What remedies are available?

➤   It is also important to consider rights in performances and moral rights – see Sections B and C of this Chapter.

Step 1	Is the work capable of copyright protection?

➤   The *CDPA* sets out the works in which copyright can subsist. In effect (although the *CDPA* does not explicitly draw this distinction), copyright works fall into 2 categories:

♦   underlying works – original literary, dramatic, musical and artistic works, *and*

♦   derivative works – works that incorporate underlying works yet attract their own copyright (eg: sound recordings, films and broadcasts).

1 Underlying works	
Literary works	➤ A 'literary work' is any work that is written, spoken or sung (excluding a dramatic or musical work) and includes: ♦ an ordinary literary work (eg: a novel, letter, poem or lyrics), *or* ♦ a table or compilation, *or* ♦ a computer program (including preparatory design material), *or* ♦ a database (ie: 'a collection of independent works, data or other materials which are arranged in a systematic or methodical way and are individually accessible by electronic or other means') (*s 3(1)*).
Dramatic works	➤ A 'dramatic work' is something capable of performance (acting, dance, or mime), eg: ♦ a play written for the theatre, *or* ♦ a screenplay for a feature film or television programme. • The expression does not extend to static scenes (*Creation Records Ltd v News Group Newspapers Ltd* [1997] EMLR 444).
Musical works	➤ A 'musical work' is a work consisting of music, but excluding any words or action intended to be sung, spoken or performed with the music. ♦ The copyright in a music for a song is separate from the copyright in the lyrics (which are protected as a literary work).

Underlying works (continued)	

Artistic works	➤ An 'artistic work' is (*s 4*):
	
	  a) a graphic work (eg: a painting, drawing, diagram, map, chart, plan or engraving), photograph, sculpture or collage, *or*
	
	  b) work of architecture (ie: a building or model for a building), *or*
	
	  c) work of 'artistic craftsmanship' (eg: hand-made artefacts).
	
	    ● A work under category (a) is protected irrespective of artistic quality, but artistic quality is required for works of architecture.
	
	    ● Category (c) protects 3-dimensional works, but aesthetic appeal is required (*Merlet v Mothercare* [1986] RPC 115).

◆ The underlying works are only protected by copyright if they are 'original'.

Requirement of 'originality'

➤ The author of a work must use his own skill and effort to create the work (ie: it must not simply be copied from somebody else).

  ◆ This is often referred to as the 'sweat of the brow' test, and it applies to all underlying works (other than databases).

    ● Eg: a drawing that reproduces an earlier drawing does not attract copyright protection (*Interlego AG v Tyco Industries Inc* [1988] 3 WLR 678).

  ◆ A higher threshold of originality applies to a database, which is only original if 'by reason of the selection or arrangement of the contents of the database the database constitutes the author's own intellectual creation' (*s 3A(2)*).

    ● It may attract protection by database right – see Section E of this Chapter.

➤ 2 identical pieces of work may be original as long as each author arrived at the end result by an independent process.

  ◆ NB: copyright is not a monopoly right. A contemporaneous (or even later) work does not infringe the copyright in another work if there has been no copying.

➤ With the exceptions of works of artistic craftsmanship and databases, there is no requirement for the work produced to have an artistic or intellectual quality (*Ladbroke (Football) Ltd v William Hill (Football) Ltd* [1964] 1 WLR 273), although a sculpture should have 'visual appeal' (*Lucasfilm Ltd v Ainsworth* [2009] EWCA Civ 1328).

➤ The requirement of extensive 'sweat of the brow' has in the past prevented certain works (or parts of works) from attracting copyright protection, eg:

  ◆ titles of books, plays and films (*Francis Day and Hunter v 20th Century Fox Corporation Ltd* [1939] All ER 192), *and*

  ◆ advertising slogans that use common-place sentences, *and*

  ◆ names of persons, as being '*de minimis*' (ie: too insubstantial for protection) (*Exxon Corp v Exxon Insurance Consultants International Ltd* [1982] RPC 69).

    ● Although a name does not attract copyright protection, it may be registrable as a trade mark (see Section L of this Chapter) and/or protectable as an unregistered right in passing-off (see Section N of this Chapter).

➤ The examples given above are not definitive. In each case it is a question of fact as to whether the 'originality' requirement has been satisfied. Eg: in *Shetland Times Limited v Dr Jonathan Wills* [1997] FSR 604 (a Scottish Court of Session case), it was held that, on the facts, copyright could have existed in headlines/titles. This decision was, however, contrary to the findings in several House of Lords cases.

➤ The requirement of originality under copyright law is an easier test to satisfy than the need for novelty under patent law: an invention is not patentable unless there is a development in the 'state of the art' – see Section I of this Chapter.

2 Derivative works	
Sound recordings	➤ A 'sound recording' is an audio-only recording of sounds or of a literary, dramatic or musical work, 'regardless of the medium on which the recording is made or the method by which the sounds are reproduced or produced' (s 5A(1)). ◆ An example is the so-called 'master recording' of a song. ➤ There is no copyright in a copy of a previous recording (s 5A(2)). ◆ Eg: there is no separate copyright in a CD or download of the master recording.
Films	➤ A 'film' is a 'recording on any medium from which a moving image may by any means be produced' (s 5B(1)). ◆ An example is a film made for cinema release or TV broadcast. ➤ There is no copyright in a copy of an existing film (s 5B(2)). ◆ Eg: there is no separate copyright in a DVD, Blu-ray or download of the film.
Broadcasts	➤ A 'broadcast' is an electronic transmission of visual images, sounds or other information which is transmitted (s 6(1)): a) for simultaneous reception by members of the public (ie: live), or b) at a time determined solely by the broadcaster for presentation to members of the public (ie: via a scheduled broadcast). ◆ Broadcast excludes any internet transmission unless (s 6(1A)): • it takes place by other means simultaneously (eg: as a 'simulcast'), or • it is transmitted live (eg: as a 'webcast'), or • it forms part of a scheduled programme service offered by the broadcaster (eg: via 'IPTV'). ➤ There is no copyright in a broadcast which infringes the copyright in another broadcast (s 6(6)).
Typographical arrangements of published editions	➤ A 'published edition' is the published edition of a literary, dramatic or musical work (s 8(1)). ◆ The copyright in the typographical arrangement protects the typesetting and layout of a published edition. • This helps publishers of public domain works to protect new editions (which could otherwise be copied freely). ➤ There is no copyright in the typography of a published edition that reproduces the typography of a previous edition (s 8(2)).

➤ A derivative work may comprise several layers of copyright, as illustrated below:

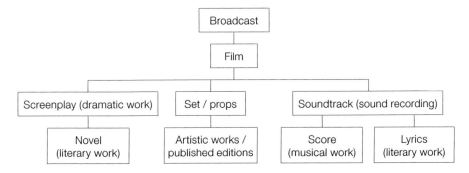

Step 2 — Is the work in a 'fixed' form?

➤ Since copyright protects the form of expression of an idea, the idea must be 'fixed' (ie: recorded) in some permanent form.

◆ In the case of a literary, dramatic or musical work, the work must be recorded 'in writing or otherwise' (s 3(2)).

● This requirement is expressed in very wide terms.

▪ Eg: a song lyric/melody will be fixed when it is recorded:

a) in written form (eg: in a musical score), *or*

b) using an electronic recording device (eg: straight to tape).

● It is irrelevant who makes the recording. A recording made without the author's consent still qualifies for fixation purposes (s 3(3)).

● NB: the originator of the work being recorded is the author of the copyright work, not the person making the recording of that work (although that person may own a separate copyright in the recording itself, as a sound recording, film or broadcast).

▪ In an interview, a journalist who writes up notes of the spoken words may use independent literary skill in doing so, in which case a further, separate copyright in the literary work comprised by the notes would arise.

◆ There is no specific requirement that an artistic work be fixed, but it is inherent in the definition of each type of artistic work that the work has taken material form.

◆ Similarly, a sound recording, film, broadcast or typographical arrangement will involve some form of fixation by its nature.

➤ The fixation criterion becomes important in cases involving allegations of copying ideas (eg: a plot for a book or a format for a TV show), as such a case will turn on how the idea has taken material form (eg: the *Da Vinci Code* case, as above).

Step 3 — Does the work qualify for UK copyright protection?

➤ Copyright is territorial by nature, being a creature of statute from country to country.

➤ In practice, qualification may be straightforward, as a work is likely to fulfil 1 or both of the usual 2 criteria for UK copyright protection, ie:

◆ *qualifying authorship* – the author of the work was, during all or a substantial part of the writing period, a 'qualifying person' (ie: broadly speaking, resident or domiciled or, in the case of company, incorporated in the UK or in a state that is a signatory to an international copyright convention) (s 154), *or*

◆ *qualifying publication* – the work was first published in (or, in the case of a broadcast, was made from a place in) the UK or such a state (ss 155 and 156).

➤ The detailed rules on qualification are beyond the scope of this Section.

Step 4	Is the work still protected by copyright?

➤ The current protection periods for copyright works are generally as follows:

Duration of copyright		

Literary, dramatic, musical or artistic work	➤ 70 years:	◆ from the end of the year in which the author dies (*s 12(2)*), *or*
		◆ if the author is unknown, from the end of the year in which the work is (*s 12(3)*):
		  ● created, *or*
		  ● made available to the public (if made available within 70 years after the end of the year in which it was created).

Sound recording	➤ 50 years:	◆ from the end of the year in which it is (*s 13A(2)*):
		  ● made, *or*
		  ● released (if released within 50 years after the end of the year in which it was made).
		
		➤ *The relatively short copyright term for sound recordings has been the subject of sustained lobbying from the recorded music industry.*
		◆ *In April 2009 the European Parliament approved a 70-year term (subject to detailed exceptions and conditions that are beyond the scope of this Section).*
		  ● *It remains to be seen whether this extension will be approved by the EU Council of Ministers.*

Film	➤ 70 years:	◆ from the end of the year in which the death occurs of the last to die of (*s 13B(2)*):
		  ● the principal director, *or*
		  ● the author of the screenplay, *or*
		  ● the author of the dialogue, *or*
		  ● the composer of the score.
		
		➤ *In summer 2009 the European Parliament asked the European Commission to conduct an assessment into whether the audiovisual sector would benefit from a similar extension of copyright term to that proposed for sound recordings.*
		◆ *The review was due to be completed by January 2010, but no findings have been published at the time of writing.*

Broadcast	➤ 50 years:	◆ from the end of the year in which it is made (*s 14(2)*).
Typographical arrangement	➤ 25 years:	◆ from the end of the year in which the edition is first published (*s 15*).
NB: each reference to 'year' is to a calendar year.		

➤ There are various exceptions, as well as rules for extensions and revivals of copyright that arose under previous *Copyright Acts*, which are beyond the scope of this Section.

Step 5	Who is the owner of the copyright?

➤ Copyright is a type of personal property that can be owned and disposed of like any other type of personal property, eg: goods or chattels (*s 90*).

➤ The first owner of a copyright work is generally its author (*s 11(1)*).

   ◆ NB: before exploiting a copyright work, a media company needs to take an 'assignment' (ie: outright transfer) or 'licence' (ie: permission for use) of it, so must first identify who the author(s) are (before considering who the current owner is).

      ● This process is commonly referred to as establishing the 'chain of title'.

➤ The 'author' of each type of copyright work is specified in the *CDPA*:

Authors of copyright works	
Literary, dramatic, musical or artistic work	➤ The person who creates it (*s 9(1)*). ◆ NB: the term 'author' has its plain meaning in this context, as the *CDPA* does not define what is meant by 'creation'. ◆ If the work is computer-generated (and there is no human author), the author is the person by whom the arrangements necessary for the creation of the work are undertaken (*s 9(3)*).

Sound recording	➤ The 'producer' (*s 9(2)(aa)*).
	
	 ◆ This means the person by whom the arrangements necessary for the creation of the work are undertaken (*s 178*).
	
	   ● NB: this is not always obvious in practice, and is a question of fact. Case law suggests that the person that pays for the arrangements is often (but not always) the producer.
	
	     ■ The recording contract should clarify which party is to be treated as the producer for these purposes.

Film	➤ The producer and the principal director (*s 9(2)(ab)*). ◆ The term 'producer' has the same legal meaning (and the same ambiguity) as noted above. ◆ The term 'director' is not defined and has its plain meaning.
Broadcast	➤ The person actually making the broadcast (or, in the case of a live relay of another broadcaster's programme, that other broadcaster) (*s 9(2)(b)*).
Typographical arrangement	➤ The publisher of the edition (*s 9(2)(d)*).

➤ Where 2 or more authors collaborate on a work, they will be joint authors if their contributions are not distinct (ie: all further a common design) (*s 10(1)*).

   ◆ Each contribution must be original (*Fisher v Brooker* [2006] EWHC 3239).

   ◆ Each author must have a direct responsibility for the resulting copyright work and not merely suggest ideas (*Robin Ray v Classic FM*, The Times 8 April 1998).

➤ If the authors' contributions are distinct, separate copyrights will arise, and the authors will own the constituent parts of the composite work as co-owners.

◆ There is no joint authorship where the contribution of one of the parties is made:

- after (*Wiseman v Wiedenfeld & Nicholson* [1985] FSR 525), *or*

- before (*Donoghue v Allied Newspapers* [1973] 3 All ER 503),

  ... the work has been created.

  ▪ There is joint authorship where the parties contribute at the same time (*Stuart v Barrett* [1992] 5 EIPR 162).

◆ Where authors are planning to collaborate, the contract between them should clearly state whether or not joint authorship is intended.

- Eg: it was found that the members of the band Spandau Ballet did not jointly own the copyright in their songs, as the contributions of certain members were essentially to the performance and interpretation of the songs rather than to their creation and composition (*Hadley v Kemp* [1999] 4 EMLR 589).

◆ The distinction between joint owners and co-owners has an important practical significance (eg: separate works may have different copyright terms and need to be transferred or licensed separately).

➤ There are 4 main exceptions to the general rule that the author is the first owner:

1   Works made in the course of employment

➤ Where a literary, dramatic, musical or artistic work or a film is made by an employee in the course of his employment, the employer is the first owner of the copyright subject to any agreement to the contrary (*s 11(2)*).

- ◆ 'Employee' has its usual meaning under employment law (*s 178*).

- ◆ It is a question of fact whether a work is created 'in the course of employment'.

  - Eg: in *Stephenson Jordan and Harrison Ltd v MacDonald and Evans* ([1952] RPC 10), copyright in lectures given by an accountant did not belong to his employer, as he was employed to advise clients rather than to give lectures.

  - Contrast *Burrows v Smith* [2010] EWHC 22, in which copyright in a game designed in the employer's time vested in the employer.

➤ For the sake of clarity, the position should expressly be dealt with in the relevant service contract (or contract for services):

Employees and self-employed contractors

➤ If the intention is that the employer will own the copyright, the contract of employment should, as 'belt and braces', include an assignment of copyright to the employer.

◆ NB: if a person is commissioning a self-employed freelancer to create a work, an assignment of copyright in any works that the freelancer creates is essential from the point of view of the commissioner, as the statutory presumption will not arise.

---

2   **Crown and Parliamentary copyright**

➤   In certain circumstances, copyright is automatically owned by the Crown or the Houses of Parliament (*s 11(3), s 163 and s 165*).

3   **Anonymous works**

➤   When an anonymous work is first published, the publisher is presumed to be the owner of the copyright (*s 104(4)*).

◆   Upon the creation of the work, the copyright then vests automatically in the 'assignee', ie: the person to whom the work has been assigned.

4   **Assignment of future copyright**

➤   It is possible to make a present assignment of future copyright (*s 91(1)*).

◆   Eg: where a record label engages a record producer to make a sound recording, the producer can, before producing the recording, assign the copyright in the recording to the label.

●   Upon the creation of the work, the copyright then vests automatically in the assignee.

➤   Once the first owner has been identified, it is necessary to identify each subsequent owner (ie: to check each link in the chain of title).

◆   Ownership of copyright can be transmitted in 3 ways (*s 90(1)*):

a) by assignment, *or*

b) under a will, *or*

c) by operation of law (eg: automatic vesting on death or bankruptcy).

●   'Operation of law' includes, on applicable facts, a constructive trust, eg: under which an author's copyright is held on trust for a commissioner (see *Vitof Ltd v Altoft* [2006] EWHC 1678).

●   NB: the latter 2 forms of transmission are otherwise beyond the scope of this Section, and are less commonly encountered in commercial practice.

◆   The chain of title may instead take the form of a chain of licences.

●   In this case, it is necessary to identify the original licensee and each subsequent sub-licensee.

➤   NB: ownership of copyright is not the same as possession of the **material** that physically embodies the copyright work.

◆   Eg: possession of a mastertape (or the digital equivalent) does not entitle the possessor to claim ownership of the copyright in the sound recording.

●   In this case, the copyright will, unless assigned to a third party, be owned by the producer of the recording.

Step 6	Will copyright be infringed?

➤ There are 2 types of infringement of copyright:

- ◆ primary infringement – relating to dealings with the copyright work itself, *and*
- ◆ secondary infringement – relating to dealings with copies of the original work.

A Primary infringement

➤ A copyright owner has 6 exclusive rights in relation to a copyright work (*s 16(1)*):

1) to copy the work, *and*

2) to issue copies of the work to the public, *and*

3) to rent or lend the work to the public, *and*

4) to perform, show or play the work in public, *and*

5) to communicate the work to the public, *and*

6) to make an adaptation of the work (or to do any of the above in relation to an adaptation).

- ◆ These are referred to in the *CDPA* as the 'acts restricted by the copyright'.

➤ Primary infringement arises if a person (*s 16(2)*):

a) does any of the restricted acts, *or*

b) authorises a third party to do any of the restricted acts,

… without the copyright owner's permission.

➤ Infringement occurs where the infringing act is done in relation to the whole or a 'substantial part' of the work (*s 16(3)*).

A 'substantial part' of the work

➤ 'Substantiality' is judged in qualitative, not quantitative terms (ie: in terms of what is taken, rather than how much is taken).

- ◆ Eg: the copying of 20 seconds of a tune (lasting 4 minutes in all) has been held to be 'substantial', as anyone hearing the 20 seconds which had been copied would have instantly recognised the tune (*Hawkes and Son v Paramount Film Service Co Ltd* (1934) 1 Ch 593).
- ◆ In *Ladbroke v William Hill* (as above), it was said that substantiality 'depends not merely on the physical amount of the reproduction but on the substantial significance of that which is taken'.
  - Eg: extracts quoted by a newspaper from a journal written by the Prince of Wales were found to form a substantial part of the journal as they expressed the Prince's personal views and were of greatest interest to the newspaper's readers (*HRH Prince of Wales v Associated Newspapers Ltd* [2006] EWHC 522).
- ◆ The cumulative effect of copying small but numerous parts may amount to copying a substantial part (*Designers Guild Ltd v Russell Williams (Textiles) Ltd* [2001] 1 All ER 700).
  - Similarly, a series of transient copies, even if copied for an instant, can amount to substantial copying (*R v Gilham* [2009] EWCA Crim 2293, in which playing a counterfeit DVD on a games console was held to involve substantial copying of artistic drawings underlying the images shown on the monitors).

➤ Each of the 6 exclusive rights is considered further below

1 Copying (s 17)

➤ In relation to a literary, dramatic, musical or artistic work, 'copying' means reproducing it in any material form, and includes storing it in any medium by electronic means (s 17(2)).

◆ For a film or broadcast, 'copying' includes making a photograph of the whole (or any substantial part) of any image forming part of it (s 17(4)).

➤ If it can be shown that the defendant had access to the claimant's work, copying is presumed (*Francis Day & Hunter Ltd v Bron* [1963] Ch 587).

◆ Access to the work need not be direct: copying from an intermediate copy without sight of the original still amounts to infringement (*Ultra Marketing (UK) Ltd v Universal Components Ltd* [2004] EWHC 468).

➤ If the copy is identical, proving infringement should be straightforward.

◆ If the copy is merely similar to the original, it is an objective test whether there is a sufficient degree of similarity between the 2 works.

➤ Partial copying often gives rise to litigation in practice. Eg:

Sampling

➤ Direct copying in the form of the 'sampling' of sound recordings is widespread in the music business.

◆ It is rare in the UK to sue over a sample of 3 seconds or less, but the test is whether the sample is a substantial part of what it was taken from (eg: a 'hook'), not whether it forms a substantial part of the new work. This is a question of fact in each case (*Produce Records Ltd v BMG Entertainment International UK and Ireland Ltd*, 19 January 1999, unreported).

Parody

➤ A parody of a copyright work can also amount to copying.

◆ There is no special test, simply an assessment of whether there has been a reproduction of the whole (or a substantial part) of the defendant's work (*Williamson Music Ltd v The Pearson Partnership* [1987] FSR 97).

---

2 Issuing copies to the public (s 18)

➤ This is a right to issue physical copies (eg: paperbacks), and it is limited in that it merely relates to issuing each copy for the first time.

◆ Once a copy has been lawfully sold (ie: to a wholesaler or customer) for the first time, the owner cannot control its subsequent exploitation, except as regards rental and lending (see below).

• This is known as the principle of 'exhaustion of rights'.

3   **Rental and lending (s 18A)**

➤   The right applies to:

a) a literary, dramatic, musical or artistic work, other than a work of:

◆   architecture in the form of a building or a model for a building, *or*

◆   'applied art' (which is not defined in the *CDPA*, but is thought, by analogy with a similar expression in the *Berne Convention* – see below – to cover articles to which an artistic work has been applied by an industrial process), *or*

b) a film or sound recording.

➤   The right entitles the owner to prohibit (*s 18A(2)*):

◆   the 'rental' of the work – essentially, its commercial rental, *or*

◆   the 'lending' of the work – essentially, free public lending.

4   **Public performance (s 19)**

➤   A copyright work cannot be performed in public without the copyright owner's permission.

◆   This restriction is critical to the music business, in which a system of collective copyright administration has long been established to facilitate the grant of public performance licences to media companies (eg: TV and radio stations and gig venues) and to other users (eg: for 'lift' or 'mood' music) – see Section A of Chapter 3.

●   There is no definition of 'public', but case law suggests that the public consists of people who are not part of the domestic or quasi-domestic circle.

5   **Communication to the public (s 20)**

➤   The right applies to a literary, dramatic, musical or artistic work, sound recording, film or broadcast.

➤   'Communication to the public' means communication to the public by electronic transmission, including (*s 20(2)*):

a) 'broadcasting' – essentially, conventional scheduled broadcast (and linked internet transmission, eg: simulcasts, webcasts and IPTV), *or*

b) 'the making available to the public of the work by electronic transmission in such a way that members of the public may access it from a place and at a time individually chosen by them' – essentially, on-demand services, eg: video-on-demand, streaming and downloads.

◆   'New media' exploitation has increasing commercial significance. Eg: there is a UK collective licensing scheme for online use of musical compositions – see Chapter 3 Section A.

6   Adaptations (*s 21*)

➤   The right applies to a literary, dramatic or musical work (*s 21(1)*).

◆   An adaptation is made when recorded in writing or otherwise (*s 21(1)*).

➤   For the following types of work, an 'adaptation' means:

Adaptations	
Literary work (except a computer program or database) *or* **Dramatic work**	➤ Either (*s 21(3)(a)*)): ◆ a translation of the work, *or* ◆ a conversion of a dramatic work into a non-dramatic work (or vice versa), *or* ◆ a version of the work in which the story or action is conveyed wholly or mainly by means of pictures in a book, newspaper, magazine or periodical (eg: converting a book into a cartoon strip).
Computer program	➤ An arrangement, altered version or translation. ◆ 'Translation' includes a version of the program in which it is converted into or out of a computer language or code or into a different computer language or code (*s 21(4)*).
Database	➤ An arrangement, altered version or translation.
Musical work	➤ An arrangement or transcription.

B Secondary infringement

➤   There are 5 acts which, without the copyright owner's permission, constitute secondary infringement of copyright:

Secondary infringement
1   Importing infringing copies (*s 22*)   ➤ This consists of importing infringing copies into the UK other than for private and domestic use.   ◆ To match the EU regime on free movement of goods, there is no infringement of copyright if the copies are lawfully imported into the UK from EEA countries (*s 27(5)*). This is the principle of 'exhaustion of rights' on an EEA-wide basis (equivalent to the principle considered above in the context of issuing copies to the public).
2   Possessing or dealing with infringing copies (*s 23*)   ➤ The relevant dealings are: a) possession in the course of business, *or*   b) selling or letting for hire (or offering or exposing for sale or hire), *or*   c) exhibiting in public or distributing in the course of a business, *or*   d) distributing otherwise than in the course of a business to such an extent as to affect the copyright owner prejudicially.

Secondary infringement (continued)

3 **Providing means for making infringing copies (s 24)**

➤ This consists of:

a) making, importing into the UK, possessing in the course of a business, selling or letting for hire (or offering or exposing for sale or hire) an article specifically designed for making copies of the work, *or*

b) transmitting the work by means of a telecommunications system (and not by way of communication to the public),

... in either case, knowing (or having reason to believe) that the article/transmission is to be used to make infringing copies.

4 **Permitting use of premises for infringing performance (s 25)**

➤ This consists of permitting a place of public entertainment (including a venue hired for one-off public entertainment) to be used for an infringing performance of a literary, dramatic or musical work.

◆ There is no infringement if the person, when giving permission, reasonably believed that the performance would not infringe copyright.

5 **Provision of apparatus for infringing performances (s 26)**

➤ In outline, this consists of supplying playback apparatus, permitting it to be brought onto premises or supplying a sound recording or film for playback with knowledge (or having reason to believe) that the apparatus/recording/film is likely to be used for an infringing public performance of a work.

➤ In each case of importing, possessing or dealing with infringing copies (ie: under ss 22 and 23), the defendant must either know or have reason to believe that the work being dealt with is an infringing copy.

◆ This involves either:

a) actual knowledge, *or*

b) constructive knowledge (ie: on the basis of facts from which a reasonable man would, with sufficient time to evaluate the facts, arrive at the relevant belief).

◆ Eg: in one case, the defendants were held to have had constructive knowledge based on, among other things, a letter before action that had been sent to them and various articles that had appeared in the press (*LA Gear Inc v Hi-Tec Sports plc* [1992] FSR 121).

Step 7	Are there any defences?

➤ An actual or implied licence to do a restricted act is a general defence to what would otherwise amount to an infringement of copyright.

  ◆ The scope of the licence must be wide enough to cover the act in question (see eg: *Grisbrook v MGN Ltd* [2009] EWHC 2520).

➤ Various statutory 'permitted acts' are set out in the *CDPA*. If a 'permitted act' takes place, there is no infringement of the copyright work (*s 16(4)(a)* and *s 28*).

  ◆ Each defence should be considered separately. The fact that a particular defence does not apply does not make any of the others ineffective *(s 28(4))*.

➤ The permitted acts more commonly encountered are as follows:

  1   Making of temporary copies (s 28A)

  ➤ Copyright in a copyright work (other than a computer program, database or broadcast) is not infringed by the making of a temporary copy:

   ◆ which is transient or incidental, *and*

   ◆ which is an integral and essential part of a technological process, *and*

   ◆ whose sole purpose is to enable:

    a) a transmission of the work in a network between third parties by an intermediary, *or*

    b) a lawful use of the work, *and*

   ◆ which has no independent economic significance.

  ➤ The scope of the temporary-copying exception is not entirely clear: the so-called '***Information Society Directive***' from which it derives (*Directive 2001/29/EC*) states that the exception should 'include acts that enable **browsing** as well as acts of **caching** to take place' (*recital 33*).

   ◆ There is little case law on the scope of the exception, which has proved controversial between rights-holders (eg: newspaper publishers) and online services (eg: news aggregators), as the extent to which the exception applies to search engines (which 'scrape' content to generate a searchable index) has yet to be tested before a court.

    • It appears that copying is only 'transient' for these purposes if (*Infopaq International A/S v Danske Dagblades Forening, Case C-5/08*):

     a) its duration is limited to what is necessary for the proper completion of the relevant technological process, *and*

     b) the copy is deleted automatically (without human intervention) once its function of enabling such completion has finished.

  ➤ The exception does not, however, prevent an aggrieved rights-holder from seeking an injunction against an information society service provider ('***ISSP***') where such ISSP has actual knowledge that a third party is using the ISSP's service to infringe copyright (*s 97A*).

2   **Fair dealing for the purposes of research and private study (*s 29*)**

➤   Fair dealing with a literary, dramatic, musical or artistic work or typographical arrangement for the purposes of research for a non-commercial purpose or private study does not infringe copyright in the work.

What is meant by 'fair dealing'?

➤   The expression 'fair dealing' is used in 3 of the permitted acts, but not defined in the *CDPA*. It has its plain meaning, but certain factors should be considered (*Hubbard v Vosper* [1972] 2 QB 84):

◆   the amount of the work that has been used (ie: the greater the amount, the less likely the use will be regarded as 'fair'), *and*

◆   whether the work was used for commercial gain, eg:

●   in *Sillitoe v McGraw-Hll Book Co (UK) Ltd* [1983] FSR 545, it was held unfair to reproduce work for commercial gain, *whereas*

●   in *BBC v British Satellite Broadcasting Ltd* [1991] 3 WLR 174, BSB's use of BBC coverage of the World Cup was held to be fair, even though it was used for commercial gain, *and*

◆   if the original work has been copied, whether the copies:

a)   deprived the owner of a sale, *or*

b)   compete with the original work.

➤   The objective of the party using the work is of prime importance (*Banier v News Group Newspapers Ltd* [1997] FSR 812).

➤   Any use for the purposes of research must be accompanied by a sufficient acknowledgement, unless this would be impossible for reasons of practicality or otherwise.

➤   It is permissible for the copying of the copyright work to be done by another person on behalf of the researcher/student (*s 29(3)*).

◆   This does not mean that one person can make many copies of the work if the result is that each is used by 'more than one person at substantially the same time and for substantially the same purpose' (*s 29(3)(b)*).

●   Eg: a lecturer is not permitted to make multiple copies of a textbook simply because he is asked to do so by each student individually, when in fact the copies will be used by the students in the same lecture.

➤   The *s 29* fair-dealing exception does not apply to sound recordings, films or broadcasts.

➤   *In a consultation (closing 31 March 2010), the UK Intellectual Property Office ('**UK IPO**') recommended expanding the s 29 exception to allow an individual to copy sound recordings, films and/or broadcasts, but only if:*

a)   *the individual is a member of an educational establishment, and*

b)   *the copying is for the purposes of a course of private study or for research at that establishment.*

---

3   **Fair dealing for the purpose of criticism or review (s 30(1))**

➤   This relates to fair dealing with a work for the purpose of criticism or review, whether of that or another work or a performance of a work.

➤   The dealing must be accompanied by a sufficient acknowledgement and the work must have been made available to the public.

◆   The acknowledgement should identify the work being copied and its author (*Sillitoe v McGraw-Hill*, as above).

➤   To plead the defence, the criticism/review need not be the only purpose of including copies of the copyright material in the derivative work, but it must be one of them.

◆   It must also have played a significant part in the decision-making process that led to the selection and inclusion of the extract from the copyright work (*Pro Sieben Media AG v Carlton UK TV Ltd* [1997] EMLR 509).

➤   The question is not whether the criticism/review is fair, but whether the extent of copying is fair in the circumstances so as to support and illustrate the criticism/review.

◆   The court looks at the derivative work as a whole, the copyright work and the criticism/review made by the former of the latter (*Pro Sieben*, as above).

4   **Fair dealing for the purpose of reporting current events (s 30(2))**

➤   Fair dealing with a work (other than a photograph) for the purpose of reporting current events does not infringe copyright in the work.

➤   The dealing must be accompanied by a sufficient acknowledgement, unless, where reporting by means of a sound recording, film or broadcast, this would be impossible for reasons of practicality or otherwise.

➤   This defence is not restricted to news events less than 24 hours old, but is concerned with the reporting of matters of current (as opposed to historical) interest or concern. The words 'reporting of current events' are words of wide and indefinite scope that should be interpreted liberally (*Pro Sieben Media AG v Carlton UK TV Ltd* [1999] 1 WLR 605, CA).

◆   The test as to whether an extract from a copyright work has been used for a purpose laid down in s 30(1) or s 30(2) is an objective one.

•   The user's subjective intentions are, however, relevant as to whether the use of the material satisfies the test of fair dealing *(Pro Sieben)*.

▪   The defence in s 30(2) did not cover a company that distributed newspaper articles to its executives to keep them up to date (*Newspaper Licensing Agency Ltd v Marks & Spencer plc, The Times, 26 January 1999*). On the facts, the articles went far beyond reporting current events (eg: included album reviews).

5   Incidental inclusion (*s 31*)

➤ This is a defence in relation to any copyright work that is incidentally included in an artistic work, sound recording, film or broadcast.

◆ Musical works or lyrics (or sound recordings of them) are not considered to have been incidentally included if deliberately included.

6   Works of unknown authorship (*s 57*)

➤ Copyright in a literary, dramatic, musical or artistic work of unknown authorship (ie: an anonymous or pseudonymous work) is not infringed if:

a) an author's identity cannot be ascertained by reasonable enquiry, *and*

b) it is reasonable to assume that:

i) copyright has expired, *or*

ii) the author died 70 years or more before the start of the calendar year in which the act in relation to the work is done.

7   Use of spoken words (*s 58*)

➤ Spoken words may amount to a literary work owned by the speaker.

➤ There is no infringement of any copyright in such work where a record of the spoken words is made (in writing or otherwise) for the purpose of reporting current events or communicating them to the public.

◆ This is subject to certain conditions (essentially, that the record and its usage do not infringe third-party rights), including that the record is a direct record of the words and not taken from a previous record or broadcast.

• This defence is widely used in the context of interviews.

8   Recording for purposes of time-shifting (*s 70*)

➤ There is no infringement of copyright in a broadcast (or in any work included in it) where it is recorded (in domestic premises for private and domestic use) solely for the purpose of enabling it to be viewed or listened to at a more convenient time.

◆ This in effect sanctions home video-taping (and the digital equivalent).

➤ It does not currently extend to so-called 'format-shifting' for convenience (eg: copying a legitimately purchased CD onto an iPod for personal use) – although the entertainment industry has for years turned a blind eye to this sort of format-shifting.

> ➤ *A private-copying exception was recommended in the influential Gowers Review of 2006 and in a first consultation by the UK IPO. In a second consultation, however (closing on 31 March 2010), the UK IPO rejected its previous proposal of a narrow UK-only format-shifting exception (due to perceived difficulties in managing such an exception) and instead encouraged the EU to consider options that benefit consumers, possibly including a broad exception to copyright for non-commercial use.*

9   **Designs**

➤   It is not an infringement of copyright in a design document/model to make a 3-dimensional article to the design (or to copy an article made to the design), unless the design is for an artistic work or a typeface (*s 51(1)*).

◆   Eg: defendants that created replica 'Stormtrooper' armour from original moulds could rely on the defence, as the armour did not amount to an artistic work (*Lucasfilm Ltd v Ainsworth* [2009] EWCA Civ 1328).

➤   Where an artistic work has, with the copyright owner's permission, been industrially produced and marketed, any person may, after 25 years from the end of the year in which such products were first marketed, produce and market 3-dimensional articles incorporating the work (*s 52*).

➤   In either case, the designs may attract protection under the design-rights regime – see Sections F, G and H of this Chapter.

10   **Miscellaneous**

➤   The permitted acts also include certain uses of copyright works:

◆   for the purpose of education (*ss 32-36*), *and*

◆   by libraries (*ss 37-44*).

> ➤ *In a consultation (closing on 31 March 2010), the UK IPO recommended:*
> *a) extension of the educational exceptions, to facilitate distance learning and the use of interactive whiteboards, and*
> *b) a new archiving and preservation exception, to enable libraries, archives, museums and galleries to make copies of any artistic works, films and sound recordings in their permanent collections for archival purposes, including format-shifting where necessary (eg: digitisation), but only where not reasonably practical to purchase another copy.*

➤   There are general defences in addition to the acts permitted under the *CDPA*:

General defences
➤ A public-interest defence has developed.
◆ The enforcement of copyright can be prevented or restricted on grounds of public interest under the *CDPA* (*s 171(3)*), although the defence itself has developed through common law (see *Lion Laboratories v Evans* (1985) QB 526).
● The test for deciding whether there is a general public policy defence to a claim for breach of copyright is whether the court can be reasonably certain that no right-thinking member of society would quarrel with its validity (*Mars UK Ltd v Teknowledge Ltd*, The Times, 23 June 1999).
➤ In certain circumstances it may be possible to raise a defence under competition law, eg: where the copyright owner:
◆ refuses to grant a licence (creating an effective monopoly in the relevant work), *or*
◆ seeks to impose unreasonable conditions of licence (such as excessive or discriminatory prices for permission to use the work), *or*
◆ behaves in any other way that abuses a dominant position in the relevant market, whether under the *Treaty on the Functioning of the European Union* ('**EU Treaty**') *Art 102* or under the *Competition Act 1998 Ch II* (see *Case T-201/04, Microsoft Corporation v Commission*, 17 September 2007).
● The issue is not common in the context of copyright (other than software) as:
■ many copyright works (eg: musical compositions and sound recordings) are collectively administered, so are available for use at set tariffs, *and*
■ there are usually alternative sources of supply of creative content.

Step 8	What remedies are available?

➤ For an actionable infringement, various civil and criminal remedies are available:

1   Civil remedies

➤ Damages (*ss 96-97*)

◆ The measure of damages is the depreciation of the value of the copyright caused by the infringement (*Claydon Architectural Metalwork Ltd v DJ Higgins & Sons Ltd* [1997] FSR 475).

◆ The court considers factors such as:

a) the fact that the infringing work may have harmed the reputation of the copyright owner by distorting the original work, *and*

b) the fee/royalty that should have been paid for use of the work.

◆ If the defendant did not know, and had no reason to believe, that copyright subsisted in the work, the claimant is not entitled to damages (but this is without prejudice to any other remedy that the claimant may have) (*s 97(1)*).

◆ The court has the power to award 'additional damages' (*s 97(2)*) and considers, in particular:

a) the flagrancy of the infringement, *and*

b) any benefit accruing to the defendant from the infringement.

➤ Account of profits (*s 96(2)*)

◆ This is a more valuable remedy than damages where the profit made by the defendant exceeds the damage suffered by the claimant.

◆ An account of profits is an alternative to damages (*Cala Homes (South) Ltd v Alfred McAlpine Homes East Ltd* [1996] FSR 36).

• The aim is to award the claimant the profits that the defendant wrongfully made from exploiting the copyright work.

◆ Even if the claimant opts for an account of damages, the court still has discretion to award additional damages under *s 97(2)* (*Cala Homes*).

• This differs from the position in Scotland, where it has been held that, if the claimant opts for an account of profits, there is no right to additional damages (*Redrow Homes Ltd v Bett Brothers plc*, Inner House of Scotland, March 14 1997).

◆ There are 2 disadvantages with this remedy:

a) it is an equitable remedy, so it is discretionary only, *and*

b) separating the profits made by the infringement from the profits made by the defendant in the ordinary course of trade can be difficult.

➤ Search order (*s 96(2)*)

◆ This allows a claimant to take an infringer by surprise and to ensure that evidence required to enforce the claimant's rights is not destroyed (*Anton Piller KG v Manufacturing Processes Ltd* [1976] Ch 55).

◆ The claimant has to satisfy 3 conditions (*Anton Piller*, as above):

a) there must be 'an extremely strong prima facie case', *and*

b) the actual or potential damage caused must be very serious, *and*

c) there must be clear evidence that the incriminating material is in the defendant's possession and a 'real possibility' that the defendant may destroy or dispose of it before an application can be made on notice.

◆ Safeguards for the defendant include the following:

a) the order is served by a solicitor independent of either party, *and*

b) the claimant gives an undertaking in damages to provide the defendant with an effective remedy should the claimant have abused his right (*Civil Procedure Rules 1998 Practice Direction 25*).

➤ Injunction (*s 96(2)*)

◆ This is an order by the court restraining the defendant from carrying out alleged infringing activities pending the full hearing of the action.

◆ The case of *American Cyanamid v Ethicon* [1975] AC 396 set out the usual 3 conditions that must be satisfied by the claimant:

a) there must be an 'arguable case', *and*

b) damages must not be an adequate remedy, *and*

c) the balance of convenience must lie in favour of granting an injunction.

◆ Injunctions (especially at the interim stage) are usually prohibitory (ie: prevent the defendant from doing an act). Mandatory injunctions (ie: requiring the defendant to do something) are rare.

➤ Delivery up of infringing articles (*s 99*)

➤ Seizure of infringing copies (*s 100*)

◆ There are 4 conditions:

a) prior notice must be given to the police, *and*

b) nothing can be seized at a regular place of business (so the remedy is aimed mainly at seizing goods from street traders), *and*

c) no force can be used, *and*

d) a notice in the prescribed form must be left at the place of seizure.

➤ Destruction of infringing articles (*s 114*)

◆ In considering whether to make such an order, the court considers whether other remedies available to the claimant would be adequate to compensate him and to protect his interests (*s 114(2)*).

2 Criminal remedies

➤ There are several criminal offences relating to:

◆ making, importing, possessing or dealing with infringing copies, *or*

◆ causing an infringing public performance or another infringing communication to the public (see *s 107*).

● For each offence, the offender must have known or have had reason to believe that the copies/acts were infringing.

● A company can be criminally liable under *s 107*, and a company's officer (or, if managing the company's affairs, any member of the company) that has consented to and/or connived in the offence can also be liable (*s 110*).

➤ The sanctions vary depending on the offence, but each offence can result in:

◆ imprisonment – up to 10 years in serious cases, *and/or*

◆ a fine – unlimited in serious cases.

● Among other powers, the court can make an order for delivery up (*s 108*) and issue a search warrant to the police (*s 109*).

III International considerations

➤ There are 2 main international conventions which provide guidelines to ensure that:

◆ the signatory states have certain minimum provisions in their copyright laws, *and*

◆ authors from other signatory states receive the same treatment as nationals of each particular state in respect of certain rights.

➤ Those 2 conventions (both of which have been amended) are:

a) the *Berne Convention 1886*, *and*

b) the *Universal Copyright Convention 1952* (known as the '**UCC**').

◆ Most countries in the world are parties to at least 1 of these conventions.

● Some countries (eg: the UK) have signed both conventions.

➤ Works that qualify for protection in overseas signatory states are afforded protection by the *CDPA* under the *Copyright and Performances (Application to Other Countries) Order 2008*.

➤ Remedies are only available on a territorial basis, so relief in the UK is only available for infringement in the UK.

   ◆ UK infringement can take the form of an international supply of copyright-protected goods to UK consumers via an overseas website (*Independiente Ltd v Music Trading Online (HK) Ltd* [2007] EWHC 533).

➤ The widespread use of the © symbol derives from the UCC:

Displaying the © symbol

➤ The UCC requires that copyright works have the © symbol displayed with the name of the copyright owner and the year of first publication.

   ◆ This is not actually required by English law, but it is advisable to display it for the purposes of international protection. The symbol acts as a notice that copyright subsists in the work.

➤ On 20 December 1996, 2 treaties were approved by the World Intellectual Property Organization (WIPO) at a conference in Geneva at which 150 different countries were represented. Both were ratified by the EU (now a legal person) on 14 December 2009.

   ◆ The first treaty is the *WIPO Copyright Treaty*:

WIPO Copyright Treaty

➤ This treaty relates to the protection of copyright in literary and artistic works and clarified certain points that had been in issue in some jurisdictions.

   ◆ Eg: it confirmed that software and databases should receive copyright protection. These aspects were implemented under EU legislation in *Directives 91/250/EC* and *96/9/EC* respectively and then under UK national legislation.

➤ The treaty also attempted to deal with problems posed by new technology, particularly the transmission of works on the Internet.

   ◆ In this regard, it gave authors of literary and artistic works an exclusive right to control the communication of their works to the public by wired or wireless means (including on-demand services). This aspect is reflected in the *CDPA* as amended.

   ◆ The second treaty is the *WIPO Performances and Phonograms Treaty*:

WIPO Performances and Phonograms Treaty

➤ The treaty relates to the rights of performers and producers of sound recordings.

   ◆ It required the introduction into UK law of various changes, including moral rights for performers (see Section C of this Chapter).

IV   Exploiting copyright

➤ A copyright owner can exploit copyright in a work:

- ◆ directly – by selling copies of the work direct to consumers, *or*
- ◆ indirectly – most commonly by giving a third party the right to exploit the work by:
  - a) assigning the copyright to the third party, *or*
  - b) licensing the copyright to the third party.

➤ Most first owners will need to secure third-party distribution, which will require an assignment or licence:

1   Assignment of copyright

➤ An assignment actually transfers 'title' in (ie: ownership of) the work.

- ◆ The assignor (ie: the person assigning) can subsequently be restrained from doing an act which infringes the rights of the assignee as the new owner of the copyright.

➤ It is possible to assign future copyright (as noted above).

- ◆ This takes effect as a transfer of ownership of the copyright as soon as the work is created (*s 91(1)*).

➤ For an assignment of copyright to be effective and to transfer legal title to the copyright (whether present or future copyright), it must be (*s 90(3)*):

- a) in writing, *and*
- b) signed by or on behalf of the assignor.

  - ◆ NB: an imperfect assignment of the legal title (eg: an oral agreement to assign) gives rise to an 'equitable assignment' if supported by valuable consideration.

  - ◆ The rights conferred by an equitable assignment include the rights:

    - i) to bring an action for copyright infringement (although generally, before judgment can be obtained, the title must be perfected or the legal owner joined as a party), *and*

    - ii) to an assignment of the legal title (except as against a purchaser of the legal title for value without notice).

➤ In light of the limitations on the rights in equity, an assignee should insist on compliance with the statutory formalities and including a 'further assurance' clause (ie: requiring compliance with any further formalities required).

- ◆ Where parties have failed to comply with the statutory formalities, it is best practice to have a written 'confirmatory assignment' signed.

➤ An assignment (whether legal or equitable) can be partial in that (*s 90(2)*):

    a) not all the rights held by the copyright owner are transferred, *and*

    b) it can be limited to a specific period of time (as opposed to being for the duration of the copyright period).

        ◆ Eg: the original owner may reserve certain rights (eg: retain ownership of copyright for a certain territory or require a reversion of rights after a certain period of time).

        ◆ It is also possible to transfer just 1 (or part of 1) of the exclusive rights conferred by copyright ownership.

            • This is often done to facilitate collective copyright administration.

                ▪ Eg: only the public performance right is transferred to the relevant collecting society, which is particularly important in the context of the music industry – see Chapter 3.

➤ If an agreement concerning film production is made between an author (of a literary, dramatic, musical or artistic work) and a film producer, the author is presumed (unless the agreement specifically provides otherwise) to have transferred to the film producer any rental right in relation to the film arising by virtue of the inclusion of a copy of the author's work in the film (*s 93A(1)*).

    ◆ The author, in return for the presumed transfer, has the right to receive 'equitable remuneration' (*s 93A(6)*) – see Section C of Chapter 4.

2 Licence of copyright

➤ A licence confers a contractual right on the licensee.

    ◆ Unlike an assignment, a licence does not transfer any title in the work.

        • So a licensee has no right to sue for copyright infringement (except as noted below).

    ◆ A licence of copyright is binding on subsequent assignees of copyright unless an assignee is (*s 90(4)*):

    a) a bona fide purchaser, *and*

    b) for valuable consideration, *and*

    c) without notice of the licence.

➤ There are 2 main types of licence:

    a) an 'exclusive licence', which authorises the licensee to the exclusion of all other persons (ie: the licensor is excluded too) (*s 92(1)*), *and*

    b) a 'sole licence', which authorises the licensee to the exclusion of all other persons (apart from the licensor).

➤ An exclusive licensee has statutory rights under the *CDPA*, subject to certain formal requirements.

Licence formalities

➤ A licensee under an 'exclusive licence' has:
  a) the same rights against a successor to the owner's title as the licensee has against the licensor (*s 92(2)*), *and*
  b) except against the owner, the same rights in relation to acts occurring after the grant of the licence as if the licence had been an assignment (eg: can bring an action in the licensee's own name) (*s 101(1)*).
    ◆ For such rights to be conferred, the exclusive licence must be (*s 92(1)*):
      i) in writing, *and*
      ii) signed by or on behalf of the copyright owner.
➤ The exclusive licensee's statutory rights are concurrent with those of the copyright owner (*s 101(2)*), but can be waived in the licence.
  ◆ NB: a non-exclusive licensee under a written licence can be granted a right to bring an action for infringement in the licensee's own name (*s 101A*), or could try to negotiate a contractual right to require the licensor to bring an action for infringement.
➤ Except as noted above, no formalities are required for the grant of a licence.
  ◆ A licence of copyright can be concluded orally.
  ◆ A licence of copyright may also be implied by conduct (eg: sending a letter to a newspaper editor will normally imply a licence to publish it).
    • It is, nonetheless, best practice to enter into written licences for evidential purposes (as well to gain the benefit of statutory rights).

➤ Whether the contract is an assignment or licence, it should cover certain key terms:

Contract terms

➤ The contract should confirm:
  ◆ the key legal terms, such as:
    • the nature of the grant of rights (ie: an assignment or licence), *and*
    • the scope of the grant of rights (in terms of media, term and territory), *and*
    • in the case of a licence, exclusivity (or non-exclusivity), *and*
    • which rights are being retained or reserved, *and*
    • warranties as to title and non-infringement of third-party rights, *and*
  ◆ the commercial terms (eg: the fee and/or royalties payable, any advances payable and the method and frequency of accounting).
➤ The grantor should ensure that the grant of rights is drafted narrowly so that the grantee receives only the minimum rights required to exploit the work.
  ◆ The grantee should ensure that the grant of rights is wide enough to prevent undue restrictions on the subsequent exploitation of the work.
➤ The contract should reflect any laws, regulations or industry practices that apply to the particular copyright content concerned.
  ◆ Eg: an author of an original artistic work is entitled to a royalty each time the work is resold involving an art market professional (*Artist's Resale Right Regulations 2006*, which are beyond the scope of this Chapter).
➤ It is important to distinguish between the copyright work itself and the physical materials (eg: a mastertape or negative) in which the copyright work is embodied.
  ◆ The contract should therefore contain provisions dealing with delivery (and, where appropriate, return) of the physical materials.

V   Digital Britain [not in force]

➤ *In November 2009 the UK government introduced the Digital Economy Bill.*

◆ *The Bill represents the culmination of a comprehensive review of UK copyright law in the digital age, which began with the 2006 Gowers Review and continued with (among other steps) a UK IPO consultation in January 2008 and the government's Digital Britain report of June 2009.*

➤ *The Bill will, if enacted, introduce a number of changes to UK copyright law designed to bring it in line with the UK's digital economy. In outline, there are 4 significant changes.*

1   Online copyright infringement

➤ *Major internet service providers ('**ISPs**') will be placed under obligations aimed at the reduction of online infringement of copyright (cl 4-17).*

◆ *This is a significant development, as ISPs have traditionally relied on the principle of 'net neutrality' (as enshrined in e-commerce laws) to escape liability for copyright infringement by users of their services. Rights-owners (eg: record labels and film studios) have, however, been hit hard by online piracy, and legislatures around the world are developing new regimes to counter the threat to the creative industries (eg: the 'three strikes and you're out' regimes that have been implemented in Japan and France).*

• *The Office of Communications ('**Ofcom**') will be responsible for specifying the procedural and enforcement aspects of the obligations through approving or adopting legally binding codes of practice.*

➤ *Every ISP that meets the qualifying criteria will have 3 main obligations:*

a) *The ISP must notify any of its subscribers if the subscriber's internet protocol (IP) address is reported by copyright owner(s) as being used to infringe copyright (cl 4).*

b) *The ISP must provide copyright owners with anonymous infringement lists with information on serious repeat infringers (cl 5).*

• *Using this information, a copyright owner can apply to court for a 'Norwich Pharmacal' order for disclosure of the infringers' names and addresses and can then bring copyright claims against them.*

c) *The ISP may also be obliged to take technical measures against serious repeat infringers to limit (or even suspend) their internet access, but this obligation will only be introduced if (following an Ofcom assessment of the notification obligations' effectiveness) the Secretary of State makes an order imposing such additional obligations on ISPs (cl 10-11).*

➤ *If the technical obligations are introduced, Ofcom must adopt a code that underpins them (cl 12).*

    ◆ *Under the code, subscribers will be entitled to challenge the imposition of technical measures by appealing to an independent person (cl 13).*

        ● *It is not clear whether a right of appeal would sufficiently safeguard subscribers' rights under the European Convention on Human Rights, ie:*

        a) *the right to a fair trial (Art 6), and/or*

        b) *the right to freedom of expression and communication (Art 10).*

            ■ *Eg: in France, the constitutional court ruled that a prior court order is required to sanction suspension of internet access.*

            ■ *In 2009 the European Parliament debated this point at length in relation to telecoms reforms and adopted an equivocal form of words confirming the right to a trial, but also leaving open the possibility of proportionate derogations.*

    ◆ *Ofcom will have the power to fine an ISP for breach of its obligations. The maximum amount is initially set at £250,000 (cl 14).*

➤ *The Secretary of State can order inclusion in the codes of provisions specifying contributions to be made by ISPs and copyright owners to costs incurred by ISPs and Ofcom in complying with the new obligations (cl 15).*

➤ *Controversially, under the draft Bill as first introduced, the Secretary of State would also have had the power to make provision by order to amend Pt I or Pt VII of the CDPA for the purpose of preventing or reducing online copyright infringement, taking account of technological developments (cl 17).*

> ➤ *The government's aim was to 'future-proof' the legislation to keep pace with technology (and determined infringers' ingenuity), but the proposed breadth of the Secretary of State's discretion – although subject to an obligation to consult with Ofcom and to obtain approval by both Houses of Parliament – has caused heated debate.*
>
>   ◆ *At the time of writing, the House of Lords has just voted down cl 17, approving instead a draft amendment that would give the High Court the power to grant an injunction against an ISP to block access to a website or mobile data network where (among other criteria) a substantial proportion of the content accessible at that location infringes copyright.*
>
>   ● *Both proposals are likely to be debated further at length in remaining Parliamentary readings of the Bill.*

2   Orphan works

➤ *The Secretary of State will have the power to make regulations authorising a licensing body to use, and to license the use of, 'orphan works' (ie: copyright works whose owner cannot be traced after a diligent search) (cl 42).*

3   *Increased criminal sanctions*

➤   *There will be a new maximum fine of £50,000 for making or dealing with infringing articles or illicit recordings (cl 43, amending CDPA ss 107 and 198).*

4   *Public lending*

➤   *For the purposes of the Public Lending Right Act 1979 (cl 44):*

a) *the term 'book' will include non-print formats (ie: audio-books and e-books), and*

b) *'lending' will mean making a book available to a library member for use away from library premises for a limited time, other than via electronic transmission.*

B Rights in performances

*References in this Section are to the Copyright, Designs and Patents Act 1988 ('**CDPA**'), unless otherwise stated.*

> I   Generally
> II   Dealing with rights in a performance
> III Role of the Copyright Tribunal

I Generally

➤ The *CDPA* creates rights for (*ss 180-205*):

   ◆ a performer (commonly referred to as performers' rights), *and*

   ◆ a person that has exclusive recording rights in a performance.

      ● These rights are separate from copyright and moral rights (*s 180(4)*) and should be distinguished from the right to prevent public performance of a copyright work (eg: a musical work), which is a right enjoyed by the copyright owner.

➤ The term 'performer' is not defined for these purposes, but its meaning can be inferred from the term 'performance', which is defined as (*s 180(2)*):

   a) a dramatic performance (which includes dance and mime), *or*

   b) a musical performance, *or*

   c) a reading or recitation of a literary work, *or*

   d) a performance of a variety act or any similar presentation.

      ◆ The rights in a performance apply to the extent that the performance is live (ie: not pre-recorded) and apply to each performer taking part in it (*s 180(2)*).

> ### Examples of 'performers'
> ➤ The types of performer covered by the *CDPA* include:
> | | |
> |---|---|
> | ◆ a musician/singer | ◆ a dancer |
> | ◆ an actor | ◆ a news presenter |

      ◆ NB: a sporting performance does not generally count as a performance.

➤ There are no requirements relating to the quality or originality of the performance (eg: each performance of the same work is a different performance).

➤ The performance need not have been performed in public (eg: it could have been recorded at a private recording studio) (*Bamgoye v Reed* [2002] EWHC 2922).

➤ Performers' rights are an important source of income for performers who do not own any copyright in the work they are performing. Eg: a session musician may not own any copyright in the music performed, but has rights in the performance.

II Dealing with rights in a performance

➤ The steps to consider when dealing with rights in a performance are as follows:

Steps	
1	Has there been a qualifying performance?
2	Is the performance still protected?
3	Will a performer's rights be infringed?
4	Will the rights of a person with recording rights be infringed?
5	Have all rights been cleared?
6	Has the performer received equitable remuneration?
7	Do any of the 'permitted acts' apply?
8	What remedies are available?

Step 1	Has there been a qualifying performance?

➤ A performance is only protected if it is a 'qualifying performance'.

♦ A performance is a 'qualifying performance' if it (s 181):

  a) takes place in a 'qualifying country', or

  b) is given by a 'qualifying individual', ie: an individual who is a citizen or subject of, or resident in, a 'qualifying country'.

♦ A 'qualifying country' means (s 206(1)):

  a) the UK, or

  b) another Member State of the EU, or

  c) to the extent designated by Order of Council, any country enjoying reciprocal protection (and for a current list of such countries see the *Performances (Reciprocal Protection) (Convention Countries and Isle of Man) Order 2003*).

Step 2	Is the performance still protected?

➤ Rights in a performance last for (s 191):

♦ 50 years from the end of the year in which the performance takes place, or

♦ if during that period a recording of it is released, 50 years from the end of the year in which the recording is released.

  ● *NB: in April 2009 the European Parliament approved an extension to 70 years. At the time of writing, it still remains to be seen whether the extended term of protection will be approved by the EU Council of Ministers.*

Step 3	Will a performer's rights be infringed?

➤ A performer's rights are infringed in relation to the whole or any 'substantial part' of a qualifying performance if a person (without the performer's consent):

◆ broadcasts the performance live (*s 182(1)(b)*), *or*

◆ makes a recording directly from the live performance or from a live broadcast of the performance (*s 182(1)(a)* and *(c)*).

● The expression 'substantial part' is interpreted by the courts in the same way as it is for copyright purposes (ie: in terms of quality and/or quantity).

● A 'recording' means a film or sound recording (*s 180(2)*).

▪ In an action under *s 182(1)*, damages will not be awarded if the defendant can show that at the time of the infringement he believed on reasonable grounds that consent had been given (*s 182(3)*).

➤ A performer's rights are also infringed in relation to a recording if a person (without the performer's consent):

◆ makes a copy of the recording (*s 182A* – defined as the *'reproduction right'*), *or*

◆ issues copies of the recording to the public (*s 182B* – defined as the **'distribution right'**), *or*

◆ rents or lends copies of the recording to the public (*s 182C* – defined as the **'rental right'** and **'lending right'** respectively), *or*

◆ makes the recording available to the public by electronic transmission in such a way that members of the public may access the recording 'from a place and at a time individually chosen by them' (eg: through on-demand services via cable, satellite or the internet) (*s 182CA* – defined as the **'making available right'**), *or*

◆ shows or plays the recording in public or communicates it to the public by electronic transmission, in circumstances where the recording was, and the defendant knows or has reason to believe that the recording was, made without consent (*s 183*), *or*

◆ imports, possesses or sells the recording or lets the recording for hire, in circumstances where the recording is, and the defendant knows or has reason to believe that the recording is, an 'illicit recording' (*s 184*).

● An 'illicit recording' is a recording that was made otherwise than for private purposes and without the performer's consent (*s 197*).

▪ If the defendant can show that an illicit recording was innocently acquired (ie: the defendant did not know or have reason to believe that the recording was an illicit recording), the only remedy available against the defendant is an award of reasonable damages in respect of the act complained of (*s 184(2)*).

Step 4	Will the rights of a person with recording rights be infringed?

➤ A 'person having recording rights' also has rights in performances under *ss 185-188*.

♦ This expression means:

    a) a party to an 'exclusive recording contract' with the relevant performer(s) for the performance in question (eg: a record company that has signed an exclusive recording contract for an artist's audio and/or visual services), *or*

    b) a third party to whom the benefit of the contract has been 'assigned' (ie: transferred outright) or, alternatively (in certain circumstances), licensed.

        ● An 'exclusive recording contract' is 'a contract between a performer and another person under which that person is entitled to the exclusion of all other persons (including the performer) to make recordings of one or more of his performances with a view to their commercial exploitation' (*s 185(1)*).

        ● The person must be a 'qualifying person', ie: *either* a 'qualifying individual' (see step 1 above) *or* a legal person formed under the law of a 'qualifying country' (again, see step 1 above) and having in such country a place of business at which substantial business activity is carried on (*s 206(1)*).

♦ The recording rights co-exist with performers' rights.

➤ The acts that infringe the rights of a person having recording rights are broadly similar to those set out in step 2 above (see *ss 186-188* for the detailed provisions).

♦ A live broadcast of a performance does not, however, infringe the rights of a person having recording rights.

➤ The practical impact of these rights is that any 'clearance' exercise (see step 5 below) must also involve any company with exclusive recording rights.

Step 5	Have all rights been cleared?

➤ A user of a performance (eg: a film producer) should 'clear' all rights in the performance (ie: acquire all rights, consents and waivers necessary to exploit the rights freely).

♦ Clearance takes 2 forms in this context:

    a) obtaining ownership of each performer's 'property rights', *and*

    b) obtaining consents and waivers in relation to each performer's 'non-property rights' and from any person having recording rights.

➤ A performer's 'property rights' are the performer's reproduction, distribution, rental, lending and making available rights (as described above) (*s 191A*). These concern recordings or broadcasts of the performances, not the performances themselves.

♦ As property rights, they can be 'assigned' (ie: transferred outright to another person) and ownership can pass by will or operation of law (*s 191B*).

    ● These rights can also be assigned in advance of a future recording (*s 191C*).

➤ A performer's 'non-property rights' (ie: all rights other than the property rights) – essentially consents – do not constitute transferable property, so cannot be assigned, although they are transmissible on the performer's death (s 192).

  ◆ Instead, to ensure that the intended forms of exploitation will not infringe performers' rights, the user should obtain each performer's prior consent to such use.

  ● The user should also obtain waivers of each performer's 'moral rights' (see Section C of this Chapter).

➤ Formalities are prescribed in the CDPA for assignment, but not for consents.

Form of clearance

➤ To have legal effect, an assignment of a performer's property rights must be in writing and signed by or on behalf of the assignor.

➤ The CDPA does not require that consent by a performer be given in writing, although it should be in writing as a matter of best practice.

  ◆ As a matter of law, it is a question of fact whether consent has been given (eg: it can be implied by conduct).

  ◆ The form of consent must cover the exact scope of subsequent exploitation. A film producer or record company usually obtains a very wide form of consent that anticipates all possible forms of exploitation.

Case law on clearance

➤ A performer may consent to having a performance recorded, but this does not necessarily also constitute consent to the sale of copies of that recording (Bassey v Icon Entertainment [1995] EMLR 596).

  ◆ By contrast, in Mad Hat Music v Pule 8 Records Ltd ([1993] EMLR 172), consent by a performer to the recording of a performance was held. on the facts, to constitute consent to both the manufacture and the sale of the recording.

➤ In the case of persons having recording rights, consent can be given for the purposes of the CDPA by (s 193(2)):

a) the person having recording rights, or

b) the performer.

  ◆ The recording rights are not assignable (s 192B), although the exclusive recording contract on which the rights depend can be assigned (s 185(2)).

  ◆ In practice, consent should be obtained from the person having recording rights (eg: the relevant record company), which is likely to have taken a grant of all relevant rights, consents and waivers from the performer, along with the exclusive right to authorise others to exploit the rights in the performer's performances.

Step 6	Has the performer received equitable remuneration?

➤ Even if all rights have been cleared, the performer will still be entitled to receive equitable remuneration for:

a) public performance of a sound recording of his performance (s 182D), and/or

b) transfer of his rental right to a producer of a sound recording or film (s 191G),

... as these rights to equitable remuneration can only be assigned by the performer to a collecting society (ie: cannot be assigned to a record company or other user).

Equitable remuneration for public performance

➤ If a commercially published sound recording (NB: not a film) of the whole or any substantial part of a qualifying performance is:

a) played in public, or

b) communicated to the public, but not via the making available right (eg: via scheduled broadcast, rather than via on-demand services),

... the performer is entitled to equitable remuneration from the owner of the copyright in the sound recording (s 182D(1)).

◆ The right to receive equitable remuneration cannot be assigned by the performer, except to a collecting society (s 182D(2)).

Equitable remuneration for the transfer of a rental right

➤ Like a copyright owner (see Section A of this Chapter), a performer has the right to receive equitable remuneration when the performer's rental right (ie: the right to control the rental of copies of the performance) is transferred (or presumed to be transferred in the case of a film production agreement – see below) to the producer of a sound recording or film (s 191G).

◆ The right to receive equitable remuneration cannot be assigned by a performer, except to a collecting society (s 191G(2)).

◆ The remuneration is payable by the person for the time being entitled to the rental right (ie: the person to whom the right has been transferred) or any successor in title (s 191G(3)).

➤ If an agreement concerning film production is made between a performer and a film producer, the performer is presumed (unless the agreement specifically provides otherwise) to have transferred to the film producer the performer's rental right relating to the film (s 191F(1)).

◆ In return for this presumed transfer, the performer has the right to receive equitable remuneration.

◆ Standard forms of engagement contain an express transfer of the right.

> ## Equitable remuneration in practice

➤ For each form of equitable remuneration, the producer and performer can negotiate and agree the amount payable by way of equitable remuneration (*ss 182D(3)* and *191G(4)* respectively).

- ◆ The performer cannot contract out.

  - ● Standard forms of engagement therefore usually provide that the fees or royalties payable to the performer are **inclusive** of equitable remuneration (subject to any collecting society entitlement under independent collective agreements negotiated by such collecting society).

  - ● The relevant collecting societies in the UK are:

    a) for public performance:

      i) Phonographic Performance Limited (PPL), *and*

      ii) Video Performance Limited (VPL),

      ... which collect on behalf of audio performers (see Chapter 3), *and*

    b) for transfer of the rental right – British Equity Collecting Society Limited (BECS), which collects on behalf of audio-visual performers.

➤ Equitable remuneration can be paid in a lump sum, so it is common (especially in the context of film production) for the producer to make a one-off payment that acts as a 'buy-out' of all rights, including equitable remuneration for future exploitation.

Step 7	Do any of the 'permitted acts' apply?

➤ There are various 'permitted acts' that may be done in relation to a performance or recording despite the rights in performances conferred by the *CDPA* (*s 189* and *Sch 2*).

- ◆ These are, in effect, defences to acts that would otherwise amount to infringement of rights in performances.

- ◆ They include – and broadly mirror the wording of – most of the 'permitted acts' that apply to copyright, such as:

  - ● fair dealing, *and*

  - ● incidental inclusion.

    - ■ See Section A of this Chapter for the permitted acts relating to copyright.

    - ■ See *CDPA Sch 2* for the permitted acts relating to rights in performances, the details of which are beyond the scope of this Section.

Step 8	What remedies are available?

➤ The civil remedies for infringement are (subject to certain exceptions):

♦ for infringement of performers' property rights – the usual remedies for infringement of property rights (*s 191I*), *and*

♦ for infringement of performers' non-property rights (or of the rights of a person having recording rights) – the usual remedies for breach of statutory duty (*s 194*).

● The general remedies include:

▪ an injunction (interim or final), *and/or*

▪ damages (or an account of profits).

➤ Specific statutory remedies include:

♦ an order for delivery-up of illicit recordings (*s 195*), *and*

♦ a right to seize illicit recordings, subject to certain prescribed conditions (eg: on advance notice to the local police and without use of force) (*s 196*).

➤ There are also criminal sanctions, which are similar to those for infringement of copyright, including an order for delivery-up (*s 199*) and the issue of search warrants (*s 200*).

♦ A company can be liable to criminal proceedings, along with its members and officers (*s 202*).

III Role of the Copyright Tribunal

➤ A person wishing to make a copy of a recording of a performance can apply to the Copyright Tribunal, which has the power to give consent if the identity or whereabouts of the person entitled to the reproduction right cannot be ascertained by reasonable enquiry (*s 190(1)*).

♦ If the Copyright Tribunal gives consent, it can make an order for payment to be made to the performer in return for the grant of consent (*s 190(6)*).

➤ In default of an agreement as to the amount that should be payable by way of equitable remuneration, either party may apply to the Copyright Tribunal, which has the power to determine or vary the amount payable (*s 182D* and *s 191H* respectively).

C Moral rights

*References in this Section are to the Copyright, Designs and Patents Act 1988 ('**CDPA**'), unless otherwise stated.*

> I   Generally
>
> II   Moral rights relating to copyright works
>
> III   Moral rights in performances

I   Generally

➤ The term 'moral rights' describes certain inalienable, non-economic rights of authors, directors and performers.

♦ The term has nothing to do with morality, but derives from the concept of *'droit moral'* under the laws of civil-law jurisdictions (eg: France).

♦ In contrast to copyright, moral rights cannot be commercially exploited.

➤ There are 4 moral rights relating to copyright works:

1) the right to be identified as the author or director of a work (known as the '**paternity right**') (*ss 77-79*), *and*

2) the right to object to derogatory treatment of a work (known as the '**integrity right**') (*ss 80-83*), *and*

3) the right against false attribution of authorship or directorship (*s 84*), *and*

4) the right to privacy in respect of certain films and photographs (*s 85*).

● Although these copyright-related moral rights do not all apply to authors, they are commonly referred to as '***authors' moral rights***'.

➤ Authors' moral rights do not constitute property and cannot be assigned (*s 94*).

♦ Eg: the paternity and integrity rights protect an author or director of a copyright work, even if he has assigned the copyright in the work to a third party.

● So moral rights do not necessarily belong to the owner of the related copyright, but remain with the person originally entitled to them.

➤ Authors' moral rights can, however, be waived (*s 87(2)*), and are often waived in contracts dealing with copyright works (eg: a film composer's agreement).

➤ Performers' moral rights were introduced with effect from 1 February 2006 by the *Performances (Moral Rights, etc.) Regulations 2006*, which amended the *CDPA*.

♦ These rights are essentially 'paternity' and 'integrity' rights for performers.

♦ The rights only relate, however, to a performance, rather than to any copyright work (eg: a film) in which that performance may be embodied.

Authors' moral rights (side tab)

Performers' moral rights (side tab)

II Moral rights relating to copyright works

➤ In the case of moral rights relating to copyright works, 5 steps should be considered:

Steps	
1	Who is entitled to the moral rights?
2	Which moral rights are involved?
3	Are the rights still protected?
4	Have the rights been waived? If not, have they been infringed?
5	What are the remedies?

Step 1 — Who is entitled to the moral rights?

➤ The persons entitled to copyright-related moral rights are as follows:

Paternity right Integrity right	➤ The author of a literary, dramatic, musical or artistic work (a '**work**') and the director of a film (ss 77(1) and 80(1)).
Right against false attribution	➤ Any person who is not the author or director of a work or film (s 84(1)).
Right to privacy	➤ The commissioner of a photograph or film for private and domestic purposes (s 85(1)).

◆ The terms 'author' and 'director' and the respective categories of copyright work are examined in Section A of this Chapter.

● NB: authors' moral rights do not apply to sound recordings, broadcasts or typographical arrangements of published editions.

➤ Moral rights remain exercisable by the rights-holder, whether or not the related copyright is subsequently assigned or licensed to a third party.

Step 2 — Which moral rights are involved?

➤ Each of the 4 copyright-related moral rights should be considered:

1 **Paternity right – the right to be identified as author or director (s 77)**

➤ The paternity right entitles authors/directors to be 'identified' with their works/films. The requirements are detailed, but broadly speaking:

◆ An identification should be made whenever the work/film is (ss 77(2)-(6)):

a) issued to the public in the form of a film or sound recording, *or*

b) published commercially, *or*

c) performed or shown in public (except for musical works), *or*

d) communicated to the public (except for musical works).

◆ An author/director is 'identified' by having the form of identification specified by the author/director (eg: a name or pseudonym) displayed in a clear and reasonably prominent way that is likely to bring the identification to the attention of the relevant public (s 77(7)).

➤ To be capable of infringement, the right must be asserted (s 78(1)-(2)):

a) by including (in an assignment of the relevant copyright) a statement that the author/director asserts the right to be identified, or

b) in writing by the author or director.

Asserting the paternity right

➤ In practice, an author or director should consider including an assertion in or on the copyright work itself. Eg:

◆ an author of a book can assert his paternity right by inserting the following wording in the front of the book: 'The author has asserted his moral rights in accordance with the provisions of the Copyright, Designs and Patents Act 1988', or

◆ a painter can be named on a picture or on its frame.

➤ The right applies to all or any substantial part of a work or film (s 89(1)).

➤ The paternity right does not apply in a number of cases specified in the CDPA (essentially where identification would be impractical), eg:

◆ a computer program, or

◆ the design of a typeface (ie: a font), or

◆ any computer-generated work, or

◆ a work/film produced in the course of employment, where the copyright originally vested in the employer, or

◆ a work/film to the extent that there is a defence of (s 79):

• fair dealing (in relation to reporting current events), or

• incidental inclusion.

2 Integrity right – the right to object to derogatory treatment (s 80)

➤ The right to object to 'derogatory treatment' of a work protects the same types of author as the paternity right, as well as directors.

◆ 'Treatment' means any addition to, deletion from, or alteration to or adaptation of the work, other than (s 80(2)(a)):

a) a translation of a literary or dramatic work, or

b) an arrangement or transcription of a musical work involving no more than a change of key or register.

> ### What amounts to 'treatment' of a work?
>
> ➤ The definition of 'treatment' entails inherent limitations.
>
> ◆ Eg: placing an artistic work in an inappropriate physical context or taking extracts of music for inappropriate uses may be damaging to an author, but does not come within the statutory definition of 'treatment', so would not infringe the author's moral rights.

◆ A treatment is 'derogatory' if it 'amounts to distortion or mutilation of the work or is otherwise prejudicial to the honour or reputation of the author or director' (*s 80(2)(b)*).

  • Eg: a singer/songwriter sued a record company proposing to release a 'Bad Boys Megamix'. The claimant successfully argued that his integrity right would be infringed (*George Michael and Morrison Leahy Music Ltd v BMG and IQ Records*, unreported).

➤ The right applies to all or any part of a work (*s 89(2)*).

➤ The integrity right does not apply in certain cases. These include (*s 81*):

a) a computer program or computer-generated work, *or*

b) a work made for the purpose of reporting current events.

3 **The right against false attribution of authorship or directorship (*s 84*)**

➤ Any person (NB: not just an author or director) has the right (*s 84(1)*):

a) not to have a literary, dramatic, musical or artistic work falsely attributed to him as author, *and*

b) not to have a film falsely attributed to him as director.

  ◆ An 'attribution' can include an implied attribution (*s 84(1)*).

  • Eg: a newspaper article written in the first person and containing words not actually used by the claimant amounted to a false attribution (*Moore v News of the World* [1972] 1 All ER 915).

  ◆ In practice, a false attribution is likely to be made in relation to a well-known personality, 'cashing in' on the personality's reputation (eg: *Clark v Associated Newspapers Ltd* [1998] 1 All ER 959).

➤ Broadly speaking, the right is infringed where a work (or copies of a work) containing a false attribution are issued, exhibited, performed or communicated to the public (*s 84(2)-(4)*).

➤ The right applies to all or **any** part of a work (*s 89(2)*).

4   **The right to privacy of certain photographs and films (s 85)**

➤ This right applies to a person who, for both private and domestic purposes, has commissioned:

◆ the taking of a photograph, *or*

◆ the making of a film.

• A commission can be made jointly, in which case each commissioner is entitled to the right (*s 88(6)*).

• The term 'commission' usually connotes payment of a fee to the photographer/film-maker (*Apple Corps Ltd v Cooper* [1993] FSR 286).

➤ NB: the private and domestic purposes are a requirement for the commissioning, not for the subject matter of the photograph/film.

◆ Eg: a married couple have a moral right to privacy in pictures taken by a photographer of a wedding that takes place in public, as long as the photographer is commissioned for the couple's private and domestic purposes (rather than, say, commissioned to take publicity shots).

Moral right to privacy and celebrities

➤ The requirement that the work be commissioned for private and domestic purposes makes this right of little use to a celebrity whose picture has been taken by:

◆ unauthorised paparazzi, *or*

◆ photographers commissioned to take press shots.

➤ The moral right to privacy gives a commissioner the right not to have (*s 85(1)*):

◆ copies of the photograph/film issued to the public, *or*

◆ the photograph/film exhibited or shown in public, *or*

◆ the photograph/film communicated to the public.

• The right is infringed by any person who does (or authorises the doing of) any of those infringing acts (*s 85(1)*).

➤ The right applies to all or any **substantial** part of a work (*s 89(1)*).

➤ Exceptions to the right include the incidental inclusion of the photograph or film in an artistic work, film or broadcast (*s 85(2)*).

◆ The right does not apply to photographs taken or films made before the date of commencement of the *CDPA*, ie: 1 August 1989.

➤ NB: there is no right of privacy as such under English law, although private information can, in line with human rights law, be protected to a certain extent as confidential information – see Section J of this Chapter.

Step 3 — Are the rights still protected?

➤ Copyright-related moral rights generally last for as long as the related copyright work is protected by copyright (*s 86(1)*).

◆ Broadly speaking, this is the life of the author/director plus 70 years.

➤ The exception to this is the right against false attribution, which lasts until 20 years after the death of the author/director (*s 86(2)*).

◆ With the exception of the right to prevent false attribution (which existed under the *Copyright Act 1956 s 43*), nothing done before the commencement of the *CDPA* (ie: 1 August 1989) infringes moral rights (*CDPA Sch 1 para 22*).

➤ Since all of the author's moral rights survive death, they pass upon the death of the author/director to that person's estate (see *s 95*).

Step 4 — Have the rights been waived? If not, have they been infringed?

➤ Copyright-related moral rights can be waived by the person entitled to them (*s 87(2)*).

◆ The waiver must be in writing signed by the rights-holder and may relate to:

● a specific work, a specified type of work or works generally, *and/or*

● existing and/or future works (*s 87(3)(a)*).

Waivers of moral rights

➤ It is accepted commercial practice in certain industries for a company (eg: a film studio or record label) to obtain a waiver of moral rights.

◆ Moral rights (especially paternity and integrity rights) often amount to an unworkable restriction on the commercial exploitation of a work.

● The company cannot always give a credit and needs editing flexibility.

◆ The company should insist on an unconditional, irrevocable waiver that extends to the company's successors and licensees (see *s 87(3)*).

➤ An author or director who is about to assign or license copyright should resist a waiver where it cannot be justified.

◆ Alternatively, it may be possible to afford the author/director:

a) a contractual right to a credit (except where it is not reasonably practicable in the context of industry practice), *and/or*

b) a right of approval over certain types of treatment.

➤ Whether the moral rights have been infringed depends upon the moral right involved (see step 2 above).

◆ The rights-holder's consent (whether express or implied) is a defence to infringement (*s 87(1)*).

| Step 5 | What are the remedies? |

➤ A breach of a moral right is a breach of statutory duty.

➤ An infringement of moral rights entitles the claimant to the usual remedies for breach of statutory duty, including damages or injunctive relief (*s 103(1)*).

   ◆ If there has been infringement of the integrity right, the court has the power to grant an injunction prohibiting the doing of any act unless a disclaimer (which has to be approved by the court) is made, disassociating the author or director from the treatment of the work (*s 103(2)*).

III Moral rights in performances

➤ A performer has 2 moral rights in relation to a 'qualifying performance':

   1) the '***paternity right***', ie: the right to be identified as the performer, *and*

   2) the '***integrity right***', ie: the right to object to derogatory treatment of the performance.

   ● A 'qualifying performance' has the same meaning as in the context of performers' economic rights – see Section B of this Chapter.

   ● NB: the rights only apply to a performance given after 1 February 2006.

➤ The same 5 steps considered above for authors' moral rights apply to performers' moral rights.

| Step 1 | Who is entitled to the moral rights? |

➤ A 'performer' is entitled to the moral rights.

   ◆ This term has the same meaning as in the context of performers' economic rights – see Section B of this Chapter.

| Step 2 | Which moral rights are involved? |

➤ Both moral rights need to be considered:

   1 Paternity right – the right to be identified as performer (*s 205C*)

   ➤ The right applies to (*s 205C(1)*):

      ◆ a live performance in public, *or*

      ◆ a live broadcast of a performance, *or*

      ◆ a sound recording of the performance (but only when communicated or issued to the public).

         ● NB: the paternity right does not apply to **audio-visual** recordings of performances (eg: films).

➤ The performer has the right to be identified in a manner likely to bring the performer's identity to the notice of the relevant public (s 205C(2)).

◆ For a group, the right can be satisfied by identifying the group as a whole rather than each performing member of the group (s 205C(3)).

➤ The right will not be infringed unless it has been asserted (s 205D(1)-(2)):

◆ in writing signed by or on behalf of the performer, or

• NB: the words 'on behalf of' allow performers to permit others (eg: managers or agents) to sign on their behalf.

◆ in an assignment of the performer's economic property rights.

➤ There are a number of exceptions to the paternity right, such as (s 205E):

◆ where it is not reasonably practicable to identify the performer or group, or

◆ in a performance given for the purposes of:

• reporting current events, or

• advertising goods or services.

2   **Integrity right – the right to object to derogatory treatment (s 205F)**

➤ The right applies to (s 205F(1)):

◆ a live broadcast of a performance, or

◆ a sound recording of the performance (but only when played in public or communicated to the public).

➤ Derogatory treatment is 'any distortion, mutilation or other modification that is prejudicial to the reputation of the performer' (s 205F(1)).

➤ Unlike the paternity right the integrity right does **not** need to be asserted.

➤ There are a number of exceptions to the integrity right, such as (s 205G):

◆ in a performance given for the purpose of reporting current events, or

◆ where modifications are made to a performance that are:

• consistent with normal editorial or production practice, or

• made (if a sufficient disclaimer of the fact is given) in order:

a) to avoid committing a criminal offence, or

b) to comply with a statutory duty, or

c) (in the case of the BBC only) to avoid broadcasting offensive material.

➤ Secondary infringement occurs where a person possesses (in the course of business) or deals with sound recordings that infringe the integrity right (s 205H).

Step 3	Are the rights still protected?

➤ A performer's moral rights last as long as the performer's economic rights in the particular performance (*s 205I*) – see Section B of this Chapter for details of the economic rights.

♦ Broadly speaking, the duration is 50 years from the end of the calendar year in which (*s 191*):

a) the performance takes place, *or*

b) (if within 50 years of the performance) a recording of it is released.

● *NB: in April 2009 the European Parliament approved an extension to 70 years. It still remains to be seen whether the extended term of protection will be approved by the EU Council of Ministers.*

Step 4	Have the rights been waived? If not, have they been infringed?

➤ Performers' moral rights can be waived, and the waiver must be in writing signed by the rights-holder (*s 205J(2)*).

♦ The practical implications of such waivers are similar to those applying to waivers of authors' moral rights – see step 4 of section II above.

➤ Whether the moral rights have been infringed depends upon the moral right involved (see step 2 above).

♦ The rights-holder's consent (whether express or implied) is a defence to infringement (*s 205J(1)*).

Step 5	What are the remedies?

➤ A breach of a moral right is a breach of statutory duty.

➤ Infringement of performers' moral rights gives rise to the usual remedies for breach of statutory duty (*s 205N(1)*).

♦ The remedies include damages and/or injunctive relief.

D Publication right

References in this Section are to the Copyright and Related Rights Regulations 1996 ('CRRR 1996'), unless otherwise stated.

➤ Publication right is a property right equivalent to copyright.

◆ It was introduced by the *CRRR 1996* (further to *Directive 93/98/EC Art 4*).

◆ Publication right arises automatically and is owned by the person who, after the expiry of copyright protection, first publishes a previously unpublished (*r 16*):

- literary work, *or*

- dramatic work, *or*

- musical work, *or*

- artistic work, *or*

- film.

  ■ These categories of copyright works are examined in Section A of this Chapter, and are referred to below as '***works***' for short.

➤ For any person proposing to publish such an unpublished work, there are 5 steps to consider as to whether publication right will arise on publication:

Steps	
1	Is the work a relevant copyright work?
2	Has the work's copyright protection expired?
3	Is the work unpublished?
4	Will the work qualify for protection on publication?
5	What rights are conferred?

Step 1	Is the work a relevant copyright work?

➤ The work must have:

a) been a work of the sort described above, *and*

b) qualified for copyright protection in the first instance.

➤ The requirements for copyright protection are examined in Section A of this Chapter.

Step 2	Has the work's copyright protection expired?

➤ Publication right can only exist if the work's period of copyright protection has expired.

◆ See Section A of this Chapter for details of the respective periods of protection.

- NB: any revival or extension of copyright under the *Duration of Copyright and Rights in Performances Regulations 1995* should be carefully considered.

Step 3	Is the work unpublished?

➤ Publication right can only exist if the work has not been previously 'published'.

- ◆ 'Publication' includes any making available to the public, such as (*r 16(2)*):

  a) the issue of copies to the public, *or*

  b) making the work available by means of an electronic retrieval system, *or*

  c) the rental or lending of copies of the work to the public, *or*

  d) the performance, exhibition or showing of the work in public, *or*

  e) communicating the work to the public.

    - The *CRRR 1996* do not specify any territorial limitation for such publication, and it is possible that publication anywhere in the world would prevent publication right from arising (although there is no case law on the point).

    - For this purpose, no account is taken of any unauthorised act of publication (*r 16(3)*). The term 'unauthorised' is not defined, but is likely to mean without the permission of the copyright owner or (where the work is out of copyright) of the person who possesses the physical medium embodying the work.

Step 4	Will the work qualify for protection on publication?

➤ The work will only qualify for publication-right protection if the work is first published (within the meaning of publication described in Step 3 above):

- ◆ within the European Economic Area ('**EEA**'), *and*

- ◆ by a publisher that is, at the time of first publication, a national of an EEA state.

    - Where 2 or more persons jointly publish the work, it will qualify for publication-right protection if any of them is a national of an EEA state (*r 16(4)*).

Step 5	What rights are conferred?

➤ The person who undertakes a qualifying publication will obtain the publication right.

- ◆ Subject to certain limited exceptions (which are beyond the scope of this Section), the owner effectively has all the rights and remedies of a copyright owner (*r 17*), but with one major difference: the right lasts for 25 years from the end of the calendar year in which the work is first published (*r 16(6)*).

- ◆ The owner does not have any moral rights in the work (*r 17(1)*).

➤ NB: in practice, publication right will have limited significance until (at the earliest) the end of 2039, the date on which copyright in most relevant works (other than certain artistic works) that were unpublished at the commencement date of the *Copyright, Designs and Patents Act 1988* ('**CDPA**') will expire (ie: at the end of the 50-year period of protection that is generally specified for such works under *CDPA Sch 1 para 12*).

E Database rights

*References in this Section are to the Copyright and Rights in Databases Regulations 1997 ('**CRDR**'), unless otherwise stated.*

I	**Databases generally**
II	**Database right**

I Databases generally

➤ In the 'information society' a database is an increasingly powerful tool.

♦ IT management systems, websites and intranets all utilise electronic databases.

● Physical databases (eg: hard-copy directories) also remain important.

♦ Certain types of structured information have a premium commercial value (eg: official sports data used for betting purposes).

➤ The increasing commercial significance of databases led to a need for new legislation to stimulate investment in databases by conferring new rights to protect databases.

♦ Before 1998, a compilation of data recorded in material form could be protected as a literary work under the *Copyright, Designs and Patents Act 1988* ('**CDPA**').

● To qualify for protection, the database had to satisfy the standard (relatively low) copyright test of 'originality' (ie: sufficient skill, judgment or effort must have been used in compiling the data).

■ In the UK this test was commonly passed, although databases did not attract copyright protection in every European jurisdiction.

● The author of the work also had to be a 'qualifying person' for copyright purposes under the *CDPA* – see Section A of this Chapter.

♦ Any confidential information that a database contains was (and remains) capable of protection under the law of confidence – see Section J of this Chapter.

● NB: there are no property rights in information itself (*Oxford v Moss* [1978] 68 Cr App Rep 183).

■ This is a fundamental principle of a free society.

♦ Subjects of data have rights under data protection law – see Section K of this Chapter. While important, these rights do not create rights of ownership.

♦ A database is unlikely to be a patentable invention (however inventive).

● To the extent that it amounts to a literary work, a method of doing business, a computer program or a presentation of information, it is not an invention (*Patents Act 1977 s 1(2)*).

History

➤ A new regime was introduced by the *CRDR*, which implemented *Directive 96/9/EC* (known as the '***Database Directive***') and came into force on 1 January 1998.

> ### 'Database right'
>
> ➤ The *CRDR* introduced a '*sui generis*' database right, ie: a special database right that is entirely independent of copyright (the '***database right***').
>
> ◆ The database right is similar to copyright in that it is a right against use (ie: not a monopoly right) that arises automatically and does not have to be registered.
>
> ◆ The aim of database right is to protect compilations of commonplace data, such as telephone directories, music charts or sports fixtures listings – especially where these would not satisfy the high thresholds of originality required for protection under many European copyright regimes.
>
> • This aim has not, in practice, been achieved in the way originally intended, as the courts' interpretation of the legislation has led to surprising limitations on the scope of protection afforded (see further below).
>
> ▪ Recognising this, the European Commission launched a consultation process in December 2005. The responses largely favoured maintaining the status quo and/or clarification of the scope of the database right, so it seems unlikely that database legislation will be reformed in the near future.

➤ A database that falls within the statutory definition of a 'database' may still be protected as a copyright literary work, as long as the database fulfils the statutory (relatively high) requirement of originality, ie: that 'by reason of the selection or arrangement of the contents of the database, the database can be said to constitute the author's own intellectual creation' (*CDPA s 3A(2)*).

◆ If a work does not fall within the statutory definition of a 'database', it can still attract copyright protection if it meets the ordinary criteria under the *CDPA*.

➤ There are therefore 3 potential options to consider:

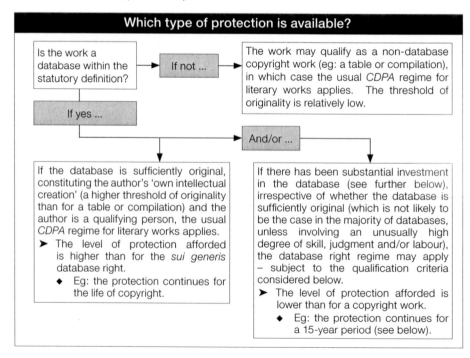

Which type of protection is available?

Is the work a database within the statutory definition? → If not ... → The work may qualify as a non-database copyright work (eg: a table or compilation), in which case the usual *CDPA* regime for literary works applies. The threshold of originality is relatively low.

If yes ...

And/or ...

If the database is sufficiently original, constituting the author's 'own intellectual creation' (a higher threshold of originality than for a table or compilation) and the author is a qualifying person, the usual *CDPA* regime for literary works applies.

➤ The level of protection afforded is higher than for the *sui generis* database right.

◆ Eg: the protection continues for the life of copyright.

If there has been substantial investment in the database (see further below), irrespective of whether the database is sufficiently original (which is not likely to be the case in the majority of databases, unless involving an unusually high degree of skill, judgment and/or labour), the database right regime may apply – subject to the qualification criteria considered below.

➤ The level of protection afforded is lower than for a copyright work.

◆ Eg: the protection continues for a 15-year period (see below).

➤ NB: copyright in a database (within the statutory meaning) and the database right can co-exist if the database is original enough to qualify for copyright protection (*r 13(2)*).

♦ In practice copyright affords stronger protection, so a rights-owner is more likely to rely on rights conferred under copyright (where utilisable) than on rights conferred under the database right.

● So the database right is of greatest relevance where (as often) there is doubt as to the originality of the database.

■ NB: the contents of a database can themselves also be copyright works (eg: articles, songs, photographs, films or sound recordings).

II Database right

➤ The extent to which a database is protected under the database right can be broken down into 7 steps:

Steps	
1	Is it a 'database'?
2	Does the database qualify for protection?
3	Who is the owner of the right?
4	How long does the right last?
5	What protection does the right give the owner?
6	Are there any defences to infringement?
7	What are the remedies?

Step 1	Is it a 'database'?

➤ The database in question must fall within the statutory definition of a 'database'.

♦ For these purposes, a 'database' is a collection of independent works, data or other materials which:

a) are arranged in a systematic or methodical way, *and*

b) are individually accessible by electronic or other means (*CDPA s 3A(1)*).

● The definition is very wide and therefore covers works such as encyclopedias, as well as more traditional forms of databases such as mailing lists.

● The definition covers all forms of media, eg: hard-copy directories, as well as electronic resources such as websites.

■ NB: the database should be carefully distinguished from its contents, which may themselves be works in which copyright and/or other rights subsist (eg: literary and graphic works posted on a webpage).

Step 2	Does the database qualify for protection?

➤ A database is protected by the database right where there has been 'a substantial investment in obtaining, verifying or presenting' its contents (r 13).

   ◆ 'Substantial' means substantial in terms of quantity or quality (or a combination of both).

   ◆ Investment is the defining characteristic of the database right.

      ● 'Investment' includes any type of investment, whether of financial, human or technical resources.

      ● The resources in question are those spent on collecting independently created contents.

         ■ Resources spent by the owner on creating the contents themselves are to be disregarded, as is the value of those contents to the owner (*British Horseracing Board Ltd v William Hill Organisation Ltd*, Case C203/02, 9 November 2004).

         ■ This has created serious difficulties for sports organisations that create contents of databases (eg: fixtures lists and player data), without spending separate and substantial resources on finding, checking or presenting those contents for the purposes of making the databases themselves.

         ■ Failure to fulfil this condition has not meant, however, that users of sports data can extract or utilise such data freely, as they may be in breach of their licence from the owner of the database (see *BHB Enterprises v Victor Chandler* [2005] EWHC 1074).

➤ There are also requirements relating to the nationality of the maker of the database (or, if made jointly, one or more of its makers) (r 18).

   ◆ If the maker is an individual, the maker must be a national of an EEA State or habitually resident within the EEA.

   ◆ If the maker is a company (or partnership), it must:

   a) have been incorporated (or formed) under the law of an EEA State, *and*

   b) at such time, have had:

      i) its central administration or principal place of business within the EEA, *or*

      ii) (in the case of a company) its registered office within the EEA, as well as being linked on an ongoing basis with the economy of an EEA State.

Step 3	Who is the owner of the right?

➤ The maker of a database is the first owner of the database right (*r 15*).

 ◆ The maker is defined as the person who 'takes the initiative in obtaining, verifying, or presenting the contents of a database and assumes the risk of investing in that obtaining, verification or presentation' (*r 14(1)*).

➤ If a database is made by an employee in the course of employment, the employer is regarded as the maker (subject to any agreement to the contrary) (*r 14(2)*).

➤ A database is treated as jointly made if 2 or more persons collaborate in obtaining, verifying or presenting its contents and share the risks of investment (*r 14(5)*).

➤ A database right may be assigned or licensed in the same way as copyright (*r 23*).

Dealings with a database

➤ Where a person commissions an independent contractor to make a database, the commissioner is likely (by assuming the investment risk) to be the first owner of the database right, although the contractor may be the author of the database if copyright arises.

 ◆ The commissioner must therefore take a full grant of rights in the database (including an assignment of copyright and database right) to secure full ownership and usage of the database.

➤ Some or all of the individual contents of a database may be protected under separate intellectual property rights (eg: as copyright works in their own right, such as films or sound recordings).

 ◆ The commissioner should take appropriate grants of rights in any such underlying works, as well as in the collection of works comprised by the database.

➤ The commissioner can then exploit the database commercially (eg: by way of an end-user licence agreement or, ultimately, a sale to a trade buyer).

Step 4	How long does the right last?

➤ The database right expires 15 years from the end of the year in which:

a) the making of the database was completed, *or*

b) the database was first made available to the public (as long as publication occurs within 15 years of its completion) (*r 17*).

➤ If there is a substantial change to the contents of the database (eg: resulting from successive updates and revisions) involving a substantial new investment, the altered database qualifies for a new 15-year period of protection of the kind described above (*r 17(3)*).

 ◆ In order to maximise protection under the database right, the owner should annually commit resources to ensuring that the database is kept up to date, thereby ensuring that a new 15-year period runs from the end of each year.

  ● In this way it is theoretically possible, in effect, to extend the period of protection indefinitely.

Step 5	What protection does the right give the owner?

➤ The owner of a database right has the right to prevent the extraction or re-utilisation of all (or a substantial part) of the contents of the database without the owner's consent (*r 16(1)*).

◆ 'Extraction' means the permanent or temporary transfer of contents of a database to another medium by any means or in any form.

● The concept of extraction is broadly construed by the courts, and includes manual copying (even if the contents are adapted as they are selected), as well as automated copying (eg: downloading) (*Directmedia Publishing GmbH v Albert-Ludwigs-Universität Freiburg*, Case C-304/07, 9 October 2008).

■ This case confirmed that, where a person has made the right kind of investment (ie: in the creation of the database itself, rather than its contents), the protection conferred by the database right is relatively extensive.

■ The case reinforced the potentially wide-ranging scope of database right, which many rights-owners feared had been severely curtailed by the various *British Horseracing Board* judgments referred to in this Section.

● Whether a transfer is permanent or temporary may affect the seriousness of the infringement, and so the quantum of damages (*Apis-Hristovich EOOD v Lakorda AD*, Case C-545/07).

● The concept of extraction is independent of the extractor's motive and of any use that the extractor may make of the data (*Apis-Hristovich*, as above).

◆ 'Re-utilisation' means making contents of a database available to the public by any means.

● The repeated and systematic extraction or re-utilisation of insubstantial parts of the contents of a database may amount to the extraction or re-utilisation of a substantial part of those contents (*r 16(2)*).

● Infringing use can be **qualitative** (using a small but significant part) or **quantitative** (using a large but less significant part) (*Database Directive Art 7(1)*).

◆ The leading case of *British Horseracing Board Ltd v William Hill Organisation Ltd* ([2001] RPC 612) shows that it is not a defence for the user of a database:

● to allege, when copying from a database that is repeatedly updated, insubstantial copying from a series of databases (as the database is viewed a single database for these purposes), *or*

● to have used intermediate media without copying direct from the database, *or*

● to have re-arranged the contents of the database without having reproduced the form of the database.

➤ The database right does not extend to protecting any software application used to create the database (*Database Directive Art 1(3)*).

◆ The software itself may qualify for protection as a copyright literary work under the *CDPA*.

Step 6	Are there any defences to infringement?

➤ A 'lawful user' of a published database (ie: a person that has a right, whether under licence or otherwise, to use a database) is entitled to extract or re-utilise **insubstantial** parts of the contents of the database for any purpose (*r 19(1)*), as long as such usage is not repeated and systematic (*r 16(2)*).

➤ A defence of 'fair dealing' for educational purposes is available to a person that extracts a **substantial** part of the contents of a published database.

 ◆ The defendant must show that (*r 20*):

  a) he is a lawful user of the part extracted, *and*

  b) the extraction is for the purpose of illustration for teaching or research and not for any commercial purpose, *and*

  c) the source of the database is indicated.

➤ A number of specially permitted acts are set out in the *CRDR*, including anything done for the purposes of (*r 20(2)* and *Sched 1*):

 ◆ parliamentary or judicial proceedings (or reporting them), *or*

 ◆ proceedings of a Royal Commission or statutory inquiry (or reporting such proceedings if held in public).

➤ In certain circumstances it may be possible to raise a defence under competition law, eg: where the owner:

 ◆ refuses to grant a licence (creating an effective monopoly in the relevant data), *or*

 ◆ seeks to impose unreasonable conditions of licence (such as excessive or discriminatory prices for access to the database), *or*

 ◆ behaves in any other way that abuses a dominant position in the relevant market, whether under the *Treaty on the Functioning of the European Union* ('**EU Treaty**') *Art 102* or under the *Competition Act 1998 Ch II* (see *Attheraces Ltd v British Horse Racing Board* [2005] EWHC 3015).

Step 7	What are the remedies?

➤ The remedies for infringement of a database right are similar to those for infringement of copyright, and include (*r 23*):

 ◆ an injunction (whether interim or final), *and/or*

 ◆ *either* damages *or* an account of the defendant's profits, *and/or*

 ◆ an order for delivery-up or destruction of infringing copies.

➤ An exclusive licensee of a database is entitled to bring proceedings in respect of infringement of the database right in his own name (*r 23*).

 ◆ This right can be waived under contract.

  ● Equally, such a right can be granted in a contract to a non-exclusive licensee.

F   Registered design right

*References in this Section are to the Registered Designs Act 1949 ('**RDA**'), unless otherwise stated.*

I   Generally
II   Is a design capable of registration?
III Registering a design
IV   Infringement
V   Dealing with registered design rights

I   Generally

➤ Design plays a key part in the success of consumer goods.

  ◆ Counterfeit goods copy not just branding, but the exact 'look' of goods.

➤ Designs are protected by 2 separate regimes:

  a) registered design rights (at UK and Community level), *and*

  b) unregistered design rights (also at UK and Community level).

    ◆ This Section examines UK registered design right ('**RDR**').

➤ RDR in the UK is governed by the *RDA* ('**RDA**').

➤ The *RDA* has been substantially amended by:

  a) the *Copyright, Designs and Patents Act 1988* ('**CDPA**'), *and*

  b) the *Registered Design Regulations 2001* ('**RDR 2001**'), *and*

  c) the *Regulatory Reform (Registered Designs) Order 2006* ('**RDO 2006**'), *and*

  d) the *Registered Designs Rules 2006* ('**RDR 2006**').

➤ The scope of protection of RDR depends on which legal regime applied at the time when the RDR was created or applied for (see *RDR 2001 r 12*).

  ◆ Applications received before the *RDR 2001* came into force on 9 December 2001 are dealt with under the previous law, which is beyond the scope of this Section.

➤ A design is often used as a trade mark – see Section L of this Chapter.

  ◆ RDR has a number of advantages in comparison with a registering a trade mark:

    a) there is no need for the owner to have used a design, *and*

    b) there are no 'distinctiveness' or 'descriptiveness' grounds of objection, *and*

    c) RDR protection covers any article to which the design is applied, whereas trade marks must be registered in particular classes of goods/services, *and*

    d) the registration process involves less extensive examination by the UK Intellectual Property Office ('**UK IPO**'), and is quicker and cheaper.

➤ The main features of the current RDR regime (ie: for RDR applications made after 9 December 2001) are as follows:

Overview of RDR regime
➤ RDR protects the **appearance** of a product.
◆ Parts of a design can be protected, as long as they are visible in normal use.
➤ RDR protects 3-dimensional and 2-dimensional designs.
◆ A sculpture is protected if it is intended to be used as a model or a pattern to be mass-produced by an industrial process.
• Single, one-off designs can be protected.
• There is no minimum number of articles that must be made to the design.
➤ The design must have 'individual character' (rather than 'eye appeal', as under the previous regime).
◆ The design must be novel worldwide (unless it fits within the exceptions).
• 'Must match' designs are now registrable (see section II below).
➤ There is a 12-month grace period for disclosure by the creator/designer, which enables filing of an application after marketing/displaying a design.
➤ RDR confers a monopoly right on the owner.
◆ The period of protection continues for 25 years from the application filing date (subject to payment of renewal fees).

II   Is a design capable of registration?

➤ In determining whether a design can be registered at the Designs Registry of the UK IPO, an applicant should consider the following steps:

Steps	
1	Does the design fall within the *s 1(2)* definition?
2	Is the design new and of individual character?
3	Does a substantive ground for refusal of registration apply?

Step 1	Does the design fall within the *s 1(2)* definition?

➤ 'Design' is defined in the *RDA* as 'the appearance of the whole or a part of a product resulting from the features of, in particular, the lines, contours, colours, shape, texture or materials of the product or its ornamentation' (*s 1(2)*).

◆ 'Product' means any industrial or handicraft item (other than a computer program), and includes packaging, get-up, graphic symbols and typefaces (*s 1(3)*).

● Accordingly, **non-visible** design features cannot be registered.

➤ RDR applies to:

◆ 2-dimensional designs (eg: a surface pattern or software icon), *and*

◆ 3-dimensional designs (eg: an ornament or article).

➤ RDR applies to the design itself, rather than a product to which the design is applied.

➤ NB: the design need not have any artistic merit.

Step 2	Is the design new and of individual character?

➤ A design can only be protected to the extent that the design:

a) is 'new' – ie: no identical (or materially identical) design has been made available to the public before the relevant date (*s 1(B)(2)*), *and*

b) has 'individual character' – ie: the overall impression produced on the informed user differs from that produced by any design that has been made available to the public before the relevant date (*s 1B(3)*).

◆ 'Made available to the public' means published, exhibited, used in trade or otherwise disclosed (*s 1B(5)(a)*).

◆ The 'relevant date' is the actual (or deemed) date of the application for the registration of the design (*s 1B(7)*) – see below for deemed priority dates.

● A factor in assessing individual character is the author's degree of freedom in creating the design (*s 1B(4)*).

■ Eg: a functional item (for which the author has limited scope for design) need not be as characterful as a decorative item.

◆ An 'informed user' need not be a design expert, but must have knowledge of products in the relevant sector.

● The courts are reluctant to allow expert evidence in an RDR action (*Procter & Gamble Co v Reckitt Benckiser (UK) Ltd* [2007] EWCA Civ 936).

➤ Certain types of disclosure are disregarded for these purposes, ie: where (*s 1B(6)*):

a) the design could not reasonably have become known before the application date in the normal course of business to persons carrying on business in the European Economic Area ('**EEA**') and specialising in the sector concerned, *or*

b) disclosure is made under conditions of confidentiality (express or implied), *or*

c) disclosure is made within the 12-month period before the application date by the designer or by a successor in title (or by any person as a result of any action taken by, or of any abuse in relation to, the designer or such successor).

   ◆ The 12-month 'grace period' in which to apply for registration after disclosure of the design allows the designer to test the market for the design (eg: to seek funding on the basis of a proven success) before incurring registration costs.

➤ In practice, a designer should carefully control disclosure of a design.

How should a design be disclosed?

➤ Although a design can be registered within the 12-month 'grace period', there is a risk that an **unrelated** disclosure of the same or a similar design by another person during that period may defeat any later application by the designer.

   ◆ To minimise this risk, the designer should apply to register the design as soon as possible following disclosure.

➤ Any marketing agreement signed before registration should include a clause protecting the confidentiality of the design.

   ◆ If the design is subsequently published in breach of the confidentiality obligations, the design can still be registered (*s 1B(6)(b)*).

Step 3	Does a substantive ground for refusal of registration apply?

➤ Aside from design features that do not qualify as a design or fail to fulfil the criteria of novelty or individual character, the following are refused registration (*s 1A*):

a) design features solely dictated by the product's technical function (*s 1C(1)*), *or*

   ◆ The test is whether the technical function dictates the appearance of the product such that there is no design freedom (*Philips Electronics NV v Remington Consumer Products Ltd*, Case C-299/99).

b) design features that must be reproduced in their exact form and dimensions so as to permit a product to be mechanically connected to (or placed in, around or against) another product so that either product can perform its function (*s 1C(2)*), *or*

   ◆ This is a 'must fit' design. In contrast, a 'must match' design is registrable.

   ◆ A design for a 'modular system' (ie: allowing multiple assembly or connection of mutually interchangeable products) can be registered (*s 1C(3)*). Eg: designs for LEGO bricks and modular furniture are registrable.

c) a design contrary to public policy or accepted principles of morality (*s 1D*), *or*

d) certain emblems (eg: coats of arms, national flags, hallmarks and controlled symbols such as the Olympic Symbol), unless registered with the consent of the person, organisation or country concerned (see *Sch A1*).

➤ The registration of a design is liable to be declared invalid on any of the above grounds, but may also be declared invalid where the design constitutes an infringement of a third party's:

♦ trade mark or rights in passing-off (*s 11ZA(3)*), *and/or*

♦ copyright (*11ZA(4)*).

 • These earlier rights are not grounds for refusal, but should be anticipated to try to ensure that the registration will not be challenged subsequently.

III   Registering a design

➤ The *RDR 2006* set out the procedure for applying for a registration.

 ♦ References to rules in this section III are to *RDR 2006*, unless otherwise stated.

➤ There are 4 stages involved in an application for registration of a design.

Stages	
1	Application
2	Examination
3	Objections
4	Registration

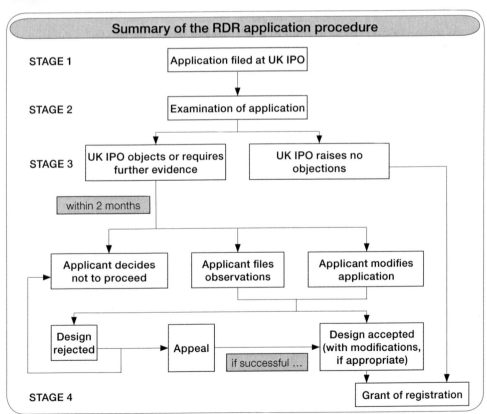

Summary of the RDR application procedure

STAGE 1 — Application filed at UK IPO

STAGE 2 — Examination of application

STAGE 3 — UK IPO objects or requires further evidence / UK IPO raises no objections

within 2 months

Applicant decides not to proceed / Applicant files observations / Applicant modifies application

Design rejected → Appeal → if successful ... → Design accepted (with modifications, if appropriate)

STAGE 4 — Grant of registration

Stage 1	Application

➤ There are 3 points for an applicant to consider.

1 Who can make the application?

➤ An application can be made by:

a) the 'owner' of the design (see *s 2* and the box below) (*s 3(2)*), *or*

b) an authorised agent of the owner (eg: a solicitor or trade-mark agent).

Ownership of a design

➤ The first owner of a design is the:

◆ author – ie: the person who creates the design, *or*

◆ commissioner – where the design is commissioned for money or money's worth, *or*

◆ employer – where the employee creates the design in the course of employment, *or*

◆ person making the arrangements necessary for the creation of the design – where the design is generated by computer such that there is no human author.

➤ The owner of a design can be of any nationality and can live outside the UK, but the owner (or the owner's agent) must have an address for service in the UK for registration purposes.

➤ Where an employee files an application and registers a design in the course of his or her employment, the design will belong to the employer.

◆ If the employee is registered as owner, the UK IPO may, at its discretion, allow for a rectification of the register.

➤ An applicant must also be the owner of any unregistered design right subsisting in the design *(s 3(3))*.

2 What must be filed?

➤ The applicant must:

a) file a completed and signed *Form DF2A* (available from the UK IPO's website), *and*

b) file an illustration of the design(s), *and*

c) with a) and b) above, send the prescribed fee for each design.

➤ The *RDR 2006* allow multiple designs to be covered in a single application, and multiple applications can be made using *Form DF2A*.

  ◆ Surplus designs can be submitted on *Form DF2B*.

  ◆ Each design is regarded as a separate piece of intellectual property and can be dealt with individually.

  ◆ For the sake of simplicity, references below are to a single design.

3   The content of the application

➤ The applicant should consider carefully what to apply to register.

What should be registered?

➤ The applicant should consider what the protectable features of the design are and how those features differ from any earlier design.

➤ The applicant should decide whether to register the design as a whole or whether to register specific features only (or both).

  ◆ Registering the features of the design separately may aid an infringement action where the infringer is only using part of the design.

➤ To assist with filing and searches, the applicant must provide details of the product(s) to which the design is to be applied.

  ◆ NB: the scope of registration is not limited to the product(s) specified.

➤ The design must be illustrated to show the features to be protected.

Illustration of the design

➤ The illustration can be a drawing, photograph or sample.

➤ It should include different views (eg: side-on or in perspective), with explanatory labels, to show all relevant features.

  ◆ The graphical representation can be supplemented, where necessary, by a brief verbal description of any features not adequately illustrated (eg: texture or materials used).

➤ The illustration should show the complete design for any repeating surface pattern, along with any repeats.

➤ The illustration can identify a part of the design that is to be protected separately (eg: by shading or circling the part). In this case, the applicant should include a written 'partial disclaimer', that specifies the features of the part that are to be protected.

➤ An application should include details of any claim to priority.

> ### Claim to priority
>
> ➤ A 'priority application' is one where the design has already been registered in a country that has signed the *Paris Convention for the Protection of Industrial Property* ('**Convention**').
>
> ◆ The countries include most developed countries and are listed in the *Designs (Convention Countries) Order 2007*.
>
> ➤ If a design has a filing date in another *Convention* country, publication in the UK after that filing date will not preclude registration of the design in the UK due to lack of novelty.
>
> ➤ The UK application is given the same filing date as the first application in the relevant *Convention* country (the 'priority date') provided that the UK application is made within 6 months of the priority date.
>
> ➤ In a priority application the applicant must, within 3 months of filing the UK application, file:
>
> a) details of the *Convention* filing, *and*
>
> b) a copy of the representation of the design that was filed in the *Convention* country.
>
> ➤ If requested by the UK IPO, the applicant must, within 3 months of the request, file a translation of all/part of any documents relating to the *Convention* filing that are not in English or Welsh (*r 7*).

➤ An applicant must elect whether:

a) to have the design published and registered by the UK IPO as soon as possible, *or*

b) to defer publication and registration (in which case the applicant must apply for the design to be published and registered within 12 months of the original application, failing which the application lapses).

◆ NB: the official publication takes place at the same time as the registration.

• The option to defer allows the applicant to market the design before it is officially published, so minimising the risk of copying before a product is launched.

◆ The form for a deferral is *Form DF2C*, and the applicant must pay a publication fee and a deferral fee.

Stage 2	Examination

➤ When the UK IPO examines the application, it:

   a) checks that all documents are in order and whether the UK IPO needs to object to the application, *and*

   b) sends the applicant a letter with the results of the examination (normally within 2 months after receiving the application).

➤ NB: in October 2006 the UK IPO ceased carrying out examination and searches of novelty and individual character.

Stage 3	Objections

➤ If the UK IPO finds grounds for refusal to register the design, it must give the applicant a written statement of objections setting out those grounds (*rr 8(1)-(2)*).

➤ The applicant may respond to the objections by:

   a) submitting written observations to the UK IPO (*r 8(3)*), *and/or*

   b) applying for a hearing (*r 8(4)*).

   ◆ There is a 2-month time limit for responding to objections.

➤ NB: in contrast to the procedure for trade-mark registration, there is no provision for:

   ◆ advertising the design, *or*

   ◆ opposing an application,

   … before registration.

➤ If the UK IPO refuses to register the design, it must give the applicant written reasons for the decision (*r 8(5)*).

➤ If the application is refused, there is a right of appeal to the Appeal Tribunal (*r 28*).

   ◆ The Appeal Tribunal may require the application to be modified.

   ◆ There is no statutory right of appeal from the Appeal Tribunal, but its decisions are subject to judicial review.

Stage 4	Registration

➤ If the UK IPO accepts an application, it will issue a certificate of registration to the applicant.

   ◆ The applicant becomes the first registered proprietor of the design right.

   ◆ The certificate confirms the date of registration and the registration number.

➤ The UK IPO must then, as soon as possible, publish a representation of the design (and can publish any other relevant material) in UK IPO's *Electronic Designs Journal* (*r 11*).

➤ The registered proprietor has an exclusive right to use (ss 7(1) and 7(3)):

a) the design, *and*

b) any design that does not produce a different overall impression on the informed user (taking into account the author's degree of freedom in creating the design).

♦ 'Use' includes making, offering, marketing, importing, exporting, using and stocking a product featuring the design (s 7(2)).

➤ The maximum duration of RDR is 25 years, but the registration must be renewed every 5 years (s 8).

♦ The applicant must submit *Form DF9A* plus the renewal fee to the UK IPO.

● If the registration is not renewed, restoration of the registration may be possible at the UK IPO's discretion.

IV   Infringement

➤ There are 3 steps to consider in relation to an infringement action:

Steps	
1	There must be an infringing act.
2	Are there any defences?
3	What are the remedies?

Step 1	There must be an infringing act

➤ RDR is infringed where, without the owner's consent, a person uses (ss 7A(1), 7(1) and 7(3)):

a) a design, *or*

b) any design that does not produce a different overall impression on an informed user (taking into account the author's degree of freedom in creating the design).

♦ 'Use' includes making, offering, marketing, importing, exporting, using and stocking a product featuring the design (s 7(2)).

● Applying the same design to a different product will infringe the RDR.

■ Eg: an album-cover design would be infringed if applied to T-shirts.

● A similar design will infringe if it reproduces key novel features.

♦ 'Overall impression' is a visual matter for which expert evidence is of little assistance (*Rolawn Ltd v Turfmech Ltd* [2008] EWHC 989).

➤ Since the owner has a monopoly right, infringement occurs even if the defendant has independently conceived the idea for the design.

➤ Since RDR is a national right created under UK law, the infringing act must occur within the UK.

    ◆ Marketing and/or importing goods for sale in the UK via an overseas website may constitute activity within the UK for these purposes (see the 'PlayStation' case, *KK Sony Computer Entertainment and Sony Computer Entertainment Europe Ltd v Pacific Game Technology (Holding) Ltd* [2006] EWHC 2509).

        ● Relevant factors in the 'PlayStation' case included that the English language was used on the website, and that prices were quoted in UK currency.

➤ The owner's exclusive rights are subject to any limitation attaching to the registration (eg: any partial disclaimer or any declaration of partial invalidity) (*s 7(4)*).

Step 2	Are there any defences?

➤ The *RDA* provides for a number of defences to infringement.

1   Non-infringing acts

    ➤ RDR is not infringed by (*s 7A(2)-(3)*):

        a) an act done privately and for non-commercial purposes, *or*

        b) an act done for experimental purposes, *or*

        c) an act done for teaching or citation purposes, provided that:

            i) the reproduction is compatible with fair trade practice and does not unduly prejudice the normal exploitation of the design, *and*

            ii) mention is made of the source, *or*

        d) the:

            i) use of equipment on overseas-registered ships/aircraft that are temporarily in the UK, *or*

            ii) importation into the UK of spare parts or accessories to repair such ships/aircraft, *or*

            iii) carrying out of repairs on ships/aircraft.

2   Exhaustion of rights

    ➤ RDR is not infringed in relation to a product featuring the design if the product has already been put onto the market in the EEA by the owner or with the owner's consent (*s 7A(4)*).

    ➤ NB: an owner can still claim for infringement where a defendant, operating outside of the EEA, has used its website to market products that can be used in the EEA, even though the website specifically states that the goods are for use outside of the EEA.

        ◆ A court looks at (among other things) the language used and the language of the manuals for the products (the 'PlayStation' case, as above).

3   Repairing a complex product

➤   It is not an infringement to repair a 'complex product' to its original appearance by replacing a component part with a similar design (s 7A(5)).

◆   A 'complex product' is a product composed of at least 2 replaceable component parts permitting disassembly and reassembly of the product (s 1(3)).

◆   This effectively allows an independent parts manufacturer to make visible spare parts for a product without infringing the product manufacturer's design.

●   This is of particular relevance to the car industry.

4   Pre-registration act

➤   RDR is not infringed by an act committed before the grant of the relevant registration certificate (s 7A(6)).

5   Innocence

➤   A claimant is not entitled to damages or an account of profits where the defendant neither knew, nor had reasonable grounds for supposing, that the design was registered (s 9(1)).

◆   A defendant is presumed to know that the design is registered where the owner marks the product with:

a)   the word 'registered' (or a similar expression or abbreviation), *and*

b)   the registration number.

◆   NB: innocence is not a defence to an injunction (or other remedies).

6   Invalidity

➤   A defendant may, by way of counterclaim, seek a declaration that the registration of the design is invalid.

◆   The grounds for invalidity are that:

a)   the design was not registrable under the *RDA, or*

b)   the person that was registered as the RDR owner is not the owner of the **design** within the meaning of the *RDA* (see above), *or*

c)   the design constitutes an infringement of a third party's rights under trade-mark law (or in passing off) or copyright (s 11ZA).

◆   If the registration is found to be valid, the claimant can apply to court for a certificate of a validity to be entered on the register (s 25(1)).

7   Use by the Crown

➤   A government department (or person authorised by such department) may use a registered design if it pays compensation to the owner (or to the exclusive licensee) in an agreed amount (or, failing agreement, as determined by the court) (s 12 and *Sch 1*).

Step 3	What are the remedies?

➤ The civil remedies for infringement include:

a) an injunction (interim or final) (s 24A(2)), and/or

b) damages or an account of profits (s 24A(2)), although an innocent infringer is exempt (s 24B and see above), and/or

c) an order for the delivery-up or destruction of infringing articles (ss 24C and 24D).

➤ A claimant must be careful not to make any groundless threats of infringement proceedings.

Groundless threats

➤ Where an owner of RDR threatens to commence proceedings against any person by any means, the person threatened may bring an action for groundless threats (ie: claiming that the owner has no grounds to bring a claim) (s 26(1)).

➤ It is a defence for the owner to show that the acts constituted (or feared acts would constitute) infringement (s 26(2)).

➤ If the action is successful, the remedies are:

a) a declaration that the threats are unjustifiable, and

b) an injunction against any continuance of the threats, and

c) damages for any loss caused by the threats (s 26(2)).

➤ The possibility of an action for groundless threats should be taken into account when drafting a letter before action.

◆ If an action for groundless threats is likely, it is safest merely to notify the potential defendant that the design is registered, as a notice to that effect does not amount to a threat of proceedings (s 26(3)).

➤ As a tactic in litigation, a potential defendant may bring an action for groundless threats even if it is questionable whether the threats are groundless to try to obtain control of the litigation and to claim damages from the owner.

➤ There are a number of criminal offences under the RDA, eg:

a) causing a false entry in the register of designs (s 34), and

b) falsely representing that a design is registered (s 35).

◆ NB: if RDR has been applied for, a designer can mark the relevant products with a notice 'registered design applied for' without committing an offence under s 35.

• See ss 33-35A for further details of the offences.

V   Dealing with registered design rights

➤ In common with other intellectual property rights, a registered design constitutes personal property, as does an application for a registered design (s 15A).

  ◆ Accordingly, a registered design (or application) is transmissible in the same way as other personal property, including under a will or by operation of law (s 15B(1)).

  ● References below to disposals of registered designs apply equally to disposals of applications.

➤ There are 2 main ways of dealing with RDR.

1   Assignment

  ➤ The owner may assign (ie: transfer title to) a registered design.

  ◆ An assignment of RDR is not effective unless it is (s 15B(3)):

  a) in writing, *and*

  b) signed by or on behalf of the assignor.

  ◆ As with other intellectual property rights, the assignment may relate to part of the RDR and/or to future RDR, although this is not expressly provided for under the *RDA*.

  ◆ If the owner also owns any UK unregistered design right ('**UDR**'), the assignment will automatically include an assignment of the UDR, unless the contract specifies otherwise (s 19(3B)).

  ➤ The assignee must register the assignment at the UK IPO (s 19) using *Form DF12A*.

2   Licensing

  ➤ An owner may grant a 'sole', 'exclusive' or 'non-exclusive' licence of RDR.

  ◆ A 'sole' licence allows only the owner and licensee to use the design.

  ◆ An 'exclusive' licence allows only the licensee to use the design (to the exclusion of all other persons, including the owner).

  ◆ A 'non-exclusive' licence allows the owner to grant third-party licences.

  ➤ An exclusive licence must be:

  a) in writing, *and*

  b) signed by or on behalf of the owner (s 15C(1)).

  ◆ An exclusive licensee has a concurrent right with the owner to bring an action for infringement of RDR (ss 7(1) and 24F).

  ◆ NB: although there are no formalities for execution of sole or non-exclusive licences, these should also be in writing and signed to provide an accurate record of the agreed terms.

➤ Any form of interest in a registered design (including any form of licence) must be registered at the UK IPO (*s 19(1)*) using *Form DF12A*.

◆ The licence must be registered if it is:

a) to bind a subsequent assignee or licensee of the RDR (*s 15B(8)*), *and*

b) (unless the court otherwise directs) to be admissible in court as evidence of the licensee's interest in the RDR (*s 19(5)*).

• An unregistered licence is, however, admissible in an application to rectify the register under *s 20*.

G Unregistered design right

*References in this Section are to the Copyright, Designs and Patents Act 1988 ('**CDPA**'), unless otherwise stated.*

I Generally

➤ Unregistered design right ('**UDR**') came into existence on 1 August 1989 under *Pt III* of the *CDPA*.

◆ Previously, designs of a 'functional nature' and designs without aesthetic qualities had only been protected by copyright, giving such designs a 50-year period of protection.

● This was anomalous in comparison with the 15-year period of protection given at that time to registered design right ('**RDR**').

■ Manufacturers could prevent the making of spare parts for their products (eg: cars or consumer goods) using their long-enduring copyright rights. This imbalance was redressed by the *CDPA*.

➤ UDR is perhaps the least well known of all the intellectual property rights.

◆ It is, however, one of the most common in existence, for 2 reasons:

a) The requirements for subsistence of UDR are relatively easy to satisfy.

● UDR applies to any aspect of the shape or configuration (whether internal or external) of the whole or part of an article (*s 213(2)*).

● There is no need for aesthetic appeal or artistic originality: the design must simply not be copied or commonplace.

● There is no exclusion for designs that serve a purely functional purpose, unlike the position with RDR.

b) In contrast with patents, RDR and trade marks (but like copyright), there is no requirement for registration.

● UDR subsists once (*s 213(6)*):

i) a design that satisfies the *CDPA* requirements is recorded in a design document, *or*

ii) an article is made to such a design.

➤ To compensate for the ease with which UDR can be acquired, UDR is a weaker right than certain other intellectual property rights.

◆ UDR is not a monopoly right to use a design: it only gives the owner an exclusive right to prevent commercial reproduction of the design (*s 226(1)*).

◆ UDR exists for only 10 or 15 years (see section II below).

◆ A licence as of right is available during the last 5 years of UDR protection (*s 237*).

II   Requirements for unregistered design right

➤ There are 7 steps to consider in assessing whether and how a design is protected by UDR under the *CDPA*:

Steps	
1	Does the design fall within the *CDPA* definition?
2	Is the design original?
3	Has the design been recorded or has an article been made?
4	Is the design excluded?
5	Does the design qualify for UDR protection?
6	Who is the owner?
7	How long does UDR protection last?

Step 1	Does the design fall within the *CDPA* definition?

➤ A 'design' is defined as 'any aspect of the shape or configuration (whether internal or external) of the whole or part of an article' (*s 213(2)*).

◆ Most designs fall within this definition because it is so broad.

➤ The term 'configuration' is widely construed by the courts.

◆ Eg: a design that can only be seen in cross-section is protected.

◆ The juxtaposition of colours in 2 dimensions (eg: on a track-suit top) has been held not to fall within the term 'configuration' (*Lambretta Clothing Co Ltd v Teddy Smith (UK) Ltd* [2004] EWCA Civ 886).

● The courts may interpret this differently following the introduction of Community unregistered design right, which protects visible aspects of a design resulting from colours (among other design features) – see Section H of this Chapter.

➤ A claimant cannot claim UDR in an underlying design **concept**. The scope of UDR is restricted to the design as **manifested** in the design document or the article made to the design (*Rolawn Ltd v Turfmech Ltd* [2008] EWHC 989).

➤ A part of design is only protected by UDR if that part itself satisfies the criteria for protection (*A Fulton Co Ltd v Totes Isotomer (UK) Ltd* [2003] EWCA Civ 1514).

Step 2	Is the design original?

➤ For a design to qualify for protection, it must be 'original' (*s 213(1)*).

   ◆ A design is 'original' if it is original in a copyright sense, ie: if it is the product of skill and labour and is not copied from an earlier design (*Ultraframe (UK) Ltd v Eurocell Building Plastics Ltd* [2004] EWHC 1785).

      ● NB: a design can be original even if the idea behind another design has been copied (*C & H Engineering Ltd v Klucznik & Sons Ltd* [1992] FSR 421).

➤ A design is not original if it is 'commonplace in the design field in question at the time of its creation' (*s 213(4)*).

   ◆ To determine whether a design is 'commonplace', the court applies a 2-stage test (*Farmers Build Ltd v Carrier Bulk Materials Handling Ltd* [1999] RPC 461):

    a) The design is compared with other designs in the field to check that it has not been copied from an earlier design.

    b) If the design is original in the copyright sense, the court assesses the degree of objective similarity (in the light of evidence submitted) between the design concerned and the design of other articles within the same design field.

      ● If the design contains aspects that are unique within the design field, it is likely that the design is not commonplace.

➤ NB: a design can be protected as a whole even if it contains several commonplace elements (*Rolawn Ltd v Turfmech Ltd* [2008] EWHC 989).

Step 3	Has the design been recorded or has an article been made?

➤ UDR does not subsist unless (*s 213(6)*):

a) the design has been recorded in a 'design document', *or*

b) an article has been made to the design.

   ◆ A 'design document' is widely defined as 'any record of a design, whether in the form of a drawing, a written description, a photograph, data stored in a computer or otherwise' (*s 263(1)*).

      ● Eg: a design existing in a basic sketch (with only approximate dimensions) qualifies for protection if an article can be made from the design (*A Fulton Co Ltd v Totes Isotomer (UK) Ltd* [2003] EWCA Civ 1514).

      ● A design will be protected at each stage of its evolution if each working design is recorded in a design document (*Società Esplosivi Industriali SpA v Ordnance Technologies Ltd* [2004] EWHC 48).

      ● It is unclear whether temporary storage of a design document is sufficient, so a hard copy should be made (*R v Gold* [1982] 2 WLR 984).

➤ UDR does not subsist in a design that was recorded (or to which an article was made) before 1 August 1989 (ie: before the *CDPA Pt III* came into force) (*s 213(7)*).

Step 4	Is the design excluded?

➤ There are 4 main exclusions from UDR protection (*s 213(3)*):

1   Construction

➤ Methods and principles of construction are not protected by UDR (*s 213 (3)(a)*).

◆ To allow protection of this type would encroach on patent law.

◆ NB: this exclusion does not preclude a design from UDR protection merely because the design serves a functional purpose (and has no aesthetic features). It is merely the method of achieving the design that cannot be protected (*Landor & Hawa International Ltd v Azure Designs Ltd* [2006] EWCA Civ 1285).

2   'Must fit'

➤ UDR does not subsist in the features of shape or configuration of an article (*s 213 (3)(b)(i)*) where those features:

a) enable the article to be connected to (or placed in, around or against) another article, *and*

b) enable either article to perform its function.

➤ This is known as the 'must fit' exclusion.

◆ UDR protection is not precluded merely because the features fit together: there must also be a functional purpose served.

• Eg: the linking part of a cuff-link would be excluded as this part attaches the cuff-link to the shirt. Without that part, the cuff-link could not perform its function.

• NB: where only part of an article must fit another article, only the design of that part is excluded from UDR protection.

◆ If an article is made up of individual component parts, the fact that the components must fit together does not necessarily exclude the article from protection when considered as a whole (*Ultraframe (UK) Ltd v Eurocell Building Plastics Ltd* [2004] EWHC 1785).

◆ Fitting need not involve actual touching: a clearance between 2 parts might fall within the exclusion if the clearance serves a functional purpose (*Dyson Ltd v Qualtex (UK) Ltd* [2006] EWCA Civ 166).

◆ A design for a cover or container for another article does not fall within the 'must fit' exclusion (*A Fulton Co Ltd v Totes Isotomer (UK) Ltd* [2003] EWCA Civ 1514).

➤ A human body part (eg: the eye-ball in the context of contact lenses) might be treated as a natural 'article' for the purposes of the 'must fit' exclusion (*Ocular Sciences v Aspect Vision Care Ltd* [1997] RPC 289).

3   'Must match'

➤ UDR does not subsist in features of shape or configuration of an article where (*s 213(3)(b)(ii)*):

a) its features are dependent on the appearance of another article, *and*

b) the designer intends it to form an integral part of the other article.

➤ This is known as the 'must match' exclusion.

◆ Eg: the design for a spare car door is dictated by the appearance of the rest of the body of the car and the designer will intend the door to be integrated into the car body. As such, it falls within the exclusion.

◆ In contrast, if there is no such dependency and the designer is free to vary the appearance of the features, the exclusion does not apply (*Dyson Ltd v Qualtex (UK) Ltd* [2006] EWCA Civ 166).

4   Surface decoration

➤ Mere surface decoration is not protected by UDR (*s 213(3)(c)*).

◆ This exclusion applies to 2-dimensional designs on the surface of products (*Dyson*, as above).

◆ UDR can subsist in 3-dimensional surface patterns.

● The fact that a surface design feature (eg: colour) extends beneath the surface does not make it a 3-dimensional feature (*Lambretta Clothing Co Ltd v Teddy Smith (UK) Ltd* [2004] EWCA Civ 886).

➤ Surface decoration can instead be protected as a registered design (see Section F of this Chapter), and a design drawing for surface decoration usually attracts copyright protection as an artistic work (*Jo-Y-Jo Ltd v Matalan Retail Ltd*, 31 March 1999, unreported).

Step 5	Does the design qualify for UDR protection?

➤ UDR subsists only if the design qualifies for UDR protection, ie: where:

a) a 'qualifying person' is the designer (or is the designer's commissioner or employer, where the design is commissioned or made in the course of employment), *or*

b) if that is not the case, articles made to the design are first marketed by a 'qualifying person' in a 'qualifying country'.

◆ A 'qualifying person' is (*s 217(1)*):

i) a citizen, subject or habitual resident of a 'qualifying country', *or*

ii) a legal person (eg: a company) formed under the law of (or carrying out substantial business activity at a place of business in) a 'qualifying country'.

◆ A 'qualifying country' means the UK, any other EU member state or any of the other countries designated as a qualifying country (ie: broadly speaking, the UK's colonies and dependencies – see the *Design Right (Reciprocal Protection) Order 1989*).

● NB: the place of creation of the design is irrelevant.

Step 6	Who is the owner?

➤ If the design qualifies for UDR protection by reference to the designer or the designer's commissioner or employer (see step 5 above), the first owner of UDR is the (*s 215(1)-(3)*):

- ◆ designer, ie (*s 214*):

  - the person who creates the design, *or*

  - in the case of a computer-generated design, the person by whom the arrangements necessary for the creation of the design are undertaken, *or*

- ◆ commissioner – if the design is created in pursuance of a commission, *or*

- ◆ employer – if (in the absence of a commission) an employee creates a design in the course of employment.

  - The term 'employee' has the usual meaning established by case law.

  - If a non-employee creates a design while acting on a company's behalf, the non-employee may, depending on the facts, hold the design on trust for the company (see *Ultraframe (UK) Ltd v Alan Clayton* [2003] EWCA Civ 1805).

➤ Alternatively, if the design qualifies for UDR protection by virtue of having been first marketed in the UK (see step 5 above), the first owner of a design is the person first marketing the design in the UK (*s 215(4)*).

➤ UDR can be jointly owned where:

- ◆ UDR arises by reference to the designer and the design is produced in collaboration by 2 or more designers whose contributions to the design are not distinct (*s 259*), *or*

- ◆ ownership of UDR is only 'assigned' (ie: transferred) in part (*s 258* – and see section V below).

Step 7	How long does UDR protection last?

➤ The period of UDR protection is the shorter of (*s 216*):

a) 15 years from the end of the calendar year in which:

  i)   the design was first recorded in a design document, *or*

  ii) (if earlier) an article was first made to the design, *or*

b) 10 years from the end of the calendar year in which articles made to the design were first made available by the owner (or with the owner's consent) for sale or hire anywhere in the world.

- ◆ NB: in practice, the protection period is likely to be the shorter 10-year period.

III   Overlap between copyright and design rights

➤   If a copyright work consists of or includes a design protected by UDR, infringement of the copyright in the work does not infringe the UDR in the work (*s 236*).

◆   Accordingly, the owner can only bring an action for copyright infringement (or, if there is any uncertainty about the subsistence of either right, can only claim for UDR infringement in the alternative).

●   The purpose of *s 236* is to prevent double recovery under what would otherwise amount to 2 separate causes of action (ie: copyright and UDR).

■   Eg: an owner's cause of action for unauthorised copying of a production drawing would be in copyright, not UDR.

●   In practice, there is little overlap between copyright works and articles made to designs, as (apart from sculptures and works of architecture) the only 3-dimensional copyright works are 'works of artistic craftsmanship' (*s 4(1)*), which require aesthetic appeal (*Merlet v Mothercare* [1986] RPC 115).

➤   In contrast, RDR can co-exist with copyright, and the owner can bring an action for infringement of RDR or copyright (or both).

➤   RDR can also co-exist with UDR, and the owner can bring an action for infringement of RDR or UDR (or both).

IV   Infringement

➤   There are 3 steps to consider in relation to an infringement action:

Steps	
1	There must be an infringing act.
2	Are there any defences?
3	What are the remedies?

Step 1	There must be an infringing act

➤   Primary infringement of UDR occurs where a person, without the owner's licence, reproduces (or authorises a third party to reproduce) the design for commercial purposes by making (*s 226(1)-(2)*):

a)   articles exactly or substantially to the design, *or*

b)   a design document recording the design to enable such articles to be made.

◆   The phrase 'for commercial purposes' means with a view to sale or hire of the article in the course of a business (*s 262(3)*).

➤ Accordingly, there are 2 classes of primary infringement (*Società Esplosivi Industriali SpA v Ordnance Technologies Ltd* [2004] EWHC 48):

1   Making class

➤ Making an article constitutes a primary infringement if it is made exactly or substantially to the design, looking at the design as a **whole** (*L Woolley Jewellers Ltd v A&A Jewellery Ltd* [2003] FSR 15).

◆ In a case of substantial reproduction, the degree of similarity between articles is to be determined (*C & H Engineering Ltd v Klucznik & Sons Ltd* [1992] FSR 421):

a) visually, *and*

b) objectively by reference to consumer opinion.

➤ As with copyright (and in contrast to RDR), a claimant must prove copying (*Rolawn Ltd v Turfmech Ltd* [2008] EWHC 989).

◆ UDR is not infringed by a person that has independently created a design (*Virgin Atlantic Airways Ltd v Premium Aircraft Interiors Group Ltd* [2009] EWHC 26).

• Expert evidence can be submitted on the similarities and differences between designs, but it is for the court to evaluate whether copying has taken place (*Virgin Atlantic*, as above).

➤ Copying part of a design can constitute infringement if that part is itself protected by UDR (*A Fulton Co Ltd v Totes Isotomer (UK) Ltd* [2003] EWCA Civ 1514).

2   Document class

➤ A defendant need not actually have made articles to the design: it is an infringement of UDR simply to have made a design document for the **purpose** of enabling articles to be made to the design.

◆ A claimant must prove this motive, along with the requisite commercial purposes (*Società Esplosivi Industriali SpA v Ordnance Technologies Ltd* [2004] EWHC 48).

➤ Secondary infringement of UDR consists of the unauthorised (*s 227(1)*):

a) commercial importation into the UK, *or*

b) commercial possession, *or*

c) sale or hire (or offering or exposing for sale or hire) in the course of a business,

… of an article that the infringer knows (or has reason to believe) is an infringing article.

◆ The test for knowledge and belief is an objective test (*Badge Sales v PMS International Group plc* [2006] FSR 1).

Step 2	Are there any defences?

➤ There are 4 main defences/exceptions to infringement.

1 Challenge to validity

➤ A defendant may challenge the validity of the UDR (eg: argue that the claimant's design is commonplace).

➤ Any party to a dispute as to the subsistence, term or first owner of UDR can refer such matter to the Comptroller-General of Patents, Designs and Trade Marks, whose decision is (unless appealed) binding on the parties (s 246(1)).

➤ The Comptroller has sole jurisdiction in these matters, except that a court or tribunal can decide any such matter (s 246(2)):

    a) on a reference or appeal from the Comptroller (ie: to the High Court – see s 251), or

    b) in proceedings in which the issue arises incidentally, or

    c) in proceedings brought with the parties' agreement or with the Comptroller's leave.

➤ The rules for proceedings before the Comptroller are set out in the Design Right (Proceedings before Comptroller) Rules 1989.

2 Innocent infringement

➤ It is a partial defence for the defendant to show that he did not know (and had no reason to believe) that (s 233):

    a) in the case of primary infringement – UDR subsisted in the relevant design, in which case the defendant is not liable in damages (but without prejudice to the claimant's other remedies, eg: injunctive relief), or

    b) in the case of secondary infringement – the article concerned was an infringing article, in which case the only remedy against the defendant is an award of damages not exceeding a reasonable royalty in respect of the infringing acts.

3 Compulsory licence

➤ In the last 5 years of the UDR term, any person is entitled as of right to a licence of the UDR, permitting that person to do anything that would otherwise be an infringement of the UDR (s 237(1)).

    ♦ If the owner and the licensee cannot agree the terms of the licence, the terms are settled by the Comptroller-General of Patents, Designs and Trade Marks (s 237(2)).

        • In the meantime, the licensee can make articles to the design.

> ➤ The terms of the compulsory licence are likely to include a royalty (determined objectively), but are likely not to include restrictions on sub-licensing or a right to terminate for breach (see *NIC Instruments Ltd's Licence of Right (Design Right) Application* [2005] RPC 1).

- ◆ The royalty base will vary depending on the facts. Examples include a per-unit retail price (*NIC Instruments*) or the licensee's net profits (*P J International Leathercrafts Ltd v Peter Jones (ILG) Ltd*, BL O/239/06, 25 August 2006).

- ◆ NB: a licensee of UDR may still infringe RDR even where the licensee has a licence as of right in relation to the associated UDR.

4   Use by the Crown

> ➤ A government department (or person authorised by such department) may use a design for supplying articles for defence and health-service purposes (or disposing of articles no longer required for such purposes) if it pays compensation to the owner (or to the exclusive licensee) in an agreed amount (or, failing agreement, as determined by the court) (*ss 240-244*).

Step 3	What are the remedies?

> ➤ The remedies for infringement include:

a) an injunction (interim or final) (*s 229(2)*), *and/or*

b) damages or an account of profits (*s 229(2)*), although:

- ◆ an innocent primary infringer is exempt from damages (*s 233(1)* and see above), *and*

- ◆ an innocent secondary infringer is liable only to damages not exceeding a reasonable royalty (*s 233(2)* and see above), *and/or*

c) an order for the delivery-up or destruction of infringing articles (*ss 230* and *231*).

> ➤ If, however, the defendant undertakes to take a licence as of right during the last 5 years of the UDR term (*s 239(1)*):

- ◆ an injunction will not be granted, *and*

- ◆ the amount recoverable by way of damages (or an account of profits) will not exceed double the amount that would have been payable by the defendant if a licence as of right had been granted before the earliest infringement, *and*

- ◆ no order for delivery-up will be made.

➤ As with RDR, a claimant must be careful not to make any groundless threats of infringement proceedings.

Groundless threats

➤ Where an owner of UDR threatens to commence proceedings against any person by any means, the person threatened may bring an action for:

   a) a declaration that the threats are unjustifiable, *and*

   b) an injunction against any continuance of the threats, *and*

   c) damages for any loss caused by the threats (*s 253(1)*).

➤ It is a defence for the owner to show that the acts constituted (or feared acts would constitute) infringement (*s 253(2)*).

➤ As with RDR, the possibility of an action for groundless threats should be taken into account when drafting a letter before action.

   ♦ If an action for groundless threats is likely, it is safest merely to notify the potential defendant that the design is protected by UDR, as a notice to that effect does not amount to a threat of proceedings (*s 253(4)*).

V   Dealing with unregistered design rights

➤ UDR is a property right (*s 213(1)*), so is transmissible as personal property (eg: under a will or by operation of law) (*s 222(1)*).

➤ There are 2 main ways of dealing with UDR.

1   Assignment

   ➤ UDR may be 'assigned' (ie: title in the UDR may be transferred).

      ♦ An assignment is not effective unless it is (*s 222(3)*):

         a) in writing, *and*

         b) signed by or on behalf of the assignor.

      ♦ An assignment may be partial (ie: limited in terms of the scope or duration of rights) (*s 222(2)*).

      ♦ Future UDR can be assigned (*s 223(1)*).

      ♦ If the UDR owner also owns RDR in the design, an assignment of the RDR automatically includes an assignment of the UDR, unless agreed otherwise (*s 224*).

2   Licensing

   ➤ A licence gives the licensee permission to do specified acts that would otherwise constitute an infringement of UDR.

➤ A licence of UDR is binding on each of the owner's successors in title, except (*s 222(4)*):

   a) a bona fide purchaser for valuable consideration without notice (actual or constructive) of the licence, *or*

   b) a person deriving title from such purchaser.

     ◆ This exception does not apply in the case of an **exclusive** licence, so all of the owner's successors are bound by the licence (*s 225(2)*).

➤ An exclusive licensee has concurrent rights with the UDR owner, so neither may proceed with an action for UDR infringement unless the other is joined as a party or the leave of the court is obtained (*ss 234-235*).

➤ For the statutory rights to apply, an exclusive licence must be (*s 225(1)*):

   a) in writing, *and*

   b) signed by or on behalf of the licensor, *and*

   c) to the exclusion of all other persons (including the licensor).

     ◆ NB: where a licensor needs to reserve any rights, the status of the exclusive licence can be preserved if the licensee grants the rights back to the licensor by way of a sub-licence.

➤ However the owner decides to deal with an UDR, the owner should take appropriate steps to confirm the subsistence and ownership of the UDR.

Managing UDR

➤ Since UDR is an unregistered right whose subsistence depends on when and how it is created and marketed, it is important to keep careful records.

   ◆ Each design document should be logged and stored securely.

   ◆ A record should be kept of related marketing activities.

     ● This is also relevant to whether a licence as of right is available.

➤ Although there is no requirement under English law to assert ownership of UDR, it is advisable to mark articles with a notice in the format:

     'Design right [*name of owner*] [*year of first marketing*]'

   ◆ NB: there is no UDR equivalent to the symbols for copyright (©), a registered trade mark (®) or an unregistered trade mark (™).

   ◆ This form of notice will assist in:

     a) putting a potential infringer on notice of the UDR, *and*

     b) rebutting an innocent-infringement defence under *s 233*.

   ◆ A licensee of UDR should be required under the licence agreement to apply such a notice to all articles made under licence.

VI   Semiconductor topography rights – summary

➤ Semiconductor topographies are protected by a special type of UDR that applies to the layout of integrated circuits.

➤ The protection of semiconductor topographies is governed by the *CDPA*, as deemed to be amended by the *Design Right (Semiconductor) Regulations 1989* ('*DR(S)R 1989*').

◆ The *DR(S)R 1989* superseded earlier regulations that provided for a free-standing 'topography right'.

● References below are to the *DR(S)R 1989*.

◆ Essentially, the protection now takes the form of UDR under the *CDPA* (subject to certain exceptions set out in the *DR(S)R 1989*).   It arises where the design in question is a 'semiconductor topography' (as defined in *r 2* – broadly speaking, a design of patterns to be fixed in or on a silicon chip).

● NB: the details of the *DR(S)R 1989* are beyond the scope of this section, but a brief summary of their effect is given below.

➤ The main exceptions to the usual UDR regime are as follows:

◆ There is a different, much wider list of qualifying countries (*r 4* and *Sch*).

● As a result, there is greater scope for first ownership via first marketing in a qualifying country (*r 5*).

● The *Design Right (Semiconductor Topographies) (Amendment) Regulations 2006* came into force on 1 August 2006.

■ These extended the scope of protection offered by UDR in semiconductor topographies to persons from countries that are members of the World Trade Organization.

◆ The 15-year period of protection (ie: where the alternative 10-year period does not apply) runs from when a design is first fixed (rather than the end of the calendar year in which the design is first fixed) (*r 6*).

◆ The owner's exclusive rights are limited by excluding the right to reproduce the design of the typography (*r 8(1)*):

● privately for non-commercial aims, *or*

● for the purpose of analysing or evaluating the design (or analysing, evaluating or teaching the concepts, processes, systems or techniques embodied in it).

◆ Licences as of right are not available during the last 5 years of protection (*r 9*).

H Community design rights

*References in this Section are to Community Design Regulation (6/2002/EC) ('**CDR 2002**'), unless otherwise stated.*

I	Generally
II	Requirements for registered Community design right
III	Applying for registered Community design right
IV	Requirements for unregistered Community design right
V	Infringement
VI	Dealing with Community design rights

I Generally

➤ A design can be protected in different countries around the world in 3 ways:

  a) at national level (eg: under UK law – see Sections F and G of this Chapter) under a series of national registrations, *and/or*

  b) throughout the European Union ('**EU**') under Community design rights ('**CDR**') (as described in this Section), *and/or*

  c) under an international system administered by the World Intellectual Property Organization (WIPO) in countries that are signatories to the *Geneva Act* of the *Hague Agreement* (which is beyond the scope of this Chapter).

➤ *CDR 2002* created a framework for EU-wide protection of designs by establishing 2 distinct rights:

  ◆ registered community design right ('**RCDR**'), *and*

  ◆ unregistered community design right ('**UCDR**').

➤ RCDR can be enforced on a pan-European basis – a significant advantage over a series of national registrations. There is a parallel disadvantage: invalidity in 1 member state will cause the right to be revoked across the whole of the EU.

  ◆ RCDR is, in other respects, similar to UK registered design right ('**UK RDR**').

   ● Unlike UK RDR, however, there is only limited examination and there is no opposition procedure, making RCDR a quicker and cheaper right to register.

    ▪ RCDR is therefore more susceptible to invalidity proceedings.

  ◆ RDCR is a true 'monopoly' right: it is not necessary to prove copying in order to bring a successful action (unlike in a copyright or UCDR claim).

  ◆ Applications can be filed at *(Art 35(1))*:

   a) the Office for Harmonization in the Internal Market ('**OHIM**') in Alicante, *or*

   b) the national registry of any EU member state, eg: the UK Intellectual Property Office ('**UK IPO**').

➤ UCDR provides EU-wide protection against unauthorised copying, but is in other respects broadly similar to UK unregistered design right ('**UK UDR**').

➤ For the purposes of both RCDR and UCDR (*Art 3*):

Definitions of 'design' and 'product'

➤ A 'design' is 'the appearance of the whole or a part of a product resulting from the features of, in particular, the line, contours, colours, shape, texture and/or materials of the product itself and/or its ornamentation'.

◆ The definition includes both 2-dimensional and 3-dimensional designs, and (unlike UK UDR) it applies to surface decoration.

➤ A 'product' is 'any industrial or handicraft item' and includes:

◆ parts intended to be assembled into a 'complex product' (ie: a product with multiple replaceable components that can be assembled/disassembled), *and*

◆ packaging, get-up, graphic symbols and typographic typefaces (eg: logos and devices that might, also or instead, be protected as trade marks).

• Computer programs are excluded from the definition.

II   Requirements for registered Community design right

➤ To be registrable, a design must:

a) fall within the definition of 'design' under *Art 3* (see section I above), *and*

b) be 'new' (*Art 4(1)*), *and*

◆ A design is 'new' if no identical design has been made available to the public (*Art 5(1)(a)*):

• before the application date, *or*

• if a right of priority is claimed (*see Art 41*), before the date of priority.

◆ Designs are 'identical' if their features differ only in immaterial details (*Art 5(2)*).

◆ As with UK RDR, there is a 12-month grace period in which to apply for registration after disclosure of the design (*Art 7(2)(b)*).

c) have 'individual character' (*Art 4(1)*).

◆ A design must produce a different overall impression on the informed user in comparison with previously disclosed designs (*Art 6(1)*).

• The 'informed user' is more discriminating than the 'average consumer' and is aware of the prior art known to specialists in the sector concerned (*Procter & Gamble Co v Reckitt Benckiser (UK) Ltd* [2007] EWCA Civ 936).

• The court compares the designs as registered, not the products actually marketed, and relatively minor differences (if not commonplace) may be sufficient to create a different overall impression (*Pepsico Inc v Grupo Promer Mon-Graphic SA*, Case R 1001/2005-3, 27 October 2006).

➤ If protection is sought for part of a complex product:

  ◆ the part must remain visible during normal use of the product, *and*

  ◆ the part's visible features must have novelty and individual character (*Art 4(2)*).

➤ A design cannot be registered (as with UK RDR):

  a) to the extent that features of the product's appearance are solely dictated by the product's technical function (*Art 8(1)*), *or*

  b) to the extent that those features must be reproduced to allow the product to fit another product (*Art 8(2)*) – the 'must fit' exclusion, *or*

    ◆ RCDR can, however, protect mutually interchangeable products within a modular system (eg: modular furniture) (*Art 8(3)*).

  c) where the design is contrary to public policy or morality (*Art 9*).

III Applying for registered Community design right

➤ Whether applying via OHIM or the UK IPO, an applicant must complete the OHIM application form, which is available:

  ◆ online on the OHIM website at www.oami.eu.int, *or*

  ◆ by downloading the form from the OHIM website and printing out a hard copy.

➤ The application must be made in an official EU language (*Art 98(1)*).

  ◆ The applicant must also use a second language (which must be Spanish, German, English, French or Italian) (*Art 98(2)*).

➤ The applicant must include in the form (*Art 36*):

  a) a request for registration, *and*

  b) details of applicant, *and*

  c) a representation of the design in a form suitable for reproduction, *and*

  d) details of the products to which the design relates.

➤ An applicant can file a single application to cover multiple designs, as long as (except in the case of ornamentation) products to which the design is to be applied all belong to the same *Locarno Agreement* class for industrial designs (*Art 37*).

  ◆ The *Locarno Agreement* system of classification separates designs into classes on the basis of products to which designs are applied.

➤ An application fee is payable (*Art 36(4)*), direct to OHIM by electronic transfer.

  ◆ For an application made via a national registry rather than direct to OHIM, an additional handling fee is payable to the national registry.

  ◆ A separate fee is payable for each design (*Art 37(2)*).

➤ OHIM only carries out a limited examination of the application, focusing on compliance with the formal requirements for registration (*Art 45*).

   ◆ OHIM will refuse to register the design if OHIM notices that the design (*Art 47*):

      a) does not fall within the definition of 'design' set out in *Art 3(a)*, or

      b) is contrary to public policy or morality.

➤ If OHIM raises any objections to the application, the applicant can either amend or withdraw the application.

   ◆ The applicant is given 2 months to remedy any deficiencies in the application.

➤ If the application is accepted, the design is registered in OHIM's register of RCDRs and the registration is published in the *Community Designs Bulletin* on the OHIM website.

➤ An applicant can request OHIM to defer the publication of the application by up to 30 months from the date of filing (or, if a right of priority is claimed, from the date of priority) (*Art 50(1)*).

   ◆ The application procedure and OHIM review still continue during the deferral period, but the publication does not take place.

      ● Deferral is useful if, for example, a designer wishes to keep the design secret until a product launch.

➤ For further details of the application procedure, see the OHIM and UK IPO websites, which provide useful guidance for applicants.

➤ The application procedure is summarised below.

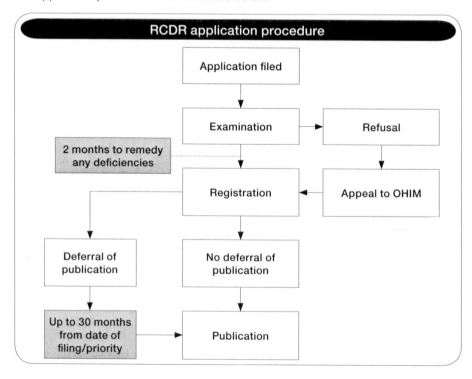

➤ The first owner of the RCDR in a design is (*Art 14*):

◆ the designer (ie: the creator of the design), *or*

◆ the employer of the designer, but only if the design was developed:

a) in the course of the designer's employment duties, *or*

b) following instructions given by the employer.

● National law can derogate from the default position that the employer is the first owner, and the employer and employee are free to come to a different contractual arrangement as to ownership (*Art 14(3)*).

● NB: in contrast to UK RDR, there is no provision for a commissioner of a design to be the first owner, so a commissioner should take a suitable grant of rights in the design (eg: an assignment – see section VI below).

■ The grant of rights should be negotiated in advance and recorded in writing (eg: in the contract of engagement).

➤ The maximum duration of RCDR is 25 years from the date of filing, but only if renewed every 5 years (*Art 12*).

◆ Renewal requests are submitted to OHIM online or by completing a renewal form.

◆ A fee is payable to OHIM for each renewal.

IV Requirements for unregistered Community design right

➤ UCDR is a right that, like UK UDR, comes into existence automatically.

➤ There are 2 requirements for UCDR to subsist (*Art 11(1)*):

a) the design must meet the requirements under *CDR 2002 Section 1*, ie: it must:

i) fall within the definition of 'design' under *Art 3*, *and*

ii) as at first publication, be new and have individual character, *and*

iii) not be excluded to the extent that its features are dictated by technical function or 'must fit' or as being contrary to public policy or morality, *and*

b) it must be 'made available to the public' within the EU (ie: published, exhibited, used in trade or otherwise disclosed such that the design would reasonably have become known to people specialising in the sector concerned and operating within the EU) (*Art 11(2)*).

➤ First ownership of UCDR is determined in the same way as for RCDR (*Art 14*).

➤ UCDR lasts for 3 years from the date of first publication in the EU (*Art 11(1)*).

◆ This is significantly shorter than for RCDR (which can last for up to 25 years).

➤ UCDR is not a monopoly right. It is necessary for a claimant to prove copying in an infringement action (*Art 19(2)*).

V   Infringement

➤ There are 3 steps to consider in relation to an infringement action:

Steps	
1	There must be an infringing act.
2	Are there any defences?
3	What are the remedies?

Step 1	There must be an infringing act

➤ RCDR is infringed if, without the owner's consent, a person 'uses' the design, including, in particular (*Art 19(1)*):

a) making, offering, marketing, importing or exporting a product to which the design is applied, *or*

b) stocking such a product for such purposes.

   ◆ RCDR is enforceable even if the infringer has not copied the design.

   ◆ NB: a claimant cannot enforce RCDR until the date of registration.

➤ UCDR is infringed if any act occurs that would infringe RCDR, but UCDR is not enforceable unless the use results from copying the design (*Art 19(2)*).

   ◆ Eg: in *Mattel Inc v Woolbro (Distributors) Ltd* (23 October 2003, unreported), the first UK case on UCDR (which settled before judgment), the defendant withdrew its defence after the claimant produced evidence of unauthorised copying of the claimant's designs for Barbie dolls.

➤ Both RCDR and UCDR are infringed if a similar design produces on the informed user the same overall impression as the protected design (*Art 10(1)*).

   ◆ In assessing the scope of protection, the court takes into consideration the designer's degree of freedom in developing the design (*Art 10(2)*).

      ● This is because a functional design is likely to be similar to other designs.

      ● Accordingly, the more functional the feature of the defendant's design, the less likely it is to have been copied (and the less likely it is that the similar feature will have individual character in the first place) (*OHIM Invalidity Division (Registered Community Design Number 16183-0001)*, 27 April 2005).

      ● Similarly, where a defendant designer has limited freedom, a slight variation over the prior art is more likely to have individual character.

Step 2	Are there any defences?

➤ The defences to infringement of RCDR or UCDR are very similar to those for UK RDR, including:

- ◆ use for private and non-commercial purposes (*Art 20(1)(a)*), *or*
- ◆ use for experimental purposes (*Art 20(1)(b)*), *or*
- ◆ reproduction for citation or for teaching purposes, where compatible with fair trade practice and mention is made of the source (*Art 20(1)(c)*), *or*
- ◆ use in connection with the equipment of (or repairs to) ships and aircraft registered in a third country when temporarily in EU territory (*Art 20(2)*), *or*
- ◆ sale of a product that has already been marketed in the EU by the owner or with the owner's consent (ie: resulting in 'exhaustion of rights') (*Art 21*), *or*
- ◆ exercise of a 'right of prior use', ie: where the defendant can show use (without copying) of the same or a similar design before the filing/priority date (*Art 22*), *or*
  - ● NB: this defence only applies to RCDR (although it is, in effect, a defence to a claim for UCDR infringement to show that the design was not copied).
  - ● If this defence succeeds, the defendant can use the design within the scope of the prior use, but cannot license the right to use the design to a third party.
- ◆ use by government for defence or security needs (*Art 23*), *or*
- ◆ invalidity of the registration (*Arts 24-26*).
  - ◆ NB: this last defence only applies to RCDR, although many of the grounds for invalidity (eg: absence of novelty or individual character) will prevent UCDR from subsisting.

Step 3	What are the remedies?

➤ An infringement claim is heard before the Community Design Court, a specially designated court of first and second instance in each EU member state (*Art 80(1)*).

➤ A Community Design Court can grant the following remedies (*Art 89*):

a) an EU-wide injunction (interim or final) restraining further infringement, *and/or*

b) an order to seize infringing products, *and/or*

c) an order to seize materials and implements used to manufacture infringing goods (if the defendant had actual or constructive knowledge of the effect for which such use was intended), *and/or*

d) any other sanctions available under national law.

- ◆ Further to the UK *Community Design Regulations 2005* ('**CDR 2005**'), the sanctions under national law also include:
  - ● damages or an account of profits (*r 1A(2)*), *and/or*
  - ● an order for delivery-up or destruction of infringing articles (*r 1B-1C*).

➤ The *CDR 2005* also provide for measures to support the *CDR 2002*, including:

 ◆ a remedy for groundless threats of infringement proceedings (*r 2*), *and*

 ◆ criminal liability for falsely representing (*r 3*):

 a) an unregistered design as an RCDR, *or*

 b) an expired RCDR as a current RCDR.

➤ Unlike UK RDR/UDR, there is no innocent-infringement defence (complete or partial) to a damages claim (*J Choo (Jersey) Ltd v Towerstone Ltd* [2008] EWHC 346).

VI Dealing with Community design rights

➤ Both RCDR and UCDR constitute property that can be dealt with in the same way as other intellectual property rights.

 ◆ References below to disposals of RCDR apply equally to disposals of RCDR applications, which also constitute transferable property (*Art 34*).

➤ There are 2 main ways of dealing with CDR.

1 Assignment

 ➤ The owner may assign (ie: transfer title to) RCDR and/or UCDR.

 ◆ An assignment of RCDR/UCDR must be for the whole area of the EU and deal with the design in its entirety (*Art 27(1)*).

 ➤ Where RCDR is assigned, the assignee's rights are not enforceable until the assignment is recorded in the register of Community designs (*Art 28*).

2 Licensing

 ➤ An owner can license (ie: grant permission to use) RCDR and/or UCDR.

 ➤ A licence of RCDR and/or UCDR can be sole, exclusive or non-exclusive (*Art 32(1)*) – see Sections F and G for the implications of these types of licence.

 ➤ It is possible to license RCDR and/or UCDR:

 ◆ for all or part of EU (*Art 32(1)*), *and/or*

 ◆ with restrictions on the permitted purposes (eg: the range of products for which the licence is granted) (*Art 32(2)*).

 ➤ A licensee may only bring an infringement action with the owner's consent, but an exclusive licensee can bring an infringement action if the owner does not bring an infringement action within an appropriate period after the licensee's request for the owner to do so (*Art 32(3)*).

 ◆ The term 'appropriate period' is not defined in *Regulation 6/2002/EC*.

 ➤ If RCDR is licensed, either party may require that the licence must be recorded in the register of Community designs and published (*Art 32(5)*).

I Patents

*References in this Section are to the Patents Act 1977 ('**PA 1977**'), unless otherwise stated.*

I	Legal framework
II	Is an invention patentable?
III	Applying for a UK patent
IV	Applying for a patent under the *EPC*
V	Applying for a patent under the *PCT*
VI	Infringement
VII	Dealing with patents

I Legal framework

➤ A patent protects a new invention that is capable of industrial application.

◆ The types of inventions covered by patent law include devices, processes, methods and chemical compounds (eg: pharmaceutical drugs).

Grounds for patentability

➤ Under UK law the general requirements for patentability are stated in the *PA 1977*. The invention must (*s 1(1)*):

a) be new, *and*

b) involve an inventive step, *and*

c) be capable of industrial application, *and*

d) not be excluded by *ss 1(2)-(3)* or *4A*.

◆ Excluded inventions include scientific theories, mathematical methods, aesthetic creations and computer programs (*s 1(2)*).

• NB: although computer programs are not patentable as such, certain software-related inventions are patentable – see step 5 of section II below.

➤ It is necessary to apply for the grant of a patent, in contrast to unregistered intellectual property rights (eg: copyright), which arise automatically.

◆ The application procedure is complex, lengthy and costly, so an inventor should seek relevant professional advice (eg: from a solicitor or registered patent agent).

➤ The grant of a patent gives the inventor a monopoly to exploit the invention for a defined period (eg: in the UK, for 20 years from the filing date of the application, as long as renewal fees are paid and the patent is not revoked for invalidity).

◆ After the protection period, the invention can be used freely by the public.

➤ To obtain the grant of a patent, the inventor must publish full details of the invention.

◆ The patent system allows industrial knowledge to develop during the life of the patent and society to benefit from the invention once the patent has expired.

➤ There are advantages and disadvantages to patent protection. An inventor should consider these before publishing the invention or applying for a patent.

Advantages ✓	Disadvantages ✗
➤ The owner of a patent ('**patentee**') has a monopoly right over the invention. ◆ Only the patentee can commercially exploit an invention (eg: through manufacturing products using it). ◆ The patentee can enforce the rights against a person that subsequently devises the same invention (even if devised entirely independently) or operates within the scope of the patent claims. ➤ A patent can be: a) a negotiating tool (eg: if the patentee is trying to find a manufacturing partner), *and* b) a revenue source (eg: if the patentee licenses an invention).	➤ In return for patent protection, a patentee consents to publication of the details of the new invention. ◆ Competitors may attempt to 'engineer around' the patent. ➤ A patent can be subject to a compulsory licence (see section VII below). ➤ Competition law may impose restrictions on a patentee's use of the patent. ➤ Obtaining patent protection is expensive (especially for a complex invention), since the inventor must pay: ◆ application and renewal fees to each relevant patent office, *and* ◆ professional costs (eg: patent agents' and translators' fees).

➤ The main alternative to patent protection is to try to protect the know-how concerned as confidential information (see Section J of this Chapter).

◆ Although it is theoretically possible to keep trade secrets confidential indefinitely, it can be extremely difficult to prevent 'leakage' in practice and may also be hard to prove that a rival's know-how has not been developed independently.

● Patent protection is therefore desirable if it can be obtained.

● Confidentiality can also be used to protect the details of the invention while it is in development, as well as the related technical know-how (eg: a particular industrial process) required to make best use of the invention.

➤ There are 3 ways in which a patent may be obtained in the UK, ie: under:

a) the *PA 1977, or*

b) the *European Patent Convention 1973* ('**EPC**'), *or*

c) the *Patent Co-operation Treaty 1970* ('**PCT**').

◆ This Section focuses on patent protection under the *PA 1977*, but examines protection under the *EPC* and (in outline only) under the *PCT*, as both forms of international protection provide protection in the UK at a national level.

➤ A UK applicant must file an application for a patent under the *PA 1977* or the *PCT* at the UK Intellectual Property Office ('**UK IPO**').

◆ An application for a patent under the *EPC* is filed at the European Patent Office ('**EPO**'), which is a supranational patent office located in Munich, Germany.

➤ Each route has advantages and disadvantages, as summarised on the next page.

PA 1977	EPC	PCT
Advantages		
✔ This is the cheapest application route. ◆ An application can be made electronically. ✔ There is no need for translations of the application into other languages. ✔ There are no long opposition proceedings following grant of the patent. ◆ NB: the duration of a patent granted after a *PA 1977* application is the same as that of the UK national patent granted after an *EPC* or *PCT* application, ie: 20 years. • Length of protection is therefore a neutral factor. ✔ The expense of High Court litigation may deter another person from seeking to revoke a patent.	✔ This route is less expensive than a *PCT* application. ✔ A registration covers most European countries (see the EPO website for a full list), giving the owner the same rights as a national patent in each jurisdiction in which the patent is granted. ✔ There is no need to file separate applications in each jurisdiction. ✔ The EPO tends to be more flexible as to the criteria for patentability than the UK IPO. ✔ The applicant can apply for 'divisional applications' (see below) to narrow the scope of protection. ✔ Opposition proceedings do not require an exchange of evidence or disclosure, so are less expensive than *PA 1977* revocation proceedings. ✔ The applicant can claim priority from other national patent applications.	✔ Only one application is needed to enable protection in a number of jurisdictions. 138 countries are signatories to the *PCT*, including all countries with significant markets. ◆ A patent protected by *PCT* can (depending on the number of jurisdictions designated in the application) result in protection in more jurisdictions than an *EPC* patent. ✔ 1 *PCT* application is cheaper than applying in separate jurisdictions. ✔ An applicant has up to 30 months after the initial filing date before jurisdictions need to be selected. ✔ An applicant can claim priority from the applicant's other patent applications for inventions filed elsewhere throughout the world.
Disadvantages		
✘ The patent protection only covers the UK. ✘ The UK courts and UK IPO are currently taking a strict view of the requirements for patentability. ✘ An applicant can only claim priority from the UK patent application. NB: each international convention allows a person with a prior application in any convention country to claim '*priority*' when applying for a patent in another convention country within a specified period after the initial filing date in the original country.	✘ The procedure is slow (in comparison with a UK patent application). ✘ After grant of the patent, opposition proceedings may be started. In certain jurisdictions the patent owner cannot start infringement proceedings until all opposition proceedings are concluded. ✘ If an *EPC* patent is successfully challenged, it is revoked in all jurisdictions covered by the application. ✘ It is not possible to have both a UK and an *EPC* application covering the same subject-matter. ✘ Translations are required.	✘ The procedure is slow (in comparison with a UK patent application). ✘ The application still undergoes a national phase in each jurisdiction designated. ✘ Translations are required.

➤ The *EPC* and *PCT* deal largely with procedural matters.

◆ Substantive issues are dealt with mainly at national level (ie: in the UK, under the *PA 1977*).

● A *PCT* 'patent' is ultimately just a national patent in each jurisdiction specified by the applicant, as the actual grant of each patent occurs at national level.

● In contrast, an *EPC* patent is granted by the EPO and operates as a bundle of national patents in each of the contracting states specified by the applicant, with each patent being governed by the relevant national law.

➤ NB: there is no EU-wide protection for patents, unlike trade marks and design rights.

◆ Although the *EPC* describes the patent obtained under it as a 'European patent', the *EPC* does not form part of EU law, but is a separate international convention.

➤ A true EU patent has been considered in detail, but has yet to come into effect.

EU patent [not in force]

➤ *The Community Patent Convention 1975, which did not come into force, aimed to provide for a single patent to cover the entire EU (in contrast to the bundle of national rights conferred by an EPC patent).*

◆ *The proposed Community patent has been referred to as an 'EU patent' since the Lisbon Treaty came into force on 1 December 2009.*

➤ *No further EU patent legislation has been enacted, but the EU Council of Ministers has agreed that in principle:*

a) *a single EU patent will cover the entire EU, and*

b) *an application must be made in English, French or German (the 3 official languages of the EPO), although, once granted, the EU patent claims should be translated into all EU languages, and*

c) *a single European and EU Patents Court ('**EEUPC**') will be established to provide a unified patent litigation system across the EU, and*

d) *the translation arrangements will be the subject of a separate regulation, to be agreed unanimously and to come into force at the same time as the EU Patent Regulation.*

➤ *There are several major issues which have not been clarified:*

◆ *Will an EU patent be expensive to obtain? Eg: does a patentee need to cover and defend all jurisdictions, particularly if certain jurisdictions within the EU have no financial or strategic benefit to the patentee?*

◆ *The costs of translating patent claims will be substantial (especially compared with a US patent, for which only 1 language is required).*

◆ *Will the grounds for objection to a patent be harmonised in each of the individual jurisdictions?*

◆ *Can a patentee's entire EU patent coverage be revoked by a single court?*

II Is an invention patentable?

A Position under UK law

➤ There are 5 steps to consider in assessing whether an invention is patentable under the *PA 1977* (or in the UK under the *PCT*, which involves a national application):

Steps	
1	Is there an invention?
2	Is the invention new?
3	Is there an inventive step?
4	Is the invention capable of industrial application?
5	Is the invention excluded?

Step 1	Is there an invention? – UK position

➤ The subject-matter of the application must amount to an 'invention' (*s 1(1)* and *Genentech Inc's Patent* [1989] RPC 147).

◆ NB: the *PA 1977* does not define the term 'invention', so the term has its ordinary meaning. It has been widely construed in practice.

➤ In practice, there is, as noted in *Genentech*, a substantial overlap between this requirement and the specific criteria for patentability under *s 1(a)-(d)*.

◆ Eg: if a device or process lacks novelty or an inventive step, it will not be an 'invention' in the ordinary sense of the word.

Step 2	Is the invention new? – UK position

➤ An invention is 'new' if it does not form part of the existing 'state of the art' (*s 2(1)*).

'State of the art'

➤ The 'state of the art' comprises, in relation to an invention:

a) any matter (whether a product, process, information or anything else) made available to the public (whether in the UK or elsewhere) before the priority date of the invention (*s 2(2)*), *and*

◆ Publication includes usage and written or oral disclosures (*s 2(2)*), but excludes a disclosure made in breach of confidence within 6 months before the filing date (*s 2(4)*).

b) the content of any other patent application that is published on or after the priority date of the invention, as long as that other application has an earlier priority date (*s 2(3)*).

◆ Ie: an earlier, as yet unpublished invention may take priority.

➤ NB: the definition of 'state of the art' does not exclude an inventor's own disclosures, so an inventor should take great care over the timing of publication of the invention.

Avoiding early disclosure

➤ A pre-application disclosure by an inventor could inadvertently form part of the state of the art, so invalidating the inventor's application at the outset.

➤ An inventor can take certain steps to try to avoid unintentional disclosure, eg:

♦ not exhibiting or publicly using the invention before filing the application, *and*

♦ ensuring that any person working on an invention signs a confidentiality agreement, *and*

♦ ensuring that any marketing agreement signed before an application is filed includes a confidentiality clause.

➤ The requirement of novelty overlaps with the requirement of an inventive step (see step 3 below), and the case law on novelty considers the 2 criteria together when approaching the question of novelty.

Disclosure and enablement

➤ The court applies an objective 2-step test to determine novelty, ie: the subject-matter of a patent application will form part of the existing 'state of the art' (and so will **not** be 'new') if an earlier patent (*Synthon BV v SmithKline Beecham plc* [2005] UKHL 59):

a) discloses matter that, if performed, would necessarily result in an infringement of the earlier patent (the 'inevitable result' test), *and*

b) is 'enabling', ie: provides suffcient information to enable a 'skilled person' to operate the invention.

♦ The concept of the 'skilled person' is examined in step 3 below.

♦ Whether an earlier patent is 'enabling' is a question of fact, ie: a question of the common general knowledge in that area of technology and what the ordinary skilled person with that knowledge would be able to do when attempting to operate the disclosed invention using the disclosed material.

'Mosaicing' documents

➤ If an invention can be arrived at by combining the teachings of 2 separate documents ('mosaicing'), an invention can still be novel.

♦ The only exception is where a document cross-refers to another document and the skilled person would read them together.

Step 3	Is there an inventive step? – UK position

➤ An invention must involve an 'inventive step' (*s 3*).

➤ It will involve an inventive step if it is not 'obvious' to a 'person skilled in the art' having regard to all matter forming part of the state of the art as at the priority date of the patent (*s 3*).

- ◆ NB: for the purposes of determining obviousness, the state of the art does **not** include unpublished patent applications (in contrast to the test for novelty).

- ◆ The test of obviousness is an objective test: the invention must be deemed inventive in the eyes of a person skilled in the art (*Mölnlycke AB v Procter & Gamble (No. 5)* [1994] RPC 49).

The skilled person
➤ The 'skilled person' is a person (or team of persons) with a wide knowledge of the area of technology relevant to the invention.   ◆ Eg: with a patent for a drug, the skilled person may be a pharmacist with 1 or 2 years' post-degree experience (*Sandoz GmbH v Roche Diagnostics GmbH* [2004] EWHC 1313).

- ◆ In deciding whether an invention is obvious the 4-step test in *Windsurfing International Inc v Tabur Marine* [1985] RPC 59 used to be applied. The test was later re-stated in *Pozzoli SPA v BDMO SA* [2007] EWCA Civ 558.

Test in *Pozzoli*

➤ The test in *Pozzoli* is also a 4-step test. The court must:
 	
 1) identify:
 	
     a) the notional person 'skilled in the art', *and*
 	
     b) that person's relevant common general knowledge, *and*
 	
 2) identify the inventive concept of the claim in question (or, if that cannot readily be done, construe it), *and*
 	
 3) identify what (if any) differences exist between:
 	
     ◆ the matter cited as forming part of the 'state of the art', *and*
 	
     ◆ the inventive concept of the claim (or the claim as construed), *and*
 	
 4) consider whether, viewed without any knowledge of the alleged invention as claimed, those differences constitute steps that:
 	
     ◆ would have been obvious to the person skilled in the art, *or*
 	
     ◆ would require any degree of invention.

- ◆ The test for obviousness is qualitative.

  - ● In determining whether an invention is obvious the court:

    - a) decides as a matter of fact what constitutes the common general knowledge of the skilled person (ie: the knowledge that the skilled person would carry around in that person's head, which can be determined by looking at textbooks in the field), *and*

    - b) considers any documents that a petitioner cites as state of the art for the purposes of assessing obviousness.

- ➤ Commercial success may, in limited circumstances, be an indication of inventiveness (*Haberman v Jackel* [1999] FSR 683).

- ➤ The burden of proving that an invention is obvious falls on a petitioner.

Step 4 | Is the invention capable of industrial application? – UK position

- ➤ The expression 'capable of industrial application' is widely defined to cover any invention that 'can be made or used in any kind of industry, including agriculture' (*s 4(1)*).

  - ◆ This requirement is easily satisfied. Eg: the criterion is likely to be met where:

    - a) the operation of the invention produces some tangible and physical result, *or*

    - b) the invention is itself a physical entity for which a practical use is specified.

  - ◆ Merely identifying a natural substance (eg: a chemical compound) will not satisfy the requirement unless an industrial use can also be shown (eg: use in a drug).

Step 5 | Is the invention excluded? – UK position

- ➤ The following are excluded from being patented:

  - a) Discoveries, scientific theories and mathematical methods (*s 1(2)(a)*), although it is possible to obtain patents for practical applications of discoveries and theories.

    - ◆ A mere idea is not patentable: there must be some physical or tangible entity to which the patent can attach.

  - b) Aesthetic creations (eg: a literary, dramatic, musical or artistic work) (*s 1(2)(b)*).

  - c) Schemes, rules or methods for performing mental acts, playing games or doing business (*s 1(2)(c)*).

    - ◆ A method is, however, patentable if it makes a substantive technical contribution to the known art, eg: where a business method is linked to a mechanical device (*Merrill Lynch's Application* [1989] RPC 561).

      - ● A 4-step approach is applied to determine whether the contribution has been made (as per the *Aerotel* case below) – the critical third limb being whether, in this context, the contribution is purely a method.

d) Computer programs (*s 1(2)(c)*).

   ◆ A software-related invention is, however, patentable if it makes a substantive technical contribution to the known art (*Fujitsu's Application* [1997] RPC 680), ie: a contribution that is more than solely a computer program (*Symbian Ltd's Application* [2008] EWCA Civ 1066).

      • A 4-step approach is applied to determine whether the contribution has been made (*Aerotel Ltd v Telco Holdings Ltd* [2006] EWCA Civ 1371):

         1) construing the claim properly, *and*

         2) identifying the actual contribution made, *and*

         3) asking whether the contribution falls solely within the excluded subject-matter (ie: whether, in the context of a software-related invention, it is purely a computer program – the key issue), *and*

         4) checking whether the actual or alleged contribution is actually technical in nature.

            ▪ Steps 3 and 4 can be conflated in the analysis (*Symbian*).

      • Accordingly, where claims to a method using a programmed computer or to a computer system to carry it out are allowable, claims to the actual computer program are also allowable in principle (*Astron Clinica's Application* [2008] EWHC 85).

      • The UK IPO published guidance on 8 December 2008 that (as previously thought) an invention solving a technical problem external to the computer or within the computer is not excluded. Further (after *Symbian*), a program making a computer run faster or more reliably can provide a technical contribution even if it only addresses a problem in the programming.

   ◆ Other forms of protection may be available (eg: copyright for software).

e) Presentation of information (*s 1(2)(d)*).

   ◆ Other forms of protection may be available (eg: under design right).

   ◆ NB: the 4 exclusions under *s 1(2)(a)-(d)* only prevent an excluded thing from being patentable to the extent that the patent relates to that thing 'as such'.

f) Inventions whose commercial exploitation would be contrary to public policy or morality (*s 1(3)*).

g) Surgical, therapeutic or diagnostic methods carried out on the human or animal body (*s 4A(1)*).

   ◆ It is, however, possible to patent an invention consisting of a substance or composition for use in any such method (*s 4A(2)*).

h) Certain biological and zoological inventions, eg: human gene discoveries, uses of human embryos, plant/animal varieties and non-microbiological processes for the production of plants or animals (see *Sch A2 para 3*).

B Position under the *EPC*

➤ The steps to consider in assessing whether an invention is patentable under the *EPC* are the same 5 steps as for the position under UK law:

Steps	
1	Is there an invention?
2	Is the invention new?
3	Is there an inventive step?
4	Is the invention capable of industrial application?
5	Is the invention excluded?

Step 1	Is there an invention? – *EPC* position

➤ The principles are the same as for UK law.

Step 2	Is the invention new? – *EPC* position

➤ The invention must not form part of the 'state of the art'.

- ◆ The 'state of the art' is defined in essentially the same way as under UK patent law, ie: (broadly speaking) what is publicly available before the filing date of the *EPC* patent application (*EPC Art 54*).

➤ Unlike UK law, the test for whether the 'state of the art' anticipates an invention requires that the state of the art disclose all the claimed technical features of an invention to a skilled person (*EPC Examination Guidelines C-IV 6.2*).

Technical features

➤ The 'technical features' of a claim are the features that define the scope of protection (*EPC Rule 43*).

- ◆ The equivalent under UK law is referred to as an 'integer' of the claim.

Step 3	Is there an inventive step? – *EPC* position

➤ *EPC Art 56* sets out the same test as *PA 1977 s 3*.

➤ Before looking at whether an invention is obvious, the EPO's Opposition Division first identifies the technical problem solved by the invention (the 'problem-and-solution approach') (*EPC Examination Guidelines C-IV 11.7*).

- ◆ Unlike in the UK, the Opposition Division determines which document represents the closest state of the art, and then determines whether an invention is 'obvious' when compared to the information in that document.

➤ 'Obviousness' is assessed according to the documents cited as being part of the state of the art and is defined in the same way as under UK law.

Test for obviousness

➤ The Opposition Division applies a 2-step objective test to determine whether an invention is 'obvious' when compared with the closest piece of prior art. An invention must (*EPC Examination Guidelines C-IV 11.4*):

   a) go beyond the normal progress of technology (rather than following plainly or logically from the prior art), *and*

   b) involve skill or ability beyond that to be expected of a person skilled in the art.

➤ The Opposition Division considers (*EPC Examination Guidelines C-IV 11.4*):

   a) any published document in the light of subsequent knowledge, *and*

   b) the general knowledge available to a person skilled in the art as at the day before the *EPC* patent application.

➤ An inventive step can involve combining disclosure of earlier documents (*EPC Examination Guidelines C-IV 11.8*).

   ◆ This can only be done where such a combination would not be obvious to the skilled person.

➤ In reaching a decision, various other indicative factors are considered, such as (*EPC Examination Guidelines C-IV 11.9*):

   a) surprising technical effect, *and/or*

   b) a long-felt want for the invention, *and/or*

   c) commercial success.

Step 4	Is the invention capable of industrial application? – *EPC* position

➤ *EPC Art 57* defines the requirement for industrial application in the same way as *PA 1977 s 4(1)*.

   ◆ NB: if there is an industrial application for the invention, this does not override any exclusion of the invention under *Art 52(2) EPC* (which sets out exclusions equivalent to those under the *PA 1977*) (*EPC Examination Guidelines C-IV 5.3*).

   • *Art 52(2) EPC* sets out exclusions equivalent to those under *PA 1977 s 1(2)*.

| Step 5 | Is the invention excluded? – *EPC* position |

➤ The exclusions set out in *EPC Arts 52-53* match those under the *PA 1977 ss 1(2), 1(3)* and *4A* (see above).

Exclusion for plant and animal varieties

➤ The scope of this exclusion is unclear (see *EPC Art 53(b)*).

♦ The exclusion does not extend to micro-biological processes or the products of such processes, both of which are patentable.

➤ The exclusion is affected by the *Biotechnology Directive 98/44/EC*, which harmonised protection of biotechnological inventions and was incorporated into the *EPC* and (via the *Patent Regulations 2000*) UK patent law.

♦ Under the *Directive*, plant and animal varieties are patentable if they are not confined to a particular variety.

● NB: plant varieties can be protected in the UK under the *Plant Varieties and Seeds Act 1964*.

● Plant breeders also have Community plant variety rights under *Regulation 2100/94/EC*. See the website of the Community Plant Variety Office for further information.

♦ The *Directive* provides farmers with exceptions to patent infringement in relation to specified seed and plant species in defined circumstances (see *PA 1977 Sch A1*).

➤ The exclusion appears to apply to transgenic animals. Note, however:

♦ The EPO Board of Appeal granted a patent covering a transgenic mouse on the basis that the invention was not a new variety of animal (*Case T 0315/03, Method for producing transgenic animals*, 6 July 2004).

● The EPO has rejected claims for transgenic mice with genes mutated by a gene-trapping construct.

Exclusion of patents for medical uses

➤ For both UK and *EPC* patent law:

♦ Only treatment by surgery, therapy and diagnostic methods are excluded (see *EPC Art 53(c)*). Other forms of treatment are not excluded.

♦ The exclusion relates to the methods of treatment (not the treatment itself), so a new drug may still be patented.

♦ The 'Swiss' form of patenting may be available, ie: a patent for substance 'X' for use in the treatment of disease 'Y'.

C Position under the *PCT*

➤ This is similar to the UK and *EPC* positions, but beyond the scope of this Section.

III Applying for a UK patent

➤ There are up to 8 stages involved in an application for the grant of a UK patent.

Stages	
1	Preparation of application
2	Submission of application
3	Preliminary examination
4	Publication
5	Substantive examination
6	Grant
7	Revocation
8	Appeal

Stage 1	Preparation of application (UK)

➤ An applicant should first consider the following:

Preliminary considerations

➤ Can the applicant can claim priority from an earlier filed application?

➤ The application should relate to a single invention or inventive concept.

➤ The application should include everything for which protection is sought, as the scope of protection cannot be broadened later in the application process.

➤ The specification must disclose the invention in a way that is clear and complete enough for the invention to be performed by a person skilled in the art (*s 14(3)*).

  ◆ This might be relatively simple for a mechanical device, but could be a lengthy and detailed exercise for a biotechnology patent.

➤ The process of seeking patent protection is often described as 'prosecuting' a patent application (and the process until the grant stage as 'prosecution to grant').

➤ An application must be made in the prescribed form (*s 14(1)*).

➤ In addition to the basic request for the grant of a patent, the application must contain the 4 items listed below (*s 14(2)*). Items 2-4 below together make up the 'specification'.

1 **Abstract**

  ➤ This is a very short summary of the nature of the invention.

  ◆ This is often used by the public and relevant offices to determine the technical area of application.

2   **Description**

➤   The description provides the details of the invention.

➤   The UK IPO suggests the following contents:

◆   a title, *and*

◆   details of the technical field, *and*

◆   the essential features or a summary of the invention, *and*

◆   the background to the invention (eg: explanation of what the invention solves), *and*

◆   the reasons for the invention (eg: highlights of its advantages), *and*

◆   1 or more examples of the invention, possibly with drawings.

•   If the applicant is claiming priority from an earlier application made in the UK or overseas within the previous 12 months (*s 5*), the description can be replaced by a reference to that earlier application (*s 15(1)(c)(ii)*).

3   **Drawings**

➤   Drawings contained in an application should comply with the UK IPO's current published requirements for technical specifications.

4   **Claims**

➤   The claims should (*s 14(5)*):

◆   clearly and concisely define the scope of protection sought, *and*

◆   relate to 1 invention only (or to a group of inventions so linked as to form a single inventive concept).

➤   The first claims are usually broad in scope (eg: a technique or formulation applicable to all drugs), with ancillary or dependent claims.

◆   If the UK IPO decides that the claims are too broad, an applicant may have to narrow the scope of the claims to more restricted claims (eg: a technique or formulation applicable to specific drugs).

➤   An applicant should draft the claims carefully to ensure that they can be clearly interpreted if there is any infringement.

> ### Scope of patent protection – practical considerations
>
> ➤   When drafting claims, an applicant should be aware that potential infringers may look to engineer around the drafted claims.
>
> ➤   In determining the scope of protection, a court will look at the latest published claims and, if they have been amended/granted, the scope of protection is determined retrospectively.

Scope of patent protection – legal principles

➤ The extent of protection conferred by a patent is determined in accordance with (*PA 1977 s 125* and *EPC Art 69*):

a) the patent claims (as interpreted by the description and any drawings contained in the specification), *and*

b) the *EPC Protocol* on interpretation of claims.

➤ In interpreting the scope of patent claims, a reasonable middle ground is sought: the patent claims are not interpreted literally, but are not interpreted as a mere guideline for variants either.

◆ The '*Improver* test' provides a 3-step approach to (but not an actual test for) interpreting the scope of patent protection (*Improver Corp v Remington Consumer Products Ltd* [1990] FSR 181, as clarified by *Kirin Amgen Inc v Hoescht Marion Roussel Ltd* [2004] UKHL 46):

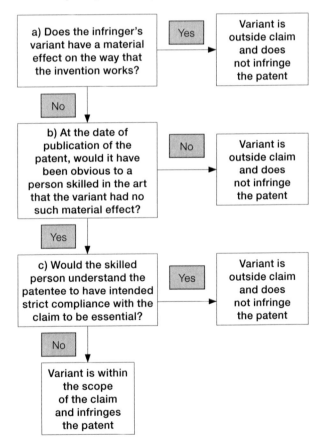

➤ NB: for a new technology, an inventor is likely to obtain wide claims; for a developed technology, the scope is likely to be narrower.

Stage 2	Submission of application (UK)

➤ The applicant must submit the application.

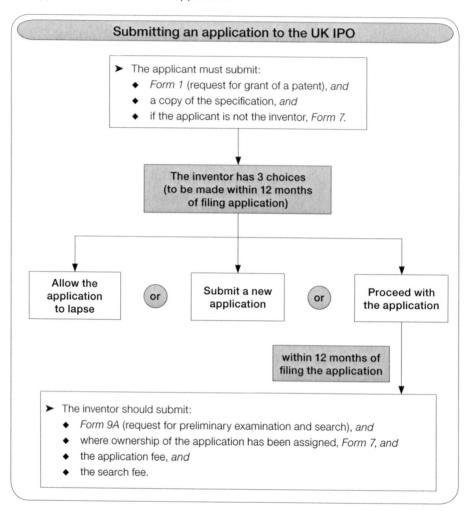

Submitting an application to the UK IPO

➤ The applicant must submit:
- *Form 1* (request for grant of a patent), *and*
- a copy of the specification, *and*
- if the applicant is not the inventor, *Form 7.*

The inventor has 3 choices (to be made within 12 months of filing application)

Allow the application to lapse — or — **Submit a new application** — or — **Proceed with the application**

within 12 months of filing the application

➤ The inventor should submit:
- *Form 9A* (request for preliminary examination and search), *and*
- where ownership of the application has been assigned, *Form 7*, and
- the application fee, *and*
- the search fee.

➤ The applicant should submit the application promptly. An early application has the following advantages and disadvantages:

Advantages ✓	Disadvantages ✗
➤ The earlier an application is submitted: • the earlier the filing date, *and* • the lower the likelihood that another person will file the same invention first.	➤ The earlier an application is submitted: • the shorter the period of time for careful drafting of the specification, *and* • the greater the chance of missing out a valid claim.

Stage 3	Preliminary examination (UK)

➤ The UK IPO conducts a preliminary examination and search (*s 15A*).

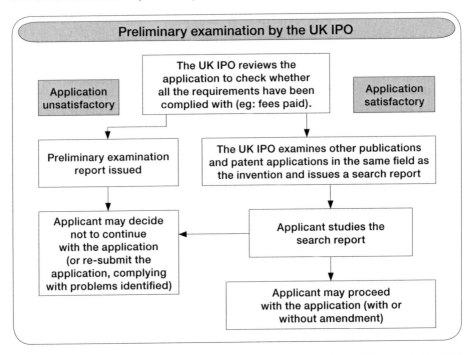

Stage 4	Publication (UK)

➤ An application is published within 18 months after the filing date or (if earlier) the claimed priority date (*s 16*).

  ◆ At the publication stage, the contents of an application and all official correspondence with the UK IPO becomes public.

    ● The published specification is called the 'A' specification.

➤ Publication has the following effects:

  a) the details of the application become part of the 'state of the art', *and*

  b) exploitation of an invention may in practice occur in jurisdictions where the invention is unprotected, *and*

  c) third parties may informally oppose the grant by supplying evidence of prior art or of pre-application disclosure.

    ◆ If an applicant decides to withdraw the application, it is advisable to do so before publication to keep out of the state of the art any aspects of the invention that the inventor may wish to develop further and/or to patent at a later date.

➤ A patentee may claim damages for infringement from the date of publication of the application, but cannot sue for infringement until the patent has been granted.

| Stage 5 | Substantive examination (UK) |

➤ An applicant must request substantive examination within 6 months of publication, or else the application is deemed to have been withdrawn (*s 17*).

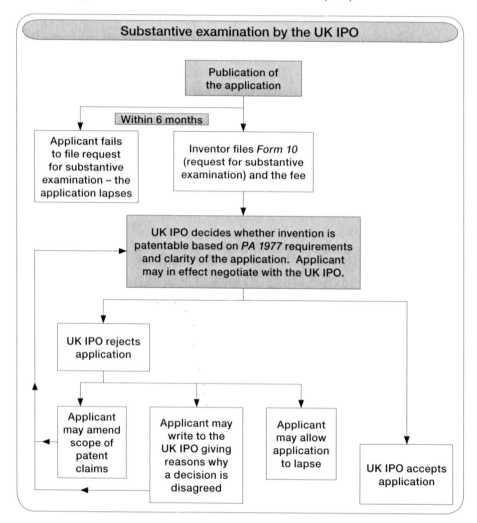

Substantive examination by the UK IPO

Publication of the application

Within 6 months

Applicant fails to file request for substantive examination – the application lapses

Inventor files *Form 10* (request for substantive examination) and the fee

UK IPO decides whether invention is patentable based on *PA 1977* requirements and clarity of the application. Applicant may in effect negotiate with the UK IPO.

UK IPO rejects application

Applicant may amend scope of patent claims

Applicant may write to the UK IPO giving reasons why a decision is disagreed

Applicant may allow application to lapse

UK IPO accepts application

| Stage 6 | Grant (UK) |

➤ Once a patent has been granted, then (subject to revocation – see below) the patentee has the right to sue anyone infringing the patent.

➤ The granted specification is called the 'B' specification.

Speeding up the process

➤ The process can take 2-4 years. It can be expedited by combining the preliminary/substantive examination stages and paying a combined fee.

➤ The rules for first ownership of a UK patent are as follows.

First ownership of a UK patent

➤ There are 3 possible first owners of a patent:

1 The inventor (or person entitled in place of the inventor)

➤ While anyone can apply, a patent will only be granted to (s 7(2)):

- the inventor (or to joint inventors – see below), *or*

- another person entitled to the whole property in the invention (eg: by law, international convention, treaty or through an agreement between the inventor and the other person).

2 An employee

➤ In contrast to other forms of intellectual property, an employee generally owns an invention. The employer owns it, however, if the invention was made during the course of normal duties for the employer (or during duties specifically assigned to the employee) and the circumstances were such that (s 39(1)):

a) an invention might reasonably be expected to result from the carrying out of those duties, *or*

b) the employee has a special obligation to further the interests of the employer's undertaking (eg: senior management).

➤ Where, because of the above exceptions, the patent belongs to the employer, a form of statutory compensation may be available to the employee where the invention (or the patent for it) is of 'outstanding benefit' to the employer and it would be just to award compensation to be paid by the employer (s 40).

- Applications under s 40 are rare.

  - If appropriate, an employer may avoid the effect of s 40 by not applying for a patent and relying on confidentiality instead.

➤ An employee cannot contract out of the above rules on ownership or compensation: any such contract is unenforceable (s 42).

➤ NB: some non-UK jurisdictions require that the employee be compensated for the invention and named as the inventor.

3 Joint owners

➤ Unless agreed otherwise, joint owners are entitled to an undivided share in the patent and must each seek the consent of the other(s) to any assignment, licence or mortgage of the patent (s 36).

- A co-owner can apply to the Comptroller for an order for a licence without the consent of the other co-owner(s) (s 37).

> ## Inventions in the 'research and development' department

> ➤ An employer should, as a matter of best practice, insist on full disclosure of work done in the department. This reduces the risk that an employee might develop an invention, leave the company and obtain a patent for the invention in the employee's name.

> ➤ Suitable measures may include:

>   a) putting disclosure obligations in the employment contract, *and*

>   b) encouraging disclosure by adopting a structured form of compensation in line with the rules on employee compensation (see above), *and*

>   c) keeping an inventory of new products and developments (eg: date-stamped and time-stamped records may provide useful evidence), *and*

>   d) ensuring that accurate, dated, laboratory notebooks are kept.

>   • This is especially important where US patent protection is sought, as, under US patent law (unlike in the UK or Europe), the patent is granted to the first to invent rather than the first to apply.

➤ A UK patent can last up to 20 years from the date of filing of the application (*s 25*).

Duration of a UK patent

> ➤ To last for the full 20-year period, the patent must not be revoked and renewal fees must be paid annually from the fifth year after the filing date.

>   ♦ To encourage patentees not to renew patents of little use to the patentee, the fees progressively increase as the patent nears its expiry date.

> ➤ A supplementary protection certificate is available for a medicinal or plant-protection invention, extending the protection after the relevant patent has expired for up to the lesser of (*Regulations 1768/92/EC* and *1610/96/EC*):

>   ♦ 5 years after such expiry date, *or*

>   ♦ 15 years from the product's first marketing authorisation in the EU.

>   • The patentee must apply for such certificate within 6 months of the grant of the patent or (if earlier) the marketing authorisation.

Stage 7	Revocation (UK)

➤ The grant of a patent does not ensure its validity. If a person believes that a patent should not have been granted (or at least not in the form in which it was granted), that person can apply for its revocation to:

a) the Comptroller of the UK IPO, *or*

b) the Patents County Court, *or*

c) the High Court (to which disputed revocations may ultimately be transferred).

➤ Revocation proceedings can be used to revoke a UK patent, the UK part of an *EPC* patent, or a *PCT* patent. There is no formal procedure for opposition in the UK.

➤ There are 5 grounds on which a patent can be revoked (*s 72*):

a) the invention is not patentable, *or*

b) the patentee was not entitled to be granted the patent, *or*

c) the patent does not disclose the invention sufficiently clearly and completely for the invention to be performed by a person skilled in the art ('insufficiency'), *or*

d) the subject-matter extends beyond the content of an application as filed, *or*

e) the protection conferred by a patent has been extended by amendment(s) that should not have been allowed.

➤ The High Court procedure is outlined below (see www.justice.gov.uk for further details). The UK IPO and County Court procedures are beyond the scope of this Section.

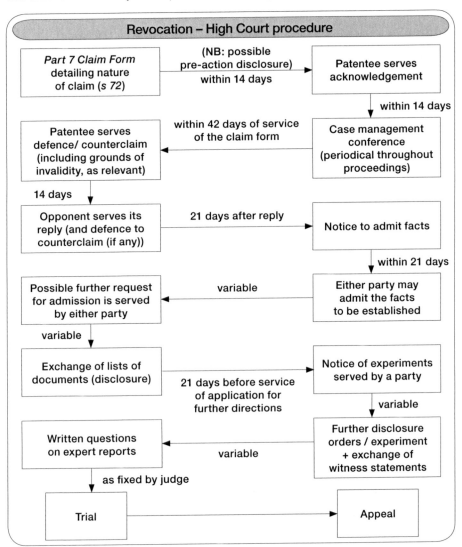

Revocation – High Court procedure

Part 7 Claim Form detailing nature of claim (*s 72*)	(NB: possible pre-action disclosure) within 14 days →	Patentee serves acknowledgement
		↓ within 14 days
Patentee serves defence/ counterclaim (including grounds of invalidity, as relevant)	← within 42 days of service of the claim form	Case management conference (periodical throughout proceedings)
↓ 14 days		
Opponent serves its reply (and defence to counterclaim (if any))	21 days after reply →	Notice to admit facts
		↓ within 21 days
Possible further request for admission is served by either party	← variable	Either party may admit the facts to be established
↓ variable		
Exchange of lists of documents (disclosure)	21 days before service of application for further directions →	Notice of experiments served by a party
		↓ variable
Written questions on expert reports	← variable	Further disclosure orders / experiment + exchange of witness statements
↓ as fixed by judge		
Trial	→	Appeal

Stage 8	Appeal (UK)

➤ A court ruling or UK IPO decision may be appealed.

♦ Either party to proceedings may appeal from most types of decision of the UK IPO Comptroller to the Patents Court, part of the High Court (*s 97(1)*).

♦ An appeal is made against the decision of a lower court on the facts or the law.

• An appellant cannot give oral evidence, nor can the appellant give evidence that was not available to the lower court.

➤ If permission to appeal is obtained , an appeal from the Patent Court can be made to the Court of Appeal (*s 97(3)*) (and from there to the House of Lords).

➤ Appeals from a decision of the Patents County Court ('**PCC**') are also possible.

♦ In such cases, an appeal is made to the Court of Appeal.

➤ The stages in an appeal to the Court of Appeal are summarised below.

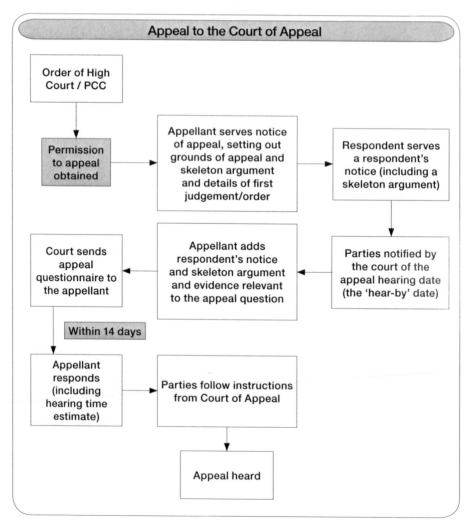

Appeal to the Court of Appeal

Order of High Court / PCC

→ Permission to appeal obtained

→ Appellant serves notice of appeal, setting out grounds of appeal and skeleton argument and details of first judgement/order

→ Respondent serves a respondent's notice (including a skeleton argument)

→ Parties notified by the court of the appeal hearing date (the 'hear-by' date)

→ Appellant adds respondent's notice and skeleton argument and evidence relevant to the appeal question

→ Court sends appeal questionnaire to the appellant

Within 14 days

→ Appellant responds (including hearing time estimate)

→ Parties follow instructions from Court of Appeal

→ Appeal heard

IV   Applying for a patent under the *EPC*

➤   The stages involved in applying for an *EPC* patent are similar to those under UK law (except that there is an 'opposition' procedure, rather than a 'revocation' procedure).

Stages	
1	Preparation of application
2	Submission of application
3	Preliminary examination
4	Publication
5	Substantive examination
6	Grant
7	Opposition
8	Appeal

➤   References in this section IV to rules are to rules of the *EPC Implementing Regulations*, which are published on the EPO website.

Stage 1 | **Preparation of application (*EPC*)**

➤   The preliminary considerations are the same as for UK law (see section III above).

◆   Eg: the application must relate to 1 invention or inventive concept (*EPC Art 82*).

➤   An *EPC* patent application is very similar to a UK application, and the specification consists of the following:

1   Abstract

➤   This is a concise summary of the invention (*R 47*).

◆   The abstract is not used to interpret the patent (*EPC Art 85*).

2   Description

➤   The description must contain (*R 42*):

a) an indication of the technical field to which the invention relates, *and*

b) a description of the prior art, citing published source documents where relevant, *and*

c) a disclosure of the invention (including the technical problem and the solution), *and*

d) a description of what is illustrated in any drawings, *and*

e) a detailed account of how the invention can be carried out, including at least 1 example, *and*

f) a statement of how the invention is capable of industrial application.

3 Drawings

➤ Drawings contained in an application should comply with the rules for form, substance and presentation set out in *RR 46*, *48* and *49* respectively.

4 Claims

➤ The claims should (*R 43*):

♦ define the scope of protection sought in terms of the technical features of the invention, *and*

♦ set out 1 independent claim only in the same category (eg: a product or process), unless the subject-matter of the application involves:

a) a plurality of interrelated products, *or*

b) different uses of a product or apparatus, *or*

c) alternative solutions to a particular problem.

➤ Another procedural difference from the UK system is that an applicant can make a 'divisional application' (*EPC Art 76*).

EPC divisional applications

➤ A divisional application is a related (but independent) application that can be filed in relation to any pending earlier *EPC* patent application (*R 36(1)*).

♦ It may be filed at any time before the date on which the *European Patent Bulletin* mentions the grant of the 'parent' application.

➤ A divisional application (*EPC Art 76(1)*):

a) cannot extend beyond the subject-matter of the original 'parent' *EPC* patent application as filed (ie: must form part of the same inventive concept as the invention), *and*

b) is treated as having the same filing date as the original application for the purposes of claiming priority.

➤ The procedure for a divisional application is the same as for an original application for a *EPC* patent, except that the application must be filed directly with the EPO (*EPC Art 76* and *R36(2)*).

Why apply for a divisional application?

➤ A divisional application is narrower in scope than the 'parent' application.

♦ It may survive an opposition (see stage 7 below), as revocation of the parent application does not necessarily result in revocation of a divisional application.

➤ A divisional application can carve out a particular aspect of an invention (eg: a specific class of drugs, rather than all drugs).

| Stage 2 | Submission of application (*EPC*) |

➤ An application can be filed at (*EPC Art 75(1)*):

- ◆ the EPO, *or*

- ◆ if the law of a contracting state so permits, at the central industrial property office or other competent authority of that state (eg: in the UK, the UK IPO).

  - ● A divisional application can only be filed at the EPO (*EPC Art 76(1)*).

    - ■ NB: if the applicant's residence or principal place of business is not within the territory of an *EPC* contracting state, the applicant must be represented by a European patent attorney throughout the application procedure (except in filing the application) (*EPC Art 133(2)*).

➤ The following must be submitted:

a) a request for grant of the *EPC* patent (*EPC Art 78(1)*) on *Form 1001, and*

b) the specification (ie: 1 or more claims, description, abstract and any drawings) (*EPC Art 78(1)*), *and*

c) where the applicant is not the inventor (or not the sole inventor), a designation of the inventor (*EPC Art 81*) on *Form 1002, and*

d) a statement of any priority being claimed (which must identify the document from which priority is claimed) (*EPC Art 87*).

➤ An application should be in:

a) English, French or German (*EPC Art 14(1)*), *or*

b) the language of any contracting state, and followed by an English, French or German translation within 3 months of filing (and no later than 13 months after the earliest priority date being claimed) (*EPC Art 14(2)* and *R 6*).

➤ All contracting states are automatically deemed to be designated upon filing of the application (*EPC Art 79(1)*).

- ◆ The designations are subject to payment of a designation fee (*EPC Art 79(2)*).

  - ● It is not possible to add further contracting states after the request for the grant of the patent is filed. Contracting states can, however, be withdrawn at any time up to grant (*EPC Art 79(3)*).

- ◆ Where there are 2 or more applicants, the respective applicants may:

  a) designate different contracting states, *and/or*

  b) jointly designate a group of contracting states (*EPC Arts 59 and 118*).

➤ Application fees are payable.

> ### EPO application fees
>
> ➤ The following fees are payable direct to the EPO (even if the application is filed with a national authority).
>
> ◆ A filing fee and a search fee must be paid within 1 month of filing an application (*Art 78(2)* and *R 38*).
>
> ◆ A claims fee is payable, within 1 month of filing the first set of claims, for each claim submitted over 10 claims (*R 45*).
>
> ◆ A designation fee is payable within 6 months of the date on which the *European Patent Bulletin* mentions the publication of the European search report (*R 39*).
>
> • An 'extension fee' is payable for extending the application to cover non-contracting states that are signatories to extension agreements (*EPC Examination Guidelines A-III 12.2*).
>
> ➤ An applicant should use *Form 1010* to communicate payment details.
>
> ◆ NB: the EPO does not send a reminder before the due date.

➤ An applicant should receive an acknowledgement of receipt of the application.

◆ If an application is filed at the UK IPO, the UK IPO will forward the application to the EPO, which will then inform the applicant of receipt.

◆ An application is deemed to be withdrawn if it does not reach the EPO within 14 months after (*EPC Art 77(5)*):

a) the application has been filed at a national registry, *or*

b) (if an applicant is claiming priority) the earliest claimed priority date.

Stage 3 | **Preliminary examination (*EPC*)**

➤ The EPO conducts a preliminary examination of the application (*EPC Arts 90-92*).

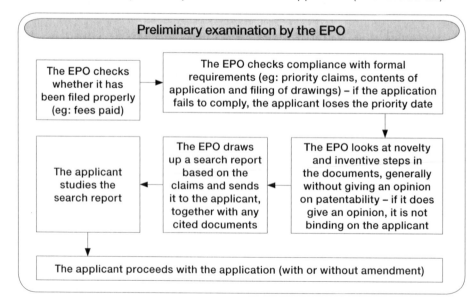

| Stage 4 | Publication (*EPC*) |

➤ An application is published as soon as possible after the expiry of 18 months from (*EPC Art 93(1)*):

   ◆ the filing date, *or*

   ◆ if priority has been claimed, the earliest priority date claimed.

      ● The applicant can request earlier publication.

➤ Publication has the same effects as for a UK patent application.

| Stage 5 | Substantive examination (*EPC*) |

➤ A request for substantive examination must be filed (and an examination fee paid) by an applicant within 6 months after the date on which the European Patent Bulletin mentions the publication of the search report (*EPC Art 94 (2)*).

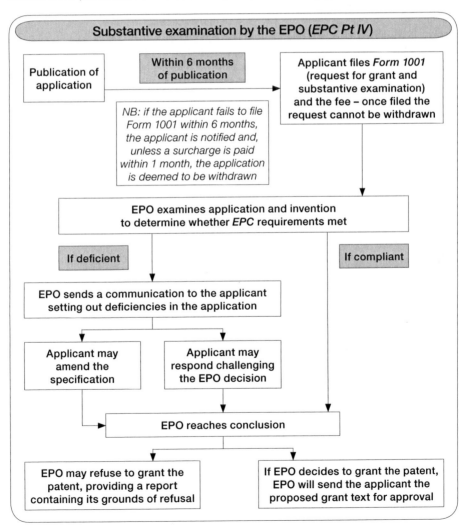

Stage 6	Grant (*EPC*)

➤ An inventor must (*EPC Art 97(2)* and *R 71(3)*):

   a) approve the text sent to it by the EPO, *and*

   b) pay a fee for grant and printing costs within 4 months of the EPO's request, *and*

   c) pay any renewal fees and additional fees that have become payable, *and*

   d) provide translations of the claims in 2 other official languages.

➤ A patent confers on the patentee, in each contracting state designated in the application, the same rights as would be conferred by a national patent (*EPC Art 64(1)*).

   ◆ Once granted, a patent is published in the *European Patent Bulletin*.

➤ The rules for first ownership of an *EPC* patent are, in outline, as follows:

Ownership of an *EPC* patent

➤ In general only an inventor (or an inventor's successor in title) is entitled to the grant of an *EPC* patent (*EPC Art 60(1)*).

➤ For an employee, the right to the grant of an *EPC* patent is determined by the law of the member state in which (*EPC Art 60(1)*):

   a) the employee is mainly employed, *or*

   b) (if this cannot be determined) the employer has its place of business.

➤ *EPC* patent protection begins from the date of filing (*EPC Art 63(1)*).

Duration of a patent under the *EPC*

➤ An *EPC* patent is effectively a bundle of national patents. Once granted, it lasts for up to 20 years from the filing date, but may in defined circumstances be extended by the national law of each contracting state (see *EPC Art 63(2)*).

   ◆ For *EPC* patents, annual renewal fees are due from the third year onwards (calculated from the filing date) (*EPC Art 86(1)*).

Stage 7	Opposition (*EPC*)

➤ Once granted, an *EPC* patent can be formally opposed.

   ◆ Any person wishing to revoke the patent must give a notice of opposition to the EPO within 9 months after publication of the grant of the patent (*EPC Art 99*).

   ◆ If the patent is opposed, an alleged infringer (if party to proceedings relating to the alleged infringement) may, after the opposition period has expired, 'intervene' in the opposition by serving a notice of intervention to the EPO within 3 months after the issue of the infringement proceedings (*EPC Art 105(1)*).

     ● The intervention is generally treated as an opposition (*EPC Art 105(2)*).

➤ In the EPO procedure, there are only 3 grounds of opposition (*EPC Art 100*):

a) the patent's subject-matter is not patentable, *or*

b) the invention has not been disclosed clearly and completely enough for it to be carried out by a person skilled in the art, *or*

c) the subject-matter extends beyond the content of the application as filed.

➤ If an opposition succeeds, the patent is revoked in all the jurisdictions in which it has been granted (*EPC Art 102(1)*).

➤ The EPO opposition procedure summarised below (see *RR 75-89*).

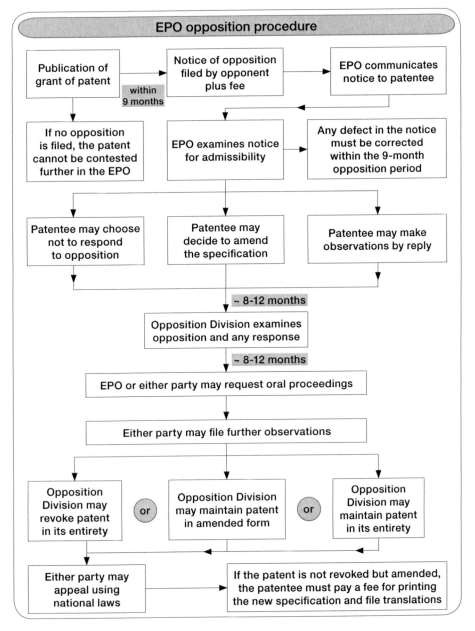

Stage 8	Appeal (*EPC*)

➤ Any party to opposition proceedings can appeal a decision of the Opposition Division (*EPC Art 109*).

Appeal from a decision of the EPO Opposition Division

➤ The appeal is made to (*EPC Arts 21-22*):

- ◆ an independent Technical Board of Appeal, which usually consists of 2 technically qualified members and 1 legally qualified member (or in special cases 3 technically qualified and 2 legally qualified), *or*

- ◆ on an important point of law, the Enlarged Board of Appeal.

➤ The appeal has suspensive effect (ie: the decision being contested has no effect until the appeal is finalised) (*EPC Art 109(1)*).

➤ The appeal procedure is summarised below (see *RR 97-103*).

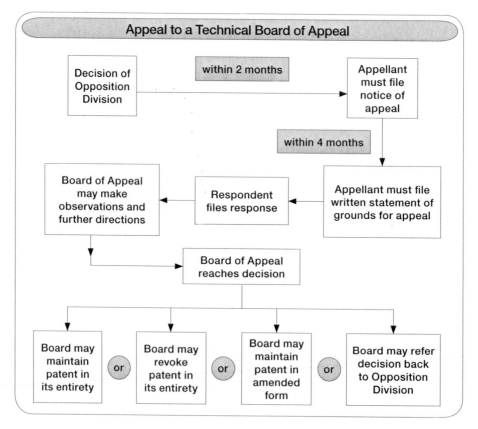

➤ NB: as an alternative to the Europe-wide opposition procedure described above, an opponent may bring revocation proceedings in any relevant state(s) at the national court, with a view to revoking the *EPC* patent at national level.

V   Applying for a patent under the *PCT*

➤ The *PCT* system enables an applicant to make a single application covering each of the *PCT* countries specified by the applicant, so eliminating the earlier national stages.

➤ The applicant files the application at the local patent office (ie: the UK IPO).

♦ The application confers priority on the applicant in all *PCT* member states.

➤ A single search of the prior art is made by an authorised international searching authority ('***ISA***') (ie: a major national or regional patent office), providing the applicant with:

a) an international search report ('***ISR***'), *and*

b) a written preliminary opinion on patentability.

♦ The applicant can request an international preliminary examination, which is conducted by an authorised international preliminary examination authority and results in an international preliminary examining report ('***IPER***').

➤ There is a single publication of the international application, which is accompanied by (or promptly followed by) publication of the ISR and later followed by publication of the written opinion (or of any superseding IPER).

➤ The application is continued in each country, and the respective national patent offices (or for Europe, if chosen by the applicant, the EPO) conduct the remaining steps (eg: substantive examination and grant).

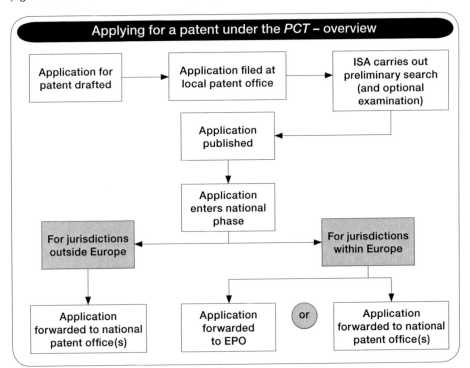

Applying for a patent under the *PCT* – overview

VI   Infringement

➤ To protect the monopoly conferred by a patent, the patentee may need to take action to prevent or stop infringement.

◆ Any infringement of an *EPC* patent is dealt with by national law (*EPC Art 64(3)*).

● This is consistent with the fact that the patent confers the same rights as would be conferred by a national patent granted in the relevant country.

■ *NB: this may change in due course. In March 2009 the European Commission recommended a unified patent litigation system for EPC patents and (if introduced) EU patents. In December 2009, the EU Council published conclusions on an enhanced European patent system. The proposals include the establishment of a European and EU Patents Court ('**EEUPC**') to provide an EU-wide unified patent litigation system.*

➤ An infringement action has the following advantages and disadvantages for the patentee:

Advantages	Disadvantages
✔ It may not be necessary to go to trial, as the action may apply sufficient pressure to force settlement.	✘ Infringement actions are often lengthy and expensive, especially where they relate to complex technology and/or involve cross-border aspects.
✔ Bringing an action may strengthen the patentee's negotiating position.	✘ An infringement action takes up valuable management time.
✔ A successful infringement action will prevent the infringer from making use of the patent.	✘ There is a risk that the infringer might counterclaim for revocation of the patent.
✔ It may also encourage other potential infringers to negotiate licences.	✘ If unsuccessful, the patentee will have to pay the defendant's legal costs.
✔ A series of actions should prevent rivals from competing in the same market during the life of the patent.	✘ Losing the action may encourage other potential infringers to infringe.

➤ There are 4 steps to consider in relation to a patent infringement action:

Steps	
1	Has there been an infringing act?
2	What is the correct procedure?
3	Are there any defences?
4	What are the remedies?

Step 1	Has there been an infringing act?

➤ Infringement occurs where, without the patentee's consent, a person (*s 60(1)-(3)*):

   a) in the case of a patented product (or product of a patented process):

      i) makes, *or*

      ii) disposes of (or offers to dispose of), *or*

      iii) uses, *or*

      iv) imports, *or*

      v) keeps,

      ... the product, *or*

   b) in the case of a patented process:

      i) uses the process (or offers it for use), *and*

      ii) knows (or ought reasonably to know) that its use would be infringing, *or*

   c) in the case of any essential means for putting the invention into effect:

      i) supplies (or offers to supply) those means, *and*

      ii) knows (or ought reasonably to know) that those means are suitable for putting, and are intended to put, the invention into effect.

         ◆ Such 'means' (eg: an invention's key components) do not include staple commercial products, unless the supply/offer is made to induce the customer to commit an infringing act of the kind described at a) or b) above.

➤ NB: each act listed above is only infringing for the purposes of UK law if the act takes place within the UK.

   ◆ International protection is available under the national laws of other countries.

➤ Any person (eg: a patentee or potential infringer) can apply to the Comptroller at the UK IPO for an opinion on whether an infringing act has occurred (*s 74A*).

UK IPO opinion on infringement and validity

➤ An opinion can be sought as to whether (*s 74A(1)*):

   a) a given act constitutes, or (if done) would constitute, patent infringement, *and/or*

   b) the invention in question is not patentable due to lack of novelty or the absence of an inventive step.

➤ The opinion is not binding on any party or for any other purposes (*s 74A(4)*).

   ◆ The aim of the opinion is to assist a potential party to proceedings to assess the merits of an action and the likely costs of the proceedings.

➤ A patentee (or an exclusive licensee of the patent) may apply to the UK IPO for a review of an opinion (*s 74B*).

   ◆ A decision made under the review procedure can be appealed to the High Court (*DLP Ltd, Re UK IPO Decision* [2007] EWHC 2669).

Step 2	What is the correct procedure?

➤ Only the owner or exclusive licensee may commence infringement proceedings (*ss 61* and *67*).

    ◆ A certified copy of the patent, evidence of registration and any relevant agreements relating to the patent rights (eg: a licence or assignment) are required.

    ◆ When deciding whom to sue, the patentee/licensee should consider which person is to be prevented from infringing (particularly where a company is involved).

➤ An infringement action can be brought in the Patent County Court or the High Court.

Choice of court

➤ The Patents County Court is less formal and less expensive than the High Court.

    ◆ A 'streamlined' court procedure may be ordered (which involves less documentation and shorter trials) where the parties agree or, in the absence of agreement and where it is deemed appropriate, the court considers proportionality, the financial position of each party, the degree of complexity and the importance of the case.

    ◆ Judgments from the Patents County Court are, however, often appealed to the High Court successfully.

➤ To place maximum pressure on an infringer, an action should be started in the High Court.

➤ Before commencing legal proceedings a letter before action should be sent.

    ◆ The threat of litigation may force an infringer into settlement negotiations.

    ◆ A patentee should seek professional advice on drafting a letter before action.

➤ A letter before action should be drafted to ensure that a potential infringer cannot counterclaim that the patentee is making 'groundless threats' and sue for injunctive relief and/or damages for any loss sustained by the threats (*s 70*).

    ◆ A patentee is not making threats if merely (*s 70(5)*):

      a) providing factual information about the patent, *and/or*

      b) making enquiries of the other person for the sole purpose of discovering whether, or by whom, the patent has been infringed.

➤ When commencing a claim the claimant should, in addition to the claim form, file a statement of case, which must at least (*CPR 63.9* and *Practice Direction 63 para 11.1*):

    a) show which claims in the patent specification are alleged to be infringed, *and*

    b) give at least 1 example of each type of infringement alleged.

| Step 3 | Are there any defences? |

➤ There are 7 main defences/exceptions to infringement.

1 Expiry

➤ It is a defence to show that the period of protection of the patent has expired (eg: where the patent has not been renewed or where, after 20 years, no supplementary protection certificate is in force).

◆ The defence only applies for the period after the patent has expired or not been renewed.

2 Invalidity

➤ Perhaps the most common form of defence is to challenge the validity of the patent and to claim that the patent should be revoked (s 74).

◆ This increases the cost of the action significantly.

➤ If a court rules the patent valid, an owner can apply for a certificate of contested validity (s 65).

◆ A certificate acts as a disincentive to defendants in future actions because, if they attempt to revoke the patent and fail, the patentee will be entitled to the costs incurred in such action.

➤ Where the court rules a patent partially invalid:

a) remedies will only be available to a patent owner for infringement of the valid part, *and*

b) damages may not be available for all of the infringing acts.

3 Limited scope of patent claims

➤ It is a defence to show that, even if the patent is valid, the patent claims do not cover the alleged infringement (known as the 'Gillette defence' after *Gillette Safety Razor Co v Anglo-American Trading Co Ltd* (1913) 30 RPC 465).

4 Private, non-commercial use

➤ It is a defence to show that the invention was used (s 60(5)(a)):

◆ privately, *and*

◆ for non-commercial purposes.

5 Experimental purposes

➤ It is a defence to show that the invention was used for experimental purposes relating to the subject-matter of the invention (s 60(5)(b)).

◆ There are a number of other scientific exceptions under the *PA 1977* (eg: in pharmaceutical and agricultural contexts). See the remaining provisions of s 60(5), which are beyond the scope of this Section.

6 Innocent infringement

➤ This is only a partial defence. Neither damages nor an account of profits will be awarded if the defendant can show that the defendant (*s 62(1)*):

a) did not know, *or*

b) had no reasonable grounds for supposing,

... that the relevant patent existed.

◆ Marking a product with 'patent' or 'patented' is not enough to put an alleged infringer on notice that a product is patented: the product must be marked with the patent number (*s 62(1)*).

7 Previous use

➤ Where a person uses an invention in the UK in good faith before the patent application is filed, that person has the right to use, and to continue to use, the invention despite the grant of a patent (*s 64(1)*).

➤ A defendant cannot, however, license the invention to any other person, although, if the previous use was in the course of business, the defendant can authorise the defendant's partners (or successors) in that business to use the invention (*s 64(1)*).

➤ There are also more general defences, such as:

◆ in the case of products already marketed within the EU, the doctrine of 'exhaustion of rights' (which permits parallel importation of such products), *and/or*

◆ defences under competition law (eg: abuse of a dominant position by the claimant in failing to grant a licence, for which there is no block exemption), *and/or*

◆ equitable bars (eg: delay or acquiesence).

Step 4	What are the remedies?

➤ The remedies for patent infringement are similar to those for other intellectual property rights and include (*s 61*):

a) an injunction (interim or final), *and/or*

◆ As in any other context, an interim injunction will not be granted if damages would adequately compensate the claimant at trial.

● Injunctions are commonly granted to prevent a generic drug from entering the market, as this would irreversibly affect the price of the patented drug.

b) damages or an account of profits, *and/or*

◆ NB: a patentee cannot sue before the patent is granted, but can recover damages for infringement that occurred between the filing date and grant of the patent.

c) delivery-up or destruction of an infringing product, *and/or*

d) a declaration that the patent is valid.

VII Dealing with patents

➤ A patent constitutes personal property, as does a patent application (*s 30(1)*).

◆ Accordingly, a patent (or application) is transmissible in the same way as other personal property, including by operation of law or under a will (*s 30(3)*), eg:

● if an individual patentee dies, the patent forms part of the deceased's estate and passes according to the deceased's will or intestacy, *or*

● if the patentee is a company, the patent forms part of its assets and passes on its liquidation to the liquidator and is held on trust for its creditors.

▪ References below to disposals of patents apply equally to disposals of patent applications. In practice, each disposal may also include a transfer or licence of rights in related know-how (ie: confidential information).

➤ There are 2 main ways of dealing with a patent.

1 Assignment

➤ A patent can be 'assigned' (ie: ownership can be transferred) (*s 30(2)*).

◆ An assignment must be in writing and signed by or on behalf of:

● the assignor – for UK patents (*PA 77 s 30(6)*), or

● the assignor and assignee – for *EPC* patents (*EPC Art 72*).

▪ If an assignment is not in writing and signed, it is void.

◆ The assignment can (and, in practice, should expressly) confer the right to bring proceedings for previous infringements (*s 30(7)*).

2 Licensing

➤ A licence can be granted under a patent (*s 30(4)* and *EPC Art 73*).

◆ A licence allows a third party to perform an act that would otherwise constitute infringement of an owner's rights.

➤ A patent licence may be limited:

a) by time, *and/or*

b) to a particular area or territory, *and/or*

c) for a particular purpose or field of application, *and/or*

d) for only part of the subject-matter of the patent.

➤ There are 3 types of patent licence:

a) Non-exclusive

◆ The patentee can grant other licences of the same invention to third parties. The patentee can also exploit the licensed invention.

b) **Sole**

- ◆ The patentee grants a licence of the invention solely to the licensee. The patentee can still exploit the invention.

c) **Exclusive**

- ◆ Only 1 person, an exclusive licensee (and sub-licensees if a right to sub-license is granted), can exploit the invention. The patentee cannot exploit the invention.

➤ A patent licence (of any type) need not be in writing to be effective.

- ◆ It is best practice, however, for a patent licence to be in writing:

    a) to provide evidence of the terms agreed, *and*

    b) to allow the licence to be registered at the UK IPO (see below).

➤ A licence can confer the right to sue for previous infringements (*s 30(7)*), but this is rare in practice – even in an exclusive licence (unless intra-group).

➤ Whatever the type of licence, a patentee should protect the patent by imposing contractual obligations or restrictions on the licensee.

- ◆ Eg: the licensee may be required to keep know-how confidential and to apply an appropriate notice to products and packaging, such as 'patented' or (in the case of a patent application) 'patent pending'.

    - • NB: it is a criminal offence to represent falsely (eg: by such a notice) that a product is:

        - ▪ patented (*s 110*), *or*

        - ▪ the subject of a patent application (*s 111*).

➤ European Competition law and the UK *Competition Act 2000* place restrictions on the terms that can be included in patent licences.

Competition restrictions on exclusive licences

➤ Licensing restrictions may amount to an anti-competitive agreement contrary to the *Treaty on the Functioning of the European Union* ('**EU Treaty**') *Art 101* and/or under the *Competition Act 1998 Ch I*.

➤ It is therefore important to consider, when drafting a licence, whether the *Technology Transfer Block Exemption* (772/2004/EC) applies (eg: in relation to the type of agreement, the parties' market share thresholds and/or types of restriction contained in the licence).

➤ If any restrictions do not fall within the 'safe harbour' created by the *Exemption*, the whole licence (in the case of 'hardcore' restrictions) or the provision (in the case of severable 'excluded' restrictions) will be subject to challenge as an anti-competitive agreement.

- ◆ Eg: the *Exemption* prohibits price-fixing and 'tie-ins', ie: where a licensee must buy a product that is neither covered by the patent nor necessary for exploitation of the licensed product.

    - • The detailed provisions of the *Exemption* are beyond the scope of this Section.

➤ The owner of a patent may, at any time after the grant of the patent, apply to the Comptroller at the UK IPO for an entry to be made in the register to indicate that licences as of right are available (s 46).

Licences as of right
➤ Offering licences as of right may be advantageous to a patentee that is having trouble exploiting an invention.
◆ Another advantage of making an entry on the register is that the renewal fee is halved.
➤ The licence fees are negotiated between the patentee and the licensee.
◆ Failing agreement the Comptroller can be asked to intervene.
➤ The licensee can insist that the patentee takes infringement proceedings on the licensee's behalf.
➤ The owner is not obliged to keep the 'offer to license' open indefinitely, and may cancel it at any time if there are no existing licences (s 47).

➤ An owner can be forced to grant a compulsory licence where (s 48):

a) 3 years have elapsed since the grant of the patent, *and*

b) the applicant shows a ground for granting a compulsory licence.

Compulsory licences
➤ There are 3 usual grounds for a compulsory licence (s 48A):
a) where demand in the UK for a patented product is not being met on reasonable terms, *or*
b) where a patentee refuses to grant a licence of an economically significant technology on reasonable terms and a patent cannot be exploited without infringing a second patent, or the development of commercial activities in the UK are being unfairly prejudiced, *or*
c) where the conditions imposed by a patentee on the manufacture or disposal of products not covered by the patent, or the development of commercial activities in the UK are unfairly prejudiced.
➤ There are special rules for patentees based in countries that are not members of the World Trade Organisation.
➤ NB: there are no such compulsory licences for semi-conductor technology.

➤ In practice, compulsory licences of patents are rarely granted in the UK.

➤ The commercial terms of an assignment or licence vary widely depending on the nature of the transaction and whether the parties are dealing at arm's length.

   ◆ An assignment may involve a one-off purchase price.

      ● It is difficult, however, to anticipate the commercial success of a patented invention, so the remuneration payable by the assignee may include deferred payments (eg: fixed instalments and/or royalties based on actual exploitation).

   ◆ A licensee often pays a per-unit royalty based on the licensed product's sale price (often with a minimum payable to incentivise the licensee to exploit the invention).

      ● The royalty base may instead be a fixed price per product or a profit share.

      ● The licensee usually bears the investment risk, so will usually retain the greater part of the proceeds (eg: 75%, with a 25% royalty payable to the licensor).

      ● The amount retained by the licensee may escalate in defined increments if the licensee achieves specified levels of turnover.

      ● Another factor in determining the royalty rate is the relevant industry sector.

         ▪ Eg: royalty rates in the pharmaceutical industry tend to be higher than the rates for exploiting a mechanical device, which in turn tend to be higher than in the electronics industry.

➤ An assignee or licensee of a patent can (but is not obliged to) register the transaction at the UK IPO (*s 32(2)(b)*).

Registration of assignments and licences

➤ Registration is strongly recommended for 2 reasons:

1) In the case of an assignment or licence (of any kind) – a third-party acquirer of property rights in the patent is not bound by the transaction unless the third party has knowledge of the transaction (*s 33*).

   ◆ Registering an assignment or licence (of any kind) puts third parties on notice of the registered interest.

2) In the case of an assignment or exclusive licence – the assignee/licensee can only be awarded costs or expenses in court or IPO proceedings relating to an infringement that occurred before registration if (*s 68*):

   a) the transaction is registered within 6 months of its completion, *or*

   b) (if registration is not feasible within that 6-month period) as soon as practicable thereafter.

➤ Since the register is public, it is common to keep the commercial terms of a licence confidential by requiring each party, at the other's request, to execute a short-form licence (a 'recordal licence') that can be submitted to the relevant patent office for registration.

J   Confidential information

I   Introduction

➤ Information is increasingly recognised as valuable property, especially in the media world where it is frequently bought and sold.

➤ Parties to a contract can agree under the contract to keep information confidential. Even if the contract is silent, the courts may imply confidentiality obligations into it.

➤ Obligations of confidence may in any event arise in equity or tort under the law of confidence. There is no requirement for a contractual relationship.

  ◆ The law of confidence is useful where information cannot be protected by:

    ● copyright (eg: because the information is not recorded in writing in the early stages of development of a creative idea), or

    ● a patent (eg: because the technology is not sufficiently inventive to attract protection).

➤ An obligation of confidence can attach to a wide range of information, eg:

  ◆ technological secrets, such as chemical formulae, or

  ◆ trade secrets, such as the way in which a particular recipe is used to make a product (eg: Coca-Cola), or

  ◆ confidential information that employees discover during the course of their employment (Robb v Green [1895] 2 QB 315), or

  ◆ confidential information that newspapers discover with a view to publication, or

  ◆ certain artistic concepts, such as a scene containing objects and people arranged for the purposes of a photographic shoot (Creation Records Ltd v News Group Newspapers Ltd [1997] EMLR 444), or

  ◆ secret aspects of an individual's private life (Argyll v Argyll [1967] Ch 302).

    ● Information relating to aspects of an individual's private life is mainly protected:

      ▪ under data protection law, to the extent that it comprises personal data for the purposes of data protection legislation (see Section K of this Chapter), and

      ▪ through the incorporation into the law of confidence of human rights law, which has led to a substantial modification of the law of confidence as it relates to private information (see section IV below).

➤ NB: certain legal restraints on breach of confidence are beyond the scope of this Section, including:

- ◆ *CDPA 1988 s 85*, which provides a limited 'moral right' of privacy in respect of certain photographs and films (see Section C of this Chapter), *and*

- ◆ statutory obligations of confidence imposed on certain public bodies, *and*

- ◆ restrictions under competition law on the exchange of information between competitors, *and*

- ◆ issues arising under foreign or international laws (eg: taxation treaties) in relation to the cross-border transfer of information.

➤ In media-related cases, it is also necessary to consider the independent and self-regulatory systems put in place by media bodies to regulate media content (eg: the restraints imposed by the Press Complaints Commission on the invasion of privacy).

- ◆ The effect of those systems is beyond the scope of this Section.

  - ● The relevant organisations are considered in the context of offensive material (see Chapter 2 Section B).

    - ■ Their websites set out the various codes, regulations, practice statements and guidance provisions.

II Breach of confidence

➤ The law of confidence is based on case law.

➤ The doctrine of breach of confidence protects against misuse or unauthorised disclosure of confidential information and can be invoked against:

- ◆ the direct recipient of the information, *and/or*

- ◆ a third party who obtains the information through a breach of confidence.

  - ● For example, if A discloses information to B in confidence and B repeats it to C, A can prevent C from publishing the information.

➤ There are 3 steps to consider in relation to a 'classical' case of breach of confidence.

- ◆ See section IV below for the steps in a case of misuse of private information.

Steps	
1	What amounts to a breach of confidence?
2	Are there any defences?
3	What are the remedies?

| Step 1 | What amounts to a breach of confidence? |

➤ 3 criteria (set out by Megarry J in *Coco v A N Clark (Engineers) Ltd* [1968] FSR 415) must be satisfied in order for the classical doctrine to be successfully invoked:

1 The information must have the necessary quality of confidence

➤ The information must be sufficiently important and have some value to it. In a commercial context, an important factor is whether the information:

a) would be of use to the claimant's competitors, *and*

b) is confidential.

◆ Trivial or useless information is not protected (*AG v Guardian Newspapers (No. 2)* [1988] 3 All ER 545) – except where it is private information that satisfies certain criteria (see section IV below).

➤ The information need not be in writing or in any other permanent form.

➤ Where the information is an idea (eg: for a copyright work such as a book or a television programme), it will not be protected unless the content is:

◆ clearly identifiable, *and*

◆ potentially attractive in a commercial sense, *and*

◆ realisable (*Fraser v Thames Television Ltd* [1983] 2 All ER 101).

2 The information must have been communicated in circumstances implying an obligation of confidence

➤ The test is whether it could be said that a reasonable person would, in the circumstances, realise that the information was confidential.

➤ An obligation of confidence can be implied from circumstances.

◆ In the case of *Fraser* (as above), Thames used an idea for a television programme against the wishes of the claimant. On the facts, it was held that the television company was under an obligation of confidence.

◆ In the case of *Creation Records Ltd v News Group Newspapers Ltd* ([1997] EMLR 444), a scene was arranged for a photo shoot for the cover of an album by the band Oasis. It was found arguable that the nature of the operation (ie: creating the scene) and imposition of security measures (eg: keeping out fans) made it an occasion of confidentiality.

➤ An obligation of confidence can be implied from the parties' relationship, eg:

◆ wherever there is a legal duty of good faith, such as exists between:

• employer and employee, *or*

• doctor and patient, *or*

• solicitor and client, *or*

◆ where appropriate, from the context of business transactions.

➤ It is no longer necessary to imply such a relationship in cases of misuse of private information (see section IV below).

3   **There must have been unauthorised use of the information to the detriment of the person communicating it**

➤   It is a question of fact in each case whether the use of the information is unauthorised.

◆   Innocent misuse by a recipient can still give rise to liability.

●   In *Seager v Copydex Ltd* [1967] 1 WLR 923, the defendants innocently used confidential information that had been given to them by the claimants, but were still held liable.

➤   The courts have doubted whether detriment is an essential element of an action for breach of confidence (see *AG v Guardian Newspapers (No. 2)* [1988] 3 All ER 545), while accepting that it will be present in most cases.

➤   In the context of an interim injunction, there need only be a **risk** of unauthorised use and (to the extent indeed required) of detriment.

Step 2	Are there any defences?

➤   There are 3 main defences to a claim for breach of confidence:

1   **Public domain**

➤   Information that is in the public domain is not protected by the law of confidence (*AG v Guardian Newspapers (No. 2)* [1988] 3 All ER 545).

◆   The position is less straightforward if the case concerns private information (see section IV below).

2   **Public interest**

➤   Use of confidential information or its disclosure may be justified where the public interest in using/disclosing the information outweighs the duty of confidence. This involves a balancing exercise by the court.

◆   This public-interest defence applies where, for example:

●   an employee discloses a wrongdoing by his or her employer, *or*

●   the police make reasonable use of the information to prevent or detect crime.

◆   The defence does not apply to use or publication that is merely 'of interest to the public' without actually being in the public interest.

●   The defence has long applied, however, to certain celebrity cases. See *Woodward v Hutchins* [1977] 2 All ER 751, in which a number of pop singers including Tom Jones attempted to prevent the publication of articles by an ex-employee about their activities on tour. It was found to be in the public interest to correct untrue images offered by performers who sought publicity to their advantage.

◆   Public interest in privacy cases is examined in section IV below.

3   **Freedom of Information**

➤   The *Freedom of Information Act 2000* provides certain defences to a public authority (eg: where required in the public interest, to disclose commercially sensitive information (*s 43*)).

4   **Innocent receipt**

➤   A third party who receives confidential information is only liable if (*AG v Guardian Newspapers (No. 2)* [1988] 3 All ER 545):

a)   notified of its confidential nature, *or*

b)   acting in bad faith.

Step 3	What are the remedies?

➤   **Injunction** – An injunction prohibiting use of the information can be obtained if damage has yet to be suffered (eg: the *Creation Records* case).

◆   See section IV below for the special considerations that apply in privacy cases.

➤   If it is too late for an injunction to be effective, other remedies are:

◆   **Damages**

●   The aim of the award is to put the claimant in the position that the claimant would have been in had the confidential information not been misused.

■   The value of the information will have to be assessed: the more valuable, the higher the damages.

◆   **Account of profits**

●   The claimant is awarded (as an alternative to damages) an amount that represents the profit made by the defendant through the misuse of the information.

◆   **Delivery-up or destruction**

●   The defendant is required to deliver up property containing the confidential information to the claimant or to destroy such property.

III   Protecting confidential information

➤   Possessors of confidential information can take several steps to protect themselves, eg:

◆   signing a non-disclosure agreement ('**NDA**') with those who will come into contact with the information, *and*

●   An NDA should be concluded at the outset of commercial negotiations, and any subsequent agreement should include express confidentiality obligations.

◆   labelling documents as 'confidential' and restricting circulation to a minimum, *and*

◆   keeping a record of all confidential documents, and ensuring that they are returned when the appropriate person has finished with them.

- inserting a clause in a relevant contract (eg: an employment contract) that restricts the extent to which information can be disclosed after the contract term, *and*

  - Broadly speaking, such a clause will only be upheld if it:

    a) protects a legitimate interest of the disclosing party (eg: employer), *and*

    b) is reasonable in terms of the scope and duration of the protection sought and the geographical area to which it applies.

- entering into a confidentiality agreement with a recipient of information.

Contents of a confidentiality agreement

➤ A definition of what is to be regarded as confidential, eg:

- commercially sensitive information about a party's (or, if the obligations are reciprocal, each party's) business and affairs, *and*

- information developed during the parties' contractual relationship, *and*

- (if appropriate) the fact and status of the negotiations and/or the existence and terms of the agreement.

  - To prevent the agreement from being held to be in restraint of trade, information in the public domain should be specifically excluded from the scope of the agreement.

  - The definition should not be too wide (eg: extending to trivial information), in case it might be held to be unenforceable (see *Faccenda Chicken v Fowler* [1986] 1 All ER 617), nor should it be too narrow to cover the information to be protected.

➤ An obligation to pay for the information (if agreed).

- The time when any such obligation arises should be stated.

➤ Restrictions on the purposes for which the information can be used.

➤ Restrictions on disclosure, together with any permitted exceptions, eg:

- a definition of any third parties authorised to receive the confidential information (eg: employees that are reasonably required to have access to the information for the performance of a party's contractual obligations), together with an obligation on the relevant party to ensure that such third parties are bound by obligations of confidence equivalent to those set out in the agreement, *and*

- an exception for disclosures specifically required by law, court order or any competent public or regulatory authority.

➤ A requirement, at the disclosing party's direction, for all copies of the information to be returned or (where specified) destroyed/erased.

➤ Survival of obligations for a specified period after termination of the agreement.

- The scope, duration and geographical area should be reasonable (as noted above) so that the provision is not in restraint of trade.

  - Technical information may remain commercially sensitive almost indefinitely (eg: the recipe for Coca-Cola), while more general business information (eg: the valuation of a company) or material where only part of the information is confidential may quickly cease to be so. These considerations affect how long an employee can be expected to keep information confidential after the end of the employment contract (Faccenda Chicken, as above), and the same principles apply to an independent contractor (*Vestergaard Frandsen A/S v Bestnet Europe Ltd* [2009] EWHC 657).

➤ If rights in confidential information are to be jointly shared, specific provisions setting out each party's rights should be included so that one party does not use the information to the other party's detriment (see *Murray v Yorkshire Fund Managers Ltd*, Times Law Reports, 18 December 1997).

IV Misuse of private information

*NB: the law described in this section IV is still developing and may have changed further since the time of writing. References below are to the Human Rights Act 1998 ('**HRA**') unless otherwise stated.*

➤ Until around 2004, 'privacy' actions were difficult to maintain.

♦ In a case of invasion of privacy there may be no contractual relationship between the publisher and the person whose privacy is invaded (so no contract to sue under).

♦ The 'classical' doctrine of breach of confidence was based on trade secrets, so a 'privacy' action required judicial ingenuity in finding a 'relationship of confidence' – especially in the absence of a general right of privacy before the enactment of the *HRA*.

➤ This gradually led to a special application of the law of confidence by taking into account the right to respect for private and family life under the *European Convention on Human Rights* ('**ECHR**') *Art 8*.

'Privacy' under human rights law
➤ Everyone has the right to respect for his private and family life, his home and his correspondence (*ECHR Art 8(1)*).   ♦ *ECHR Art 8* was enshrined in domestic UK law under the *HRA*, which came into force on 2 October 2000.   ➤ As between non-state bodies, the *HRA* does not give rise to a free-standing cause of action, so claims must be brought under existing domestic law (*Venables v News Group Newspapers Ltd* [2001] 1 All ER 908).   ➤ UK courts and tribunals must, however, take into account the decisions and opinions of the European Court of Human Rights (*s 2*) and give effect to legislation in a way which is compatible with *ECHR* rights (*s 3*).

♦ In the leading case of *Campbell v Mirror Group Newspapers Ltd* [2004] UKHL 22, the House of Lords acknowledged that the law of breach of confidence had been developed to provide a remedy for the 'wrongful disclosure of private information', describing the essence of the action as 'misuse of private information'.

♦ In *Von Hannover v Germany* (2005) 40 EHRR 1, the European Court of Human Rights recognised an obligation on the courts of member states to interpret legislation in a way that would protect an individual from an unjustified invasion of private life.

● It was held that the courts had to strike a 'fair balance' between the competing interests under *Art 8* and *Art 10* (the right to freedom of expression).

♦ In *Douglas v Hello!* [2005] EWCA Civ 595, the Court of Appeal went so far as to comment *obiter* that it would have upheld an injunction it had lifted previously.

➤ NB: the courts have consistently stopped short of confirming the existence of a separate cause of action in 'privacy' as such.

- ◆ There is no 'tort of privacy' (*Wainwright v Home Office* [2003] 3 WLR 1377), but the courts have clearly established a distinct action in confidence for misuse of private information.

➤ In the context of private information, the 'classical' doctrine of breach of confidence now appears to be applied in a modified way in 3 respects:

1   New human rights test

> ➤ The values enshrined in *ECHR Arts 8* and *10* are now 'part of the cause of action' (*Campbell v Mirror Group Newspapers Ltd* [2004] UKHL 22).
>
>   - ◆ The courts must apply the law of confidence so as not to act 'in a way which is incompatible with a Convention right' (*Douglas v Hello!* [2005] EWCA Civ 595).

2   No need for a relationship of confidence

> ➤ A claimant need no longer demonstrate a specific relationship of confidence between the parties.
>
>   - ◆ The law now imposes a duty of confidence whenever a person 'receives information he knows or ought to know is fairly and reasonably to be regarded as confidential' (*Campbell*, as above).

3   Unauthorised use/detriment

> ➤ The third limb of the 'classical' doctrine under *Coco v Clark* is still required (ie: unauthorised use/detriment), but *de facto* assumes less significance than in other contexts, in that unauthorised use and detriment are inherent in invasion of privacy.

➤ It is also now clear that the rights under *Arts 8* and *10* apply as much in disputes between one individual and a non-governmental entity (eg: a newspaper) or another individual as they do between an individual and a public authority (*Campbell*, as above).

➤ From the pattern that has emerged from the leading cases, there appear to be 4 steps to consider in relation to an action for misuse of private information:

Steps	
1	Is there a reasonable expectation of privacy? – the 'threshold test'
2	Does privacy outweigh freedom of expression? – the 'balancing exercise'
3	Are there any defences?
4	What are the remedies?

| Step 1 | Is there a reasonable expectation of privacy? – threshold test |

➤ For an action for misuse of private information to succeed, the claimant must have a 'reasonable expectation of privacy' (*Campbell v Mirror Group Newspapers Ltd* [2004] UKHL 22).

  ◆ This 'threshold test' sets a minimum requirement for protection.

➤ There is a reasonable expectation of privacy where:

  ◆ the information is obviously private, *or*

  ◆ its disclosure would cause 'substantial offence' to a 'reasonable person of ordinary sensibilities' placed in the claimant's position (test in *Campbell*, as above).

    ● The more intimate the information, the more likely it is to pass the test.

➤ Case law suggests that the threshold is set quite low. The courts have recognised privacy where, on the face of it, it might appear to be absent or to have been lost:

  ◆ Where a public figure or celebrity has forfeited an expectation that some parts of his life will be kept private, he may still retain rights of privacy in other parts of his life, even parts closely linked to those where privacy rights have been forfeited (*HRH Prince of Wales v Associated Newspapers Ltd* [2006] EWHC 522).

  ◆ Information can be private even if obtained in public or semi-public places – see *Campbell* (as above) and *Von Hannover v Germany* (2005) 40 EHRR 1), and *Wood v Commissioner of Police for the Metropolis* ([2008] EWCA Civ 414), in which the taking and retention of photographs of a person in a public street by the police without explanation or sufficient cause was found disproportionate.

    ● Relevant factors appear to include that the place is 'secluded' (ie: a place to which the claimant has gone with the clear intention of enjoying privacy), or that, where the information was obtained in a fully public place, the information is 'obviously private' or 'offensive in some other way'.

      ■ A photograph of someone 'popping out to get some milk' is, however, unlikely to attract protection (an *obiter* comment in *Douglas v Hello!* [2005] EWCA Civ 595).

  ◆ Information which may be exploited for commercial value can be private, even where similar information has been, or is about to be, published. A claimant can, in effect, rely on a right of 'publicity' by showing (in addition to the usual requirements of the threshold test) that:

    ● the claimant reasonably intended to profit commercially by using/publishing the information, *and*

    ● the defendant knew (or ought to have known) of this intention, and knowingly obtained it without authority (test in *Douglas*, as above).

  ◆ Information will not necessarily fail the threshold test if it is 'banal, inconsequential or anodyne' or 'trivial', as long as it relates to a matter expressly addressed in *Art 8* (eg: the 'home') (*Ash v McKennitt* [2006] EWCA Civ 1714).

    ● The trivial nature of such information could still be relevant to the 'balancing exercise' to be conducted if the threshold test is satisfied (see step 2 below).

➤ NB: rights in misuse of private information extend to:

♦ information communicated orally or via any media, including photographs (as in all of the leading cases) or film footage (ie: not just to written information), *and*

♦ private relationships with other persons, including adulterous relationships (*CC v AB* [2006] EWHC 3083) and sadomasochistic sex (*Mosley v News Group Newspapers Ltd* [2008] EWHC 1777), *and*

♦ false allegations about private behaviour (*P, Q and R v Quigley* [2008] EWHC 1051), *and*

♦ to corporate information, in that companies have a right to privacy – albeit probably more limited than for individuals (*R v BSC, ex p BBC* [2000] 3 All ER 989).

Step 2	Does privacy outweigh freedom of expression? – balancing exercise

➤ If the threshold test is satisfied, a balance must be struck between the protection of privacy and freedom of expression.

♦ For an action in misuse of private information to succeed, that balance must come down in favour of protecting the right to privacy.

> ### Freedom of expression under human rights law
>
> ➤ Everyone has the right to freedom of expression. This right includes freedom to hold opinions and to receive and impart information and ideas without interference (*ECHR Art 10*).

➤ Each case turns on its facts as to where the balance lies (*A v B plc* [2002] EWCA Civ 337).

➤ The House of Lords has identified 4 general principles to be applied:

1) neither Article has actual or presumptive precedence over the other, *and*

2) where the values under each Article conflict, an 'intense focus' on their comparative importance is required, *and*

3) the court must take account of justifications for interfering with each right, *and*

4) the harm caused by any such interference must be proportionate to the benefits achieved by favouring one right over the other (*Re S (FC) (A Child)* [2004] UKHL 47).

➤ According to *Von Hannover v Germany* ((2005) 40 EHRR 1), the 'decisive factor' in balancing the competing rights is the contribution of the information to a 'debate of general interest'.

♦ The public interest is likely to be engaged where:

• in the context of public figures who exercise official functions, intrusion into their private life is 'necessary in a democratic society' (*Von Hannover*, as above), *or*

• in the context of extra-marital affairs, the relationships are not particularly permanent or stable (*A v B*, as above).

- ◆ The case of *Ash v McKennitt* ([2006] EWCA Civ 1714) suggests that 'formulaic' claims to public interest (eg: in the context of a 'kiss and tell' story) may be subjected to greater scrutiny.

➤ Factors favouring the protection of privacy include:

- ◆ the voyeuristic quality of photographs – a 'particularly intrusive' means of invading privacy (*Theakston v Mirror Group Newspapers Ltd* [2002] EWHC 137), *and*

  - In *Theakston*, the fact of the claimant's visits to a brothel could be published, while photographs of those visits could not.

  - In *Mosley v News Group Newspapers Ltd* ([2008] EWHC 1777), the public did not need to see photographs of 'every gory detail'.

- ◆ where the subject of a photograph is a child, especially if the parents (even if celebrities themselves) have kept the child out of the public eye (*Murray v Big Pictures Ltd* [2008] EWCA 446).

➤ The courts have often prevented the publication of photographs taken:

- ◆ without the claimant's consent, *or*

- ◆ with the claimant's consent, but exploited commercially in a way which the claimant did not approve, *or*

- ◆ in public, but depicting what could not be seen by the naked eye.

Step 3	Are there any defences?

➤ 2 'defences' can be identified from the case law. These could equally be characterised as instances of failure to satisfy the respective threshold and balancing tests.

1 **No reasonable expectation of privacy**

  ➤ *Incidental inclusion*

  - ◆ A person who appears only incidentally (eg: in a photograph) cannot, as a general rule, object to publication (*Campbell v Mirror Group Newspapers Ltd* [2004] UKHL 22).

  ➤ *Public domain*

  - ◆ It is generally a defence to prove that the information concerned was:

    - in the public domain, *and*

    - so generally accessible that, in the circumstances, it cannot be regarded as confidential (*Ash v McKennitt* [2006] EWCA Civ 1714).

      - ▪ The public domain defence does not apply in the context of photographs, where, due to their particularly intrusive quality, each new or repeat viewing amounts to a fresh invasion of privacy (*Douglas v Hello!* [2005] EWCA Civ 595).

      - ▪ Blogging has been characterised as an essentially public activity (*The Author of A Blog v Times Newspapers Ltd [2009] EWHC 1358*).

2 **Public interest**

➤ It is a defence to show that the right of the media to impart information to the public outweighs the claimant's privacy rights, such that the public have a legitimate interest in receiving that information (*A v B plc* [2002] EWCA Civ 337).

➤ The public interest is likely to be engaged in the context of misconduct by politicians or other public figures who exercise official functions (*Von Hannover v Germany* (2005) 40 EHRR 1).

◆ Publication of such information is likely to be properly in the public interest, rather than merely 'of interest to the public'.

➤ Claimants (eg: celebrities) may forfeit their right to protection of otherwise private information where they:

◆ choose to publicise certain aspects of their life (especially those showing them in a favourable light), *and/or*

◆ mislead, or present a false image to, the public about those aspects.

• In such circumstances, the public interest in publication may outweigh the interest in protecting the claimant's privacy.

➤ Case law suggests that a very high degree of misdemeanour on the claimant's part must be demonstrated to trigger a defence of public interest in cases involving celebrities who court publicity (*Ash* v *McKennitt* [2006] EWCA Civ 1714).

➤ Disclosure is not justified by mere immorality or depravity or even by a minor crime committed on private premises (*Mosley v News Group Newspapers Ltd* [2008] EWHC 1777).

◆ In *Mosley*, the claimant had participated in private sexual activity involving roleplay as a German officer. This was distinguished from roleplay with a Nazi theme, which would have engaged the public interest.

➤ NB: the right to privacy may be forfeited on public interest grounds even if it is, on the face of it, protected by contractual confidentiality restrictions.

◆ See *Beckham v Gibson,* 29 April 2005, unreported, in which a nanny formerly employed by David and Victoria Beckham was held, on the facts, to be justified in disclosing information in breach of her service contract.

Step 4	What are the remedies?

➤ The remedies are the same as for any other action for breach of confidence, ie:

◆ an injunction restraining the misuse/disclosure of private information, *and/or*

◆ damages or an account of profits, *and/or*

◆ an order for delivery-up/destruction of property containing the private information.

➤ Special rules apply to interim injunctions in cases of misuse of private information:

Interim injunctions in privacy cases

➤ When hearing an application, the court will not apply the normal threshold test under *American Cyanamid v Ethicon Ltd* [1975] AC 396 (ie: that there is a serious case to be tried).

➤ Instead, in accordance with *s 12(3)*, the court will not restrain publication before trial unless satisfied that the applicant is 'likely' to establish that publication should not be allowed.

  ◆ In *Cream Holdings Ltd v Banerjee* [2004] UKHL 44, the House of Lords characterised the requisite degree of likelihood as 'more likely than not', but allowed that, in 'exceptional cases' (eg: disclosures that might destroy confidentiality), a flexible approach might be justified.

  ◆ The courts have been slow to find instances of such 'exceptional cases' (eg: the court found otherwise in *A & B v Channel Four*, 6 July 2005 and *John v Associated Newspapers Ltd*, 23 June 2006, both unreported).

➤ If the privacy-specific 'likelihood' test is satisfied, the court will then consider the usual 'balance of convenience' test for interim injunctions.

  ◆ In doing so, the court is more likely than in other contexts to grant an interim injunction, since an award of damages is, for the reasons given above, unlikely to be an adequate remedy at trial (see *Douglas v Hello!* [2005] EWCA Civ 595).

    ● This has given rise to a series of comprehensive gagging orders that are commonly described in the media as 'super-injunctions'.

      ■ The availability of super-injunctions may be on the wane following the decision in *LNS v Persons Unknown* ([2010] EWHC 119) (the '*John Terry*' case), in which the High Court lifted a super-injunction that had previously been in place in relation to a famous footballer's extra-marital affair.

  ◆ An injunction will not be granted if:

    ● it is a 'futile gesture' because the material is already widely available via other media (*Mosley v News Group Newspapers Ltd* [2008] EWHC 687), *or*

    ● the application is really brought to protect commercial interests rather than privacy (see the '*John Terry*' case (as above), in which the court did not accept that the footballer's right against interference with his private life outweighed the newspaper's right to freedom of expression where his primary objective appeared to be to protect his reputation, in particular with his sponsors).

➤ Injunctive relief is likely to be the principal remedy. The damages awarded in the leading cases have been modest in scale compared to the costs of the cases and are, as the Court of Appeal accepted in *Douglas* (as above), unlikely to deter newspapers or magazines with a large circulation.

  ◆ In *Douglas*, the Court of Appeal rejected a claim for substantial damages on the basis of a licence fee that the defendant would otherwise have had to pay to acquire the publication rights. The basis of the claim was distress (eg: hurt feelings, upset and affront), not a notional loss of profits.

  ◆ Damages of £60,000 were awarded in *Mosley* (as above), but exemplary damages were rejected.

➤ An account of profits may equally be an ineffective remedy – except in the context of a 'kiss and tell' story, where a rival publisher may have paid a large sum for a story.

  ◆ Profits derived from misuse/disclosure may be hard to quantify, as it may be impossible to demonstrate that any increase in sales resulted from publication of the information. There may even be no profits where a large fee has been paid by the publisher (eg: to a paparazzo photographer).

➤ Misuse of private information has 3 key practical implications for the media.

1   Private information is not transferable

➤ It is clear from *Douglas v Hello!* ([2005] EWCA Civ 595) that private information is not transferable, and this was confirmed in OK!'s appeal to the House of Lords ([2007] UKHL 21).

◆ Private information is not property that can be owned and transferred, and does not amount to an intellectual property right.

- It can only be protected by a right of action against a person who unlawfully invades privacy.

➤ In that sense, the rights to a story can be 'sold', but cannot be 'acquired', ie: cannot be bought such that the publisher literally owns the information.

◆ Eg: in *Douglas*, the co-claimant publisher OK! had not acquired any enforceable interest in the **private** information.

- OK! was held, on appeal to the House of Lords, to have acquired an interest only in **commercially confidential** information applying the ordinary *Coco v Clark* principles.

◆ A publisher using private information under licence only acquires the right to use/disclose it in a way which would otherwise be unlawful.

◆ In the event of misuse by a third party (eg: a rival publisher), the publisher has no direct cause of action against it, unless the information is protectable as commercially confidential information.

2   'Acquiring' rights to a story

➤ Since the ownership of private information cannot be transferred to a publisher (and it may be difficult to establish enforceable rights in commercially confidential information), a publisher should, in order to protect 'exclusives', require the person that (as it were) 'owns' the information to enter into a contractual obligation:

◆ to bring proceedings to protect that information (perhaps under an indemnity from the publisher to the 'owner'), *and/or*

◆ to assign the claim in misuse of private information to the publisher (ie: rather than purporting to transfer the information itself).

- Such contractual protections assist in assuring the commercial value of the deal to the publisher.

3 Clearing a story for publication

➤ It remains uncertain, given the relatively rapid and recent development of the law of privacy, how the threshold or balancing tests will be applied to a given set of facts.

◆ The balancing exercise involves an assessment of proportionality, and the large number of dissenting judgments in the leading cases illustrates the fact that it is inherently difficult to predict the outcome of such an assessment.

➤ This makes it hard for a publisher to determine whether a given article might be actionable on privacy-based grounds.

◆ In cases of doubt, it is advisable to take a cautious approach to publication, especially as recent case law has shown a marked tendency to favour the protection of privacy over freedom of expression.

● Clear themes are, however, beginning to emerge from the large number of cases in the privacy area in recent years, which should begin to make the outcome of privacy cases more predictable.

➤ NB: a publisher should also bear in mind that privacy is also protected in other ways under legislation, including under:

◆ the *Protection from Harassment Act 1997*, which creates criminal and civil liability for a course of conduct amounting to harassment, and is relevant to cases of 'stalking', *and*

◆ the *Regulation of Investigatory Powers Act 2000*, which creates criminal and civil liability for unlawful interception of communications (including post, email and telephone conversations).

K Data protection

*References in this Section are to the Data Protection Act 1998 ('**DPA**'), unless otherwise stated.*

I	Generally
II	Application
III	Notification
IV	The data protection principles
V	Rights of data subjects
VI	Exemptions
VII	Enforcement

I Generally

➤ Due to the widespread availability of personal computers and internet access, personal data can easily be transferred from individuals to organisations and stored.

◆ Such personal information can be misused, eg: to access a bank account or to send 'junk mail'. It can also be sensitive, eg: containing private details.

➤ Laws have been enacted across Europe to protect the security and use of personal data. The main UK legislation is the *DPA*.

DPA
➤ The *DPA* came into force on 1 March 2000.   ◆ The *DPA* implemented *European Directive 95/46/EC*.

➤ The *DPA* sets out controls over the use of personal data (eg: in relation to direct marketing) and imposes sanctions for the unlawful use of personal data.

◆ The *DPA* confers various rights on individuals in relation to personal data, including several rights relating to the processing of personal data.

➤ Breach of the *DPA* can result in criminal and civil sanctions and, increasingly, adverse publicity.

➤ The Information Commissioner ('**Commissioner**') is responsible for enforcement of the *DPA*.

◆ The Information Commissioner's Office ('**ICO**') is based in Wilmslow, Cheshire, with regional offices in Northern Ireland, Scotland and Wales.

● The Commissioner's website at www.ico.gov.uk provides useful guidance on compliance with the *DPA*.

➤ NB: although 'data' is often used as a singular word in speech, this Section treats 'data' as a plural word – in line with the *DPA*.

➤ The *DPA* contains a number of key definitions that are critical to understanding the scope and purpose of the Act (*s 1(1)*).

Key definitions	
'Data'	➤ 'Data' means information: ♦ processed by means of equipment operating automatically or recorded with the intention that it should be so processed (eg: a computer database), *or* ♦ recorded as part of a structured filing system or intended to form part of such a system (eg: a card database sorted by name), *or* ♦ forming part of certain accessible health, education or public records (see *s 68*), *or* ♦ recorded and held by a public authority.
'Personal data'	➤ 'Personal data' means data relating to a living individual who can be identified from: ♦ that data, *or* ♦ that data and other information which is in (or likely to come into) the possession of a 'data controller' (see below). ➤ The data must: a) identify the individual, *and* b) relate to the individual in a way that might affect his privacy (*Durrant v Financial Services Authority* [2005] EWCA Civ 1746).
'Data subject'	➤ A 'data subject' is the individual who is the subject of personal data.
'Data controller'	➤ A 'data controller' is the person who (either alone or jointly or in common with other persons) determines the purposes for which and the manner in which any personal data are, or are to be, processed.
'Processing'	➤ Data 'processing' is very widely defined. It includes obtaining, recording or holding (or carrying out any operation(s) on) data, and includes organising, adapting, altering, retrieving, consulting, using, disclosing, aligning, combining, blocking, erasing and/or destroying data.
'Data processor'	➤ A 'data processor' is any person (other than an employee of the data controller) who processes data on the data controller's behalf.

II Application

➤ The definition of 'personal data' is fundamental to the scope of application of the *DPA*, since the *DPA* only imposes restrictions on the use of personal data.

➤ The *DPA* applies to a data controller where the data controller (*s 5*):

♦ is established in the UK and the data are processed in the context of that establishment, *or*

♦ is established outside the EEA but uses equipment in the UK for processing the data otherwise than for the purposes of transit through the UK.

III   Notification

➤ In general, a data controller cannot process personal data without being entered on the registry maintained by the Commissioner (*s 17(1)*).

◆ To be included in the register, a data controller must give a '***notification***' to the Commissioner.

➤ There are 2 steps to consider in relation to notification:

Steps

1 Is notification required?

2 If so, how must the Commissioner be notified?

Step 1	Is notification required?

➤ The following flowchart shows whether notification is required (see *ss 16-26*).

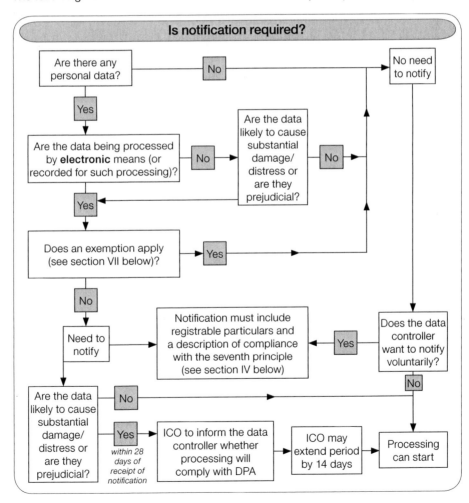

Step 2	If so, how must the Commissioner be notified?

➤ Registrable particulars have to be provided to the ICO, including (*s 16(1)*):

- ◆ the data controller's name and address (which should be the registered office if the data controller is a company), *and*

- ◆ the name of any representative nominated to oversee the data protection requirements, *and*

- ◆ a description of the data and the categories of data subject to which the data relates, *and*

- ◆ a description of the purpose(s) for which data are to be processed, *and*

- ◆ a description of any intended recipient(s) of the data, *and*

- ◆ the names of any countries or territories outside the EEA to which the data controller directly or indirectly transfers (or intends to transfer) the data, *and*

- ◆ where there is other data for which notification is not required (eg: manually recorded data), a statement of that fact.

    - ● The ICO provides model-form notifications and guidance on how to complete them.

➤ An annual fee is payable under a 2-tier structure (introduced from 1 October 2009 by the *Data Protection (Notification and Notification Fees) (Amendment) Regulations 2009*):

- a) A controller with an annual turnover of at least £25.9 million and 250 or more staff, and a public authority with 250 or more staff, have to pay a £500 fee.

    - ◆ There is an exception for charities and small occupational pension schemes.

- b) Other controllers have to pay a £35 fee.

➤ The data controller must provide a statement that there has been compliance with the seventh data protection principle (ie: concerning data security – see section IV below), setting out the measures for protection of the data (*s 18*).

IV The data protection principles

➤ A data controller must comply with 8 '**data protection principles**' (*s 4* and *Sch 1*).

- ◆ NB: there are exemptions from compliance – see section VII below.

Principles	
1	Fair processing
2	Purpose of processing
3	Relevance of data
4	Accuracy of data
5	Retention of data
6	Rights of data subjects
7	Security measures
8	International transfer of data

First principle	Fair processing

'Personal data shall be processed fairly and lawfully.'

➤ The first principle is the most important of all the principles in practice.

➤ Various requirements must be satisfied to comply with the first principle.

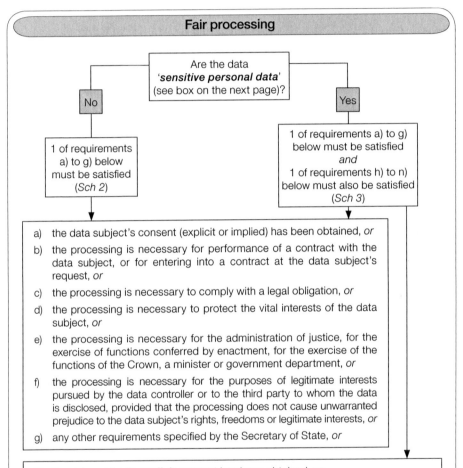

Fair processing

Are the data *'sensitive personal data'* (see box on the next page)?

No → 1 of requirements a) to g) below must be satisfied (*Sch 2*)

Yes → 1 of requirements a) to g) below must be satisfied *and* 1 of requirements h) to n) below must also be satisfied (*Sch 3*)

a) the data subject's consent (explicit or implied) has been obtained, *or*

b) the processing is necessary for performance of a contract with the data subject, or for entering into a contract at the data subject's request, *or*

c) the processing is necessary to comply with a legal obligation, *or*

d) the processing is necessary to protect the vital interests of the data subject, *or*

e) the processing is necessary for the administration of justice, for the exercise of functions conferred by enactment, for the exercise of the functions of the Crown, a minister or government department, *or*

f) the processing is necessary for the purposes of legitimate interests pursued by the data controller or to the third party to whom the data is disclosed, provided that the processing does not cause unwarranted prejudice to the data subject's rights, freedoms or legitimate interests, *or*

g) any other requirements specified by the Secretary of State, *or*

h) the data subject's **explicit** consent has been obtained, *or*

i) the processing is necessary for the exercise/performance of any right/obligation conferred/imposed by law on the data controller in connection with employment, *or*

j) the processing is necessary to protect the vital interests of a third person, but only where consent cannot be given, the data controller cannot reasonably be expected to obtain consent or the consent is unreasonably withheld, *or*

k) the processing is carried out by a body not established or conducted for profit and existing for political, philosophical, religious or trade-union purposes under restricted circumstances (eg: that there are appropriate safeguards), *or*

l) information has been made public deliberately by the data subject, *or*

m) the processing is necessary for legal or medical purposes in restricted conditions (eg: where undertaken by a health professional), *or*

n) the data relate to racial or ethnic origin and processing is necessary in restricted circumstances.

➤ NB: even if a data controller can satisfy the requirements described above, there is still a requirement to ensure that processing is **generally** fair.

➤ The additional requirements depend on whether the personal data are 'sensitive'.

Sensitive personal data
➤ 'Sensitive personal data' are data relating to the data subject's (*s 2*): a) racial or ethnic origin, *or* b) political beliefs, *or* c) religious or other similar beliefs, *or* d) trade union membership, *or* e) physical or mental health conditions, *or* f) sexual life, *or* g) actual/alleged commission of a criminal offence (and any related proceedings, the disposal of such proceedings and the sentence).   ● NB: the processing of sensitive personal data is specifically permitted under certain *Orders*, which are beyond the scope of this Section.

➤ For data to be processed fairly, it must also be fairly obtained.

Fair data capture

➤ Data is fairly obtained if obtained from an authorised person (eg: the data subject) (*Sch I Pt II para 1*). Obtaining data is known as 'data capture'.
 	
➤ Each data subject must be provided with the following information:
 	
    ◆ the identity of the data controller (or his representative), *and*
 	
    ◆ the purposes for which the data are being processed, *and*
 	
    ◆ any further information necessary, having regard to the specific circumstances of the processing, to enable the processing to be fair (*Sch I Pt II para 2*).
 	
➤ The data controller must provide this information:
 	
    ◆ on first obtaining the data from the data subject, *or*
 	
    ◆ in the case of data not obtained from the data subject, on first processing the data or first disclosing the data to a third party (*Sch I Pt II para 2*).
 	
➤ Where the data has not been obtained from the data subject, provision of information to the data subject is not required where:
 	
    ◆ the provision would involve a disproportionate effort, or
 	
    ◆ where recording or disclosing the data is required by law (except under a contractual obligation) (*Sch I Pt II para 3*).
 	
➤ The information is commonly provided to data subjects in the form of a 'fair processing notice' or 'data capture notice' (eg: in a website privacy policy).
 	
➤ ICO guidance suggests that, for a data controller to rely on a data subject's consent, it must be freely given, specific and informed consent, but need not necessarily be in writing.

Second principle	Purpose of processing

'Personal data shall be obtained only for one or more specified and lawful purposes, and shall not be further processed in any manner incompatible with that purpose or purposes.'

➤ The specified purpose(s) may be set out (*Sch 1 Pt II para 5*):

   a) in a notice given to the data subject under the first principle, *or*

   b) in the notification to the Commissioner.

➤ Where data is disclosed to a third party, the purpose to which that third party will put the data must also be considered.

Third principle	Relevance of data

'Personal data shall be adequate, relevant and not excessive in relation to the purpose or purposes for which they are processed.'

➤ A data controller must regularly check personal data held to ensure continuing compliance with this principle.

Fourth principle	Accuracy of data

'Personal data shall be accurate and, where necessary, kept up to date.'

➤ A data controller must take reasonable steps to ensure the accuracy of data.

➤ Where a data subject notifies a data controller that the data are inaccurate, the data controller is not breach of this principle if the data records are updated to indicate that the data subject's view that the data are inaccurate (*Sch 1 Pt II para 7*).

Fifth principle	Retention of data

'Personal data processed for any purpose or purposes shall not be kept for longer than is necessary for that purpose or those purposes.'

➤ The *DPA* does not specify how long is necessary, and this can be difficult to ascertain in practice.

   ◆ A data controller should incorporate compliance with this principle into an overall data retention policy.

      ● Care should be taken to ensure compliance with other legislation requiring data to be retained for specific periods.

         ■ Eg: the *Data Retention Directive 2006/24/EC* requires the retention of certain customer data for 12 months to aid the security services. It was implemented in the UK by the *Data Retention (EC Directive) Regulations 2009*, which replaced earlier 2007 regulations and now apply to providers of fixed-line and mobile telephony services, as well as to internet service providers.

Sixth principle	Rights of data subjects

'Personal data shall be processed in accordance with the rights of data subjects under this Act.'

➤ This principle is contravened where the data controller fails (*Sch 1 Pt II para 8*):

- ◆ contrary to *s 7*, to comply with a data subject's right to access personal data, *or*

- ◆ contrary to *s 10*, to cease processing data if the processing is causing (or likely to cause) substantial damage or distress to any person, *or*

- ◆ contrary to *s 11*, to comply with a notice requiring the data controller to cease processing for the purposes of direct marketing, *or*

- ◆ contrary to *s 12*, to comply with a notice requiring the data controller not to make any decision significantly affecting the data subject (eg: an evaluation of creditworthiness) based solely on automatic processing (or fails to reply to that notice in the prescribed manner).

  - • See section V below on these rights.

Seventh principle	Security measures

'Appropriate technical and organisational measures shall be taken against unauthorised or unlawful processing of personal data and against accidental loss or destruction of, or damage to, personal data.'

➤ This is perhaps the most difficult principle for a data controller to comply with.

- ◆ Eg: in October 2007 HM Revenue & Customs lost 25 million child benefit records contained on 2 CDs.

  - • The Commissioner is particularly concerned to ensure compliance with this principle where non-encrypted personal data is held on portable devices such as laptops.

➤ The security measures must be appropriate having regard to the state of technological development and the cost of implementing the measures (*Sch 1 Pt II para 9*).

- ◆ The measures must ensure a level of security appropriate to (*Sch 1 Pt II para 9*):

  - a) the harm that might result from unauthorised processing or accidental loss, destruction or damage, *and*

  - b) the nature of the data being protected.

    - • A general description of the measures must be specified as part of the data controller's notification requirements – see section III above.

➤ The data controller must take reasonable steps to ensure the reliability of employees that have access to personal data (*Sch 1 Pt II para 10*).

➤ A data controller is not 'off the hook' where using a third party to process data.

Third-party processing

➤ If processing is to be carried out by a third party (*Sch 1 Pt II para 11-12*):

◆ the data controller must choose a third party providing sufficient guarantees in relation to data security measures and take reasonable steps to ensure compliance with those measures, *and*

◆ the processing must be carried out under a contract (which must be made or evidenced in writing) under which the third party can only act on instructions from the data controller, *and*

◆ the contract must require the third party to comply with obligations equivalent to those imposed on the data controller by the seventh principle.

➤ These provisions are particularly relevant where the data controller has outsourced any processing (eg: processing of pensions data).

Eighth principle	International transfer of data

'Personal data shall not be transferred to a country or territory outside the European Economic Area (EEA) unless that country or territory ensures an adequate level of protection for the rights and freedoms of data subjects in relation to the processing of personal data.'

➤ Whether the country/territory ('*country*') to which data are being transferred ensures an 'adequate' level of protection is assessed, in particular, according to (*Sch 1 Pt II para 13*):

a) the nature of the personal data, *and*

b) the country of origin of the information contained in the data, *and*

c) the final destination of the information, *and*

d) the purposes for which and period during which the data are intended to be processed, *and*

e) the law in force in the country in question, *and*

f) the international obligations of that country, *and*

g) the relevant codes of conduct or other rules in force in that country, *and*

h) any security measures taken in respect of the data in that country.

◆ The European Commission has decided that a number of countries ensure an adequate level of protection, including Switzerland, Canada (subject to certain conditions), Argentina, Guernsey and the Isle of Man.

The US *Safe Harbor* scheme

➤ The USA is not on this 'white list', but the European Commission considers that data is adequately protected if sent to the USA under the *Safe Harbor* scheme.

◆ If a US recipient company signs up to the scheme, it agrees:

• to comply with 7 principles of data-handling, *and*

• to be held responsible for compliance by the Federal Trade Commission or other applicable supervisory bodies.

■ Certain types of company (eg: financial services providers) cannot sign up to the scheme. A list of companies signed up to the scheme is published at www.export.gov/safeharbor.

➤ The Commissioner has indicated that it is not a breach of the eighth principle if data are transmitted from the UK to another EEA country through a non-EEA country.

➤ The eighth principle does not apply if the transfer is (*Sch 1 Pt II para 14* and *Sch 4*):

a) consented to by the data subject, *or*

b) necessary to facilitate entry into, or to perform, a contract between the data subject and the data controller, *or*

c) necessary to conclude or perform a contract between the data controller and a third party, provided that the contract is entered into at the data subject's request or is in the data subject's interests, *or*

d) necessary for reasons of substantial public interest, *or*

e) necessary for legal proceedings, obtaining legal advice or establishing, defending or exercising legal rights, *or*

f) necessary to protect the data subject's vital interests, *or*

g) part of the personal data on a public register and any person to whom the data are transferred complies with any conditions of inspection of the register, *or*

h) made on terms of a kind approved by the Commissioner (or the transfer is authorised by the Commissioner) as ensuring adequate safeguards for data subjects' rights (see box below on ex-EEA transfers of data).

◆ Under exception h), there are 2 different ways of ensuring adequate safeguards in the case of transfers to ex-EEA countries that do not have an adequate level of protection (and for which there is no 'safe harbour' scheme):

---

1 Model contract clauses

➤ The European Commission has adopted (and the Commissioner has authorised) model contract clauses for ex-EEA transfers of data from:

a) controller to processor, *or*

b) controller to controller.

◆ Under each version, the data importer agrees to process data in accordance with certain standards (to overcome any deficiencies in protection under local law) and the parties confer third-party rights on data subjects to enforce the contract.

● There are 2 alternative sets of model clauses for a controller-to-controller contract (the later version being less onerous for both controllers).

▪ The model clauses are annexed respectively to *Decision 2002/16/EC* (replaced by *Decision 2010/87/EU* with effect from 15 May 2010), *Decision 2001/497/EC* and *Decision 2004/915/EC*.

---

2 Binding corporate rules

➤ If a UK company transfers data to other group members in different jurisdictions, the transfer will comply with the eighth principle if it is governed by a set of legally binding corporate rules ('**BCRs**') that have been approved by the Commissioner.

◆ Detailed guidance has been published on BCRs by the EC Article 29 Data Protection Working Party (including a checklist and framework), but no set of BCRs has been formally adopted and few UK groups of companies have adopted BCRs (due to the lengthy/costly process to put BCRs in place).

V Rights of data subjects

➤ A data subject has 6 rights in relation to personal data held by a data controller.

1 Right of access to personal data (*ss 7-9*)

➤ A data subject is entitled to be informed by the data controller whether the data subject's personal data are being processed by the data controller (or by a third party on the data controller's behalf) (*s 7(1)(a)*).

◆ A data controller must give a data subject a description of (*s 7(1)(b)*):

a) the personal data, *and*

b) the purposes for which the data are being (or to be) processed, *and*

c) the recipients (or classes of recipients) to whom the data are or may be disclosed.

◆ A data subject is entitled to receive (in an intelligible form) (*ss 7(1)(c)-(d)*):

• the information constituting the data, *and*

• any information available to the data controller as to the source of the data, *and*

• the logic involved in any automated decision-taking (unless the logic is a trade secret).

◆ The information constituting the data must be supplied in permanent form, unless such supply is not possible or would involve disproportionate effort or the data subject agrees otherwise (*s 8(2)*).

◆ It may be impossible for the data controller to respond without disclosing a third party's personal data. If so, the data controller need not respond unless the third party has consented or it is reasonable to respond without such third party's consent (*ss 7(4)-(6)*).

➤ The data subject's request must be in writing. This includes email (*s 7(2)(a)*).

➤ The data controller may generally charge a small administration fee for responding to the request (up to a prescribed limit – typically £10) (*s 7(2)(b)*).

➤ The data controller must comply with the request promptly and in any event within the prescribed period (typically 40 days) from the date of receipt of the request or, if later, receipt of the fee (*ss 7(7)-(8)*).

◆ A data controller need not comply with a request where the data controller has complied with an identical or similar request by the data subject, unless a reasonable interval has elapsed between compliance with the previous request and the making of the current request (*s 8(3)*).

➤ If the data controller fails to comply with a request for information, the data subject can apply for a court order requiring compliance (*s 7(9)*).

➤ The following flowchart shows whether a disclosure should be made in response to a data subject's access request:

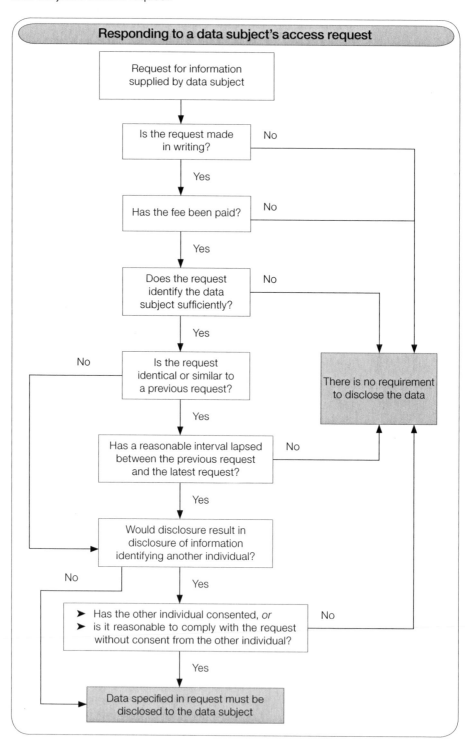

Responding to a data subject's access request

Request for information supplied by data subject

Is the request made in writing? — No

Yes

Has the fee been paid? — No

Yes

Does the request identify the data subject sufficiently? — No

Yes

No — Is the request identical or similar to a previous request?

Yes

Has a reasonable interval lapsed between the previous request and the latest request? — No

Yes

There is no requirement to disclose the data

Would disclosure result in disclosure of information identifying another individual?

No

Yes

➤ Has the other individual consented, *or*
➤ is it reasonable to comply with the request without consent from the other individual? — No

Yes

Data specified in request must be disclosed to the data subject

2   **Right to prevent processing likely to cause damage or distress (*s 10*)**

➤ Where processing of personal data causes (or is likely to cause) substantial, unwarranted damage/distress to the data subject or another, the data subject can, on written notice, require the data controller within a reasonable time to cease (or not to begin) processing the data (or processing the data for a specified purpose or in a specified manner) (*s 10(1)*).

➤ This right does not apply where the processing is (*s 10(2)*):

♦ consented to by the data subject, *or*

♦ necessary for performance of a contract or to facilitate entry into a contract at the data subject's request, *or*

♦ necessary to comply with a legal obligation (other than a contractual obligation), *or*

♦ necessary to protect the data subject's vital interests, *or*

♦ necessary for the administration of justice or the exercise of public functions, *or*

♦ in any other cases prescribed by the Secretary of State (NB: no such cases have yet been prescribed).

➤ Within 21 days of receiving a notice from the data subject, the data controller must send a written notice to the data subject stating (*s 10(3)*):

♦ that the data controller has complied (or intends to comply) with the notice, *or*

♦ the reasons for regarding the notice as unjustified and the extent (if any) to which the data controller has complied (or intends to comply).

➤ If the data controller fails to comply with a notice, the data subject can apply for a court order requiring the data controller to comply (*s 10(4)*).

3   **Right to prevent processing for purposes of direct marketing (*s 11*)**

➤ A data subject can, on written notice, require the data controller within a reasonable time to cease (or not to begin) processing the personal data for the purposes of 'direct marketing' (*s 11(1)*).

♦ 'Direct marketing' means communication (by whatever means) of any advertising or marketing material that is directed at particular individuals (*s 11(3)*).

• NB: this right applies even where the data subject has previously given consent to direct marketing.

➤ If the data controller fails to comply with a notice, the data subject can apply for a court order requiring the data controller to comply (*s 11(2)*).

4   **Rights in relation to automated decision-taking (s 12)**

➤   A data subject can, by written notice, require a data controller to ensure that no decision significantly affecting the data subject is based solely on processing the personal data by automatic means (s 12(1)).

♦   Such decisions specifically include evaluation of the data subject's performance at work, creditworthiness, reliability or conduct (s 12(1)).

➤   The data controller must, even if no such notice has been received, promptly notify the data subject if such a decision is taken (s 12(2)(a)).

♦   The data subject can, within 21 days of receiving such notice, give written notice requiring the data controller to reconsider the decision or to take a decision on a basis that is not solely automated (s 12(2)(b)).

●   The data controller must respond within 21 days in writing, indicating the compliance steps the data controller intends to take (s 12(3)).

➤   A decision may be taken on an automated basis if it is 'exempt', ie: if (ss 12(5)-(7)):

a) it is:

i)   taken in connection with entry into (or in the course of performing) a contract with the data subject, or

ii) authorised or required by any enactment, and

b) either:

i)   the decision's effect is to grant a request of the data subject, or

ii) steps have been taken to safeguard the data subject's legitimate interests.

➤   If a data controller fails to comply with these requirements, the data subject can apply for a court order requiring the data controller to reconsider the decision or to take a decision on a basis that is not solely automated (s 12(8)).

5   **Right to compensation for breach of the DPA by the data controller (s 13)**

➤   A data subject is entitled to apply to the court for compensation for damage (or damage and distress) suffered as the result of any breach of the requirements of the DPA by a data controller (s 13(1)).

♦   NB: compensation is not generally payable for distress alone.

♦   Damages for distress alone can only be claimed where the breach relates to the processing of personal data for 'special purposes' (ie: journalistic, artistic or literary purposes, which are largely exempt from the provisions of the DPA – see section VI below).

➤   It is a defence for the data controller to show that he has taken all reasonable care to comply with the relevant requirement (s 13(3)).

6 Rights in relation to inaccurate data (s 14)

➤ The data subject is entitled to apply to the court for an order requiring the data controller, where reasonably practicable, to rectify, block, erase or destroy (s 14(1)):

◆ inaccurate personal data, and

◆ any other personal data that contain an expression of opinion based on such inaccurate data.

➤ The data controller may also be ordered to notify third parties to whom the data have been disclosed of the rectification, blocking, erasure or destruction (s 14(3)).

➤ The court may instead order compliance with the fourth principle (ie: relating to accuracy of data – see section IV above) (s 14(2)).

VI Exemptions

➤ The table below summarises the main circumstances in which a data controller is exempted from the need to comply with the notification requirements, the data protection principles and the rights of data subjects.

Exemptions	
Exemption from:	**Scope of exemption:**
All notification requirements, data protection principles and rights of data subjects	➤ Safeguarding national security (s 28). ◆ A certificate is required from a minister. ➤ Processing for domestic purposes (s 36).
The first principle (only as regards fair data capture – Sch 1 Pt II para 2) and the right of access to data (if prejudicial to the relevant matter – s 7)	➤ Order of Secretary of State relating to defined data (s 30). ➤ Processing for the discharge of defined functions (s 31). ➤ Protection of the armed forces (Sch 7). ➤ Conferring honours or judicial appointment (Sch 7). ➤ Assessing suitability for Crown or ministerial employment (Sch 7). ➤ The data controller's management forecasting or planning (Sch 7). ➤ Negotiations between data controller and data subject (Sch 7). ➤ Corporate finance service in defined circumstances (Sch 7). ➤ Information covered by legal professional privilege (Sch 7). ➤ Information available to public by or under enactment (s 34). ➤ Prevention of crime, apprehension of offenders, assessment or collection of tax, and discharge of statutory functions (s 29).
Right of access to data (s 7)	➤ Where compliance would result in self-incrimination (Sch 7). ➤ Confidential references given by the data controller in defined circumstances (Sch 7). ➤ Information relating to examination marks and scripts (Sch 7).

Exemptions (continued)	
Exemption from:	**Scope of exemption:**
Second and fifth principles	➤ Research purposes in defined circumstances (*s 33*).
First principle (except *Sch 2-3* conditions) and second to fifth principles	➤ Where disclosure of data is required by any enactment or law or by a court order (*s 35*). ➤ Where data is available to the public by or under an enactment (*s 34*).

All data protection principles (except the seventh), and rights to prevent processing, to require rectification and relating to automated decision-taking	➤ Personal data processed only for 'special purposes' and in defined circumstances (*s 32*).
	
	   ◆ The 'special purposes' are:
	
	     ● the purposes of journalism, *and/or*
	
	     ● artistic purposes, and/*or*
	
	     ● literary purposes (*s 3*).
	
	 ➤ The defined circumstances are, broadly speaking, that the data controller reasonably believed that publication was in the public interest.
	
	 ➤ This exemption is significant for journalism, especially as for *DPA* purposes the term 'data' includes photographs (*Douglas v Hello! Ltd* [2005] EWCA Civ 595).
	
	   ◆ Eg: a newspaper successfully used this exemption in a case brought by the model Naomi Campbell (*Campbell v Mirror Group Newspapers Ltd* [2002] EWCA Civ 1373).
	
	   ◆ In contrast, the exemption was not available to the magazine publisher in the *Hello!* case (as above), since the publisher could not demonstrate a reasonable belief that publication would be in the public interest.
	
	 ➤ NB: the exemption in respect of a data subject's right of access only applies **until** the time of publication.

Fourth principle and right to require rectification	➤ Information available to public by or under enactment (*s 34*).
Provisions on enforcement and unlawful obtaining or disclosure of data	➤ Safeguarding national security (*s 28*). ◆ A certificate is required from a minister.
Miscellaneous	➤ The Secretary of State may by order make further exemptions where necessary for the safeguarding of the interests of the data subject or the rights of other individuals (*s 38*).

VII   Enforcement

➤ The Commissioner is responsible for enforcing compliance with the data protection principles (*ss 40-50*).

◆ The Commissioner is an independent officer appointed by the Crown.

◆ NB: the Commissioner can enforce the data protection principles against both those who have notified under the *DPA* and those who are exempt from notification.

➤ The Commissioner can serve an '***enforcement notice***' upon a data controller that is in breach of any of the data protection principles (*s 40*).

◆ An enforcement notice may require a data controller (*s 40(1)*):

● to take, or to refrain from taking, specified steps, *or*

● to refrain from processing personal data (or personal data of a specified type), either altogether or for a specified purpose or in a specified manner.

◆ In deciding whether to serve an enforcement notice, the Commissioner must consider whether the breach has caused (or is likely to cause) any person damage or distress (*s 40(2)*).

◆ An enforcement notice must state the principle(s) believed to have been contravened and the reasons for such belief (*s 40(6)*).

◆ An enforcement notice may be cancelled or varied in certain circumstances, eg: when the Commissioner considers that the notice, or part of it, need not be complied with to ensure compliance with the relevant data protection principle(s) (*s 41(1)*).

➤ Any person who is, or believes himself to be, directly affected by any processing of personal data can make a '***request for assessment***' as to whether it is likely or unlikely that the processing has been or is compliant with the *DPA* (*s 42*).

◆ On receiving a request for assessment, the Commissioner must make an assessment, unless the Commissioner has not been supplied with sufficient information to enable the Commissioner to identify the person making the request and the processing in question. The Commissioner has a wide discretion in deciding how to make an appropriate assessment (*s 42(2)*).

◆ The Commissioner must notify the person who made the request:

a) whether the Commissioner has made an assessment, *and*

b) to the extent the Commissioner considers appropriate, of any view formed or action taken (*s 42(3)*).

➤ On receiving a request for assessment or to determine compliance with the data protection principles, the Commissioner may serve an '***information notice***' on a data controller stating the information required from the data controller (*s 43(1)*).

➤ The Commissioner may serve a '*special information notice*' on a data controller where the Commissioner has reasonable grounds for suspecting that personal data are **not** being processed:

a) only for 'special purposes' (ie: journalistic, artistic and/or literary purposes – see section VI above), *or*

b) with a view to the publication by any person of any journalistic, literary or artistic material that has not been previously published by the data controller (*s 46(1)*).

◆ The purpose of special information notice is ascertain whether those grounds of suspicion are justified, in which case the Commissioner can make a '*determination*' to that effect (*s 45*).

◆ NB: in a case of processing for special purposes, the Commissioner cannot serve an enforcement notice unless a determination has taken effect and an order for leave has been obtained from the court for the notice to be served (*s 46*).

➤ A data controller on whom an enforcement notice, information notice or special information notice has been served may appeal against the notice to the General Regulatory Chamber of the First-tier Tribunal or (for complex or important proceedings only) the Administrative Appeals Chamber of the Upper Tribunal (*ss 48* and *70(1)*).

◆ All such notices should include (*ss 40, 43* and *44*):

● details of the right of appeal, *and*

● the time limit for compliance (which must not be less than the time limit set for appeal, unless the matter is urgent), *and*

● if the Commissioner considers that urgent compliance is required, a statement of that fact and the reasons.

◆ The grounds for appeal are that:

a) the notice was not brought in accordance with the law, *or*

b) the Commissioner should have exercised his discretion differently (*s 49(1)*).

➤ Non-compliance with any such notice renders the data controller guilty of a criminal offence, unless the data controller can show that the data controller exercised all due diligence to comply with the notice (*s 47*).

◆ Each offence is punishable by a fine of up to £5,000 on summary conviction or an unlimited fine if convicted on indictment (*s 60*).

● NB: there are certain other criminal offences under the DPA, which are beyond the scope of this Section (see *ss 21, 22, 24, 55, 56, 59* and *61* and *Sch 9*).

■ The Commissioner can apply to a circuit judge for a warrant to enter and search premises suspected to contain evidence of an offence under the *DPA* or of breach of the data protection principles (*Sch 9*).

➤ The following flowchart summarises the enforcement process.

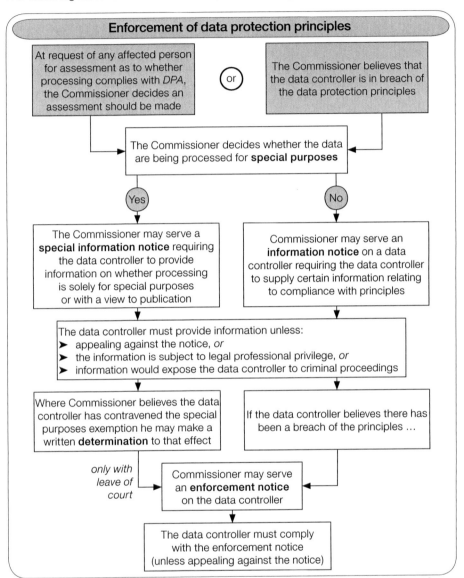

Enforcement of data protection principles

At request of any affected person for assessment as to whether processing complies with *DPA*, the Commissioner decides an assessment should be made

or

The Commissioner believes that the data controller is in breach of the data protection principles

The Commissioner decides whether the data are being processed for **special purposes**

Yes / **No**

The Commissioner may serve a **special information notice** requiring the data controller to provide information on whether processing is solely for special purposes or with a view to publication

Commissioner may serve an **information notice** on a data controller requiring the data controller to supply certain information relating to compliance with principles

The data controller must provide information unless:
➤ appealing against the notice, *or*
➤ the information is subject to legal professional privilege, *or*
➤ information would expose the data controller to criminal proceedings

Where Commissioner believes the data controller has contravened the special purposes exemption he may make a written **determination** to that effect

If the data controller believes there has been a breach of the principles …

only with leave of court

Commissioner may serve an **enforcement notice** on the data controller

The data controller must comply with the enforcement notice (unless appealing against the notice)

➤ *Tough civil sanctions are due to come into force shortly: the Commissioner will be able to impose a fine on any data controller that deliberately or recklessly commits a serious breach of the data protection principles of a kind likely to cause substantial damage or substantial distress (ss 55A-55E, as amended by the Criminal Justice and Immigration Act 2008 s 144).*

◆ *The maximum fine will be £500,000.*

➤ Aside from legal sanctions, failure to comply with the *DPA* can result in adverse publicity, causing significant damage to the data controller's reputation.

L Trade marks

*References in this Section are to the Trade Marks Act 1994 ('**TMA**'), unless otherwise stated.*

I	Generally
II	Is a mark capable of registration?
III	Registering a trade mark
IV	Protecting a trade mark
V	Revocation and invalidity
VI	Dealing with trade marks
VII	Trade-mark searches
VIII	Other types of registrable marks

I Generally

➤ A trade mark is an indication of the origin of goods or services.

➤ Registration of a trade mark provides a particularly valuable form of protection.

  ◆ A registered trade mark often commands a high commercial value. In markets where branding is of prime importance (eg: sports goods), trade marks often represent a significant proportion of a company's assets.

  ◆ The duration of protection is potentially indefinite: the right will continue to exist, provided that renewal fees are paid every 10 years (*ss 42-43*).

  ● No other intellectual property right affords such extensive protection .

  ◆ Registration confers a monopoly right on the owner to use the mark.

  ● There is no need to prove copying in an infringement action, so the right affords stronger protection to an owner than copyright or unregistered design right.

  ◆ An owner that cannot protect a brand as a registered trade mark may have a remedy in the common-law tort of passing-off – see Section N of this Chapter.

  ● In comparison with an action for infringement of a registered trade mark, an action in passing-off is time-consuming, costly and uncertain in outcome.

  ◆ An owner should also consider registered design – see Section F of this Chapter.

➤ There are limits on the protection afforded to the owner of a registered trade mark.

Limitations of a registered trade mark

➤ The various defences to trade-mark infringement impose limits on the owner's monopoly right – see section IV below. Eg:

  ◆ Uses are permitted where in accordance with 'honest practices' (*s 11*).

  ◆ The *TMA* allows an advertiser to use a rival's registered trade mark for 'comparative advertising' (ie: where comparing its goods or services with those of its rival).

  ● The advertiser must also comply with other applicable laws (eg: the *Consumer Protection from Unfair Trading Regulations 2008* and the *Business Protection from Misleading Marketing Regulations 2008*) – see Chapter 5 Section A.

➤ This Section deals with UK registered trade marks.

◆ A person that wishes to obtain international trade-mark protection may apply for protection:

● **nationally** – on a case-by-case basis, *or*

● **throughout the EU** – by applying for a Community Trade Mark ('*CTM*') – see Section M of this Chapter, *or*

● **internationally** – through the World Intellectual Property Organisation (WIPO) under the *Madrid Protocol* (conferring a bundle of separate national rights).

▪ International registrations are beyond the scope of this Chapter.

➤ In the UK, an application is made to the UK Intellectual Property Office ('**UK IPO**').

➤ For the sake of brevity, where the terms '*goods*' (or a '*product*') or '*trade marks*' are used below in this Section, they include (respectively) services and 'service marks', unless a distinction is drawn.

◆ NB: the term 'service mark' is not used in the *TMA*, but is used under US trade-mark law and commonly appears in international contracts.

➤ The key issues in relation to the registration and protection of trade marks include:

◆ whether a mark is registrable, *and*

◆ how to register a trade mark, *and*

◆ what amounts to infringement.

● These are examined in sections II-IV below.

II Is a mark capable of registration?

➤ There are 3 steps to consider in assessing whether a mark is registrable:

Steps	
1	The mark must fall within the *s 1* definition.
2	There must be no absolute grounds for refusal of registration.
3	There must be no relative grounds for refusal of registration.

Step 1	The mark must fall within the *s 1* definition

➤ A trade mark must be capable of:

◆ being represented graphically, *and*

◆ distinguishing goods of one undertaking from those of another (*s 1(1)*).

● The criterion of graphical representation is straightforward in the case of words and images, but can also apply to words/images that describe a mark (eg: musical notation in the case of a sound mark).

➤ There are 8 types of registrable mark. Types 1-5 are specifically mentioned in *s 1(1)*. Types 6-8 are recognised by the UK IPO as falling within the scope of *s 1(1)*.

1   Words (including personal names, slogans and domain names)

➤ Words form the largest category of registered trade marks.

◆ Many brand names are registered trade marks. The top 3 global brands in 2009 according to market-research business Interbrand were 'Coca-Cola', 'IBM' and 'Microsoft'.

◆ Descriptive words cannot usually be registered as a word mark.

• Eg: slogans can be difficult to register as they are often descriptive. A sufficiently distinctive way of portraying a descriptive message might succeed. Eg: Marks & Spencer plc successfully registered 'THE SHOES YOUR FEET HAVE BEEN ACHING FOR'.

◆ Domain names are registrable. In assessing a domain name the UK IPO usually ignores the suffix (eg: '.com' or '.co.uk').

2   Designs

➤ There are 2 common forms of design mark:

a) **Character designs**

◆ These are often in the form of a symbol or cartoon-style character and may be used alongside the name of a brand.

◆ Symbols have become increasingly important. Eg: Nike has dispensed with its name for many products and uses solely its 'swish' symbol to distinguish itself from competitors.

b) **Stylised word designs**

◆ The style of lettering is often a distinctive part of a mark. This is considered a separate form of mark from the word itself.

• A stylised word logo (eg: the well-known 'Virgin' logo) therefore requires 2 separate forms of registration:

■ the word itself as a word mark, *and*

■ the stylised design of the word as a graphic device.

◆ If a word is descriptive (so may not be protectable as a word mark), it can still be registered as a stylised logo. The registration would only protect the design, rather than the word itself.

3   Letters

➤ Individual letters offer a way to distinguish goods. They generally have no descriptive meaning, even if the letters stand for a longer name. As such, letters (eg: in the form an acronym) are more likely to be registrable.

◆ Eg: 'IBM' is a registered trade mark, and it would have been easier to register than 'International Business Machines'.

4   **Numerals**

➤ Numerals are rarely registered as trade marks. This is because:

♦ the use of numerals as a mark is quite rare, *and*

♦ it can be difficult for the mark to become distinctive of goods.

5   **The shape of goods or their packaging**

➤ The shape of a product is often an important means of distinguishing it from other products in the same market.

➤ The *TMA* made it possible for the shape of the product or its packaging to be protected as a registered trade mark. Eg:

♦ The shape of a Coca-Cola bottle was not registrable before the *TMA*, but it is now registered.

♦ The triangular shape of a Toblerone bar is registered as a trade mark.

➤ A shape can be represented graphically by photographs or drawings.

➤ NB: there are limitations under *s 3(2)* on the type of shapes that may be registrable – see step 2.

6   **Colours**

➤ Colours (or colour combinations) are distinct from designs because they do not have to be defined by shape.

♦ Eg: the specific turquoise colour used by Heinz on cans of baked beans can only be used for that product.

7   **Sounds**

➤ Sounds can be registered as trade marks. Sound marks are of particular value in the context of radio advertising, where a distinctive jingle or tune is often used to create an identity for a product or service. Eg: the tune accompanying the insurer Direct Line's adverts is registered as a mark.

➤ A sound can be represented graphically by the use of musical notation or by wave patterns.

8   **Smells**

➤ Smells can, in theory, be registered as trade marks.

♦ It is difficult, however, to overcome the practical requirement to register the mark graphically (*Sieckmann v Deutsches Patent- und Markenamt*, Case-273/00, 12 December 2002).

➤ Smells have also yet to make much impact as registered trade marks, perhaps because they cannot be transmitted through traditional forms of marketing.

➤ A single product (and/or its packaging) may incorporate several types of mark.

Use of multiple marks on a single product

➤ Where registrable, each individual mark is protected separately.

◆ Eg: a product could be sold under a brand name in a stylised word format in conjunction with:

● a character design, *and*

● a distinctive form of packaging, *and*

● a distinctive colour, *and*

● a distinctive tune.

▪ Each of these is considered a 'mark' under the *TMA* and would, if sufficiently distinctive and not within the grounds for refusal of registration (see steps 2 and 3), be registrable.

▪ Whether it is, in financial terms, worth applying to register all of these features is a commercial decision.

| Step 2 | There must be no **absolute** grounds for refusal of registration |

➤ There are 7 'absolute grounds' on which registration can be refused.

1   The mark is not distinctive (*s 3(1)*)

➤ A mark is not distinctive in 4 circumstances, ie: where:

1) The mark cannot be represented graphically and/or cannot distinguish goods (*s 3(1)(a)*).

2) The mark is devoid of distinctive character (*s 3(1)(b)*).

◆ A word that describes the goods with which it is associated would be considered for refusal under this head. Eg:

● FROOT LOOPS was not registrable by Kelloggs because the name was descriptive of the product (a loop-shaped cereal containing fruit), so was lacking in distinctive character (*FROOT LOOPS Trade Mark* [1998] RPC 240).

● Also, the phonetic equivalent of an unregistrable word is itself unregistrable (*Electrix Ltd v Electrolux* [1959] RPC 283).

▪ Eg: the word 'Electrix' was unregistrable, as it is a mere mis-spelling of, and indistinguishable in sound from, 'Electrics'.

◆ In a borderline case (eg: where a mark is not entirely descriptive), EC law suggests that the application should be refused where one possible meaning of the mark is descriptive (see the 'Wrigley's Doublemint' case – *OHIM v Wm Wrigley Jr Company, Case C-191/01P*, 23 October 2003).

3) The mark consists exclusively of signs or indications that may serve to designate the characteristics of the goods (*s 3(1)(c)*).

- The *TMA* seeks to avoid providing a monopoly right for words that would ordinarily be used to indicate the characteristics of the goods, including the following:

  - kind (eg: 'computer' for PCs), *or*

  - quality (eg: '100% silk' for clothes), *or*

  - quantity (eg: '6-pack' for beers), *or*

  - intended purpose (eg: 'dog food'), *or*

  - value (eg: 'pence'), *or*

  - time of production (of goods) or of rendering (of services) (eg: '1-hour service' for a photography service), *or*

  - geographical origin (eg: 'Parma' ham and 'Melton Mowbray' pork pies) (*s 3(1)(c)*).

- Eg: EUROLAMB was refused registration because it indicated the geographical origin of the goods (it was held to be no different from calling a product European Lamb). The mark was also refused on the basis that it lacked distinctive character (*EUROLAMB Trade Mark* [1997] RPC 279).

  - There are, in fact, very limited circumstances in which geographical indications may be registered. See the UK IPO's online *Manual of Trade Mark Practice para 35* for further information.

    - NB: in addition, separate to the trade-mark registration procedure it may be possible to posit geographical indications through EC law (*Council Regulation 510/2006/EC*).

4) The mark consists exclusively of signs or indications that are customary in the current language or the bona fide and established practices of the trade (*s 3(1)(d)*).

- Marks that become established terminology to describe goods or features are excluded.

  - Eg: a mark (such as 'escalator') that has become generic within a trade before registration will be refused.

- An existing registered mark may also be revoked on similar grounds – see section V below.

➤ An otherwise non-distinctive mark can become distinctive in practice:

> ### Acquired distinctiveness
>
> ➤ If a mark has in fact acquired a distinctive character through use, it is registrable despite s 3(1)(b)-(d) (see above).
>
> ◆ Eg: CARPHONE WAREHOUSE has acquired distinctiveness in relation to the provision of telephone equipment.

2 **The mark consists exclusively of a useful shape** (s 3(2))

➤ A mark cannot be registered if the shape:

a) results from the nature of the goods themselves, *or*

b) is necessary to obtain a technical result, *or*

c) gives substantial value to the goods.

◆ NB: goods or packaging created in a sufficiently distinctive shape can be registered, if the shape is does not fall within these categories.

➤ Eg:

◆ An application to register an application for 'a chewy sweet on a stick' was refused because both the sweet and stick were entirely functional (*Swizzels Matlow Ltd's Trade Mark Application* [1998] RPC 244).

◆ The shape of a toaster was not registrable since it was not inherently distinctive. The shape needed to go beyond that necessary to achieve a technical result (*Dualit Ltd's Trade Mark Application*, The Times, 19 July 1999).

3 **The mark is contrary to public policy or morality** (s 3(3)(a))

➤ Eg: an application to register JESUS for goats has been rejected (*Basic Trademark SA's Application*, BL O/021/05).

4 **The mark is likely to deceive the public** (s 3(3)(b))

5 **The mark is prohibited under UK or EC law** (s 3(4))

6 **The mark is a specially protected emblem** (s 3(5))

➤ A list of specially protected emblems is given in s 4. These include the Royal Arms and the Union Jack (subject to certain exceptions).

7 **The application is made in bad faith** (s 3(6))

➤ Dishonesty is not a requirement for establishing bad faith (*Harrison v Teton Valley Trading Co Ltd* [2004] EWCA Civ 1028).

➤ In practice, category 1 (ie: lack of distinctiveness) is the most frequently cited absolute ground for refusal, and the other categories are less common.

| Step 3 | There must be no **relative** grounds for refusal of registration |

➤ The 'relative grounds' for refusal prevent the registration of a mark that is the same or similar to an 'earlier mark' (ie: one that is already in use in business). The earlier mark may (but need not) be registered and different rules apply to each situation.

1 Where the earlier mark is registered (s 5(1)-(3))

➤ An application for registration will be refused where there already exists:

a) an **identical mark** in relation to **identical goods** (or services), *or*

- ◆ Eg: an application to use 'Kelloggs' for cereals would be refused.

b) a **similar mark** in relation to **identical goods** (or services) *and* there is a likelihood of confusion on the part of the public, *or*

- ◆ Because the earlier mark need only be **similar**, there is an additional requirement of customer confusion.

- ◆ Eg: an application to use 'Chelloggs' for cereals would be refused.

c) an **identical mark** in relation to **similar goods** (or services), *and* there is a likelihood of confusion on the part of the public, *or*

- ◆ Because the goods (or services) to which the earlier mark relates need only be **similar**, there is an additional requirement of customer confusion.

- ◆ Eg: an application to register 'Kelloggs' for marmalade would probably be refused.

d) a **similar mark** in relation to **similar goods** (or services), *and* there is a likelihood of confusion on the part of the public, *or*

- ◆ Because the earlier mark and the goods (or services) to which the earlier mark relates need only be **similar**, there is an additional requirement of customer confusion.

- ◆ It is perhaps less likely for a customer to be confused under this ground than for the grounds b) and c) above, because under ground d), both the earlier product and mark are only **similar** to the new product and mark.

- ◆ Eg: an application to register 'Chelloggs' for marmalade would probably be refused.

e) an **identical or similar mark** for **any goods** (or services) (ie: whether in relation to similar or dissimilar goods/services), *and*

- i) the earlier mark has established a reputation, *and*

- ii) the later mark would take unfair advantage of, or be detrimental to, that reputation.

- ◆ NB: this ground e) used to apply only to **dissimilar** goods or services. The restriction was removed by the *Trade Mark (Proof of Use etc.) Regulations 2004*.

- ◆ There are 2 additional requirements because the type of goods (or services) for which the earlier mark is used can (but need not) be unrelated.

  - • Eg: an application to register 'Kelloggs' or 'Chelloggs' for running shoes would be unlikely to be refused registration under grounds a)-d), because the goods for which the new mark is used are not similar goods.

    - ■ The mark may, however, be refused registration under ground e) if the later mark is shown to be taking advantage of, or to be detrimental to, the reputation of the earlier mark. Detriment may exist where the goods associated with the later mark are of a poor quality.

2   **Where the earlier mark is not registered** (*s 5(4)*)

➤ Even if an existing mark is unregistered, registration of a new mark will be refused if the use of the new mark is liable to be prevented by virtue of:

a) any law protecting the existing mark as an unregistered trade mark (eg: under passing-off – see Section N of this Chapter), *or*

b) any other earlier rights (eg: copyright or design rights).

III   Registering a trade mark

➤ Any person that owns a trade mark may apply to the UK IPO for registration (directly or using a trade-mark agent).

- ◆ There must be an address in the UK to which all correspondence can be sent.

➤ The *Trade Mark Rules 2008* set out the procedure for applying for a registration.

➤ There are 5 stages involved in an application for registration of a trade mark.

Stages	
1	Application
2	Examination
3	Objections
4	Publication and opposition
5	Registration

Stage 1	Application

➤ The applicant must:

- ◆ fill in *Form TM3* (or online using *Form e-TM3*), including the following:

  - the applicant's name and address for service, *and*

  - the types of goods/services to which the trade mark is to be applied, *and*

  - a request that the trade mark be registered, *and*

  - a representation of the mark, *and*

    - The representation of the mark must be clear and depict the essential features that are to be protected (*CREOLA Trade Mark* [1997] RPC 507).

  - a statement that the applicant:

    a) is currently using the mark for the named classes of goods/services, *or*

    b) has a genuine intention to do so, *or*

    c) is allowing a third party to do so, *and*

- ◆ submit the *Form TM3* (or *Form e-TM3*) and the appropriate fee.

➤ An applicant must decide which of 45 classes of goods/services to apply for.

- ◆ The classification system is known as the International Classification. It is based on the *Nice Agreement 1957.*

➤ Once a mark is registered in a class, a monopoly right is conferred on the mark for that class only.

- ◆ The applicant can register a mark for any number of classes on *Form TM3* (although such registration must be justified). Subsequent registration for additional classes, while possible, requires an additional fee (see the fee list for details).

  - The appropriate form for registration of additional classes is *Form TM3A.*

- ◆ Goods are in classes 1 to 34, and services are in classes 35 to 45.

  - Each class covers a list of goods/services of a similar type.

- ◆ By way of example, the main classes of goods relevant to technology and media companies are:

Class	Types of goods/services included
9	➤ Photographic, cinematographic, recording and telecommunications apparatus, data processing equipment, computer hardware and software, downloadable electronic publications, compact discs, digital music, computer games equipment and mobile phone accessories.
16	➤ Paper; printed matter; photographs; artists' materials; printers' type.
25	➤ Clothing, footwear and headgear.

◆ By way of example, the main classes of services relevant to technology and media companies are:

Class	Types of services included
35	➤ Advertising, electronic data storage, online advertising services, production of TV and radio adverts, and data processing.
38	➤ Telecommunications, email and internet services, and broadcasting.
41	➤ Entertainment, online entertainment, sporting and cultural activities, online games services and the provision of online electronic publications.
42	➤ Scientific and technological services, industrial analysis and research services, design and development of computer hardware and software, computer programming, creating and hosting websites, and design services.

➤ Since April 2008 an applicant can make a 'fast track' application online.

   ◆ A fast-track application is examined within 10 business days of filing.

➤ An applicant that has applied to register a trade mark in an overseas country can make a 'priority application' (ie: in effect backdating the effective date of the UK application).

Priority applications

➤ For the applicant to claim priority:

   ◆ the applicant must have first applied to register the mark in a country:

      ● which is party to the *Paris Convention*, *or*

      ● with which the UK has a special agreement, *and*

   ◆ that application must have been made no more than 6 months ago.

➤ The effect is that the date of the application in the overseas country is used as the date for the present application in the UK. For example:

   ◆ A company registers a mark in France (as a national application).

   ◆ A competitor tries to register the same mark in France and is refused.

   ◆ The competitor tries to register the mark in the UK.

   ◆ As long as the original applicant applies to register the mark in the UK within 6 months of filing in France, the competitor will be prevented from registering the mark in the UK.

➤ A street name is registrable if there is no connection between the name and goods:

Street names

➤ Eg: an application to register the name 'Saville Row' for glasses was refused because glasses are used in the fashion industry and the tailoring businesses in Saville Row would be commercially affected by registration (*Saville Row Trade Mark* [1998] RPC 155).

Stage 2	Examination

➤ The UK IPO considers whether the mark is capable of registration.

- ◆ The UK IPO considers whether:

  a) the mark falls within the definition of a mark in the *TMA, and*

  b) whether it is outside the absolute grounds for refusal.

- ◆ If there are earlier trade-mark registrations that are the same or similar to the one applied for, the UK IPO notifies the applicant and the owner of the earlier mark.

  - Owners of earlier CTMs will not, however, be notified (unless such owners have opted in to the notification system).

➤ Either objections are raised (see step 3) or the application is accepted and published (see step 4) .

Stage 3	Objections

➤ If the UK IPO raises objections to the application, the applicant may either:

- ◆ offer written arguments, *or*

- ◆ request an oral hearing.

➤ Either way, the applicant should anticipate possible objections:

Overcoming objections

➤ Eg: if an objection is likely to be raised due to a:

- ◆ **lack of distinctiveness** – the applicant should provide evidence of previous use by which the mark has in fact become distinctive, *or*

- ◆ **pre-existing mark** – the applicant should consider reducing the number of classes or narrowing the specification within a particular class.

Stage 4	Publication and opposition

A Publication

➤ The application is published in the *Trade Marks Journal* if:

a) there are no objections, *or*

b) the applicant has overcome the objections made by the UK IPO, *or*

c) the applicant chooses to proceed in spite of an earlier trade mark.+

- The *Trade Marks Journal* gives opportunities to interested parties (including the owners of earlier marks that the UK IPO has notified – see step 2) to assess new trade marks.

  - Any person may object to the application within 2 months of publication (extended to 3 months on request).

B Opposition

➤ An opposition is made by sending *Form TM7* and the relevant fee to the UK IPO.

- ◆ The original applicant may then make a counter-statement.

- ◆ Both parties may adduce evidence before the Registrar at a hearing.

- ◆ The Registrar then notifies the parties of the Registrar's decision in writing.

Stage 5	Registration

➤ The mark is registered once 2 months have passed since publication in the *Trade Marks Journal* without opposition (subject to a possible 1-month extension).

- ◆ Where a trade mark is opposed, the application may be considerably delayed and may not proceed to registration.

➤ The UK IPO sends a certificate of registration to the applicant containing:

- ◆ the classes of goods or services for which the mark is registered, *and*

- ◆ a representation of the mark.

➤ The applicant then becomes the first owner of the registered trade mark.

- ◆ The duration of the rights conferred by registration is indefinite, provided that:

  - • a renewal fee is paid every 10 years, *and*

  - • the mark is not revoked or found to be invalid – see section V below.

➤ In the case of a straightforward application (ie: for a mark that appears to be registrable and where registration is not opposed), the application would usually proceed to registration in 4-6 months.

IV Protecting a trade mark

➤ Even though an owner has registered a mark, others may try to use the mark or attempt to register themselves as proprietor of an identical or similar mark. An owner may have to defend a mark through:

- ◆ infringement proceedings (dealt with below), *and/or*

- ◆ opposition proceedings, *and/or*

- ◆ avoiding revocation of the mark (ie: its removal from the register) through actively promoting the use of the mark.

➤ There are 4 steps to consider in relation to an infringement action:

Steps	
1	The mark must be registered.
2	There must be an infringing act.
3	Are there any defences?
4	What are the remedies?

Step 1 — The mark must be registered

➤ Regardless of how well-known a mark is, an **unregistered** trade mark cannot benefit from the *TMA* (except that an unregistered mark cannot usually be registered by someone other than the owner).

   ◆ Nonetheless, alternative remedies such as passing-off may be available.

Step 2 — There must be an infringing act

➤ Registration provides an owner with the **exclusive** right to use the mark for the classes of goods/services for which it is registered.

   ◆ Ie: subject to certain exceptions, if another person uses the same or similar mark on the same or similar goods or services, the owner can sue for infringement.

➤ For there to be an infringing act, 2 criteria need to be satisfied:

   1   There must be use of the mark in the course of trade

   ➤ A person uses a mark in the course of trade if that person (*s 10(4)*):

   a) affixes it to goods or packaging, *or*

   b) offers for sale, markets, or stocks goods under the mark, *or*

   c) offers or supplies under the mark, *or*

   d) imports or exports goods under the mark, *or*

   e) applies it to business paper or uses it for advertising.

   ➤ In *Marks & Spencers v One in a Million Ltd* [1998] FSR 265, use in the course of trade was held to be broader than use as a trade mark: 'use in the course of trade' was held to involve use in the course of a business.

      ◆ The infringing activity must take place in the UK.

   ➤ Non-visual use may amount to infringement: 'smell' and 'sound' marks may be infringed.

➤ Suppliers of infringing material (eg: printers) may be joined in the proceedings.

◆ The supplier must know (or have reason to believe) that use of the mark was not authorised by the owner.

• In *Trebor Bassett Ltd v The Football Association Ltd* ([1997] FSR 211), the publication of cards bearing photographs of football players wearing the England football strip using the 'Three Lions' logo did not constitute use of the logo on the cards.

2   **The mark must infringe the existing registered mark**

➤ There are 5 criteria for deciding whether the new mark infringes the existing mark, which are equivalent to the 5 relative grounds of refusal for registration where there are a earlier registered rights. Ie: it is an infringement to use:

a) an **identical mark** in relation to **identical goods** (or services), *or*

b) a **similar mark** in relation to **identical goods** (or services), *if* there is a likelihood of confusion on the part of the public, *or*

c) an **identical mark** in relation to **similar goods** (or services), *if* there is a likelihood of confusion on the part of the public, *or*

d) a **similar mark** in relation to **similar goods** (or services), *if* there is a likelihood of confusion on the part of the public, *or*

e) an **identical or similar mark** for **any goods** (or services) (ie: whether in relation to similar or non-similar goods/services), *if*:

i)   the earlier mark has established a reputation, *and*

ii) the later mark would take unfair advantage of, or be detrimental to, that reputation (*s 10(1)-(3)*).

➤ The criteria can be summarised as follows:

Section	Mark	Goods/ services	Confusion?	Reputational damage?
10(1)	➤ Identical	➤ Identical	➤ Not required	➤ Not required
10(2)(a)	➤ Identical	➤ Similar	➤ Required	➤ Not required
10(2)(b)	➤ Similar	➤ Identical/ similar	➤ Required	➤ Not required
10(3)	➤ Identical/ similar	➤ Any	➤ Not required	➤ Required

➤ Case law has clarified the scope of these criteria:

◆ *Identical* – If there are insignificant differences, the later mark may still be deemed to be identical to the earlier mark (*LTJ Diffusion v Sadas Verbaudet*, C-291/00, 20 March 2003). Eg: the marks 'WEBSPHERE' and 'web-sphere' were found to be identical (*IBM Corp v Web-Sphere Ltd* [2004] EWHC 529).

- In *Arsenal Football Club plc v Reed* ([2003] All ER 865), the defendant – a local trader of unofficial Arsenal FC merchandise – argued that use of the Arsenal mark was not use in a trade mark sense, but was merely a 'badge of allegiance'. The Court of Appeal rejected this view and held that circulation of unofficial Arsenal-branded goods affected Arsenal FC's ability to guarantee the origin on the goods and so was an infringing act.

  ▪ Following this case, use of a mark that is identical to an earlier mark will be infringing if it jeopardises the guarantee of the origin of the goods.

◆ *Likelihood of confusion* – A likelihood of confusion:

- is assessed:

  ▪ at the time when the defendant's goods were first sold (*Levi Strauss & Co v Casucci SpA*, Case C-145/05, 27 April 2006), *and*

  ▪ by taking into account all factors relevant to the circumstances of the case (eg: the visual, aural or conceptual similarity of the earlier and later marks, based on the overall impression given by those marks, in light of their distinctive and dominant components) (*Sabel BV v Puma AG*, Case C-251/95, 11 November 1997), *and*

- can be inferred from the circumstances even in the absence of evidence (*Mont Blanc Simplo GmbH v Sepia Products Inc*, The Times, 2 February 2000), *and*

- is not implied merely by a likelihood that the public would believe that the claimant's and defendant's goods have the same (or an associated) origin (*Marca Mode CV v Adidas AG*, Case C-425/98, 22 June 2000).

◆ *Reputation* – To have a reputation, a mark has to be known by a significant part of the 'relevant public', which is determined by taking into account the following factors in relation to the mark, ie:

a) market share, *and*

b) intensity, geographical extent and duration of use, *and*

c) size of investment (*General Motors Corp v Yplon SA*, Case C-357-97, 14 September 1999).

- *Unfair advantage* – 4 factors are taken into account (*L'Oréal SA v Bellure NV* [2006] EWCH 2355):

    a) whether there is a deliberate similarity between the marks, *and/or*

    b) the extent to which the claimant's mark is well-known, *and/or*

    c) whether the similarity enables the defendant to charge a higher price for the product, *and/or*

    d) whether the defendant's goods benefited from the claimant's promotion of the claimant's goods.

    - The ECJ has held that (*L'Oréal SA v Bellure NV*, Case C-487/07):

        - An advantage taken of a mark's distinctive character or repute may be unfair, even if the use of the mark is not detrimental to its distinctive character or repute (or, more generally, to its proprietor)

        - To determine unfair advantage requires a 'global assessment', taking into account all factors relevant to the circumstances of the case (eg: the strength of the mark's reputation, the degree of distinctive character of the mark, the degree of similarity between the marks at issue, and the nature and degree of proximity of the goods/services concerned).

Step 3	Are there any defences?

➤ The most commonly cited defences to trade-mark infringement are set out below.

1   Claimant's failure to prove infringement

➤ Since infringement is not always clear-cut, perhaps the most common defence is simply to prove that the claimant has failed to make out a case of infringement. It is in effect, therefore, a defence to show that:

- the claimant consented to the use (*s 9(1)*), *or*

- there has been no infringing use under *s 10*.

2   Use relating to the claimant's genuine goods

➤ It is a defence to show that:

    a) the defendant has used the existing registered trade mark to identify goods or services belonging to the owner of that mark, *and*

    b) the use is in accordance with honest practices in industrial or commercial matters, *and*

    c) it is not such as to take unfair advantage of, or cause damage to, the distinctive character or reputation of the mark (*s 10(6)*).

➤ This defence covers 2 different situations:

- where the defendant is a trader (eg: a retailer of branded goods) that is selling the goods in question in the ordinary course of business, *or*

- where the defendant is engaging in comparative advertising.

➤ The rules on comparative advertising have been consolidated under *Directive 2006/114/EC* (the '**Comparative Advertising Directive**'), which was implemented in the UK in May 2008 by the *Business Protection from Misleading Marketing Regulations 2008* – see Chapter 5 Section A.

- ◆ There is, at the time of writing, considerable uncertainty about the extent to which *s 10(6)* remains relevant to comparative advertising.

  - On a referral from the Court of Appeal in *O2 Holdings Ltd v Hutchinson 3G Ltd* [2006] EWHC 2571, the ECJ held that use of a rival's mark in comparative advertising can constitute trade-mark infringement if it gives rise to a likelihood of confusion between the marks.

  - The ECJ did not, however, rule on a number of questions referred to the ECJ about the interaction between *s 10(6)* and the *Comparative Advertising Directive*.

  - It is possible that the old case law on *s 10(6)* may no longer be relevant, so it is beyond the scope of this Section. Section A of Chapter 5 examines the new legislative regime.

3   Use of a registered trade mark in the same class

➤ Where the claimant and defendant each have a trade mark registered for the same class of goods/services, the defendant will not have infringed the claimant's mark if the defendant uses the defendant's mark within the relevant class (*s 11(1)*).

4   Honest use

➤ There are 3 related defences under *s 11(2)*:

a) the use by a person of that person's own name or address, *or*

- ◆ This applies where a company uses its own registered or trading name (*Scandecor Developments v Scandecor Marketing* [2001] 2 CMLR 30).

b) the use of indications concerning the kind, quality, quantity, geographical origin or other characteristics of goods or services, *or*

c) the use of a trade mark where it is necessary to indicate the intended purpose of a product or service (in particular, as accessories or spare parts).

➤ In order to rely on the defences under *s 11(2)*, the use must be in accordance with 'honest practices in industrial or commercial matters'.

- ◆ The 'honest use' test is objective. There would be no honest use where the business is trading on another's goodwill, but would be where the name had been used years before use of the mark was questioned.

5   **Earlier right**

➤   A registered trade mark is not infringed by the use, in the course of trade in a particular locality, of an 'earlier right' (essentially, an unregistered trade mark that is protected under passing-off) which applies only in that locality (s 11(3)).

6   **'Exhaustion of rights'**

➤   A registered trade mark is not infringed by its use in relation to goods that have been put on the market in the European Economic Area under that trade mark by the owner or with the owner's consent (s 12).

◆   This allows goods to be imported into the UK and sold by the defendant in parallel to goods sold by the claimant under the same mark.

➤   Where a mark is declared invalid, there is no infringement from the date of registration (s 47(6)) – which in effect provides a defence from that date.

7   **Disclaimer or limitation**

➤   An owner may have restricted the rights conferred by a mark by:

a)   **disclaimer** – ie: disclaiming any right to the exclusive use of a specified element of a trade mark, *or*

b)   **limitation** – ie: agreeing that the rights conferred by registration will be subject to a specified limitation (territorial or otherwise).

8   **Attack on validity of registration**

➤   A registered trade mark can be revoked (under s 46) or declared invalid (under s 47) – see section V below.

➤   Where a mark is revoked, there is no infringement from the date on which the grounds for revocation existed (s 46(6)) – which in effect provides a defence from that date.

9   **Acquiescence or delay**

➤   It is a defence under general equitable principles to show that the claimant acquiesced in the infringement or unconscionably delayed in bringing an action for infringement.

◆   Acquiescence for a continuous 5-year period may also give rise to a declaration of invalidity – see s 48 and section V below.

Step 4	What are the remedies?

➤ The remedies for trade-mark infringement are similar to other remedies for an infringement of intellectual property rights. They are:

   ◆ an injunction (interim or final), *and/or*

   ◆ damages or an account of profits (*s 14*), *and/or*

   ◆ erasure of the mark, or if not possible, destruction of the offending items (*s 15*), *and/or*

      ● Note, however: the High Court cannot order the Registrar of Companies to change a company name comprising an infringing mark (*Halifax plc v Halifax Repossessions Ltd* [2004] EWCA Civ 331).

   ◆ delivery-up of the offending items (*s 16*).

➤ There are several criminal offences created under the *TMA* relating to the unauthorised use of trade marks (*s 92*).

   ◆ Eg: a person commits an offence where offering goods for sale or hire:

      ● under a mark that is identical to (or likely to be mistaken for) an existing registered trade mark, *and*

      ● with a view to gain for himself or another or with intent to cause loss to another, *and*

      ● without the owner's consent (*s 92(1)*).

         ▪ In the 'Teletubbies' case, it was held that liability is 'near strict', ie: it is not necessary to prove knowledge of infringement or intent to infringe (*Torbay DC v Singh* [1999] 2 Cr App R 451).

   ◆ The maximum penalties are:

      ● on summary conviction – up to 6 months' imprisonment and/or a fine of up to £5,000, *or*

      ● on indictment – up to 10 years' imprisonment and/or an unlimited fine.

➤ NB: an owner of intellectual property rights may apply to HM Revenue and Customs to seize goods coming into the UK where the rights-owner suspects that such goods infringe their intellectual property rights.

   ◆ See the *Goods Infringing Intellectual Property Rights (Customs) Regulations 2004*.

V Revocation and invalidity of a trade mark

A Revocation

➤ Any person may apply to the Registrar of Trade Marks or to court for revocation (*s 46*).

◆ A trade mark may be removed from the register where (*s 46(1)*):

a) the owner has not put the mark to genuine use (unless there are proper reasons for non-use) or consented to its use within 5 years of registration, *or*

b) the owner has suspended use for 5 years, *or*

c) the mark has become a generic term for the goods or services for which it is registered, *or*

d) the mark is liable to mislead the public, particularly as to the nature, quality or geographical origin of the goods/services for which the mark is used.

➤ For categories a) and b), the burden is on the owner to prove genuine use of the mark (*s 100*).

◆ Use must relate to the range of goods for which the mark was registered (*Hachette Filipacchi Presse v Safeway Stores plc,* CH1996-H-7401).

➤ For a market-leading product, the risk of genericisation under category c) is high.

Risk of generic use

➤ For the owner of a particularly popular trade mark, the main risk of revocation stems from the possibility that the mark might become a generic term for the type of goods to which it is applied.

◆ 'Aspirin', 'escalator' and 'linoleum' were all once registered trade marks, but became victims of their own success, suffered the fate of 'genericide' and have been removed from the register.

➤ The owner can try to prevent generic use as follows:

a) each reference to the mark should be distinguished when combined with other text (eg: through use of capitals, quotation marks or a different font and/or typeface), *and*

b) a word mark should not be used on its own as a noun or verb (eg: 'to conduct a *Google* search', rather than 'to google'), *and*

c) where a graphic logo and word form a single registration, the constituent parts should not be used separately unless they are registered separately as well, *and*

d) steps should be taken to try to prevent and/or correct any generic use of the mark in marketing materials, listings or the media.

B Invalidity

➤ Any person may apply to the Registrar or court for a declaration that a registered mark is invalid (ss 47-48).

♦ The application is based on the absolute and/or relative grounds for refusal to register a mark.

• Eg: a registered mark has been declared invalid because an earlier mark that was confusingly similar had been registered previously (Gromax Plasticulture Ltd v Don & Low Nonwovens Ltd [1999] RPC 367).

➤ Where the owner of an earlier mark has acquiesced to the use of a later registered mark for 5 years continuously, the owner of the earlier mark loses the right (s 48):

a) to apply for a declaration of invalidity, and

b) to oppose the use of the later mark, unless the later mark was applied for in bad faith.

VI Dealing with trade marks

➤ A trade mark is personal property (s 22). Accordingly:

♦ The owner may assign or license the trade mark (ss 24 and 28).

♦ The original owner may restrict (ss 24(2) and 28(1)):

a) the classes of goods or services for which the mark is to be licensed or assigned, and/or

b) the duration of assignment or license, and/or

c) the geographical area in which the mark can be used.

➤ For an assignment or licence to be valid, it must be in writing and signed by the assignor/licensor (ss 24(3) and 28(2)).

➤ Although there is no statutory requirement to do so, the assignee/licensee should register the assignment (using Form TM16) or licence (using Form TM50) as soon as possible.

♦ If an assignment or licence is not registered within 6 months of the transaction, remedies will not be available for the period between the transaction and registration (s 25(4)).

♦ If an assignment or licence has not, at any given time, been registered, the transaction is ineffective against a person acquiring a conflicting interest in ignorance of it (s 25(3)(a)).

➤ Unless agreed otherwise, a licensee (but not an exclusive licensee) may ask the owner to bring proceedings on the licensee's behalf (*s 30*).

   ➤ An owner may grant an exclusive licence that allows the licensee to use the trade mark to the exclusion of all others including the owner (*s 29(1)*).

      ◆ An exclusive licence may allow the licensee all the rights and remedies of the licensor (*s 31*).

         • An exclusive licensee can bring proceedings in the licensee's own name.

         • Such rights and remedies run concurrently with those of the owner.

➤ Where the owner licenses a registered trade mark, the owner should impose contractual restrictions on the licensee to ensure suitable control over the use of the trade mark by the licensee (and by any permitted sub-licensees).

   ◆ Eg: quality control is important to the protect the reputation and value of the brand.

VII Trade-mark searches

➤ It is often advisable to conduct trade-mark searches, eg:

   ◆ to establish whether a new mark can registered (or whether there are earlier marks that might prevent registration), *or*

   ◆ as part of a 'due diligence' exercise when acquiring a trade mark.

➤ The following searches can be conducted:

1 Online search

   ➤ The UK IPO maintains a searchable register of UK registered trade marks on its website at www.ipo.gov.uk/tm.

      ◆ The website also provides guidance and information on applying for and managing registered trade marks. Eg: the online Manual of Trade Marks Practice provides detailed practical guidance on the approach taken by the UK IPO in examining trade-mark applications.

2 Public inspection

   ➤ Any person may inspect the UK IPO's trade marks register between 9.00 a.m. and 5.00 p.m. (Monday to Friday).

      ◆ The search rooms are located at the UK IPO's London and Newport offices. Advance notice must be given to the Central Enquiry Unit. Since the register is public, copies may be made and removed.

3 New trade marks

   ➤ The *Trade Marks Journal* is published weekly on the UK IPO website and provides details of prospective new trade marks.

VIII Other types of registrable marks

➤ In addition to the ordinary trade mark, there are 2 special forms of trade mark:

1 Collective marks (s 49)

➤ A collective mark enables the members of an association that owns the mark to display the mark to show a business connection with the association.

◆ An example is FEDERATION OF MASTER BUILDERS.

➤ The association may allow authorised businesses to apply the mark, provided that the users comply with the regulations specified by the association.

➤ An application should be made on the same form as for ordinary trade marks (Form TM3).

◆ The procedure is the same as for ordinary trade marks, except that the applicant must submit regulations governing the use of the mark.

2 Certification marks (s 50)

➤ A certification mark provides an indication as to a **characteristic** of the product or service. The characteristics include:

◆ origin, or

◆ material, or

◆ mode of manufacture of goods, or

◆ performance of services, or

◆ quality, or

◆ accuracy.

• An example of a certification mark is the 'woolmark' that certifies the type of material used in a woollen product.

▪ NB: a certification mark covers many of those areas that are refused under the absolute grounds for refusal under s 3(1)(b).

➤ The owner will usually be a trade association or governing body.

◆ The registered owner has exclusive rights in the mark and can permit others to use the mark, provided that the other product possesses the relevant characteristics.

➤ An application should be made on Form TM3.

◆ The procedure is the same as for ordinary trade marks except that:

a) the applicant must submit regulations governing the use of the mark, and

b) the absolute grounds of refusal relating to the above characteristics do not apply.

M Community trade marks

*References in this Section to '**CTMR 09**' are to Regulation 207/09/EC (which replaced, and is a consolidated version of, Regulation 40/94/EC).*

*References in this Section to '**CTMR 95**' are to the Rules set out in Regulation 2868/95/EC.*

I	Generally
II	Is a mark capable of registration as a CTM?
III	Registering a CTM
IV	Protecting a CTM
V	Revocation, invalidity and surrender
VI	Conversion into national rights
VII	Dealing with CTMs

I Generally

➤ There are 3 ways of registering a trade mark in the UK:

a) an application to the UK Intellectual Property Office ('**UK IPO**') for a UK-only trade-mark registration, *or*

b) an application to the Office for Harmonization in the Internal Market ('**OHIM**') for a 'Community trade mark' ('**CTM**'), *or*

   • A CTM is a single registration applying throughout the European Union.

c) an application to the World Intellectual Property Organisation (WIPO) for an international trade-mark registration under the *Madrid Protocol*.

   • This gives rise to a bundle of national registrations. The rules and procedure for international registrations are beyond the scope of this Chapter.

➤ Some advantages and disadvantages of a CTM are shown in the table below.

Advantages	Disadvantages
✓ A single registration extends across all EU member states.	✗ An application may be refused due to a conflict in a single EU member state.
✓ A unitary right is easier to enforce, as proceedings need only be brought in 1 country.	✗ Damages for infringement only run from the date of registration (not application).
✓ It may be converted into national rights if required – see section VI below.	✗ If a CTM is converted into national rights, national application fees are payable in addition to the CTM fee.
✓ It is cheaper than applying for national rights in each country.	✗ An application must be made in 1 of 5 languages.
✓ There is no need to use a CTM in every EU member state to avoid a risk of revocation for non-use.	✗ A CTM cannot be assigned separately in each country: it must be assigned for the whole of the EU – see section VII below.

➤ Intellectual property professionals (eg: trade-mark agents) can help with choosing the appropriate registration route.

♦ Information is also available via the registries' websites:

- UK IPO – at www.ipo.gov.uk.

- OHIM – at www.oami.europa.eu.

- WIPO – at www.wipo.org.

➤ In March 2009, to encourage small and medium enterprises in the EU to obtain CTM protection, the EU Fees Committee approved a 40% reduction in the total fees for registering a CTM.

II   Is a mark capable of registration as a CTM?

➤ For a mark to be registrable as a CTM, it must be capable of (*CTMR 09 Art 4*):

a) graphical representation, *and*

b) distinguishing the goods or services of an 'undertaking' (ie: a business) from those of another.

♦ *CTMR 09 Art 4* gives the following examples of types of registrable mark:

- words (including personal names), *or*

- designs, *or*

- letters, *or*

- numerals, *or*

- the shape or packaging of goods.

➤ A mark is not registrable if any **absolute** ground for refusal applies (*CTMR 09 Art 7*).

Absolute grounds for refusal of CTM registration
➤ The absolute grounds for refusal are broadly the same as under the *Trade Marks Act 1994* ('**TMA**') (see Section L of this Chapter). Eg: the mark must not (*CTMR 09 Art 7(1)*):
♦ be devoid of distinctive character, *or*
♦ be descriptive of the relevant goods/services, *or*
♦ be customary in the language/practice of the trade, *or*
♦ consist exclusively of a useful shape, *or*
♦ be deceptive.
➤ The absolute grounds apply even if they only apply in **part** of the EU (*CTMR 94 Art 7(2)*).

Absolute grounds for refusal of CTM registration (continued)

➤ NB:

    a) bad faith is not an absolute ground, *and*

    b) marks consisting exclusively of signs/indications that have become customary in any EU language will be refused (*CTMR 09 Art 7(1)(d)*).

       ● If a word mark is in a dictionary of the language concerned, this ground is presumed to be present.

➤ Where a mark is devoid of distinctive character, the absolute grounds do not apply if the mark has in fact become distinctive through use (*CTMR 09 Art 7(3)*).

    ◆ It is not enough that such 'use' is only in a 'substantial part' of the EU: it must be 'throughout' the EU (*Ford Motor Co v OHIM (Trade Marks and Designs)* (T-91/99) 2 CMLR 276).

➤ A CTM cannot be contested in a new country acceding to the EU if the CTM was valid before enlargement of the EU (*CTMR 09 Art 165(2)*).

➤ OHIM will only refuse registration on **relative** grounds if an application is opposed successfully by the owner of an earlier right – see section III below.

III   Registering a CTM

➤ Any natural or legal person (including an authority established under public law) can apply to register a CTM (*CTMR 09 Art 5*).

➤ There are 6 stages involved in an application to register a CTM.

Stages	
1	Filing
2	Examination
3	Search for earlier marks
4	Publication and opposition
5	Appeal
6	Registration

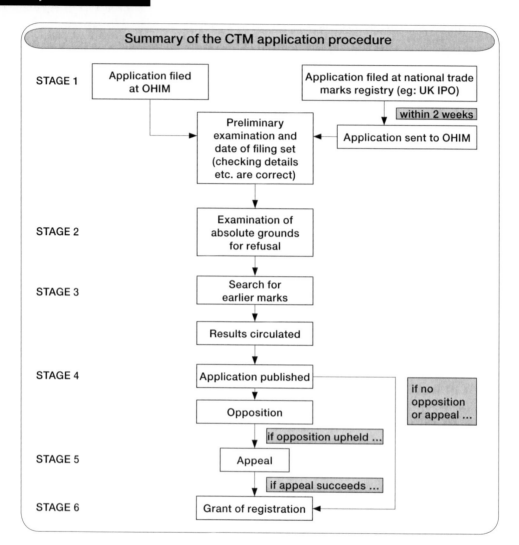

Summary of the CTM application procedure

STAGE 1 — Application filed at OHIM / Application filed at national trade marks registry (eg: UK IPO)

within 2 weeks → Application sent to OHIM

Preliminary examination and date of filing set (checking details etc. are correct)

STAGE 2 — Examination of absolute grounds for refusal

STAGE 3 — Search for earlier marks → Results circulated

STAGE 4 — Application published → Opposition

if no opposition or appeal ...

if opposition upheld ...

STAGE 5 — Appeal

if appeal succeeds ...

STAGE 6 — Grant of registration

Stage 1	Filing

➤ The application must be filed at:

  ◆ the trade marks registry of any EU member state (ie: in the UK, the UK IPO), *or*

  ◆ OHIM at its office in Alicante (*CTMR 09 Art 25*).

➤ The application must contain (*CTMR 09 Art 26*):

  a) a request for registration, *and*

  b) information identifying the applicant, *and*

  c) a list of goods and services for which the mark is to be registered, *and*

  d) a representation of the mark.

➤ The application fee is payable within 1 month of the request for registration if not included with the application (*CTMR 95 r 9(1)*).

➤ The application may also contain (*CTMR 95 r 9(3)*):

◆ details of any other application from which priority is claimed, *and/or*

Claiming priority (*CTMR 09 Art 29*)
➤ Claiming priority from an earlier application effectively allows the filing date to be back-dated by up to 6 months.
➤ Priority can be claimed where the CTM application is:
◆ for the same mark and covers the same goods or services, *and*
◆ filed within 6 months after the earlier application.
➤ Priority can also be claimed where goods to which the mark is affixed have been presented at an officially recognised international exhibition within 6 months before filing the CTM application.

◆ a claim to seniority (although seniority can be claimed after registration).

Seniority (*CTMR 09 Art 34*)
➤ Claiming seniority allows the owner of an earlier national registration to abandon that registration without losing the rights attached to it.
➤ Seniority can be claimed for any number of earlier registrations in an EU member state that cover the same mark and the same goods/services.
◆ When an earlier mark is surrendered or lapses, the owner of the CTM is treated as having the same rights as the owner would have had if the earlier registration had been maintained.
➤ The applicant should provide seniority details to OHIM within 3 months after filing the CTM.

➤ The application may also contain details of a 'collective mark' (ie: a mark owned by a trade association for use by its members to indicate membership – see *CTMR 09 Art 66*).

➤ The application can be filed in the official language of any EU member state, but the application must indicate 1 of the official OHIM languages as a second language.

◆ Opposition proceedings may be conducted in this second language.

◆ The official OHIM languages are English, French, Italian, German and Spanish.

◆ If the application is not filed in 1 of the 5 official OHIM languages, OHIM will arrange to have the application translated into the language indicated by the applicant (*CTMR 09 Art 119*).

Stage 2	Examination

➤ The Examination Division at OHIM will examine the application to confirm that it complies with the requirements listed in stage 1 above (*CTMR 95 r 9(1)*).

  ◆ If there are deficiencies that cannot be remedied, the application will be refused.

  ◆ If there are deficiencies that can be remedied, OHIM will allow the deficiency to be remedied within 2 months (*CTMR 95 r 9(2)*).

  ◆ If OHIM is satisfied with the application, a date of filing will be given to the application.

➤ OHIM will then look at the application in further detail, considering, in particular, whether there are any absolute grounds for refusing the application (*CTMR 95 r 11*).

➤ In 2008 OHIM published new examiners' guidelines, which should be taken into account by an applicant when preparing an application for submission.

Stage 3	Search for earlier marks

➤ OHIM will check the CTM register for any conflicting marks and provide the applicant with a search report (*CTMR 09 Art 38(1)*).

➤ At the applicant's request and on payment of a fee (*CTMR 09 Art 147(4)*), OHIM will also forward the application to the registries of certain other EU member states, which will also perform a search of their own records within 2 months (*CTMR 09 Art 38(3)*).

  ◆ France, Germany, Ireland, Italy, Portugal, Sweden and the UK are excluded from carrying out this search.

  ◆ The search results are returned to OHIM and promptly forwarded to the applicant.

➤ The search report(s) obtained are not definitive and do not necessarily give an accurate indication of whether an opposition is likely.

Stage 4	Publication and opposition

A Publication

➤ A application that is not refused is published (*CTMR 09 Art 39*). It is published in the *CTM Bulletin*.

  ◆ Publication should occur within 1 month after the OHIM (and, where requested, national) search report(s) have been sent to the applicant (*CTMR 09 Art 38(7)*).

  ◆ Upon publication, OHIM will inform any owners of earlier CTMs or earlier CTM applications (NB: not national trade marks or national applications) cited in the CTM search report (*CTMR 09 Art 38(7)*).

➤ The date of publication in the *CTM Bulletin* is the date from which damages may be calculated in infringement proceedings.

B Opposition

➤ OHIM will not refuse an application on the grounds that it conflicts with an earlier mark unless registration is opposed.

➤ A notice of opposition can only be filed by the proprietor of an 'earlier trade mark'.

Definition of an 'earlier trade mark'
➤ An earlier trade mark is an earlier (*CTMR 09 Art 8(2)*):   a) CTM, *or*   b) trade mark registered in an EU member state or at the Benelux Trade Mark Office, *or*   c) trade mark registered under international arrangements which have effect in an EU member state or in the EU, *or*   d) application for any of the above (subject to registration), *or*   e) well-known unregistered trade mark.

➤ An opponent can oppose a CTM only on **relative** grounds for refusal. These grounds are set out in *CTMR 09 Art 8*.

◆ The relative grounds for refusal are equivalent to those set out in the *TMA* (see Section L of this Chapter) and can be summarised as follows:

Article	Mark	Goods/ services	Confusion on part of public?	Reputational damage?
8(1)(a)	➤ Identical	➤ Identical	➤ Not required	➤ Not required
8(1)(b)	➤ Identical	➤ Similar	➤ Required	➤ Not required
8(1)(b)	➤ Similar	➤ Identical/ similar	➤ Required	➤ Not required
8(5)	➤ Identical/ similar	➤ Any (see below).	➤ Not required	➤ Required

● NB: *CTMR 95 Art 8(5)* has not in fact been amended (as the *TMA* has) specifically to allow the ground for refusal to apply to **any** goods (ie: rather than only to **dissimilar** goods/services).

● In practice, however, OHIM allows this where the earlier mark:

a) has a reputation in the EU or relevant EU member state, *and*

b) registration of the later mark would be detrimental to the earlier registration, irrespective of whether the later mark would apply to the **same, similar or dissimilar** goods (*Adidas-Salomon AG v Fitness World Trading Ltd*, Case C-408/01 [2003] ECR I-12537).

➤ The opposition notice must be filed at OHIM within 3 months of the publication of the application (*CTMR 09 Art 41(1)*).

- ◆ The notice must contain details of (*CTMR 95 r 15(2)*):

  - the application being opposed, *and*

  - the opponent's earlier trade mark.

- ◆ The opposing person must provide a translation of the notice if the notice is not in (*CTMR 09 Art 119*):

  a) an OHIM official language, *or*

  b) 1 of the languages indicated in the application.

➤ The applicant is notified of the opposition only after any deficiencies in the opposition have been remedied (*CTMR 95 r 17*).

- ◆ The OHIM indicates that proceedings will commence 2 months from receipt of the notification unless the application is withdrawn or amended (*CTMR 95 r 18*).

  - For these purposes, the applicant can only amend the application to restrict it to unopposed goods/services.

  - The 2-month period is designed as a 'cooling off' period and can be extended up to 24 months if both parties agree.

- ◆ NB: during the examination of the opposition, each of the parties may be invited by OHIM to file 'observations' on communications from the other party or issued by OHIM (*CTMR 09 Art 42(1)*).

➤ Third parties (ie: other than the applicant and the owner of an earlier trade mark) can make observations to OHIM after publication of the application.

Observations by third parties

➤ Third-party observations may be made by (*CTMR 09 Art 40*):

- ◆ any natural or legal person, *and/or*

- ◆ any group or body representing manufacturers, suppliers, traders or consumers.

  - This is the only way for third parties to object before the grant of registration of a CTM.

  - Observations may only be made in respect of the **absolute** grounds for refusal.

➤ Third-party observations will be copied to the applicant, who may comment on them.

➤ An applicant can resist an opposition, on legal or practical grounds.

Defences to opposition proceedings

➤ An applicant has 4 choices:

a) to amend the application to avoid the opposition (*CTMR 09 Art 43*), *or*

b) if feasible, to negotiate a co-existence agreement with the opponent, *or*

c) to object to the opposition and to argue the opposite of the opponent's claims, *or*

d) where the opposition is based on an earlier registration that was registered over 5 years ago, to request proof of use during the 5 years preceding the date of publication of the application (*CTMR 09 Art 42(2)*).

♦ This can place pressure on an opponent and increase the opponent's costs.

● If an opponent is unable to establish use within the preceding 5 years, the opposition fails.

➤ The main stages of opposition proceedings are summarised below.

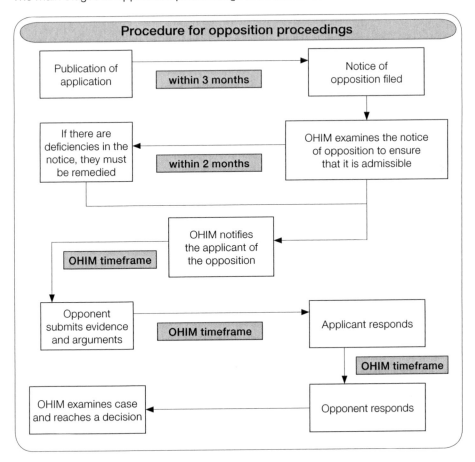

Procedure for opposition proceedings

Publication of application → within 3 months → Notice of opposition filed

OHIM examines the notice of opposition to ensure that it is admissible

If there are deficiencies in the notice, they must be remedied ← within 2 months

OHIM notifies the applicant of the opposition

OHIM timeframe

Opponent submits evidence and arguments → OHIM timeframe → Applicant responds

OHIM timeframe

OHIM examines case and reaches a decision ← Opponent responds

Stage 5	Appeal

➤ Any person adversely affected by an OHIM decision may appeal against it (see *CTMR 94 Arts 58-65*).

➤ The appellant must file:

   ◆ a notice of appeal within 2 months ... *and*

   ◆ grounds of appeal within 4 months,

   ... after notification of OHIM's decision not to register an applicant's mark as a CTM (*CTMR 09 Art 60*).

➤ The notice of appeal is sent to the department within OHIM that made the decision.

   ◆ If the department considers the appeal admissible and well founded, it will rectify its decision.

   ◆ If a decision is not rectified within 1 month, it is automatically remitted to OHIM's Board of Appeal (*CTMR 09 Art 61(2)*).

➤ There is a further right of appeal from a decision of the Board of Appeal to the European Court of Justice (*CTMR 09 Art 65*).

Stage 6	Registration

➤ Once granted, a registration gives the owner rights to prevent the use of similar or identical trade marks by third parties (*CTMR 09 Art 9*).

   ◆ Damages for infringement can be claimed from the date of publication of the registration (*CTMR 09 Art 9(3)*).

➤ The registration of a CTM is renewable every 10 years from the date of filing (*CTMR 94 Arts 46-47*).

   ◆ The owner must pay a renewal fee, as well as a fee for each class of registration (over 3 classes) (*CTMR 95 r 30*).

      ● The fee is doubled in the case of collective marks.

IV Protecting a CTM

➤ The protection afforded by registration of a CTM is very similar to the protection afforded by a UK trade-mark registration (*CTMR 09 Art 9*).

   ◆ An owner may protect a mark by:

     a) taking infringement proceedings (see below), *and/or*

     b) opposing a later registered mark, *and/or*

     c) avoiding revocation of the mark (see section V of this Chapter).

➤ A CTM must be registered before an infringement action can be brought.

➤ The definition of an infringing act under *CTMR 09 Art 9* is equivalent to that under the *TMA* (see Section L of this Chapter).

♦ The criteria for infringement concern use in the course of trade within the EU, and can be summarised as follows:

Article	Mark	Goods/ services	Confusion on part of public?	Reputational damage?
9(1)(a)	➤ Identical	➤ Identical	➤ Not required	➤ Not required
9(1)(b)	➤ Identical	➤ Similar	➤ Required	➤ Not required
9(1)(b)	➤ Similar	➤ Identical/ similar	➤ Required	➤ Not required
9(1)(c)	➤ Identical/ similar	➤ Any (see *Adidas-Salomon* case above).	➤ Not required	➤ Required

● NB: where the claimant must prove reputational damage, the claimant must show that the infringing use takes unfair advantage of, or is detrimental to, a reputation **within the EU**.

➤ If a CTM is infringed in **any** of the EU member states, the owner can take action against the infringer in the CTM courts of:

a) the EU member state in which the **defendant** is domiciled (or, if not domiciled in any EU member state, has an establishment), *or*

b) if the defendant is not domiciled and has no establishment in the EU, the EU member state in which the **claimant** is domiciled (or, if not domiciled in any EU member state, has an establishment), *or*

c) if neither party is domiciled or has an establishment in the EU, Spain, *or*

d) where *Regulation 44/2001/EC* applies, the jurisdiction chosen by the parties (*CTMR 94 Art 94*).

♦ NB: this effectively confers a pan-European jurisdiction on the relevant CTM court.

➤ An owner can also bring an action in a particular EU member state if an infringing act is threatened or committed in that EU member state (*CTMR Art 97(5)* and *98*).

♦ In a case of infringement in multiple territories, the owner can therefore choose to bring proceedings on a territory-by-territory basis or to bring a single action in a CTM court with pan-European jurisdiction.

➤ The international jurisdictional rules are summarised below.

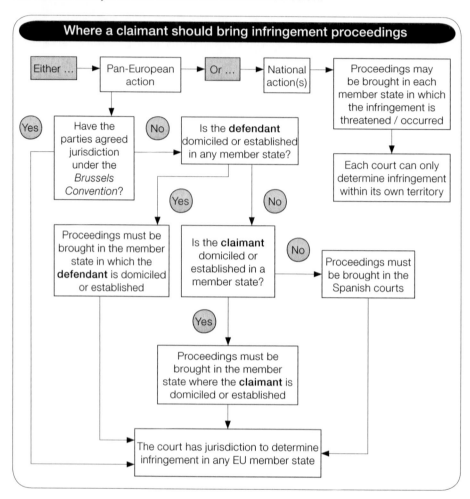

➤ *Directive 2004/48 EC* provides for the harmonisation of EU laws relating to enforcement of intellectual property rights. This is in recognition of their business significance.

◆ The *Directive* was implemented into UK law by the *Intellectual Property (Enforcement, etc.) Regulations 2006*.

➤ The defences are similar to those to infringement of a UK registered trade mark, eg:

◆ use of a mark in accordance with honest practices (*CTMR 09 Art 12*), or

◆ on parallel imports where CTM rights have been 'exhausted' by being marketed in another EU member state (*CTMR 09 Art 13*).

➤ The remedies for infringement are:

◆ an injunction (interim or final), *and/or*

◆ any other remedy available under the law of the EU member state in which the infringing act was threatened or committed (eg: damages or an account of profits, and/or destruction or delivery-up of the offending items) (*CTMR 09 Art 102*).

V   Revocation, invalidity and surrender

A   Revocation

➤ Any person can apply to revoke a CTM.

◆ An application is made to the OHIM, unless an application is by way of counter-claim in infringement proceedings (*CTMR 09 Art 51*).

➤ The grounds for revocation of a CTM are that:

a) there has been no genuine use of the CTM in the EU for 5 consecutive years, *or*

b) the CTM has become a generic name for the relevant type of product/service, *or*

c) as a result of its use, the CTM is liable to mislead the public (*CTMR 09 Art 51(1)*).

➤ Where grounds for revocation only exist in respect of certain goods and services, a CTM is revoked only as regards those goods and services (*CTMR 09 Art 51(2)*).

➤ If a CTM is revoked, it is revoked as a whole. There are no 'parts' of a CTM.

B   Invalidity

➤ Any person can apply to invalidate a CTM if relying on **absolute** grounds, ie: that:

a) a CTM was registered contrary to any of the absolute grounds of refusal under *CTMR 09 Art 7* (unless it has in fact become distinctive through use), *or*

b) the applicant acted in bad faith when filing the application (*CTMR 09 Art 52*).

◆ Eg: the shape of goods that is necessary to obtain a technical result will be refused registration, even if the result achieved could be achieved by other shapes or using a different technical solution (*Lego Juris A/S v OHIM*, Case T-270/06, 12 November 2008 – a case relating to the shape of a Lego brick).

◆ OHIM considers all relevant factors (subjective and objective) (*Chocoladefabrikenn Lindt & Sprungli AG v Franz Hauswirth GmbH*, Case C-529/07).

➤ Only the owner of an earlier right can apply to invalidate the CTM if relying on **relative** grounds, ie:

a) the relative grounds in opposition proceedings (see section III of this Chapter), *or*

b) where the use of the CTM may be prohibited further to another earlier right (eg: copyright, either under EC legislation or national law) (*CTMR 94 Art 52*).

◆ In a case of the same/similar goods/services, all factors that characterise the relationship between the goods/services should be taken into account, eg:

● their respective natures, purposes and methods of use, *and*

● whether they compete with or complement each other (*Commercy AG v OHIM*, Case T-316/07, 22 January 2009)

▪ In *Commercy*, no confusion was found, since the earlier mark related directly to software services, but the later mark related to the use of computer technology only to facilitate other services.

➤ Whether the applicant relies on absolute or relative grounds for invalidity:

◆ An application is made to OHIM, unless it is by way of counter-claim in infringement proceedings (*CTMR 09 Arts 52(1)* and *53(1)*).

◆ The CTM is invalid only in respect of the goods/services for which the relevant ground of invalidity exists (*CTMR 09 Arts 52(3)* and *53(5)*).

➤ Where the owner of an earlier mark has knowingly acquiesced to the use of the CTM for a continuous period of 5 years, that person loses the right (*CTMR 09 Art 54*):

a) to apply for a declaration of invalidity, *and*

b) to oppose the use of a later mark, unless the later mark was applied for in bad faith.

C Surrender

➤ An owner may 'surrender' a CTM in respect of some or all of the goods/services for which it is registered (*CTMR 09 Art 50*).

◆ To 'surrender' means to declare in writing to OHIM that the owner is permanently giving up protection.

● If a CTM has been licensed and the licence has been registered, the owner must prove to OHIM that the licensee has been notified of the intention to surrender.

VI Conversion into national rights

➤ The owner of a CTM can apply under *CTMR 09 Arts 112-114* to convert a CTM into a national trade mark where:

a) a CTM application has been refused, withdrawn or deemed withdrawn, *or*

b) a CTM ceases to have effect (*CTMR 09 Art 112(1)*).

➤ It is not possible to convert to a national trade mark in an EU member state where grounds for revocation or invalidity apply (*CTMR 09 Art 112(2)*).

➤ On conversion, a new national application procedure begins.

◆ The applicant is still entitled to claim the same:

● filing date ... *and/or*

● priority date ... *and/or*

● seniority date (in an EU member state where seniority has been claimed),

... as the CTM (*CTMR 09 Art 112(3)*).

VII Dealing with CTMs

➤ A CTM constitutes personal property (*CTMR 09 Art 16(1)*).

  ◆ Accordingly, a CTM may be:

    a) 'assigned' (ie: ownership of the CTM may be transferred), *or*

    b) 'licensed' (ie: permission to use the CTM may be granted).

➤ To be effective, an assignment of a CTM must be in writing and signed by both parties (*CTMR 09 Art 17(3)*).

  ◆ An assignment of a CTM may relate to some or all of the registered goods/services (*CTMR 09 Art 17(1)*), but can only be assigned in its entirety in geographical terms: the registration cannot be split into separate territories (*CTMR 09 Art 16(1)*).

  ◆ Where a whole 'undertaking' (ie: a whole business) is transferred, a CTM is also transferred, unless there is an agreement to the contrary or circumstances clearly dictate otherwise (*CTMR 09 Art 17(2)*).

➤ A licence of a CTM may:

  a) relate to some or all of the registered goods/services, *and/or*

  b) cover the whole or part of the EU, *and/or*

  c) be exclusive or non-exclusive (*CTMR 09 Art 22(1)*).

    ◆ A non-exclusive licensee of a CTM can only bring infringement proceedings if the owner consents (*CTMR 09 Art 22(3)*).

    ◆ An exclusive licensee can bring proceedings if the owner is given a formal notice and the owner does not bring infringement proceedings within an appropriate period (*CTMR 09 Art 22(3)*).

➤ An assignment or licence should be promptly registered at OHIM, as third parties are, in the absence of actual knowledge of the transaction, not affected by the rights protected by the CTM until the transaction has been registered (*CTMR 09 Art 23(1)*).

  ◆ An assignee cannot invoke any rights arising from registration of the CTM until the assignment has been registered (*CTMR 09 Art 17(6)*).

➤ Either party to the transaction can register the transaction (*CTMR 09 Arts 17(5) and 22(5)*).

N Passing-off

I   Protection of goodwill

➤ An action in passing-off protects the 'goodwill' in a business, product or service.

   ◆ 'Goodwill' is the distinctive feature that makes the customer prefer that business, product or service to those of competitors in the same market.

      ● It can take many forms, including words, designs and the shape of goods.

➤ There is considerable overlap between a mark in relation to which goodwill can subsist, and a mark which is capable of registration as a trade mark.

Passing-off and infringement of registered trade marks

➤ It is therefore important to consider a claim for infringement of a registered trade mark as an alternative to (or in addition to) an action in passing-off.

   ◆ An action in passing-off is invariably more difficult to prove (and is often more costly), as the claimant must prove all 3 necessary elements (see below).

➤ The principal aim of bringing an action in passing-off is to prevent one person from benefiting from the goodwill attaching to the business, product or service of another.

➤ Strictly speaking, a remedy in passing-off is not an intellectual property right, but a remedy in tort.

   ◆ A right of action accrues when a person commits a civil wrong, ie: 'passes off' the business, goods or services of another as his own.

➤ There are generally 3 elements to a passing-off action (*Consorzio del Prosciutto di Parma v Marks & Spencer plc* [1991] RPC 351):

Passing-off – the 3 necessary elements

Element 1 – goodwill – attaching to the claimant's goods or services
Element 2 – misrepresentation – by the defendant leading (or likely to lead) to customer confusion as to the origin of the goods or services, causing ...
Element 3 – damage – to the claimant.

➤ NB: there is an 'extended' form of passing-off with 5 elements. It applies eg: where a class of traders relies on collective goodwill, and is beyond the scope of this Section.

II   Element I – existence of goodwill

➤   There are 6 steps to consider:

Steps	
1	What is meant by 'goodwill'?
2	What is the distinguishing feature?
3	How long has the mark been used?
4	Does goodwill exist in the UK?
5	Are there any limits on the extent of goodwill?
6	Who owns the goodwill?

Step 1	What is meant by 'goodwill'?

➤   'Goodwill' is a legal term of art that has been developed through case law, but has never been precisely defined. Broadly speaking, it is the feature (or combination of features) of a business that makes it more valuable than the sum of its parts and sets it apart from another business. It has been characterised variously as:

◆   something that distinguishes a business, product or service from another business, product or service of the same type, *or*

◆   the reason why customers prefer one particular brand to other brands in a similar product range, *or*

◆   something that provides an identity for a business, product or service, *or*

◆   the 'attractive force' in obtaining financial support (*British Diabetic Association v Diabetic Society Ltd* [1995] 4 All ER 812).

➤   A person's business, products and/or services are referred to below as such person's '***goods***' for short.

Step 2	What is the distinguishing feature?

➤   Goodwill may subsist in a number of features (including those described below), as long as each feature distinguishes a claimant's goods from those of a rival.

1   **Words**

➤   It is important to distinguish between different types of word, because goodwill is more likely to attach to certain types of word than others.

a)   **Invented words**

◆   An invented word does not describe the goods to which it relates.

•   Its purpose is to distinguish the goods from rival goods, so it is relatively easy to prove that goodwill exists in this type of word.

b) Descriptive words

- ◆ These refer to a characteristic or the geographical origin of goods.

- ◆ It is difficult to prove the existence of goodwill in a descriptive word. Many well-known names (such as 'shredded wheat') have failed (*Shredded Wheat Co Ltd v Kellogg (GB) Ltd* (1940) 57 RPC 137).

  - • Goodwill does not necessarily exist in a descriptive word where that word is used together with a brand name. So, in the 'Horlick's Malted Milk' case (*Horlick's Malted Milk Co v Summerskill* [1917] 34 RPC 63), goodwill did not subsist in the words 'malted milk' on their own. The same principle applied to McCain's Oven Chips (*McCain International Ltd v Country Fair Foods Ltd* [1981] RPC 69).

- ◆ Goodwill does not attach to a descriptive word unless it has established a secondary meaning to the customer.

  - • Eg: the word 'Champagne' is associated with the French region, and it also has a secondary meaning to the customer as a drink (*Bollinger v Costa Brava Wine Co Ltd* [1959] 3 All ER 800).

- ◆ The word does not, however, have to lose its original meaning.

  - • In the example above, goodwill still attaches to the word 'Champagne' even though it also denotes the region.

- ◆ For geographical words, once a secondary meaning has been established, it does not matter that the business has moved from its original location. So 'Chartreuse', the name of a liqueur originally made in the Grande Chartreuse monastery, was held to be distinctive even though production had moved to a different location (*Lecouturier v Rey* [1910] AC 262).

c) Business names

- ◆ Goodwill may subsist in a business name. If the name is descriptive, the claimant must show that it has become so distinctive that a substantial proportion of the public associate it with the claimant's business.

d) Authors' names

- ◆ Goodwill may exist in an author's name or *nom de plume*, and such goodwill is usually owned by the author rather than the publisher.

  - • Eg: a prominent politician brought a successful action against a newspaper publisher which had used his name in conjunction with a series of fake diaries. The court held that a significant proportion of the public would be confused into believing that he had written the articles (*Clark v Associated Newspapers Ltd* [1998] RPC 261).

  - • The publisher had also infringed his moral right against false attribution of authorship under *CDPA s 84* – see Section C of this Chapter.

e) **Names of fictional characters**

♦ Although goodwill may exist in a story itself, it does not usually exist in the names of fictional characters. Consequently a company may be able to publish further stories using the same fictional names, even though the author of the original story may not consent.

f) **Titles**

♦ Since copyright does not usually exist in the title of a work, passing-off may be the only potential remedy available to a claimant.

• Eg: the owner of the Daily Mail was able to show goodwill in the title and brought a successful action against the proposed publication of the 'Evening Mail' (*Associated Newspapers v Express Newspapers* [2003] EWHC 1322).

• Nevertheless, it is rare for a title to acquire goodwill, because it is often descriptive of the work's contents and, as mentioned above, it is difficult to acquire goodwill in a descriptive name.

g) **Generic names**

♦ A brand name may become a victim of its own success. Effectively, the word becomes so popular that the public no longer associates it with a particular brand, but with the general type of goods that it represents.

• Eg: the word 'Hoover' eventually lost the goodwill that used to attach to it, because the word became synonymous with vacuum cleaners generally and did not distinguish a particular make.

2 **Devices**

➤ 'Device' is a broad term describing any visual image that distinguishes goods.

♦ Devices include logos, signs, pictures and/or stylised words or letters.

➤ Unlike with words (see above), there are rarely any issues of descriptiveness, and it is therefore relatively easy for goodwill to be found in a device.

3 **Letters and numbers**

➤ The initials of words are often used as business or product names, eg: HMV (His Master's Voice) or EMI (Electrical and Musical Industries).

♦ Initials are likely to be distinctive (and so be part of protectable goodwill), as they hide the descriptive meaning behind the initials. The customer instead associates the initials with the business or goods.

➤ The use of numbers for goods is quite rare, although it is possible. For example, goodwill was found to attach to the perfume '4711'.

♦ Goodwill cannot, however, subsist in the smell of a perfume (*L'Oréal SA v Bellure NV* [2006] EWHC 2355).

4   Get-up

➤ As a basic rule, get-up is the style by which a product is defined and includes various features, eg: the colours, size and shape of goods or their packaging.

◆ Following the 'Jif Lemon' case (*Reckitt & Colman Products Ltd v Borden Inc* [1990] 1 All ER 873), get-up includes any feature of packaging or shape of the article itself, provided that it is distinctive of the origin of the goods.

• In that case, the House of Lords decided that it was possible for a lemon-shaped bottle to amount to protectable goodwill.

▪ It was previously thought that goodwill could not attach to the mere shape of an article.

➤ In practice, it is usually difficult to prove distinctiveness solely from the get-up of a product alone, because the appearance of the article often includes the brand name or logo. For goodwill to exist in the get-up, the customer must be able to distinguish the goods on the basis of the get-up alone.

◆ In the 'Penguin Biscuits' case (*United Biscuits (UK) Ltd v ASDA Stores Ltd* [1997] RPC 513), the owner of the Penguin biscuits brand failed in a claim for registered trade mark infringement of the name Penguin, but succeeded in a passing-off claim on the basis that the defendant had sold 'Puffin' biscuits using very similar packaging to that of the claimant.

➤ Examples of what has, and has not, been held to be distinctive get-up in a product are:

◆ Distinctive:

✓ The Coke bottle.

✓ The Financial Times 'pink' paper.

✓ The grey colour of a Soda Stream bottle.

◆ Not distinctive:

✗ The different colours of Rizla roll-up papers.

✗ The Rubik's Cube.

➤ NB: the degree of copying that is permissible is a question of fact in each case, so it is not possible to derive a general legal principle from a particular case.

◆ Rather, the cases should be used:

• as a guide to establish the types of feature that the courts take into account, *and*

• by way of analogy to support a particular claim.

5 Merchandising features

➤ The name/likeness of a real or fictional character may be applied to goods.

- ◆ The 'Ninja Turtles' case (*Mirage Studios v Counter-Feat Clothing Co Ltd* [1991] FSR 145) marked a change in the approach of the courts to the recognition of goodwill in character merchandising.

  - • It was held that goodwill does not attach to intended (rather than actual) exploitation of characters through merchandising. For goodwill to exist, a mark must acquire a reputation in the merchandising field that distinguishes it from other goods.

  - • If, therefore, a celebrity or the creator of a character has not actually created character-related merchandising products, no goodwill attaches to the character for merchandising purposes.

➤ The name or likeness of a band or sports team can also be applied to merchandise. Vendors have often been sued for selling unlicensed merchandise (eg: *Arsenal Football Club plc v Matthew Reed* [2003] EWHC 2695).

6 Domain names

➤ Goodwill can subsist in a domain name if it is sufficiently distinctive.

- ◆ In a case concerning the domain name phone4u.co.uk, it was held that a lower standard of distinctiveness is required for actionable goodwill to exist compared with that required for registration of the domain name as a trade mark (*Phones 4u Ltd v phone4u.co.uk Internet Ltd* [2006] EWCA Civ 244).

Step 3	How long has the mark been used?

➤ Goodwill needs to be established through use of the mark in business.

- ◆ The period can be as little as 3 weeks (*Stannard v Reay* [1967] RPC 589), but it is a question of fact in each case.

  - • Massive advertising campaigns and use of the internet can establish goodwill very quickly (eg: the games console 'Wii' and the search engine 'Google').

➤ Goodwill can also exist before the start of trading, although activity such as marketing must have created the goodwill (*Glaxo plc v GlaxoWellcome Ltd* [1996] FSR 388).

➤ Goodwill can continue to exist even where a business has ceased trading. This is relevant where the former business resumes trading.

- ◆ Goodwill can, in certain circumstances, survive for a very long time after the activity that generated it. Eg: in the 'Word Cup Willie' case, goodwill arising from the 1966 World Cup had survived despite non-use of a logo for around 36 years (*Jules Rimet Cup Ltd v The Football Association Ltd* [2007] EWHC 2376).

- ◆ A claim cannot, however, succeed where a claimant has totally 'abandoned' a business and the related goodwill (*Sutherland v V2 Music Ltd* [2002] EMLR 28).

Step 4	Does goodwill exist in the UK?

➤ The basic rule is that a person must conduct business within the UK to generate goodwill in the UK.

  ◆ This is because, properly speaking, goodwill attaches to a business (and/or to the goods/services of the business as a whole), rather than to a particular mark.

    ● So a person cannot generate goodwill in a territory without conducting business there.

➤ When applying this principle to foreign businesses that have a presence in the UK, the courts have made differing decisions that are hard to reconcile.

  ◆ There is some confusion in the relevant case law about the extent to which a claimant must actually trade in the UK, rather than merely having established a reputation in the UK (eg: through advertising).

    ● A supplier does not need an established place of business in the UK.

      ● Eg: a French manufacturer was found to have goodwill in the UK by selling cars abroad to English customers who brought the cars into the UK (*Panhard et Levassor SA v Panhard Levassor Motor Co Ltd* (1901) 18 RPC 405).

    ● In the Sheraton restaurant case, a provider of services abroad was able to prevent the establishing of services under the same name in the UK (*Sheraton Corp of America v Sheraton Motels Ltd* [1964] RPC 202).

      ■ There was evidence of actual commercial activity in the UK, as the claimant maintained an office in London through which bookings were taken.

    ● Conversely, the Crazy Horse Saloon of Paris, which was well known in the UK, could not prevent the establishing of a similar-named restaurant here (*Bernadin (Alain) et Cie v Pavilion Properties Ltd* [1967] RPC 581).

      ■ Its reputation was only based on publicity distributed via travel agencies.

    ● In the 'Hit Factory' case, a counter-claim by a US-based business to use a studio name already in use in the UK failed due to the absence of an actual 'trade connection'.

      ■ What was required was a presence of customers in the UK, irrespective of where the goods/services themselves were supplied (*Pete Waterman v CBS United Kingdom Ltd* [1993] EMLR 27).

    ● In several recent cases from other common-law jurisdictions (which have only persuasive authority), the courts have held that goodwill generated through advertising rather than actual trading was sufficient to support a claim in passing-off (eg: the Indian case *WHIRLPOOL Trade Mark* [1997] FSR 905).

Step 5	Are there any limits on the extent of goodwill?

➤ There are 2 possible limits on the extent of goodwill:

   a) Field of activity

     ◆ Goodwill is limited to the field of activity in which the distinguishing feature is used (*Wombles Ltd v Wombles Skips Ltd* [1977] RPC 99).

   b) Geography or locality

     ◆ Goodwill is limited to the topographical area in which the goods are known.

Step 6	Who owns the goodwill?

➤ Even if goodwill subsists, a claimant should ensure that the goodwill is actually owned by the claimant at the time of bringing the claim.

   ◆ It may not always be clear which person has generated goodwill in the first place.

     ● Eg: there may several persons involved in a distribution chain (such as a manufacturer, a distributor and a sub-distributor), in which case it may not be clear who owns the goodwill in the goods.

       ■ In such circumstances, the person recognised by the public as the source of the goods will generally be the owner (*MedDen Inc v Passion for Life Products Ltd* [2001] FSR 30).

       ■ Eg: in *Jules Rimet Cup Ltd v The Football Association Ltd* ([2007] EWHC 2376), the FA was found to own goodwill in the 'World Cup Willie' logo due to the massive publicity for the 1966 World Cup, even though various third parties had produced 'World Cup Willie' merchandise at the time.

     ● Goodwill belongs to a subsidiary company (and not to the parent company) where that subsidiary has built goodwill up through use (*Scandecor Development AB v Scandecor Marketing AB* [1999] FSR 26).

       ■ This applies even where the parent owns the registered trade mark.

     ● Goodwill attaches to the business, rather than its individual employees.

   ◆ Goodwill can be jointly owned.

     ● Eg: 'collective goodwill' can be owned jointly and severally by a class of traders such as producers of Champagne (*J Bollinger SA v Costa Brava Wine Co Ltd* [1960] Ch 262).

     ● One joint owner can sue another where one co-owner's business is prejudiced by customer confusion created by a misrepresentation made by the other co-owner (eg: *Sir Robert McAlpine Ltd v Alfred McAlpine plc* [2004] EWHC 630).

   ◆ Goodwill is personal property that can be disposed of as the owner wishes.

     ● Eg: goodwill can:

       ■ be transferred (eg: sold) to another person, *or*

       ■ pass under a will or by operation of law.

➤ In practice, therefore, it is advisable to ensure that, before the start of a transaction (eg: between supplier and distributor) or a working relationship (eg: between one group company and another, between employer and employee or between joint venturers), ownership of goodwill is dealt with in the relevant contract(s) between the parties.

◆ This should include, where necessary, an 'assignment' (ie: outright transfer of ownership) to the appropriate person – even if simply as a 'belt and braces' confirmation of the ownership of goodwill.

III   Element 2 – misrepresentation causing confusion

➤ There are 3 steps to consider:

Steps	
1	There must have been a misrepresentation ...
2	... made by a trader in the course of trade ...
3	... leading to confusion (in the mind of the customer)

Step 1	There must have been a misrepresentation ...

➤ A misrepresentation is generally a false representation as to the source of goods.

➤ The most common form of misrepresentation is where the defendant passes off his own goods as those of the claimant.

◆ The defendant may instead pass off the claimant's goods as his own, making his own goods more marketable (which is known as 'reverse' or 'inverse' passing-off).

➤ The misrepresentation need not take the form of a specific statement, but can be implied by conduct (eg: through the defendant's use of the claimant's marks).

◆ For example, the use of the name 'Bizplan Building' as a name for a software package was held to be a misrepresentation of 'Business Plan Builder', (*Jian Tools for Sales Inc v Roderick Manhattan Group Ltd* [1995] FSR 924).

➤ The misrepresentation must be operative in the customer's mind at the point of sale (*Bostik Ltd v Sellotape GB Ltd* [1994] RPC 556) or, if there is no actual point of sale (eg: for a free-to-air TV programme), at the time of consumption or use, disregarding any initial misleading impression that is quickly dispelled (*Knight v Beyond Properties Pty Ltd* [2007] EWHC 405).

➤ The misrepresentation need not have been intentional or negligent.

◆ Eg: it is irrelevant whether the misrepresentation was made with an intention to deceive. Even if the statement is literally true, it amounts to a misrepresentation if it creates a false impression and causes confusion as to the source of the goods (*Reddaway v Banham* [1896] AC 199).

Step 2	... made by a trader in the course of trade ...

➤ 'Trader' is defined broadly by the courts and includes charities.

◆ Eg: in *British Diabetic Association v Diabetic Society Ltd* [1995] 4 All ER 812, the claimants, who had charitable status, could bring an action in passing-off.

| Step 3 | ... leading to confusion (in the mind of the customer) |

➤ The claimant must show, on the balance of probabilities, that the misrepresentation leads (or is likely to lead) to confusion in the mind of the customer.

  ◆ This is a question of fact in each case, although the courts usually take into account certain factors (eg: similarities between the marks, the nature of the market for the goods, the parties' positions within that market, and patterns of consumption).

➤ The business making the misrepresentation must usually be engaged in a similar field of activity as the business being misrepresented.

  ◆ What amounts to a similar field of activity is a question of fact in each case.

    ● The internationally famous department store 'Harrods' could not claim passing-off against 'Harrodian School', because there was sufficient difference between the 2 fields of activity to avoid confusion in the mind of the public (*Harrods Ltd v The Harrodian School Ltd* [1996] RPC 697).

    ● The makers of 'Lego Bricks' were able to claim passing-off for the use of the word 'Lego' to sell plastic garden equipment. The court accepted that the similar field of activity was production of plastic objects, so the claimants were able to show that confusion existed in the mind of the public (*Lego Systems A/S v Lego M Lemelstrich Ltd* [1983] FSR 155).

➤ It is important to identify the class of customer for the goods, because the more knowledgeable the customer, the less likely he is to be confused.

  ◆ A substantial proportion of customers must be confused. It is not enough for a small number of customers to be confused.

    ● It is 'ordinary sensible members of the public' who must be confused. The relevant type of customer is more than the 'moron in a hurry' (*Morning Star Cooperative Society Ltd v Express Newspapers Ltd* [1979] FSR 113), but not a sophisticated, well-informed customer (*Sir Robert McAlpine Ltd v Alfred McAlpine plc* [2004] EWHC 630).

  ◆ Many passing-off claims have failed because the claimant could not adduce sufficient evidence of customer confusion.

    ● Customer surveys are often adduced as evidence, but, to be effective, must be conducted fairly and the results must be representative of a relevant cross-section of customers (*Imperial Group plc v Philip Morris Ltd* [1984] RPC 293).

    ● In a case of virtually identical products, it may be enough that confusion is certainly likely to occur, even if there is no evidence of actual confusion (*Kitfix Swallow Group Ltd v Great Gizmos Ltd* [2008] EWHC 2723).

➤ It does not matter that the misrepresentation made about the claimant's goods is in fact true. The key is whether the statement caused confusion.

  ◆ Eg: in comparative advertising, a supplier must make it as clear as possible that there is no connection between the supplier's goods and the competitor's goods.

    ● NB: even a disclaimer as to the status of goods (eg: a notice that a fanzine is 'unofficial') may, on the facts, not be sufficient to provide a defence.

IV   Element 3 – damage

➤ The claimant must show that the claimant has suffered (or is likely to suffer) damage to the claimant's goodwill as a result of the misrepresentation.

➤ There are 3 main heads of damage:

1   Loss of sales

➤ The claimant needs to show actual or likely loss of sales.

◆ Eg: this occurs where a customer buys the defendant's goods believing them to be the claimant's goods.

2   Damage to reputation

➤ A claimant suffers damage reputation in a mark where the defendant's goods are of an inferior quality.

◆ Since the customer believes that the inferior goods are produced by the claimant, the reputation of the claimant is lowered.

➤ The damage may also take the form of an erosion or dilution of distinctiveness, eg: where use of another person's exclusive right to use a mark undermines that person's competitive position in the market.

3   Restriction of chance to expand into a new market

➤ A claimant might be prevented from entering a new market where the defendant attempts to establish an identical or similar mark in that market.

◆ This head is harder to prove, as the claimant is in effect trying to protect a monopoly over a mark or other identifying feature in a potential market.

• Some well-known claimants have, however, been successful in this respect.

▪ Eg: the photographic equipment producer Kodak managed to prevent the use of its name in association with bicycles (*Eastman Photographic Materials Co Ltd v John Griffiths Cycle Corp Ltd* (1898) 15 RPC 105).

◆ To succeed under this head, the claimant usually needs to prove the existence of a fraudulent misrepresentation.

V Defences

➤ Each of the following 4 'defences' is essentially a deficiency in 1 of the 3 elements required for passing-off. They are that the claimant's mark:

◆ is not distinctive, *or*

◆ has ceased to be distinctive and has become generic, *or*

◆ is descriptive and has not acquired a secondary meaning, *or*

◆ has been completely abandoned.

➤ The most common defences are where:

◆ the defendant adds material to distinguish the defendant's mark from that of the claimant so as to prevent the likelihood of confusion, *or*

◆ the defendant uses the defendant's own individual name as a trading name, even if confusion is caused, *or*

● NB: use of the defendant's own name as a trade mark (ie: as a mark applied to a product) will not be a defence, even if honestly used.

◆ the defendant has equal rights to use the mark (eg: where the defendant has been using the mark for some time), *or*

◆ the claimant has actively consented to the defendant's use of the mark, *or*

◆ there is an equitable bar to the claim, eg:

● an 'estoppel' (ie: where the claimant's assertion of rights is inconsistent with some affirmative action by the claimant), *and/or*

● acquiescence by the claimant in the defendant's use of the mark, *and/or*

● delay on the claimant's part in bringing the claim.

▪ In the case of the defences in equity, the court decides whether it is unjust for the claimant to enforce the claimant's rights.

➤ NB: since passing-off need not be intentional, innocence is not a defence (*Gillette UK Ltd v Edenwest Ltd* [1994] RPC 279).

VI Remedies

➤ Remedies for passing-off include:

◆ an injunction (whether interim or final), *and/or*

◆ damages or (alternatively) an account of the defendant's profits, *and/or*

◆ an order for delivery-up or destruction of the infringing articles.

VII Objection to company name under *Companies Act 2006*

➤ Any person (ie: not only a company) has a right under the Companies Act 2006 (‘**CA 2006**’) to object to a company name that another person has registered at Companies House if that company name is:

a) the same as a name in which the objector has goodwill, *or*

b) sufficiently similar to such a name that its use in the UK would be likely to mislead by suggesting a connection between the company and the objector (*CA 2006 s 69(1)*).

➤ This right of objection came into force on 1 October 2008.

➤ The term ‘goodwill’ is not defined, but is stated to include ‘reputation of any description’ (*CA 2006 s 69(7)*).

◆ NB: registration of a company name does not confer any intellectual property rights on the registrant, but the company name may constitute (or contain) a mark in which another person has goodwill and/or which can be registered as a trade mark.

➤ To exercise the right, the objector must apply to a company names adjudicator (*CA 2006 s 69(2)*).

◆ The Secretary of State appoints company names adjudicators, including a Chief Adjudicator (*CA 2006 s 70*).

● The Chief Adjudicator's office is at the Intellectual Property Office in Newport, and is known as the Company Names Tribunal.

◆ The *Company Names Adjudicator Rules 2008* regulate proceedings before company names adjudicators, including the procedural rules for applications, fees, filing of evidence, case management, hearings, timing and costs.

➤ Where the objector can establish either ground for objection, the company has a defence if it can show that the name was adopted legitimately, ie: if (*CA 2006 s 69(4)*):

a) its name was registered before the start of the activities on which the objector relies to show goodwill, *or*

b) it is:

i) operating under the name, *or*

ii) proposing to do so (having incurred substantial start-up costs), *or*

iii) dormant (having formerly operated under the name), *or*

c) its name was registered in the ordinary course of a company-formation business and the company is available to sale to the objector on the standard terms of that business (ie: as an ‘off the shelf’ company), *or*

d) it adopted its name in good faith, *or*

e) the objector's interests are not adversely affected to any significant extent.

➤ NB: each of defences a), b) and c) is defeated if the objector shows that the main aim of the company (or any of its members or directors) in registering the name was (*CA 2006 s 69(5)*):

◆ to obtain money (or other consideration) from the objector, *or*

◆ to prevent the objector from registering the name.

● In effect, the right of objection is aimed at preventing the practice of 'squatting' on a company name by making an opportunistic registration (which is similar to 'cybersquatting' in the context of domain names).

➤ If the applicant is successful, the adjudicator will order the respondent to change its name to one that does not offend (*CA 2006 s 73(1)*).

◆ The adjudicator must publish the decision, giving reasons for it (*CA 2006 s 72*).

● Eg: in December 2008, the Company Names Tribunal ordered a company named 'Coke Cola Limited' to change its name, finding that its use in the UK would be likely to mislead by suggesting a connection between the company and the existing company The Coca-Cola Company Limited.

◆ If the company fails to change its name by the deadline specified in the order, the adjudicator may determine a new name for the company (*CA 2006 s 73(4)*).

➤ The unsuccessful party can appeal the decision to the High Court, whose powers include determination of a new name for the company (*CA 2006 s 74*).

➤ In practice, there are two routes for objecting to a company name:

Objecting to a company name

➤ A legitimate operating company can raise a defence to an objection under *CA 2006 s 69*, so the success of the application will turn on whether there was an 'opportunistic registration' (eg: where someone registers variants of a well-known company name to try to get that company to buy the registrations).

◆ For this reason, the Company Names Tribunal does not consider an objection unless an opportunistic registration is suspected.

➤ Where a company believes that another company's name is too similar to, or 'too like', its own company name (but no opportunistic registration is suspected), the company can make an objection to Companies House.

◆ Companies House has the power, acting on the Secretary of State's behalf, to direct a company to change its name (*CA 2006 s 67*).

● Under Companies House practice at the time of writing, an offending company is offered a limited right of appeal to Companies House. If directed to change its name, it must make the change (and register the change at Companies House) within 12 weeks.

◆ In considering whether one name is 'too like' another, Companies House only takes into account the 'visible appearance or sound' of the names, but not 'external factors' (such as geographic location, trading activities, registered trade marks and likelihood of confusion). Eg: Companies House would accept the registration of 'H & S Consultants (Cardiff) Limited' even if there is an existing 'H & S Consultants Limited'.

● NB: the registration would not prevent the existing company from bringing an action in passing-off.

2 Content Clearance

This Chapter examines:

A   Defamation

*References in this Section are to the Defamation Act 1996 ('**DA 1996**'), unless otherwise stated.*

I   Content clearance – introduction

➤ The right to free speech is the hallmark of a free press, but it can conflict with 3 other fundamental values of society: reputation, decency and the right to a fair trial.

- ◆ The causes of action examined in this Chapter are based on those 3 values:

    - *reputation* – defamation, malicious falsehood and 'false privacy', *and*

    - *decency* – actions relating to offensive material (see Section B), *and*

    - *the right to a fair trial* – prosecution for contempt of court (see Section C).

- ◆ Unsuccessful defendants to such actions face legal and regulatory sanctions, as well as practical and commercial consequences.

- ◆ For this reason, it is usual to 'clear' media content before publication.

➤ Perhaps the most commonly encountered restriction on media freedom is the law of defamation.

II   Defamation generally

➤ Defamation is a tort derived from case law and statute.

- ◆ A claimant must prove that the relevant material is:

    a) defamatory, *and*

    b) reasonably understood to identify the claimant, *and*

    c) published by or on behalf of the defendant.

- ◆ Libel (see below) is also a crime, but will only be prosecuted in extremely serious cases where the public interest requires (*Gleaves v Deakin* [1979] 2 WLR 665).

- ◆ NB: although defamatory content may be a gesture or an image (eg: a waxwork), the content of defamation claim almost invariably consists of words. For the sake of simplicity, such content is described below as a 'statement' or 'words'.

➤ Defamation can be sub-divided into libel and slander:

Libel	Slander
➤ Libel is defamation in writing or some other permanent form (eg: newspapers, magazines and books).	➤ Slander is defamation that occurs by the spoken word or some other transient form.
➤ It also includes words: ◆ broadcast on television or radio (*Broadcasting Act 1990 s 166(1)*), or ◆ spoken in a film (*Youssoupoff v MGM Pictures Ltd* (1934) 50 TLR 581), or ◆ spoken in a theatre production (*Theatres Act 1968 s 4(1)*), or ◆ written in an email (*Western Provident v Norwich Union*, July 4, 1997, unreported). ➤ Libel is actionable *per se* (ie: the claimant does not need to prove actual damage). ◆ Proof of actual damage may, however, lead to a higher award of damages.	➤ Unlike libel, slander generally requires proof of special damage (usually financial loss) before an action can be brought. ➤ Special damage need not be shown where the claimant is imputed: ◆ to be unfit, dishonest or incompetent in the claimant's office, profession or trade, *or* ◆ (if a woman) to be unchaste, *or* ◆ to have committed a criminal offence punishable by imprisonment, *or* ◆ to have an infectious disease.
➤ The status of online material is uncertain. Webpages and newsgroup postings probably constitute libel. 'Chat' posted to an internet bulletin board is more akin to slander than libel (*Smith v ADVFN plc* [2008] EWHC 1797). Internet-phone statements are probably slander.	

➤ The court of first instance is the High Court. County courts do not have jurisdiction.

➤ If the case goes to trial, each party generally has the right to have the action tried by a jury (*Supreme Court Act 1981* ('**SCA 1981**') *s 69(1)*).

◆ This right is exercised in most cases. Trial by jury is favoured by claimants because juries are considered more likely to award a higher level of damages.

➤ The case will be heard by judge alone where:

a) the judge determines that the trial will require prolonged examination of documents or accounts or scientific or local investigation which cannot 'conveniently' be made with a jury (*SCA 1981 s 69(1)*), or

> ➤ In determining 'convenience', the factors that the judge will consider include:
>
> ◆ logistical difficulties in handling documents in a jury box, *and/or*
>
> ◆ whether the number and/or complexity of the documents will substantially increase the duration and expense of the trial, *and/or*
>
> ◆ any risk that the jury may not understand complex documents (*Beta Construction v Channel Four* [1990] 1 WLR 1042).

b) neither party applies for trial by jury (*SCA 1981 s 69(1)*), or

c) there is an application for summary disposal of the claim (*DA 1996 s 8(5)*).

➤ In a jury trial, most issues of fact are decided by a jury.

◆ The judge has the discretion to withdraw all or part of a party's case from the jury if it has no real prospect of success (*Civil Procedure Rules 1998* ('**CPR**') *Pt 24.2*).

III   Approaching defamation problems

➤   In an action for libel or slander, the steps set out below should be considered.

◆   An overriding consideration for the claimant is whether bringing a claim will ultimately exacerbate damage to reputation by giving allegations wider publicity.

Steps	
1	Check the limitation period, jurisdiction and applicable law.
2	Are the words defamatory?
3	Do the words refer to the claimant?
4	Have the words been published?
5	Who can sue?
6	Who can be sued?
7	Are there any defences?
8	What are the remedies?
9	Who will pay the costs?

Step 1	Check the limitation period, jurisdiction and applicable law

1   Limitation period

➤   For material published after 3 September 1996, the limitation period is 1 year from the date of publication (*Limitation Act 1980 s 4A*).

◆   Despite this relatively short period:

●   The court retains a discretion to allow the claim to be brought out of time if it considers it equitable to do so (*Limitation Act 1980 s 32A*).

●   Each repetition of defamatory words gives rise to a new cause of action (*Duke of Brunswick v Harmer* (1849) 14 QB 185) and a fresh limitation period.

■   So the limitation period for internet defamation does not start to run while publication continues, as each 'hit' gives rise to a fresh limitation period (*Loutchansky v Times Newspapers Ltd* [2001] EWCA Civ 1805).

2   Jurisdiction

➤   In international contexts (eg: internet defamation), it is necessary to check whether the English courts will accept jurisdiction.

➤   Put simply, where the defendant is domiciled in England, the English courts will generally accept jurisdiction, subject to the doctrine of *forum non conveniens*.

◆   Under this doctrine, an English court will decline jurisdiction if it is more appropriate for a case to proceed in a foreign court.

3   Applicable law

➤   If an English court accepts jurisdiction, English law generally applies if the forum of jurisdiction and place of publication are the same.

◆   Publication takes place where the defamatory material is heard or read (*Bata v Bata* (1948) WN 366) and, in an internet context, where the website is accessed or downloaded by the user (*Loutchansky v Times Newspapers Ltd* [2001] EWCA Civ 1805).

◆   Defamation claims are excluded from the scope of *Regulation 864/2007/EC* (known as 'Rome II'), which establishes applicable law for other torts.

➤   If the statement is published abroad, there must be a good cause of action under both English law and the law of the country of publication (the rule of 'double actionability' under *Boys v Chaplin* [1971] AC 356).

◆   The detailed rules on applicable law and jurisdiction are beyond the scope of this Section.

Step 2	Are the words defamatory?

➤ There are 4 points to consider:

1   Defamatory meaning

➤ There is no definition of what is 'defamatory'. Juries are commonly directed that a defamatory statement is one that 'tends to lower the claimant in the estimation of right-thinking members of society generally' (*Sim v Stretch* [1936] 2 All ER 1237). Alternative categories are statements that tend:

♦ to expose the claimant to 'hatred, contempt or ridicule', *and/or*

♦ to cause others to 'shun or avoid' the claimant.

● NB: defamation need not involve discredit or moral blame.

♦ In *Berkoff v Burchill* [1997] EMLR 139, a statement that a person was hideously ugly would not make people 'shun or avoid' him, but could expose him to 'ridicule', so was capable of being defamatory.

♦ The claimant need not show that a statement is false, but may need evidence to that effect to rebut a defence of justification (see below).

2   Function of judge and jury

➤ The judge considers whether the statement is **capable** of bearing a defamatory meaning. If so, the jury decides whether they are **actually** defamatory. If not, the matter will be withdrawn from the jury.

➤ What was subjectively meant by the statement is irrelevant.

♦ The jury must look at its whole context and its effect on an ordinary, reasonable and fair-minded reader (*Charleston v News Group Newspapers Ltd* [1995] AC 65).

● The jury must also look at an article as a whole. In *Charleston*, the claimants argued unsuccessfully that an article was defamatory if readers only looked at the headline and illustration.

3   Innuendo

➤ Where appropriate, the court considers 'natural and ordinary' meaning.

♦ In *Lewis v Daily Telegraph* ([1964] AC 234), a news report that police were enquiring into an individual's affairs was held, on the facts, not to be defamatory, as the ordinary reader would not, simply from reading the report, presume that the individual was guilty.

➤ The court may also find that a statement is defamatory by implication, even if not defamatory when taken at face value. This is known as '*innuendo*'.

♦ In *Hayward v Thompson* ([1981] 3 WLR 470), a report of police inquiries was held, on the facts, capable of implying guilt on the suspects' part.

➤ There are 2 types of innuendo:

a) **'True' (or 'legal') innuendo**

- This arises where words are defamatory to persons with special knowledge of information not apparent from the actual words.

  - True innuendo must be specifically pleaded in the statement of claim (*CPR Sch 1, RSC Ord 82 r 3*).

- Examples include:

  - a depiction of a sportsman with a branded bar of chocolate, which is defamatory to those who know that this violates his amateur status (*Tolley v JS Fry & Sons Ltd* [1931] AC 333), *and*

  - a reference to an ordinary word, which is defamatory to those who understand a technical or slang sense of the word (eg: 'snort' – see *Gowrie v Express Newspapers plc*, 1986, unreported).

b) **'False' (or 'popular') innuendo**

- This arises where words give rise to an inference that is discernible without additional information.

  - False innuendo need not be specifically pleaded, but it is best practice for the claimant to plead the alleged meaning.

- In *Hayward* the plain inference was that the suspects were guilty.

4   Ruling on meaning

➤ Either party may apply to court for a ruling at any time on whether the statement is capable of:

a) having any meaning attributed to it in a statement of case, *or*

b) being defamatory of the claimant, *or*

c) bearing any other meaning defamatory of him (*CPR Pt 53 PD 4*).

➤ A ruling is typically sought at a preliminary stage.

- Eg: a defendant may wish to challenge a meaning pleaded in the particulars of claim, or the claimant may wish to challenge a meaning pleaded in the defence).

➤ If the judge rules that the words are not capable of having the meaning pleaded, that meaning and consequential parts of the statement of case are struck out, but the unsuccessful party is usually permitted to amend the statement of case to plead a meaning that they are capable of bearing.

- Where the words are not capable of bearing any defamatory meaning at all, the statement of case is struck out altogether.

Step 3	Do the words refer to the claimant?

➤ Defamation is only actionable if the claimant is identifiable as the person defamed.

   ◆ The words may simply refer to the claimant by name, or may otherwise identify the claimant, eg: by reference to:

      ● a particular post/position that the claimant holds (eg: 'the captain of the England rugby team' or 'the Archbishop of Canterbury'), *or*

      ● a nickname or description of the claimant's physical peculiarities.

➤ The test is whether a reasonable reader would understand the words to refer to the claimant.

   ◆ If the claimant is only identifiable via extrinsic facts that are not widely known, the words must have been communicated to people with knowledge of the facts.

➤ There are 3 common instances of identification issues:

   1 Coincidence

      ➤ A writer can be responsible for defamation even if the writer does not know of the claimant's existence (eg: where a claimant happens to share the same name as the intended target, whether real or fictional – see *Hulton v Jones* [1909] 2 KB 444). This is known as 'unintentional defamation'.

         ◆ The 'offer of amends' defence (see below) mitigates the harshness of this rule for an innocent publication of defamatory words.

      ➤ The principle has not been applied in a 'lookalike' case.

         ◆ In *O'Shea v Mirror Group Newspapers Ltd* ([2001] EMLR 943), it was held that a publisher would bear an impossible burden to check for resemblances, which would be an unjustifiable interference with the right to freedom of expression under the *European Convention on Human Rights Art 10*.

            ● It remains to be seen whether the same approach will be taken in future cases of coincidental naming (or even class defamation – see below).

   2 Class defamation

      ➤ If the words refer to a group (eg: a political party), only an individual who is specifically identifiable may sue.

         ◆ This depends on the group's size and the words used (*Knupffer v London Express Newspapers Ltd* [1944] AC 116).

   3 Companies

      ➤ Directors can sue if it is well known that they control the company.

| Step 4 | Have the words been published? |

➤ Defamation is not actionable unless the words complained of have been 'published' (ie: communicated to one or more third parties).

◆ It can be sufficient for the words to be communicated solely to one person other than the claimant (eg: in a letter), although the extent of publication will ultimately affect the level of damages that may be awarded to the claimant.

● In a case of internet defamation, a very small readership (*Jameel v Dow Jones & Co Inc* [2005] EWCA Civ 75) or a very short posting (*Carrie v Tolkein* [2009] EWHC 29) may be considered too insignificant to found a defamation claim.

➤ There is no restriction on the medium in which the words are communicated (eg: they can be published in writing, spoken, broadcast or transmitted online).

➤ The form of publication is not restricted to factual articles or programmes (eg: songs, fiction and drama can be defamatory).

| Step 5 | Who can sue? |

➤ Individuals can sue, both for financial loss and injury to feelings.

➤ As a general rule, a company (whether trading or, in rare cases, non-trading) can sue, but only for damage to its reputation and goodwill.

◆ A company may sue for libel without pleading or proving special damage, if the publication has a tendency to damage it in the way of business (*Jameel v Wall Street Journal Europe (No. 2)* [2006] UKHL 44).

◆ A company can claim that a publication directed at officers or employees is defamatory of the company, but only if it can be implied that the company condoned, or failed to exercise due care in relation to, their actions.

➤ A minor (ie: a person under 18) and a mental patient may sue, but only if an adult (known as a 'litigation friend') brings the case on the claimant's behalf.

➤ The following persons cannot bring a defamation claim:

◆ *Personal representatives* – as a defamation claim is personal to the deceased.

◆ *Governmental bodies* – eg: a local authority, state-run trading company or political party (although the officers of such body can bring a claim if defamed in person).

◆ *Associations without separate legal personality* – except trade unions and partnerships, who may sue in their own name.

◆ *Spouses* – where the allegation is communicated only to the other spouse.

Step 6	Who can be sued?

➤ A publisher is liable for any publication that:

 ◆ the publisher intends to be published, *or*

 ◆ the publisher can reasonably anticipate will be published, *or*

 ◆ is published due to lack of care on the publisher's part.

➤ Defamation is a strict liability tort.

 ◆ Every repetition of a defamatory statement by a third party gives rise to a fresh cause of action, and each person who repeats it will be liable as though such person were the originator of it (*Cutler v McPhail* [1962] 2 WLR 1135).

➤ Accordingly, every person that in any way participates in, or is responsible for, the publication can potentially be sued.

 ◆ Eg: if a journalist writes a defamatory article which is published in a newspaper, the people who could be sued – ignoring any possible defences – include the journalist, editors, printers, distributors and newsagents.

 ● The company publishing the newspaper can also be sued as a result of its employees' or agents' acts under the principle of vicarious liability.

 ● In practice, a single case may be brought against the publisher, editor and journalist.

 ▪ It is unusual for printers and distributors to be sued, although see *Major v WWR Publications*, *The Times*, January 28, 1993.

 ◆ *DA 1996 s 1* provides a defence in cases of innocent dissemination – see below.

➤ NB: there are restrictions on suing the Crown and foreign states (including diplomats and other state officers), which are beyond the scope of this Section.

Step 7	Are there any defences?

➤ In the majority of defamation cases, the claimant can make out a *prima facie* case and the real issue is whether the defendant can establish a defence.

➤ 8 defences should always be considered. The first 4 are the most common.

A Justification

➤ Once the claimant has proved that the words are defamatory, they are presumed to be false.

➤ 'Justification' requires the defendant to prove that the words in question are factual (rather than a matter of opinion) and are true or substantially true.

 ◆ If successfully pleaded, justification is a complete defence.

➤ The defendant must show that the significant part (the so-called 'sting') of the words is true (*McKenna v Mirror Group Newspapers Ltd* [2006] EWHC 1996).

➤ Immaterial errors will not defeat the defence. There is no need to justify every allegation, as long as the words not proved do not materially injure the claimant's reputation 'having regard to the truth of the remaining charges' (*Defamation Act 1952 s 5*).

◆ In assessing whether errors are material, the jury has to weigh up the seriousness of what has been proved against the seriousness of what has not been proved.

➤ In the particulars of defence, the defendant must state the precise meaning to be attributed to the words that the defendant seeks to justify (known as the '*Lucas-Box* particulars' after the case of *Lucas-Box v News Group Newspapers Ltd* [1986] 1 WLR 147).

◆ If a publication contains 2 or more distinct defamatory statements and the claimant only complains of 1, the defendant cannot assert the truth of the other by way of justification (*Cruise v Express Newspapers plc* [1999] QB 931).

◆ The defendant need not have evidence of justification at the time of service of the defence, but the particulars of justification may be struck out on an interim application if it is clear from disclosure that the requisite evidence will not be forthcoming (*McDonald's Corp v Steel (No 1)* [1995] 3 All ER 615).

➤ Raising a plea of justification can be dangerous. If it is unsuccessfully pleaded, damages are likely to be increased, as the defendant will have repeated the defamation in court and subjected the claimant to cross-examination.

➤ Justification will not be defeated by 'malice' on the part of the defendant (see below), except in the case of an imputation relating to a 'spent' criminal conviction (*Rehabilitation of Offenders Act 1974 s 8(4)*).

B Fair comment

➤ 'Fair comment' relates to opinions that, by their nature, cannot be true or false.

➤ 5 elements must all be shown for the defence to be successfully pleaded:

1 The statement must be one of comment or opinion (as opposed to fact)

➤ There is no straightforward test to differentiate between facts (which have to be justified) and comment (to which this defence applies).

◆ A pure value-judgment is comment (eg: to say that a man committed a crime is a factual allegation; to say that it was disgraceful is comment).

◆ A statement which begins with phrases such as 'it seems to me' is more likely to be comment, although the context may suggest otherwise.

◆ A statement leaving a reader to draw his own conclusions is more likely to be factual. An inference of fact can, however, amount to comment.

◆ A satirical or ironic statement may appear to be factual but, from its context, be understood by a reasonable reader not to be a factual statement (*John v Guardian News & Media Ltd* [2008] EWHC 3066).

2   There must be a sufficient factual basis

➤   The comment must be based on true (or sufficiently true) facts.

◆   It is not necessary for every fact upon which the comment is based to be true, so long as the expression of opinion is fair comment 'having regard to such of the facts alleged or referred to in the words complained of as are proved' (*Defamation Act 1952 s 6*).

◆   This requirement does not apply where the supporting facts are protected by absolute or qualified privilege (see below).

●   Eg: a journalist may comment fairly on a privileged report of court proceedings, even if the evidence before the court turns out to be unfounded.

3   The statement must be objectively fair

➤   To be fair, the comment must be capable of being honestly held.

◆   The test is whether a fair-minded man, even if holding strong, obstinate and/or prejudiced views, could honestly hold the views expressed by the defendant (*Silkin v Beaverbrook Newspapers Ltd* [1958] 2 All ER 516).

●   So, in practice, extreme views can be fair comment.

4   The comment must be on a matter of public interest

➤   Public interest has been widely defined. The matter must affect the public at large in such a way that 'they may be legitimately interested in, or concerned at, what is going on or what may happen to them or others' (*London Artists Ltd v Littler* [1968] 1 WLR 607).

5   The defendant must not have acted with 'malice'

➤   'Malice' on the defendant's part defeats the defence of fair comment. It is for the claimant to assert and prove malice.

◆   In the context of fair comment, 'malice' does not mean spite, animosity or any other intent to injure.

◆   The claimant must show that the defendant did not genuinely hold the view that he expressed (*Brandon v Bower (No. 2)* [2002] QB 737).

●   This is a subjective test, so a defendant who makes a mistake in good faith has not acted with malice.

◆   If the claimant asserts malice, the defendant will be required in disclosure to provide evidence relevant to his state of mind.

●   This will widen the range of documents to be produced.

●   The judge decides whether the evidence is sufficient before handing the case to the jury.

C Absolute privilege

➤ On 'privileged' occasions, freedom of expression takes precedence over the protection of reputation.

   ◆ This is necessary to ensure the proper functioning of the government and the courts, and to protect the contribution by the media and members of the general public to the public interest.

➤ It is a complete defence to a defamation claim to show that a statement is protected by 'absolute privilege'.

   ◆ This is the case even where the defendant was actuated by 'malice' (which defeats 'qualified privilege' – see further below).

➤ Statements protected by absolute privilege include:

   ◆ a statement made in Parliament or select committee (*Bill of Rights 1688 Art 9*), *and*

   ◆ official reports of Parliamentary proceedings (*Parliamentary Papers Act 1840*), *and*

   ◆ a statement made during the course of judicial or quasi-judicial proceedings (ie: proceedings before a court or tribunal, as opposed to administrative proceedings, which are not privileged).

➤ A contemporaneous, fair and accurate report of the proceedings of any UK court or tribunal (or of certain European and international courts and tribunals) is also covered by absolute privilege (*DA 1996 s 14*).

   ◆ Whether a report is published 'contemporaneously' depends on how often the publication is issued.

      • Eg: a daily newspaper should publish a report on the following day, but a monthly magazine could publish it in the next edition.

➤ As a general rule, absolute privilege only attaches to the maker of the statement.

   ◆ If it is subsequently broadcast or reported, the person responsible for publication is not protected by absolute privilege (although the defence of 'qualified privilege' may be available – see below).

      • Note, however, that:

         a) a defamation action will be stayed if Parliamentary privilege prevents a defendant from raising a defence (*Allason v Haines* [1996] EMLR 143), *and*

         b) an MP may waive the protection of privilege where the MP's conduct in Parliamentary proceedings is in issue in defamation proceedings (*DA 1996 s 13).*

D   Qualified privilege

➤ 'Qualified privilege' derives from common law and statute. It falls into 3 categories:

1   General common-law doctrine

➤ Qualified privilege arises where the person making a communication has a legal, social or moral 'duty or interest' to make it to the recipient and the recipient has a corresponding duty or interest to receive it (*Adam v Ward* [1917] AC 309).

♦ Eg: qualified privilege attaches to a reference given by an employer, a response to questioning by police officers, a report of misconduct to public authorities and (in appropriate cases) a business communication.

2   Responsible journalism – *Reynolds* qualified privilege

➤ The leading case of *Reynolds v Times Newspapers Ltd* ([1999] 3 WLR 1010) extended the general common law doctrine to protect the media where a defamatory statement is published on a matter of public interest.

♦ The House of Lords held that the 'duty/interest' test (see 1 above) should be applied, taking into account all the circumstances of the publication. It was recognised that the media have a duty to publish material that is genuinely in the public interest, and that the public have an interest in receiving it.

♦ The court was also prepared to reduce the 'duty/interest' test to an analysis of 'whether the public was entitled to know the particular information'.

➤ In *Reynolds*, the House of Lords identified 10 non-exhaustive factors that a court should consider in determining whether such 'right to know' arises (the weight to be given to each to vary from case to case):

a) the seriousness of the allegation, *and/or*

b) the extent to which the subject-matter is of public concern, *and/or*

c) the source of the information, *and/or*

d) the steps taken to verify the information, *and/or*

e) the status/provenance of the information, *and/or*

f) the urgency/currency of the matter, *and/or*

g) whether comment was sought from the claimant, *and/or*

h) whether the gist of the claimant's side of the story was published, *and/or*

i) the tone/neutrality of the piece, *and/or*

j) the circumstances and timing of the publication.

➤ The following principles emerge from the cases applying *Reynolds*:

- ◆ The duty to publish only arises if a defendant behaves 'responsibly' (*Loutchansky v Times Newspapers Ltd (No. 1)* [2002] QB 321).

- ◆ The duty to publish must exist at the time of publication, and defendants cannot adduce facts in evidence that were not known to them at the time of publication (*Loutchansky*, as above).

- ◆ Neutral reporting (eg: not adopting allegation as fact or 'taking sides') on a matter of public interest is a weighty factor in favour of according privilege (*Galloway v Telegraph Group Ltd* [2006] EWCA Civ 17).

➤ The House of Lords confirmed (by a narrow majority) that the 'duty/interest test' should continue to be applied, but with greater flexibility (*Jameel v Wall Street Journal Europe (No. 2)* [2006] UKHL 44).

➤ In *Jameel*, the House of Lords 'restated' the *Reynolds* principles and took a 3-stage approach to applying them:

- ◆ *Public-interest threshold test* – As a minimum requirement, the article as a whole must concern a matter of public interest.

  - • In the first analysis, there need not be a separate public-interest justification for each item of information, provided that there is one for the 'thrust' of the article.

- ◆ *Justified inclusion test* – The inclusion of a defamatory allegation must be justifiable and serve a public purpose.

  - • Allowance must be made for editorial judgment as to whether its inclusion was necessary. It must form part of the story reported.

  - • The more serious the allegation, the more it should make a real contribution to the public-interest element in the article.

- ◆ *Responsible journalism test* – The final question is whether the defendant behaved fairly and responsibly in gathering (eg: verifying) the information and publishing it (eg: affording opportunity to comment and considering timing of publication), as measured by an objective standard of care.

3   **Reports of proceedings**

➤ *DA 1996 s 15* provides a statutory defence of 'qualified privilege'.

- ◆ The defence covers:

  - • reports of proceedings of certain public bodies and organisations, *and*

  - • related extracts and other documents.

- ◆ See *s 15* for full details and see the table on the next page.

Qualified privilege under *DA 1996 s 15*	
Qualified privilege attaches to ….	
… all items listed in *DA 1996 Sch I Pt I*	… all items listed in *DA 1996 Sch I Pt II*
These include 'fair and accurate' reports of proceedings in public of: a) any legislature, *or* b) any court, *or* c) any public inquiry, *or* d) any international organisation or conference, in each case, anywhere in the world.	These include 'fair and accurate' reports of proceedings of: a) public meetings/sittings in the UK of local authorities and certain other local or statutory bodies in the UK, *or* b) general meetings of UK public companies, *or* c) bona fide public meetings held in any EU member state, *or* d) findings of cultural, trade, sporting and charitable associations in any EU member state. ◆ Press conferences are treated as public meetings for the purposes of *Sch I Pt II* (*Turkington v Times Newspapers Ltd* [2001] 2 AC 227).
➤ NB: none of the *Sch I Pt I* items are subject to 'explanation or contradiction' (see right-hand column).	➤ NB: a defendant cannot claim qualified privilege under *Sch I Pt II* if the claimant can show that the claimant asked the defendant to publish in a suitable manner a reasonable letter or statement 'by way of explanation or contradiction', and that the defendant refused or neglected to do so (*s 15(2)*). ◆ This effectively gives the claimant a limited right of reply.

➤ *DA 1996 s 15(4)* preserves the residual protection at common law for fair and accurate reports of Parliamentary or judicial proceedings.
 	
  ◆ This protection is useful where a report does not satisfy the criteria for:
 	
    • absolute privilege under *s 14*, *or*
 	
    • qualified privilege under *s 15*.	

➤ Qualified privilege is defeated if the defendant was actuated by 'malice'.

  ◆ 'Malice' in this context means that the defendant:

    • did not honestly believe the truth of the statement, *or*

    • was reckless as to whether the statement was true or false.

      ▪ Contrast absolute privilege, which is not defeated by malice.

  ◆ Malice is unlikely to defeat *Reynolds* qualified privilege if the journalist has behaved 'responsibly', especially where suitable steps have been to taken to verify the allegations made.

E Innocent dissemination

➤ The law protects those who play an innocent or subordinate part in distributing material that contains defamatory statements. There are 2 defences:

1 Common-law defence

➤ At common law, the defendant has to show that:

- ◆ he did not know that the material contained the words in question, *and*

- ◆ he did not know that the material was likely to contain the words, *and*

- ◆ his lack of knowledge was not due to his negligence (*Vizetelly v Mudie's Library* [1900] 2 QB 170).

➤ NB: the significance of this defence has been reduced considerably since the statutory defence (see below) came into force.

- ◆ It has nonetheless been an important consideration in internet defamation cases (see below).

2 Statutory defence

➤ The defence under *DA 1996 s 1* does not expressly supersede the common law, but is of greater practical significance, as it effectively provides express protection to defined categories of defendant.

➤ There is in effect a 2-stage test. The defendant must show that:

a) the defendant was not the 'author' (ie: originator), 'editor' (ie: responsible editor') or 'publisher' (ie: commercial publisher) of the statement, *and*

- ◆ This limb of the test protects intermediaries, such as (*s 1(3)*):

  - • printers and distributors of printed material, *and*

  - • producers and distributors of films or sound recordings containing defamatory material, *and*

  - • makers of electronic apparatus used to access or copy defamatory material, *and*

  - • broadcasters of live programmes with no control over the statement made (eg: live phone-ins), *and*

  - • providers of online services (such as the internet) with no control over the content of the material provided.

b) the defendant took reasonable care in relation to its publication, and did not know, and had no reason to believe, that what the defendant did caused or contributed to the publication of a defamatory statement.

- ◆ This limb is only available to a defendant that is not aware that the defendant is disseminating defamatory material (and whose lack of such awareness is not due to negligence).

➤ Innocent dissemination is of particular relevance to internet service providers ('*ISPs*'):

Innocent dissemination via the internet

➤ In *Godfrey v Demon Internet Ltd* [2001] QB 201 (the first case on the *s 1* defence), it was held that:

- ◆ the ISP was a 'publisher' at common law of subscribers' postings to its newsgroup service, *and*

- ◆ it was *not* a 'publisher' for the purposes of the *s 1* defence, but could not satisfy the additional requirements of the defence once it had been informed of the defamatory content of the posting and then failed to remove it for a period of 10 days.

➤ If, however, an ISP performs 'no more than a passive role' in facilitating postings on the internet, then (subject to the question of its actual or constructive awareness that defamatory content has been posted):

- ◆ it is *not* a 'publisher' at common law, *and*

- ◆ it can rely on the *s 1* defence, *and*

- ◆ it can also rely on the 'mere conduit', 'caching' and 'hosting' defences under the *Electronic Commerce (EC Directive) Regulations 2002 rr 17-19 (Bunt v Tilley* [2006] EWHC 407).

  - • The *Bunt* case absolves an ISP from the need to monitor postings on a routine basis (which would be an intolerable burden).

  - • The e-commerce defences provide a similar immunity, which is lost (for 'caching' and 'hosting') if the ISP has actual or constructive knowledge of the illegal information and/or (on becoming aware) fails to act 'expeditiously' in removing, or disabling access to, it.

➤ NB: it is not clear, at the time of writing, whether an ISP or website operator might be liable as a 'publisher' where customers use its hyperlinks or search-engine functions to access defamatory material.

- ◆ The liberal tendency of the decided cases suggests that the ISP or website operator would not generally be liable.

➤ Various points of best practice emerge for ISPs and website operators:

Minimising liability for online services

➤ An ISP or website operator should:

- ◆ maintain a passive role where community content (eg: 'social networking' content) is provided online, *and*

- ◆ not initiate transmission of the content or select the recipients, *and*

- ◆ not contribute material or select, modify or assert editorial control over content transmitted, in case it becomes an 'author' or 'editor', so defeating the *s 1(1)* defence, *and*

- ◆ operate a suitable 'notice-and-take-down' procedure (ie: removing any allegedly defamatory material as soon as it is put on notice that it is allowing access to defamatory material), *and*

- ◆ remove defamatory material from online archives (or, in borderline cases, post warnings about the possible falsity of the content), *and*

- ◆ include the right to remove content in the website's terms of use, taking into account consumer-legislation requirements to act reasonably.

F Consent to publication

➤ It is a complete defence for the defendant to prove that the claimant consented (whether expressly or impliedly) to publication of a defamatory statement.

   ◆ The proof must be clear and unequivocal.

G Release/accord and satisfaction

➤ It is a complete defence for the defendant to prove that a claim has been settled by agreement in circumstances where a claimant attempts to pursue a claim despite such agreement.

   ◆ This is known as:

   ● 'release' where the agreement is by way of deed, *or*

   ● 'accord and satisfaction' where the claimant surrenders his claim in return for consideration provided by the defendant (eg: publication of an apology and/or payment of damages and costs).

H Offer of amends

➤ *DA 1996 ss 2-4* sets out an 'offer of amends' procedure.

   ◆ This operates as a means of settling the dispute (if the offer is accepted) or as a defence (if the offer is rejected).

   ● The procedure is essentially a damage-limitation exercise, rather than a substantive defence.

➤ An 'offer of amends' is a written offer (which must be expressed to be made under *DA 1996 s 2*) (*s 2(4)*):

a) to make a suitable correction of the statement complained of and a sufficient apology, *and*

b) to publish the correction and apology in a manner that is reasonable and practicable in the circumstances, *and*

c) to pay the claimant such compensation (if any) and such costs as are agreed or determined by the court to be payable.

   ◆ The offer must be made before serving a defence (*s 2(5)*).

   ● Although the statute does not specify an injunction as a remedy, the court has a general power to grant an injunction against repetition and a defendant will often volunteer an undertaking not to repeat the statement complained of.

➤ The offer may be made in relation to the statement as a whole or only in relation to part of it. An offer as to part is a 'qualified offer' (*s 2(2)*), which must be stated as such and must specify the defamatory meaning to which the offer relates (*s 2(3)*).

   ◆ A qualified offer only operates as a defence in relation to the defamatory meaning specified in the offer.

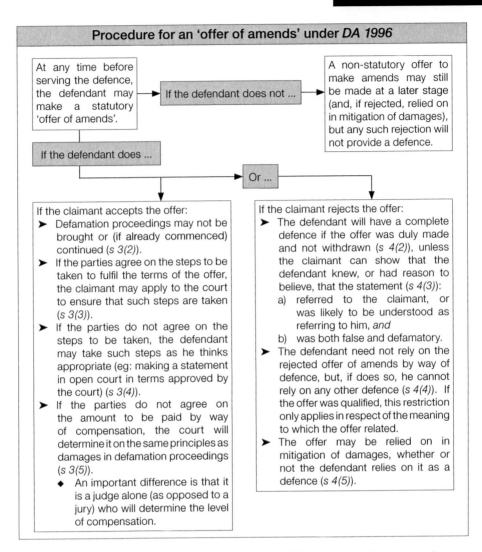

Procedure for an 'offer of amends' under *DA 1996*

At any time before serving the defence, the defendant may make a statutory 'offer of amends'.

If the defendant does not ...

A non-statutory offer to make amends may still be made at a later stage (and, if rejected, relied on in mitigation of damages), but any such rejection will not provide a defence.

If the defendant does ...

Or ...

If the claimant accepts the offer:
➤ Defamation proceedings may not be brought or (if already commenced) continued (*s 3(2)*).
➤ If the parties agree on the steps to be taken to fulfil the terms of the offer, the claimant may apply to the court to ensure that such steps are taken (*s 3(3)*).
➤ If the parties do not agree on the steps to be taken, the defendant may take such steps as he thinks appropriate (eg: making a statement in open court in terms approved by the court) (*s 3(4)*).
➤ If the parties do not agree on the amount to be paid by way of compensation, the court will determine it on the same principles as damages in defamation proceedings (*s 3(5)*).
  ◆ An important difference is that it is a judge alone (as opposed to a jury) who will determine the level of compensation.

If the claimant rejects the offer:
➤ The defendant will have a complete defence if the offer was duly made and not withdrawn (*s 4(2)*), unless the claimant can show that the defendant knew, or had reason to believe, that the statement (*s 4(3)*):
  a) referred to the claimant, or was likely to be understood as referring to him, *and*
  b) was both false and defamatory.
➤ The defendant need not rely on the rejected offer of amends by way of defence, but, if does so, he cannot rely on any other defence (*s 4(4)*). If the offer was qualified, this restriction only applies in respect of the meaning to which the offer related.
➤ The offer may be relied on in mitigation of damages, whether or not the defendant relies on it as a defence (*s 4(5)*).

➤ The 'offer of amends' defence may be appropriate if the defendant has a weak case or wishes to 'cut his losses'.

➤ The practical alternative in such circumstances is to try to settle the dispute. The 2 most commonly encountered methods of settling a defamation dispute are a negotiated settlement and the procedure under *CPR Pt 36*.

Negotiated settlement

➤ The aim of a negotiated settlement is to draw up a settlement agreement. Normal contractual principles apply.

  ◆ The settlement process can involve, with the court's permission, the reading of an agreed statement in open court.

  ◆ If money is paid into court in full settlement, either party may apply for leave to make a unilateral statement in open court.

> ## Part 36 offer/payment
>
> ➤ The defendant could make a *Part 36* offer/payment under *CPR Pt 36*.
>
> ◆ It will be hard to assess the appropriate amount to pay into court given the unpredictable size of any award of damages, so it is usual to seek counsel's advice and to try to assess the claimant's position during any settlement negotiations that precede the *Part 36* offer.
>
> ➤ If at trial the claimant fails to better the *Part 36* payment, the claimant usually has to pay the defendant's costs incurred after the expiry of the normal 21-day time-limit for acceptance (*CPR Pt 36.14*) – a major deterrent in a defamation action.
>
> ◆ Where a defendant sues 2 or more defendants and accepts a *Part 36* payment from one but not all of them, then, in any action that goes ahead, the claimant's recovery of damages are capped at the amount by which any award exceeds such payment and the claimant is not generally entitled to his costs of the claim unless there is such an excess.
>
> ➤ The procedural aspects of *Part 36* are beyond the scope of this Section.

Step 8 | What are the remedies?

➤ There are 2 main remedies:

1 **Damages**

> ➤ The purpose of damages is generally to compensate the claimant, rather than to punish the defendant. Compensatory damages fall into 2 categories:
>
> ◆ *general damages* – which vindicate the claimant and compensate for injury to reputation and (if an individual) to feelings, *and*
>
> ◆ *special damages* – which generally compensate for any financial loss suffered as a result of the defamation (eg: loss of earnings).
>
> • If, however, a claimant proves that a defendant deliberately or recklessly defamed him on the basis that the commercial benefit would outweigh any damages payable, punitive or exemplary damages may be awarded (*Cassell & Co Ltd v Broome* [1972] AC 1027).
>
> ➤ The amounts awarded range from nominal to substantial sums.
>
> ➤ Since 1991, the Court of Appeal has had the power under the *Courts and Legal Services Act 1991 s 8* to substitute its own award of damages without having to order a retrial.
>
> ◆ In *John v Mirror Group Newspapers Ltd* ([1997] QB 586), the Court of Appeal reduced compensatory damages from £75,000 to £25,000 and exemplary damages from £275,000 to £50,000.

➤ As a result of the *John* case, juries can be addressed by counsel and the judge on quantum and can be referred to awards in personal injury cases.

♦ The jury are not obliged to attempt direct comparisons. If they do, the award of damages may be relatively low, as awards for serious personal injuries are comparatively low (eg: around £30,000 for loss of sight in one eye). Damages will only in exceptional cases exceed the maximum personal injury award (ie: around £200,000 for quadriplegia) (*Jones v Pollard* [1997] EMLR 233).

♦ NB: juries should not be informed of previous jury awards (*John*).

➤ Quantum is still difficult to estimate. The relevant factors are as follows:

Quantum of defamation damages – factors

➤ *Seriousness of the allegation* – The more closely a statement relates to the claimant's 'integrity, professional reputation, honour, courage, loyalty and the core attributes of his personality', the more serious the damage is likely to be (*John*, as above).

➤ *Size of readership* – A local newspaper is likely to damage reputation less than a newspaper with national circulation.

♦ A large membership of a 'social networking' website or high level of 'hits' may increase damages in an internet defamation case (*Firsht v Raphael* [2008] EWHC 1781).

➤ *Special damage* – Damages will be increased if the defamation caused the claimant 'special damage' (eg: financial loss or loss of opportunity).

➤ *Aggravating factors* – Damages are 'aggravated' (increased) by:

a) a malicious motive or improper conduct on the defendant's part (*Keith-Smith v Williams* [2006] EWHC 860), *and/or*

b) an unsuccessful plea of justification (even if in good faith) or injurious conduct on the defendant's part during litigation.

➤ *Mitigating factors* – Damages are 'mitigated' (reduced) by:

a) responsible conduct on the defendant's part (eg: prompt publication of an apology), *and/or*

b) there being an element of truth in the allegations, even if insufficient to establish justification, *and/or*

c) the claimant's bad reputation or improper conduct, *and/or*

d) in practical (even if not legal) terms, a favourable impression made by the defendant on the jury at trial, *and/or*

e) the 'clearing' of the claimant's name or recovery of damages in previous defamation actions relating to similar allegations.

---

2 Injunctions

- ➤ A claimant may seek an interim or permanent injunction restraining the defendant from publishing/repeating the statement or similar imputations.

  - ◆ A defendant who breaches the injunction can be fined or imprisoned for contempt of court.

- ➤ Interim injunctions are rarely granted in defamation cases, as they run contrary to the right to freedom of expression (*Fraser v Evans* [1969] 1 QB 349).

  - ◆ NB: the general principles for interim injunctions set out in *American Cyanamid v Ethicon* ([1975] AC 396) do not apply in defamation cases.

- ➤ Case law has set minimum criteria for obtaining an interim injunction:

  - ◆ the statement must be unarguably defamatory, *and*

  - ◆ there must be evidence that the defendant intends to publish or to repeat the defamatory statement or similar imputations, *and*

  - ◆ where a defendant states an intention to rely on a substantive defence, such defence must be unarguable or clearly raised in bad faith.

- ➤ If the defendant intends to rely on a defence of justification at trial, the court will not grant an interim injunction unless the words are so manifestly untrue that the defence will fail (*Bonnard v Perryman* [1891] 2 Ch 269).

  - ◆ There can be exceptions to this rule, but neither improper conduct on the defendant's part nor potential damage to the claimant will normally constitute such an exception (*Holley v Smyth* [1998] QB 726).

    - • The same test of manifest untruth applies to facts supporting fair comment (*Fraser v Evans* [1969] 1 QB 349).

    - • If the defendant intends to rely on qualified privilege at trial, the claimant must show overriding evidence of express malice to obtain an injunction (*Herbage v Pressdram Ltd* [1984] 2 All ER 769).

- ➤ The difficulty of obtaining interim injunctions in defamation actions has led claimants to apply instead for interim injunctions restraining breach of contract or breach of confidence (where arguable on the same facts).

➤ Unless the claim is disposed of summarily (see section IV below), the court cannot order a defendant to apologise.

Apologies

- ➤ If the case is settled before trial (as most cases are), it is a common provision of the settlement agreement that the defendant make an apology, often in the form of an agreed statement to be read out in open court.

- ➤ The Press Complaints Commission's *Code of Practice* requires newspapers and magazines that are party to defamation actions to publish a fair and accurate report of the outcome and to publish an apology where appropriate (*para 1* of the *Code*).

Step 9	Who will pay the costs?

➤ Defamation cases are notoriously expensive.

 ◆ A jury trial is likely to last longer than a case heard by judge alone.

   ● A jury trial can be further protracted by extensive examination and cross-examination of witnesses.

 ◆ A conditional fee agreement can lead to a large uplift in costs (eg: *King v Telegraph Group Ltd (Costs)*, 2 December 2005, where success fees of 100% (solicitors) and 67% (counsel) were held appropriate for prospects of success estimated at 60%).

➤ Costs are a therefore a significant consideration, especially as:

 ◆ in many defamation actions, the costs exceed the damages obtained, *and*

 ◆ legal aid is not available to claimants or defendants in defamation cases.

➤ As a general rule, the winner pays the loser's costs (*CPR Pt 44.3(2)*). Note, however:

 ◆ The winner may not recover all of its costs after assessment (eg: in the *King* case, the amount allowed after detailed assessment of costs was around 65% of the claimant's bill, since the claimant's base costs were disproportionate).

 ◆ The court may deprive the winning party of part of its costs where it raises issues that do not succeed, or of all of its costs where its conduct has been improper.

 ◆ Where the claimant fails to better a *Part 36* offer/payment, the court will usually order that the claimant should bear its costs incurred after the latest date on which the claimant could, without need for court permission, have accepted the offer.

 ◆ Where nominal damages are awarded (eg: because the defamation is trivial or there are substantial mitigating factors), the court will:

   ● make no order as to costs (ie: each side bears its own costs), *or*

   ● exceptionally, order the claimant to pay a contribution to the defendant's costs (*Grobbelaar v News Group Newspapers Ltd* [2002] UKHL 40).

IV   Summary disposal of a defamation claim

➤ Under *DA 1996 s 8* either party may apply for summary disposal of the claim. Alternatively, the court may invoke the procedure of its own initiative. The court may:

 ◆ dismiss the claim if satisfied that the claim has no realistic prospect of success and there is no reason why it should proceed to full trial (*s 8(2)*), *or*

 ◆ give judgment for the claimant and grant summary relief if satisfied that (*s 8(3)*):

   a) there is no defence to the claim which has a realistic prospect of success and there is no other reason why the claim should proceed to full trial, *and*

   b) (where the defendant or court has invoked the procedure) summary relief will adequately compensate the claimant for the wrong he has suffered.

249

➤ If judgment is given for the claimant, the court may (*s 9(1)*):

- ◆ make a declaration that the statement was defamatory, *and/or*

- ◆ order publication of a suitable correction and apology, *and/or*

- ◆ award damages of up to £10,000, *and/or*

- ◆ grant an injunction against publishing or repeating the defamatory words.

  - • NB: the court hearing is without a jury (*s 8(5)*).

➤ The *s 8* procedure does not supersede the court's general power under *CPR Pt 24* to grant summary judgment if a party's statement of case has no realistic prospect of success and there is no other reason why the claim should be tried (*CPR Pt 24.2*).

- ◆ The regimes under *s 8* and *CPR Pt 24* run in parallel. The 2 main differences are:

  - a) the court can dispose of all or any part of a party's case under *Pt 24*, but only the case in its entirety under *s 8*, *and*

  - b) if a claimant obtains summary judgment on liability under *Pt 24*, the jury assesses damages in the usual way without limit (unlike the *DA 1996* £10,000 limit).

➤ Neither regime overrides the court's general power under *CPR Pt 3.4* to strike out where a party's statement of case discloses no reasonable case or is an abuse of process or where a party has failed to comply with a rule, practice or court order.

- ◆ *CPR Pt 3.4* assists a party where the other's statement of case has a real prospect of success, but ought to be struck out on procedural grounds.

V   Clearing potentially defamatory content

➤ In practice, media editors should 'clear' potentially defamatory content (and edit it as necessary) before publication. The steps to be considered include the following:

Clearance checklist

➤ Get the facts straight.
- ◆ Ensure that any allegations are true and can be proved in a court of law.
  - • Remember that it is for the defendant to prove the truth of the words when raising a defence of justification – not for the claimant to prove their falsity.
- ◆ Ensure that there are reliable witnesses and satisfactory documentary evidence before publication.

➤ Do not repeat an unsubstantiated rumour or quote defamatory allegations made by others.
- ◆ Stating 'allegedly' and/or presenting 'both sides of the story' is not necessarily enough to prevent a libel action.

➤ Do not rely on literal meaning.
- ◆ Check whether the words are or might be defamatory by implication.

➤ Do not exaggerate.
- ◆ Choose words carefully, and avoid hyperbole.
- ◆ Avoid unjustifiable inferences – even if drawn from true facts.

VI   Malicious falsehood

➤ The law of malicious falsehood (or 'injurious falsehood') can provide a separate cause of action in tort where a false statement has been made about someone which, although it causes damage, is not defamatory.

➤ To bring a successful claim, the claimant must prove 5 elements:

1   A false statement …

➤ The statement may be oral or written, and the burden is on the claimant to prove that it is false (unlike in defamation, where the words are presumed to be false and the burden is on the defendant to show that they are true).

◆ In *Kaye v Robertson* ([1991] FSR 62), the claimant won where a newspaper reported, untruthfully, that he had consented to an exclusive interview.

◆ As with defamation, the meaning of words may be disputed. The rules of construction and procedure are similar to those in defamation.

2   Published to a third party …

➤ As with defamation, the statement must be published.

3   Referring to the claimant (or to the claimant's goods or property) …

➤ As with defamation, an element of identification is required (albeit wider).

4   Made with 'malice' …

➤ A defendant acts with 'malice' if the defendant knew that the statement was false or was reckless as to whether it was true or false.

5   Causing (or likely to cause) damage to the claimant

➤ Damage must be the 'direct and natural result' of publication (*Kaye v Robertson* [1991] FSR 62).

➤ It must generally be shown that publication caused (or is likely to cause) 'special damage' to the claimant (ie: financial loss or damage capable of being estimated in monetary terms). Note, however:

◆ In appropriate cases, damages are awarded to compensate for injury to feelings (*Khodaparast v Shad* [2000] 1 WLR 618).

◆ Proof of special damage is not required if the statement is 'calculated':

• to cause pecuniary damage and is published in writing or other permanent form (ie: akin to libel rather than slander), *or*

• to cause pecuniary damage to the claimant in respect of any office, profession, calling, trade or business held or carried on by him at the time of publication (*Defamation Act 1952 s 3(1)*) (like slander actionable *per se*).

■ 'Calculated' in this context simply means 'likely' (*Stewart-Brady v Express Newspapers plc* [1997] EMLR 92).

➤ The cause of action generally protects a claimant's commercial interests.

♦ In *Grappelli v Derek Block (Holdings) Ltd* ([1981] 1 WLR 822), the well-known violinist Stéphane Grappelli succeeded in his claim in malicious falsehood, but failed in his claim in defamation.

● His concert promoters stated (falsely) that he was so ill that he might never perform again.

■ The statement did not lower his reputation, but did damage his career.

➤ It is often possible to plead defamation or malicious falsehood on the same facts.

♦ To do so might imply a weakness in the defamation claim as regards proof of defamatory meaning.

➤ Malicious falsehood has the following disadvantages and advantages for a claimant:

Malicious falsehood v defamation	
Disadvantages for a claimant	**Advantages for a claimant**
✘ The claimant must prove the falsity of the statement.	✓ There is no need to prove any loss of reputation.
✘ The claimant must prove malice.	✓ Personal representatives can bring an action after the death of the complainant, as malicious falsehood is a property tort.
✘ The claimant must normally prove special damage.	
✘ There is no right to trial by jury, so the amount of any award of damages is likely to be lower than in a defamation claim.	✓ There is greater likelihood of obtaining an interim injunction to prevent publication or repetition of the statement (*Kaye v Robertson* [1991] FSR 62).
	✓ Trial by judge alone is shorter (so less expensive) and more predictable than trial by jury.
	♦ NB: legal aid is no longer available for malicious falsehood, so there is now no difference in the availability of public funding (see the *Access to Justice Act 1999 Sch 2 para 1(f)*).

♦ Overall, defamation is usually more advantageous to the claimant, unless there is a specific reason to bring a claim in malicious falsehood.

● The most common reason to bring a claim in malicious falsehood (rather than defamation) is an inability to prove loss of reputation.

VII 'False privacy'

NB: the law described in this section VII is still developing at the time of writing.

➤ It appears that an alternative means of redress for false statements may be provided by an action in what has been described by lawyers (but not with judicial authority) as 'false privacy'.

◆ This action is simply an application of the action for misuse of private information, in which a claimant must show:

a) a reasonable expectation of privacy (the 'threshold test'), *and*

b) that the right to privacy should take precedence over freedom of expression (the 'balancing exercise').

• See Section J of Chapter 1.

➤ In 'classical' cases of breach of confidence, false information cannot be regarded as confidential (*Interbrew SA v Financial Times Ltd* [2002] EMLR 446).

➤ In a case of misuse of private information, however, the question is whether the information is **private**, not whether it is true or false, and the truth or falsity of the information is irrelevant (*McKennitt v Ash* [2006] EWCA Civ 1714).

◆ The truth or falsity of the information may be relevant to an assessment of whether freedom of expression should outweigh protection of privacy (under the 'balancing exercise' to be conducted as part of the 2-stage test in such a case), but, even if the information is shown to be false, that does not defeat a claim for misuse of private information (*McKennitt*, as above).

• Eg: in *P, Q and R v Quigley* ([2008] EWHC 1051), the defendant was restrained from publishing online a 'novella' showing claimants P and Q (thinly disguised) as participating in wholly fictitious sexual activities.

▪ The expectation of privacy was found to be 'plainly engaged'.

▪ The balancing exercise came down clearly in favour of restricting publication, as there was 'no conceivable public interest in making such scurrilous allegations' (per Eady J).

• Note, however, that the damages arising from false allegations about private information may not be significant if those allegations are not also defamatory.

▪ Eg: in *Firsht v Raphael* ([2008] EWHC 1781), the damages awarded for misuse of private information through the creation of a malicious profile page on Facebook were relatively modest in comparison with the damages awarded for the defamatory material posted on the page.

➤ It is unclear which rules should be applied in an application for an injunction that is brought on both privacy and defamation grounds (*RST v UVW* [2009] EWHC 2448).

➤ It appears that a claimant can bring a claim for misuse of private information even if the claimant has lost a defamation action (see *H v Tomlinson* [2008] EWCA Civ 1258).

B Offensive material

I	Civil regulation
II	Obscenity
III	Possession of extreme pornography
IV	Protection of children
V	Inciting racial hatred
VI	Inciting hatred on grounds of religion or sexual orientation

I Civil regulation

➤ Various sanctions can be imposed for publication of material that offends against public standards of propriety.

◆ The term 'offensive material' is not a legal term of art, but is a convenient catch-all for the different types of offensive or harmful material considered in this Section.

● In determining whether media content is offensive, it is necessary to consider both the criminal law and the civil system of media regulation. The criminal offences that relate to offensive material are examined in sections II-VI below.

➤ Various organisations regulate offensive material in the media industry.

Organisation	Regulation
Office of Communications (Ofcom)	➤ Ofcom is the independent regulator for the UK communications sector, with responsibilities for television, radio, telecommunications and wireless services.
	➤ One of Ofcom's duties is to provide 'adequate protection for audiences against offensive or harmful material'.
	➤ As required under the *Communications Act 2003* and *Broadcasting Act 1996*, Ofcom has drawn up the *Broadcasting Code*. The second (and current) version came into effect on 16 December 2009 and applies to TV and radio programmes broadcast on or after that date, including repeats.
	➤ Certain sections of the *Broadcasting Code* apply to offensive material. Eg: broadcasters must:
	◆ not broadcast material that might seriously impair the physical, mental or moral development of under-18s, and must exclude content unsuitable for under-15s from TV programmes broadcast before the 'watershed' (which is, for most TV services, 9 p.m., with the exclusion period resuming again at 5.30 a.m.) (*s 1*), *and*
	◆ provide adequate protection for members of the public from the inclusion in programmes of harmful and/or offensive material (of which non-exhaustive illustrations are given) (*s 2*), *and*
	◆ exclude material likely to encourage or incite the commission of crime or to lead to disorder (*s 3*), *and*
	◆ ensure that programmes do not involve any abusive treatment of religious views and beliefs (*s 4*).

Organisation	Regulation
Ofcom (cont.)	➤ Ofcom has the power to impose statutory sanctions for non-compliance with the *Broadcasting Code*, including: ◆ directing the broadcaster not to repeat a programme or to broadcast a correction or Ofcom's findings, *and/or* ◆ imposing a fine (subject to prescribed maxima, eg: a maximum of £250,000 in the case of the BBC or S4C), *and/or* ◆ shortening a licence period (in certain circumstances) or revoking a licence (not applicable to the BBC, S4C or Channel 4).
British Broadcasting Corporation (BBC)	➤ The BBC has preserved some self-regulatory functions, but the programme standards set by Ofcom apply. ➤ The BBC imposes strict *Editorial Guidelines* on producers, including guidelines on offensive material (*s 8*). It operates a 'watershed' policy for TV, but has more flexible scheduling for radio.
Advertising Standards Authority (ASA) **Broadcast Committee of Advertising Practice (BCAP)** **and** **Committee of Advertising Practice (CAP)**	➤ The ASA is the independent body set up by the advertising industry to oversee the advertising self-regulatory system. ◆ BCAP regulates the content of TV and radio commercials. • CAP regulates the non-broadcast advertising industry. ➤ The ASA and BCAP exercise powers contracted out by Ofcom to set and enforce standards under the *Communications Act 2003* s 319. ➤ The ASA administers codes of conduct for both broadcast and non-broadcast advertising. Each code contains restrictions on the inclusion of offensive material, eg: ◆ *BCAP Television Advertising Standards Code* • Adverts must not cause serious or widespread offence against generally accepted moral, social or cultural standards or offend against public feeling (*s 6*). ◆ *BCAP Radio Advertising Standards Code* • Each radio station must take account of the sensitivities of all sections of its audience when deciding on the acceptability or scheduling of adverts (*s 9*). ◆ *British Code of Advertising, Sales Promotion and Direct Marketing* (known as the '**CAP Code**') (ie: the non-broadcast code) • Marketing communications should contain nothing that is likely to cause serious or widespread offence. Particular care should be taken to avoid causing offence on the grounds of race, religion, sex, sexual orientation or disability (*r 5.1*). ◆ See Chapter 5 Section A for further details of these *Codes*. ➤ If the ASA receives a complaint about offensive material, it can launch a formal investigation, and the ASA Council will rule on the matter. If the complaint is upheld, the advertiser must change or withdraw the advert and cannot use the advertising approach in any future marketing communications. ◆ If the advertiser does not comply, it may face a number of consequences (but not a fine). Eg: the ASA may: • ask media companies to refuse to run the advert, *and/or* • publish the ruling on the ASA website, leading to bad publicity for the advertiser.

Organisation	Regulation
Clearcast **and** **Radio Advertising Clearance Centre (RACC)**	➤ Clearcast is an advisory body that advises commercial TV stations on what is likely to be acceptable advertising content. ➤ RACC provides a similar pre-vetting service for radio stations. ◆ NB: the advance-clearance service does not guarantee that a complaint under the *BCAP Codes* will not be upheld by the ASA if a breach of the *BCAP Codes* is subsequently found.
British Board of Film Classification (BBFC)	➤ The BBFC is the non-governmental, independent regulator of the UK film and video industry. ➤ It classifies: ◆ films on behalf of the local authorities who license cinemas under the *Licensing Act 2003, and* ◆ videos (and computer games with video footage or grossly violent or sexual content) under the *Video Recordings Act 1984*. ➤ Films are classified according to content (see Chapter 4 Section F). Each classification determines the age group able to see the film. ➤ Since May 2008 the BBFC has run 'BBFC.online', a self-regulatory scheme for classification of all forms of digital content delivery.
Interactive Software Federation of Europe (ISFE)	➤ The IFSE is the body that has been running the self-regulatory *Pan-European Game Information* (*PEGI*) age-rating system since 2003. This is designed to ensure that minors are not exposed to interactive games that are unsuitable for their particular age group. ◆ The *PEGI* system is jointly adminstered on the IFSE's behalf by the Netherlands Institute for the Classification of Audiovisual Media ('**NICAM**') and the Video Standards Council (see below). ◆ Since 2007, the IFSE has also run *PEGI Online*, a related system which confers a seal of approval on online game providers that volunteer to comply with the *PEGI Online Safety Code* (*POSC*). ➤ The whole *PEGI* system is supported by all major console manufacturers and by publishers and developers of interactive games throughout Europe (including the UK).
Video Standards Council (VSC)	➤ The VSC is a self-regulatory body that administers a *Code of Practice* and *Code of Practice Rules* designed to promote high standards within the video industry and the computer games industry. ➤ The *Practice Rules* are supplemented by *Guidelines* for various categories of member on (among other things) offensive material.
Association for Television On-Demand (ATVOD)	➤ ATVOD is a self-regulatory body that protects the consumers of on-demand audiovisual content services. Its members are expected to adhere to its *Code of Practice*, including taking all reasonable efforts to ensure: a) protection of under-18s from unsuitable content, and protection of all users from indecent marketing communications, *and* b) the availabilty of adequate information about the nature of content before it is viewed (preamble to the *Code*). ➤ The *Code* is supplemented with *Guidance Notes* (eg: *no 5*, on the protection of human dignity and against harm and offence).

Organisation	Regulation

PhonepayPlus	➤ PhonepayPlus regulates UK premium-rate services (known as '**PRS**') whose cost is charged to telephone bills or pre-pay accounts.
	
	  ◆ PRS examples include phone-in TV voting services (the subject of widespread scandal in 2007) and mobile-delivered 'wallpapers'.
	
	    ● PhonepayPlus acts as Ofcom's agent in carrying out the day-to-day regulation of the PRS market on Ofcom's behalf.
	
	➤ PhonepayPlus regulates the content and promotion of PRS through a *Code of Practice* (see eg: *para 5.3* on harm and offence).
	
	➤ PhonepayPlus investigates complaints and has the power:
	
	  a) to fine a service provider, *and/or*
	
	  b) to bar access to a service provider's services, *and/or*
	
	  c) to bar the individual behind a service provider from running other services under a different trading name.

Independent Mobile Classification Body (IMCB, a PhonepayPlus subsidiary)	➤ The IMCB is the UK's independent classification body for picture-based content delivered to mobile devices (including still and moving images, audio-visual materials and mobile games). ➤ Content providers are required to use the IMCB *Classification Framework* (which includes examples of offensive content in *s 2*) and to self-classify content as '18' where inappropriate for under-18s.
Internet Watch Foundation (IWF)	➤ The IWF is an independent, self-regulatory body that monitors illegal content on the internet, with particular reference to images of child sexual abuse hosted anywhere in the world and to images of criminally obscene/racist content hosted in the UK. ➤ It operates a 'hotline' reporting system, alerting internet service providers ('**ISPs**') to potentially illegal content on their systems and at the same time inviting the police to investigate the publisher.
ICRA	➤ The ICRA (formerly the Internet Content Rating Association) is part of an international organisation, the Family Online Safety Institute. ◆ Website operators voluntarily rate their content according to ICRA descriptors. End users (eg: parents of young children) can use filtering software to block access to unsuitable material.
Press Complaints Commission (PCC)	➤ The PCC is the self-regulatory body that monitors the editorial content of newspapers and magazines (and their related websites). ◆ It investigates complaints under a *Code of Practice* drawn up by the editors of national and regional newspapers/magazines. ➤ The *Code* restricts reporting of offensive material in specific ways (eg: *para 7*, restricting identification of children in sex cases, and *para 12*, prohibiting any racial or other potentially discriminatory references unless genuinely relevant to the story). ➤ Any publisher judged to have breached the Code must print the PCC's adjudication in full and with due prominence.

➤ For further details of these organisations and their roles, visit the relevant websites.

  ◆ The websites set out the full text of the *Codes*, along with guidance on their interpretation, and provide information on the various complaints procedures.

II   Obscenity

*References in this section II are to the Obscene Publications Act 1959 ('**OPA 1959**'), unless otherwise stated.*

➤ This section focuses on the criminal offences relating to obscene 'articles' under the *OPA 1959*.

◆ The common-law offences of 'corrupting public morals' and 'outraging public decency' are of limited application and beyond the scope of this Chapter, as are the various statutory offences relating to the performance of obscene plays and the supply of obscene or indecent goods or services.

➤ There are 4 steps to consider in relation to the 2 offences under the *OPA 1959*:

Steps	
1	Is there an obscene article?
2	Has an offence been committed?
3	Is there a defence?
4	What are the penalties?

Step 1	Is there an obscene article?

➤ An article is obscene if:

◆ 'its effect or (where the article comprises two or more distinct items) the effect of any one of its items is, if taken as a whole, such as to tend to deprave and corrupt persons who are likely, having regard to all relevant circumstances, to read, see or hear the matter contained or embodied in it' (*s 1*).

➤ This definition contains 4 elements:

1   **There must be an 'article'**

➤ An article means 'any description of article containing or embodying matter to be read or looked at or both, any sound record, and any film or other record of a picture or pictures' (*s 1(2)*).

◆ This includes recorded matter that is incorporated in TV programmes (*s 1(4)-(6)*).

◆ The definition is so wide that it is not usually difficult to show the existence of an 'article'.

2   **The article must be 'taken as a whole'**

➤ The general rule is that an article cannot be split up into different parts when considering whether it is obscene.

◆ Eg: a 2-hour-long film would not be obscene simply due to short obscene scenes. If, however, a film contains distinct items, the effect of the individual items is considered (*R v Goring* [1999] Crim LR 670).

➤ Magazines are an exception, in that the publication can be considered on an item-by-item basis (*R v Anderson* [1972] 1 QB 304).

 ◆ In *Anderson*, the majority of features in a magazine were innocuous, but, for instance, one advert contained explicit references to oral sex and one picture showed school-children engaging in sexual activities. Each obscene item was enough to make the whole article obscene.

3 **The articles must 'tend to deprave and corrupt' ...**

➤ The article must go further than merely to shock or disgust readers. Case law suggests that the article must have a **morally** corrupting effect.

 ◆ An article is not necessarily obscene merely because it is 'repulsive, filthy, loathsome or lewd' (*R v Anderson*, as above).

4 **... persons 'likely' to read, see or hear the content**

➤ One must consider the article's 'likely' audience and whether that audience (rather than people in general) will be depraved and corrupted.

 ● A **significant proportion** of the 'likely audience' has to be depraved and corrupted (*R v Calder and Boyars Ltd* [1969] 1 QB 151).

  ▪ What represents a 'significant proportion' is a question for the jury to decide.

 ◆ Minority categories within the likely audience should not be disregarded unless they are numerically negligible (*Goldstar Publications Ltd v DPP* [1981] 2 All ER 257).

Step 2	Has an offence been committed?

➤ The first offence is to 'publish' an obscene article (irrespective of whether the publication is 'for gain') (*s 2*).

 ◆ 'Publishing' an article means:

  a) distributing, circulating, selling, letting on hire, giving, lending, offering it for sale or for letting on hire (*s 1(3)(a)*), or

  b) (where the matter is audiovisual or audio content) showing, playing or projecting it, or (where the matter is data stored electronically) transmitting those data (*s 1(3)(b)*), or

  c) (where the matter is recorded) including it in a TV programme (*s 4*).

 ◆ NB: the offence is one of strict liability, so there is no need for the prosecution to establish an **intent** to 'publish'.

  ● This is particularly relevant in the context of a live broadcast, where the broadcaster may be liable for showing material provided by a third party.

➤ The second offence is to possess an obscene article with a view to publishing it 'for gain' (*OPA 1959 s 2*, as amended by *Obscene Publications Act 1964 s 1*).

◆ This amendment closed a gap in the *OPA 1959* whereby it was not an offence to display obscene articles in a shop for sale (which is not technically regarded as an 'offer' – see *Fisher v Bell* [1960] 3 WLR 919).

• NB: the person standing to 'gain' can be a person other than the defendant.

➤ In the context of a film or video, it is highly unlikely that an offence will have been committed where the film or video has been classified by the BBFC.

◆ While the Director of Public Prosecutions ('**DPP**') has the power to prosecute cinemas and video distributors:

• local authorities will, in practice, only license the showing of films that have been classified by the BBFC, *and*

• the DPP has indicated that BBFC-approved videos will not be prosecuted as being obscene.

Step 3	Is there a defence?

➤ There are 3 main defences:

1 Innocent publication or possession

➤ It is a defence for the defendant to prove that he did not examine the article and he had no reasonable cause to suspect that publishing it (or possessing it with a view to publication) would make him liable to conviction (*s 2(5)*).

2 The 'public good' defence

➤ It is a defence if 'publication of the article in question is justified as being for the public good on the ground that it is in the interests of science, literature, art or learning, or of other objects of general concern' (*s 4(1)*).

◆ Whether something is for the 'public good' is a question for the jury, who may hear expert evidence as to the merits of the article in question (*s 4(2)*) and will have to weigh those merits up against (see *R v Calder and Boyars Ltd* [1969] 1 QB 151):

a) the size of the article's likely audience, *and*

b) the nature of the article's capacity to deprave and corrupt, *and*

c) the strength of its tendency to deprave and corrupt.

◆ Case law suggests that the phrase 'other objects of general concern' is to be construed narrowly in terms of the 4 examples preceding it.

➤ If the article published is a film or soundtrack, the definition of public good differs in that the article must be shown to be 'in the interests of drama, opera, ballet or any other art, or of literature or learning' (*s 4(1A)*).

3   The 'aversion' defence

➤   In *R v Anderson* ([1972] 1 QB 304), it was held that material might 'shock in the first instance', but then 'tend to repel', ie: have an 'aversive' effect.

◆   Aversion is not strictly speaking a defence: if successfully pleaded, the article in question will not be found to be obscene because it does not tend to 'deprave or corrupt'.

➤   NB: it is unlikely that a defence can be successfully raised on human rights grounds, ie: that national obscenity laws contravene the right to freedom of expression under the *European Convention on Human Rights* ('**ECHR**') *Art 10*.

◆   In *Handyside v UK* ([1976] 1 EHRR 737), the court found a conviction on grounds of obscenity to be 'necessary in democratic society' and within the UK's margin of appreciation.

Step 4	What are the penalties?

➤   Both offences are triable either way. A defendant is liable (*s 2(1)*):

◆   *on summary conviction* – to be fined up to £5,000 or imprisoned for up to 6 months, *or*

◆   *on conviction on indictment* – to an unlimited fine and/or to imprisonment for up to 5 years.

➤   The police have powers of search and seizure, and the court can order the forfeiture of offending material (*s 3*).

III   Possession of extreme pornography

➤   Possession of an obscene article for publication is an offence under the *OPA 1959 s 2* (as amended), but only if the possession is 'for gain'.

➤   The *Criminal Justice and Immigration Act 2008* ('**CJIA 2008**') made it an offence for any person to be in possession of an 'extreme pornographic image', irrespective of whether the possession is 'for gain' (*s 63(1)*).

◆   The offence was introduced to try to combat the regrettable increase in the availability of extreme pornography due to the ease of distribution via the internet.

●   The relevant sections of the *CJIA 2008* came into force on 26 January 2009.

➤   The offence is relevant to content creators and users, as it introduced a new legal concept of an 'extreme pornographic image', as distinct from the concept of an 'obscene article'.

◆   It is also of particular relevance to ISPs and website operators, as they provide the main means of transmission of extreme pornography and the *CJIA 2008* introduces a new class of content that is subject to a 'notice-and-take-down' procedure.

➤ There are 4 steps to consider in relation to the offence contrary to *CJIA 2008 s 63*:

Steps	
1	What is an 'extreme pornographic image'?
2	Has an offence been committed?
3	Is there a defence?
4	What are the penalties?

Step 1	What is an 'extreme pornographic image'?

➤ There are 3 elements to the definition:

1 **An 'image' that is ...**

    ➤ An 'image' is (*s 63(8)*):

        a) a moving or still image (produced by any means), *or*

        b) data (however stored) that can be converted into an image.

2 **... 'pornographic' *and***

    ➤ An image is 'pornographic' if it must 'reasonably be assumed to have been produced solely or principally for the purpose of sexual arousal' (*s 63(3)*).

        ◆ If an image forms part of a **series** of images, the question whether the image is pornographic is determined by reference to:

            a) the image itself, *and*

            b) the context (if any) in which it occurs in the series.

3 **... 'extreme'**

    ➤ An image is 'extreme' if:

        a) it portrays, in an explicit and realistic way, an act:

            i) threatening a person's life, *or*

            ii) resulting (or likely to result) in serious injury to a person's anus, breasts or genitals, *or*

            iii) involving sexual interference with a human corpse, *or*

            iv) involving intercourse or oral sex performed by a person with an animal (whether dead or alive), *and*

        b) a reasonable person looking at the image would think that any such person or animal was real (*s 63(7)*), *and*

        c) the image is 'grossly offensive, disgusting or otherwise of an obscene character' (*s 63(6)*).

➤ The offensive element is more clearly defined than in the depravity/corruption test under the *OPA 1959*, so is more likely to be satisfied in applicable cases.

Step 2	Has an offence been committed?

➤ Proceedings for an offence under *s 63* may not be instituted except by, or with the consent of, the DPP (*s 63(10)*).

➤ The prosecutor must show 2 elements, ie: that:

  a) the image possessed was an extreme pornographic image, *and*

  b) the person possessed the image (which is a question of fact).

➤ It is a strict-liability offence, so there is no need to show **intent** to possess.

  ◆ NB: there is a defence of innocent possession – see step 3 below.

➤ The offence specifically applies to an ISP based in the UK or in the European Economic Area ('**EEA**') (*s 68* and *Sch 14*).

  ◆ An non-UK ISP based in the EEA can only be prosecuted if the prosecution (*Sch 14 para 2*):

    a) is necessary for the purposes of the 'public interest objective' (ie: the pursuit of public policy), *and*

    b) relates to an information society service that prejudices that objective (or presents a serious and grave risk of prejudice to that objective), *and*

    c) is proportionate to that objective.

      ● NB: there are special e-commerce defences – see step 3 below.

➤ The offence does not apply to an 'excluded image', ie: an image that forms part of a series of images contained in a recording of the whole or part of a video for which a classification certificate has been issued by a designated authority under the *Video Recordings Act 1984* (ie: in practical terms, the BBFC) (*s 64(1)-(2)*).

  ◆ An image is not, however, an 'excluded image' if:

    a) it is contained in a recording of an 'extract' (eg: a single image or short excerpt) from a classified video, *and*

    b) it must reasonably be assumed to have been extracted (with or without other images) solely or principally for the purpose of sexual arousal (*s 64(3)*).

Step 3	Is there a defence?

➤ It is a defence for the defendant to prove that the defendant:

  a) had a legitimate reason for being in possession of the image, *or*

  b) had not seen the image concerned and did not know, nor had any cause to suspect, it to be an extreme pornographic image, *or*

  c) without any prior request by or on behalf of the defendant (*s 65(2)*):

    i) was sent the image concerned, *and*

    ii) did not keep it for an unreasonable time.

➤ The *CJIA 2008* provides 3 defences that mirror the defences under *Directive 2000/31/EC* (known as the '***E-commerce Directive***'), as implemented under UK law by the *Electronic Commerce (EC Directive) Regulations 2002* ('***ECR***').

1   Mere conduit

➤ An ISP that provides access to a network or transmits information for a network user is not liable if the ISP did not (*CJIA 2008 Sch 14 para 3* – compare *ECR r 17*):

   a) initiate the transmission, *or*

   b) select the receiver of the transmission, *or*

   c) select or modify the information contained in the transmission,

   as long as the information is stored for no longer than reasonably necessary for the transmission.

2   Caching

➤ An ISP that temporarily stores ('caches') information on its server for the sole purpose of facilitating oward transmission to subsequent service users is not liable in respect of that information, as long as the ISP (*CJIA 2008 Sch 14 para 4* – compare *ECR r 18*):

   a) does not modify the information, *and*

   b) complies with any conditions attached to having access to the information, *and*

   c) acts 'expeditiously' to remove, or to disable access to, the information on obtaining actual knowledge of the fact that:

      i)   the information has been removed from the network, *or*

      ii) access to it has been disabled, *or*

      iii) a court or an administrative authority has ordered such removal or disablement.

3   Hosting

➤ An ISP that stores ('hosts') information for a service user is not liable in respect of that information, as long as the ISP (*CJIA 2008 Sch 14 para 5* – compare *ECR r 19*):

   a) had no actual knowledge that, at the time the information was provided, it contained any offending material, *or*

   b) on obtaining such knowledge, 'expeditiously' removed, or disabled access to, the information.

➤ There is a limited defence for participation in consensual acts, which is beyond the scope of this Section (see *s 66*).

Step 4	What are the penalties?

➤ The offence is triable either way. A defendant is liable (*s 67*):

- ◆ *on summary conviction* – to be fined up to £5,000 and/or imprisoned for up to 12 months, *or*

- ◆ *on conviction on indictment* – to an unlimited fine and/or to imprisonment for:

  a) up to 3 years for possession of images portraying life-threatening acts or serious injury contrary to *s 63(7)(a)-(b)*, *or*

  b) up to 2 years for possession of images portraying necrophilia or bestiality contrary to *s 63(7)(c)-(d)*.

IV   Protection of children

➤ Where children are featured in material for publication, offensive material may be 'indecent' (as well as obscene).

➤ There are 2 statutes that create criminal offences relating to indecency with children:

1   Sexual Offences Act 2003

➤ The *SOA 2003* repealed the *Indecency with Children Act 1960*, but introduced new offences of indecency towards children under the age of 16, including facilitating commission of a child sex offence (*s 14(2)*).

2   Protection of Children Act 1978

➤ The *PCA 1978* created offences under *s 1* in relation to any indecent photograph or pseudo-photograph of a child under the age of 18.

- ◆ Related case law suggests that 'indecent' means shocking, disgusting and revolting to ordinary people (*Commissioners of Customs and Excise v Sun & Health Ltd*, 29 March 1973, unreported).

- ◆ 'Pseudo-photograph' means a computer-generated or other image that appears to be a photograph (*s 7(7)*).

- ◆ 'Photograph' means a photograph, film or still, or a tracing or other image (whether made by electronic or other means) that (*s 7*):

  a) is not itself a photograph or pseudo-photograph, *but*

  b) is derived from the whole or part of a photograph or pseudo-photograph (or a combination of either or both).

- ◆ Both definitions include (*s 7*):

  a) electronic data (however stored) that are capable of conversion into photographs/pseudo-photographs, *and*

  b) copies of photographs/pseudo-photographs.

- It is an offence for a person (*s 1(1)*):

  a) to take an indecent photograph or pseudo-photograph of a child (ie: a person under the age of 18) or to permit it to be taken, *or*

  b) to distribute or show it, *or*

  c) to possess it with a view to its being distributed or shown by that person or others, *or*

  d) to publish (or to cause the publication of) any advertisement likely to be understood as conveying that the advertiser distributes or shows such indecent photographs or pseudo-photographs or intends to do so.

    - Downloading and/or printing computer data of indecent images constitutes 'taking' photographs (*R v Bowden* [2001] QB 88).

➤ There are certain defences to charges under these *Acts* and, understandably, serious penalties on conviction (which are beyond the scope of this Section).

V   Inciting racial hatred

References in this section V are to the Public Order Act 1986 ('**POA 1986**'), unless otherwise stated.

➤ Incitement of hatred of certain groups of persons is prohibited under the *POA 1986*.

  ◆ The *POA 1986* creates criminal offences that are relevant to all forms of publication via the media.

➤ There are 4 steps to consider in relation to the criminal offences of inciting racial hatred contrary to *Part III* of the *POA 1986*:

Steps	
1	What is 'racial hatred'?
2	Has an offence been committed?
3	Is there a defence?
4	What are the penalties?

Step 1	What is 'racial hatred'?

➤ 'Racial hatred' is defined as 'hatred against a group of persons defined by reference to colour, race, nationality (including citizenship) or ethnic or national origins' (*s 17*).

  ◆ NB: the group of persons need not be located in the UK.

  ◆ Case law on the *Race Relations Act 1976* is likely to have a bearing on the construction of the word 'ethnic'.

    - In *Mandla v Dowell Lee* ([1983] 1 All ER 1062), Sikhs were found to be a racial group defined by ethnic origins, although not biologically distinguishable from other Punjabis.

- It was held in *Mandla* that an ethnic group must regard itself (and must be regarded) as a distinct community, whose essential characteristics are:

  a) 'a long shared history, of which the group is conscious as distinguishing it from other groups, and the memory of which it keeps alive', *and*

  b) 'a cultural tradition of its own'.

Step 2	Has an offence been committed?

➤ Proceedings under *Part III* of the *POA 1986* may only be instituted with the consent of the Attorney-General (*s 27(1)*).

➤ It is an offence for a person to do any of the following 5 acts:

- to use inflammatory words or behaviour or to display any inflammatory written material … (*s 18*), *or*

- to publish or distribute inflammatory written material … (*s 19*), *or*

- to distribute, show or play a recording of inflammatory visual images or sounds … (*s 21*), *or*

- to broadcast a TV or radio programme involving inflammatory visual images or sounds … (*s 22*), *or*

- to possess inflammatory written material or a recording of inflammatory visual images or sounds with a view to publication … (*s 23*),

… in each case:

  a) with an intention to stir up racial hatred, *or*

  b) in circumstances where racial hatred is likely to be stirred up by such act.

  - NB: the term 'inflammatory' is used above as a shorthand for the statutory words 'threatening, abusive or insulting'.

  - The statutory term 'written material' includes any sign or other visible representation (*s 29*).

  - Any natural or legal person is liable to prosecution under the offences, except that the persons liable to prosecution under the *s 22* offence are:

    i) the broadcaster, *and/or*

    ii) the producer or director, *and/or*

    iii) the person recorded making the incitement.

➤ NB: the offence under *s 20* (presenting or directing a performance of a play involving the use of inflammatory words or behaviour) is beyond the scope of this Section.

Step 3	Is there a defence?

➤ There are no statutory defences available where the defendant can be shown to have **intended** to stir up racial hatred.

➤ Where the defendant is **not** shown to have intended to stir up racial hatred, it is a defence for the defendant to prove that:

    ◆ for a *s 18* offence:

      ● *if inside a dwelling* – he had no reason to believe that his words, behaviour or written material would be heard or seen by a person outside that or another dwelling, *or*

      ● *whether inside or outside a dwelling* – he did not intend his words, behaviour or written material to be, and was not aware that they might be, inflammatory, *or*

    ◆ for an offence under *ss 19, 21* or *23*: he was not aware of the content of the material and did not suspect, and had no reason to suspect, that it was inflammatory, *or*

    ◆ for a *s 22* offence:

      ● *all defendants* – he did not know, and had no reason to suspect, that the material was inflammatory, *or*

      ● *broadcaster, producer or director only* – he did not know, and had no reason to suspect, that the programme would involve inflammatory material, and it was not reasonably practicable in the circumstances to secure the removal of the material, *or*

      ● *producer, director or person recorded only* – he did not know, and had no reason to suspect, that the programme would be broadcast or that, in the circumstances, racial hatred was likely to be stirred up.

➤ Under the *Electronic Commerce (EC Directive) Regulations 2002* (which provide ISPs with a general immunity from criminal sanctions in certain defined circumstances), an ISP has a defence against storage/transmission of racially inflammatory material where it:

  a) acts as a 'mere conduit' (*r 17*), *and/or*

  b) merely provides 'caching' services (*r 18*), *and/or*

  c) merely provides 'hosting' services (*r 19*).

    ◆ These 3 defences are the defences on which the 3 ISP defences for storage/transmission of extreme pornographic images were based (almost verbatim) – see above.

➤ Human rights law may also provide a defence.

    ◆ In *Jersild v Denmark* ([1994] 19 EHRR 1), the maker of an investigative documentary containing interviews with racist youths was convicted at first instance, but the conviction was found on appeal to violate his right to freedom of expression under *ECHR Art 10*.

Step 4	What are the penalties?

➤ All 5 offences are triable either way. A defendant is liable (*s 27*):

♦ *on summary conviction* – to be fined up to £5,000 and/or imprisoned for up to 6 months, *or*

♦ *on conviction on indictment* – to an unlimited fine and/or to imprisonment for up to 7 years.

➤ The police have powers of search and seizure (*s 24*), and the court can order the forfeiture of offending written material or recordings (*s 25*).

VI   Inciting hatred on grounds of religion or sexual orientation

*References in this section VI are to the Public Order Act 1986 ('**POA 1986**'), unless otherwise stated.*

➤ A new *Part IIIA* of the *POA 1986* was introduced by the *Racial and Religious Hatred Act 2006* ('**RRHA 2006**'). It came into force on 1 October 2007.

♦ The *RRHA 2006* was designed to fill a gap in protection for religious groups who are effectively targets of bigoted hatred (but not covered by the definition of 'racial hatred') – most notably, the British Muslim community in the aftermath of '9/11' and the subsequent invasions of Afghanistan and Iraq.

• *Part IIIA* effectively mirrors the existing *Part III*, but protects religious (rather than racial) groups.

➤ The offences, defences and penalties replicate the equivalent provisions of the racial-hatred legislation almost verbatim (see *ss 29B-29N*).

♦ *Part IIIA* specifically applies to UK-based and (where required by public policy) other EEA-based ISPs by virtue of the *Electronic Commerce Directive (Racial and Religious Hatred Act 2006) Regulations 2007* ('**ECDR 2007**').

• Under the *ECDR 2007*, ISPs have mere-conduit, caching and hosting defences.

➤ The steps to be considered are therefore virtually the same as for racial hatred, the main difference being the definition of 'religious hatred', ie: 'hatred against a group of persons defined by reference to religious belief or lack of religious belief' (*s 29A*).

♦ NB: it is not just deists, but atheists and humanists who are protected.

♦ *Part IIIA* specifically protects freedom of religious expression, ie: it does not prohibit or restrict (*s 29J*):

• discussion, criticism or expressions of antipathy, dislike, ridicule, insult or abuse of:

▪ particular religions or the beliefs or practices of their adherents, *or*

▪ any other belief system or the beliefs or practices of its adherents, *or*

• proselytising or urging adherents of a different religion or belief system to cease practising their religion or belief system.

➤ As with the racial-hatred offences, the consent of the Attorney-General is required for prosecution for the offences of inciting religious hatred (*s 29L*).

➤ The introduction of offences relating to incitement of religious hatred (which are not limited to the Christian religion) rendered the law of 'blasphemy' obsolete.

Abolition of 'blasphemy'

➤ With effect from 8 July 2008, the *CJIA 2008 s 79* abolished the common-law offences of:

   a) 'blasphemy' (ie: speaking blasphemous words), *and*

   b) 'blasphemous libel' (ie: publishing a blasphemous document).

➤ NB: the law of blasphemy had been much more limited in scope than the name might suggest.

   ◆ The offences were limited to content that was 'contemptuous, reviling, scurrilous or ludicrous matter' relating to God, Jesus Christ, the Bible or the tenets of the Anglican faith (*Whitehouse v Lemon* [1979] AC 617).

   ◆ There had only been 1 successful prosecution since 1922.

   ◆ The secular disposition of the courts was illustrated for the last time by the House of Lords' refusal in early 2008 to grant leave to appeal against the High Court's ruling that no prosecution for blasphemous libel could be brought against the BBC for broadcasting *Jerry Springer: The Opera* (*R (on the application of Stephen Green) v City of Westminster Magistrates' Court*, 5 December 2007, unreported).

➤ *The scope of Part IIIA is to be expanded by the CJIA 2008 (s 74 and Sch 16) to extend to the incitement of hatred on grounds of sexual orientation. The changes have not come into force at the time of writing.*

Inciting hatred on grounds of sexual orientation (not yet in force)

➤ *All offences, defences, penalties and procedures applying to religious hatred under ss 29B–29N will also apply to 'hatred on the grounds of sexual orientation', ie: hatred against a group of persons defined by reference to sexual orientation (whether towards persons of the same sex, the opposite sex or both) (s 29AB).*

➤ *The amended Part IIIA will also protect freedom of expression (in terms of sexual orientation) in that neither:*

   a) *the discussion or criticism of sexual conduct or practices, nor*

   b) *the urging of persons to refrain from or modify such conduct or practices,*

   will be taken of itself to be threatening or to be intended to stir up hatred (s 29JA).

➤ *In January 2010 the government issued in draft form the Electronic Commerce Directive (Hatred against Persons on Religious Grounds or the Grounds of Sexual Orientation) Regulations 2010 ('**ECDR 2010**').*

   ◆ *The ECDR 2010 will implement the 'E-Commerce Directive' (Directive 2000/31/EC) in the light of the widening of the offences in Part IIIA of the POA 1986 and will replace and revoke the ECDR 2007. The ECDR 2010 mirror the provisions of the ECDR 2007 but for the broadening of scope to include the new offences.*

C Contempt of court

*References in this Section are to the Contempt of Court Act 1981 ('**CCA**') unless otherwise stated.*

I	Generally
II	Strict liability contempt
III	Other statutory contempts
IV	Intentional contempt
V	Defamation proceedings

I Generally

➤ The media cannot always enjoy unlimited freedom of expression if the right to a fair trial is to be upheld. The law of contempt of court protects the integrity of court proceedings and ensures that news likely to affect the outcome of a trial is not reported.

➤ The 2 types of contempt of court most commonly encountered are:

a) disrupting the court process by publishing material that could prejudice or interfere with legal proceedings, *and*

b) disobeying court orders.

◆ This Section is solely concerned with a).

➤ The rules on contempt of court apply to both broadcast and non-broadcast media.

II Strict liability contempt

➤ Strict liability contempt is a criminal offence under the *CCA*.

◆ It applies to a publication that creates a substantial risk that the course of justice in the proceedings in question will be seriously impeded or prejudiced (*s 2(2)*).

● 'Publication' includes any speech, writing, broadcast or other communication in whatever form, which is addressed to the public at large (or any section of the public) (*s 2(1)*).

● 'Proceedings' means those taking place in any UK court, tribunal or other body exercising the judicial power of the State (*s 19*) and so includes proceedings of employment tribunals and mental health review tribunals, but excludes proceedings of administrative bodies such as licensing authorities.

◆ The rule applies only if the proceedings in question are 'active' (see below).

➤ The 'strict liability' nature of the rule means that the prosecutor does not have to prove **intent** to interfere with the course of justice (*s 1*).

➤ Questions relating to strict liability contempt can be broken down into 4 steps:

Steps	
1	Was there a 'substantial risk' of 'serious prejudice'?
2	Are the proceedings active?
3	Who is liable and are there any defences?
4	What are the penalties?

Step 1	Was there a 'substantial risk' of 'serious prejudice'?

➤ The prosecutor has to prove that:

a) there was a 'substantial risk', *and*

  ◆ The risk must be more than a mere possibility (ie: a theoretical risk is not enough). Each case must be considered on its own facts.

  ● There need be no actual prejudice, as long as the risk is substantial. The term 'substantial':

    ▪ does not mean 'weighty', but rather 'not insubstantial' or 'not minimal' (*MGN Pension Trustees Ltd v Bank of America National Trust and Saving Association and Credit Suisse* [1995] EMLR 99), *and*

    ▪ means more than 'merely incidental' (*AG v English* [1983] 1 AC 116).

  ● A 9-month period elapsing between a TV news report and trial has been held not to create a 'substantial' risk (*AG v ITN*, Times, 12 May 1994).

  ● In *AG v Morgan* ([1998] EMLR 294), the layout and design of an article was such that, although there would be a considerable lapse of time between publication and trial, the risk of recollection by a juror of the substance of the article was a substantial one.

b) the risk was such that proceedings would be 'seriously prejudiced'.

  ◆ 'Seriously prejudicial' material includes compromising photographs and reports of previous convictions, assertions of guilt and confessions.

  ● Eg: in *AG v Express Newspapers* ([2004] EWHC 2859), publishing the name, club and pixellated photograph of a footballer defendant created a serious risk of prejudicing a rape trial where identification was an issue.

  ◆ In a jury trial, it is thought more likely that the publication of material relating to the trial will seriously prejudice the outcome: jurors are assumed to be influenced by reports in the media.

  ◆ In a trial by magistrate, it is thought less likely that the outcome will be seriously prejudiced: professional magistrates (especially stipendiaries) are viewed as harder to influence than people sitting as lay justices.

  ◆ A judge in a civil case is regarded as unlikely to be affected by media reports.

Step 2	Are the proceedings active?

➤ The proceedings to which the publication refers must be active at the time of publication, otherwise the strict liability rule will not apply (*s 2(3)*). *Sch 1* sets out when proceedings can be regarded as active:

◆ **Proceedings at first instance (*Sch 1 para 1 - 14*)**

- Criminal proceedings become active from the first to occur of the following:

  a) arrest without warrant, *or*

  b) issue of a warrant for arrest, *or*

  c) issue of a summons to appear, *or*

  d) service of an indictment or other document specifying the charge.

- Criminal proceedings cease to be active upon:

  a) acquittal or sentence, *or*

  b) any other verdict, finding or decision which an end to the proceedings, *or*

  c) discontinuance for the following reasons:

    ▪ withdrawal of the charge or summons, *or*

    ▪ discontinuance under the *Prosecution of Offences Act 1985 s 23*, *or*

    ▪ where the arrest is without warrant – on release (otherwise than on bail) without charge, *or*

    ▪ where there is an arrest warrant – on expiry of 12 months from the date of the warrant (unless the defendant is arrested in such period), *or*

    ▪ a finding that the defendant is unfit to be tried or to plead.

- Civil proceedings become active from the time:

  a) when arrangements for the hearing are made, *or*

  b) if no such arrangements are made, when the hearing begins.

- Civil proceedings cease to be active when the proceedings are disposed of, discontinued or withdrawn.

◆ **Appellate proceedings (criminal or civil) (*Sch 1 para 15*)**

- Appellate proceedings become active when they are commenced by:

  a) application for leave to appeal or to apply for review, or notice of such an application, *or*

  b) notice of appeal or of application for review, *or*

  c) any other originating process.

- Appellate proceedings cease to be active when the proceedings are disposed of, abandoned, discontinued or withdrawn.

Criminal proceedings

Civil proceedings

Appellate proceedings

| Step 3 | Who is liable and are there any defences? |

➤ Any person responsible for publishing the offending material can be liable.

◆ Case law suggests that those who are potentially liable for contempt include editors, proprietors, publishers, printers, distributors and reporters, whether in relation to print media or other media such as television or radio broadcasting.

➤ A prosecution of strict liability contempt can only be brought by or with the consent of the Attorney-General (s 7), but private parties can seek an injunction to stop publication.

➤ There are 3 defences under the CCA to a charge of strict liability contempt:

1   Innocent publication or distribution

➤ A publisher is not guilty if, at the time of publication, he did not know, and had no reason to suspect, that the relevant proceedings were active (s 3(1)).

➤ A distributor of a publication containing material in contempt of court is not guilty if, at the time of distribution (having taken all reasonable care), he does not know that it contains such material and has no reason to suspect that it is likely to do so (s 3(2)).

2   Contemporaneous report of proceedings

➤ A person is not guilty in respect of a fair and accurate report of legal proceedings that are held in public if such a report is published contemporaneously with the proceedings and in good faith (s 4(1)).

◆ In these circumstances, the court can still order that the publication of any report of the proceedings (or any part of the proceedings) be postponed for such period as the court thinks necessary to avoid a substantial risk of prejudice to those or other proceedings (s 4(2)).

3   Discussion of public affairs

➤ A publication made as, or as part of, a discussion in good faith of affairs or matters of general public interest is not a contempt if the risk of prejudice to the legal proceedings is merely incidental to the discussion (s 5).

◆ This defence is important for the media as it enables the media to discuss matters of general public interest, even though a possible side-effect is that active proceedings might be prejudiced.

• The defence was raised successfully in the case of AG v English ([1983] 1 AC 116), in which the Daily Mail had, in the week of the trial of a doctor accused of murder for allowing a baby with Down's Syndrome to die of starvation, published a critique of the practice of terminating medical support to deformed babies.

• The defence depends on the existence of good faith. A person with an improper motive cannot rely on it. The burden of negating good faith or proving bad faith rests on the prosecutor (AG v English, as above).

| Step 4 | What are the penalties? |

➤ Strict liability contempt is an offence that is triable summarily, without a jury. The sanctions that can be imposed by the court include:

◆ in the case of committal by a 'superior court' (see below) – imprisonment for up to 2 years or an unlimited fine (s 14), and/or

◆ in the case of committal by an inferior court – imprisonment for up to 1 month or a fine of up to £2,500 (s 14), and/or

◆ an injunction restraining repetition of the act of contempt.

● 'Superior court' is defined in s 19, and includes a county court.

● Substantial fines have been imposed.

■ Eg: in AG v News Group Newspapers Ltd ([1989] QB 110), a newspaper proprietor was fined £75,000 for publishing articles intended to prejudice the fair trial of a defendant accused of rape.

➤ Strict liability contempt is punishable (among other sanctions) by:

◆ a fine (subject to the rules under s 14 described above), and/or

◆ an injunction restraining the commission or repetition of a contempt, and/or

◆ a summary award of damages for breach of an undertaking which also constitutes a breach of contract, and/or

◆ an order to pay the costs of the claimant's application.

III   Other statutory contempts

➤ Various other acts amount to contempt of court under the CCA, including:

1   Disclosure of jury deliberations

➤ It is contempt of court to obtain, disclose or solicit details of statements made, opinions expressed, arguments advanced or votes cast by jury members during the course of deliberations in any proceedings (s 8(1)).

◆ NB: it is not a contempt of court to publish an interview with a juror about the juror's opinion of a trial after the verdict has been given (as the proceedings have at that stage come to an end).

2   Publication of films/recordings of proceedings

➤ It is a contempt of court (s 9(1)(b)):

◆ to publish a recording of proceedings made by means of any instrument for recording sound, or any recording derived directly or indirectly from it, by playing it in the hearing of the public or any section of the public, or

◆ to dispose of it or any recording so derived with a view to publication.

3   Unjustified refusal to disclose a source

➤ Sources of information are generally protected from disclosure by *s 10*, but it is a contempt of court to refuse to disclose such source where the court is satisfied that disclosure is necessary in the interests of justice or national security or for the prevention of disorder or crime (*s 10*).

➤ NB: there are various restrictions on reporting of proceedings in legislation other than the *CCA*, which are beyond the scope of this Section.

◆ These restrictions cover, for instance, courts sitting in private, cases pending trial at the Crown Court, anonymity for victims of sexual offences, anonymity for defendants and witnesses in Youth Court hearings, protection of children, indecency, fraud and divorce, wardship/adoption and other family matters.

IV   Intentional contempt

➤ Legislation is not the only source of law for contempt. There is a parallel offence at common law (eg: *AG v Hislop* [1991] 1 QB 514) which applies if it can be shown that:

◆ a publication has caused a 'real risk' of impeding or interfering with the administration of justice, *and*

◆ the defendant has deliberately **intended** to impede or interfere with the administration of justice.

● Intent is inferred if it is obvious that the publisher must have seen that publication would create a real risk of prejudice (*AG v News Group Newspapers Ltd* [1989] QB 110).

➤ Case law suggests that, for the purposes of this offence, proceedings must be pending or imminent (or at least reasonably likely to occur) at the time of publication.

◆ NB: there is no requirement that the proceedings be 'active' (eg: *AG v Times Newspapers Ltd* [1992] 1 AC 191).

● So the prosecutor will rely on intentional contempt where no proceedings are currently active against a defendant, but proceedings are likely (eg: where, before the arrest of a suspect, a newspaper 'scoop' reveals criminal activity and the DPP is likely to bring a prosecution).

➤ Examples of offending publications at common law include articles that have:

◆ disclosed information that the defendant was prevented from disclosing under his service contract (*AG v Punch Ltd* [2003] 1 All ER 289), *or*

◆ contained material that was the subject of an injunction (*AG v Times Newspapers Ltd*), *or*

◆ brought to the attention of readers, including potential jurors, damaging facts that would be inadmissible as evidence in imminent criminal proceedings (*AG v News Group Newspapers Ltd* [1989] QB 110).

➤ The persons who may be liable for intentional contempt at common law are the same as those who may be liable under the *CCA* (see section II above).

➤ NB: there are other common-law offences that are beyond the scope of this Section, such as the (possibly obsolete) charge of 'scandalising the court', ie: lowering the court's authority (eg: by publishing scurrilous abuse of the court or personal attacks on a judge's character).

V   Defamation proceedings

➤ Special rules apply to civil proceedings for libel and slander.

   ◆ If a defendant has *prima facie* support for the defence of justification, then, unless the strict liability rule is invoked (*Thomson v Times Newspapers Ltd* [1969] 3 All ER 648):

   ● the claimant cannot obtain an interim injunction to restrain repetition by a defendant of the material alleged to be defamatory, *and*

   ● any repetition of such material by the defendant will not in general amount to a contempt of court.

   ◆ Where, however, a publication amounts to 'comment' for defamation purposes (see Section A of this Chapter), it may be restrained by injunction or punished as a contempt of court if it (*AG v Hislop* [1991] 1 QB 514):

   ● goes beyond mere repetition of such material, *or*

   ● is comment prompted by the issue of the claim form, *or*

   ● is intended to prejudice the fair trial of issues raised in the defamation proceedings.

3 Music Industry

This Chapter examines:

A   Overview

*References in this Section are to the Copyright, Designs and Patents Act 1988 ('**CDPA**'), unless otherwise stated.*

I	Copyright, performance rights and the music industry
II	Music industry organisations
III	Enforceability of music contracts – introduction
IV	Restraint of trade
V	Undue influence
VI	Contracts with minors

I   Copyright, performance rights and the music industry

➤ Money generated in the music industry is mainly derived from the exploitation of:

 ◆ copyright (whether in musical compositions, lyrics or sound recordings), *and*

 ◆ performers' rights.

  ◆ Successful artists also earn from live concerts and from exploiting their name and likeness rights (eg: through merchandising, endorsements and sponsorship).

➤ This Chapter focuses on the core intellectual property and related rights that underpin the music industry.

Copyright and the music industry – basic principles

➤ Recorded music involves 3 separate copyrights:

 a) copyright in the music as a musical work, *and*

 b) copyright in the lyrics as a literary work, *and*

 c) copyright in the recording of the music as a sound recording.

➤ The author of a copyright work is the person who creates it (*s 9(1)*).

 ◆ The same person may write both the lyrics and music (eg: Carole King), or 2 or more separate people may be involved (eg: Syreeta Wright writes the lyrics and Stevie Wonder writes the music).

  • Ultimately, the copyright in both the music and the lyrics will normally be assigned to a publishing company (see Section D of this Chapter). For this reason, music and lyrics are treated below as if they constitute a single copyright work (the '**song**').

 ◆ In relation to a sound recording, the author is the 'producer' (ie: the person who makes the necessary arrangements for the making of the recording) (*ss 9(2)(aa)* and *178*). In most cases, this will be a record company.

➤ The author of the copyright work is also its first owner (*s 11*).

Performers' rights and the music industry – basic principles

➤ A musician has statutory rights under *CDPA Pt II* in each performance by the musician, whether as a vocalist, instrumentalist or both (*s 180(2)(b)*).

♦ The rights of commercial significance are the artist's 'economic rights' as a performer, which are examined in Section C of this Chapter.

● If an artist's performance is recorded and exploited (eg: by being sold or broadcast), the artist's consent must be obtained to avoid infringement of the artist's rights as a performer.

● An artist also has a right to receive 'equitable remuneration' from the owner of the sound recording in respect of public performance (*s 182D*) and rental (*s 191G*) of the recording of the performance.

➤ A musician also has contractual rights in each recorded performance under a contract with a record company (or a session musician agreement).

➤ A performer's rights in a recorded performance of a song should be carefully distinguished from the public performance rights which, under *s 16(1)(c)-(d)*:

♦ the songwriter(s) control as owner(s) of the copyright in the song, *and*

♦ the record company controls as owner of the copyright in the sound recording.

➤ The other key right in a song is the right to reproduce the song in a recording (*s 17*). As first owner of the copyright in the song, the songwriter(s) exclusively control the right for a record company to reproduce the song in a master sound recording (together with the related right to manufacture multiple copies of the 'master' for sale to the public).

➤ Each recording of a song therefore involves a complex rights position.

♦ Eg: where a singer-songwriter writes and performs a song with a view to a commercial release by a record label, 5 main, independent rights are involved:

a) the right controlled by the songwriter to allow the reproduction of the **song** and manufacture of records or digital equivalents (the '**mechanical right**'), *and*

b) the songwriter's exclusive right to control the public performance, broadcast or digital dissemination of the **song** (the '**performing right**'), *and*

c) the record label's exclusive right to control the public performance, broadcast or digital dissemination of the **sound recording** of the song (the '**phonographic performance right**'), *and*

d) the statutory rights of the songwriter and any other performers in their **performances** irrespective of copyright (the '**performers' rights**'), *and*

e) the contractual rights in **performances** that each performer has under the relevant recording contract or session agreement (the '**contractual rights**').

● NB: other rights are also involved (eg: authors' and performers' moral rights), and these are examined in Sections C and D of this Chapter.

➤ The 5 main rights listed above give rise to 5 different income streams when recorded music is exploited. The following table illustrates the revenue streams flowing from each right. NB: a single songwriter is assumed below for the sake of simplicity.

Rights	Income stream

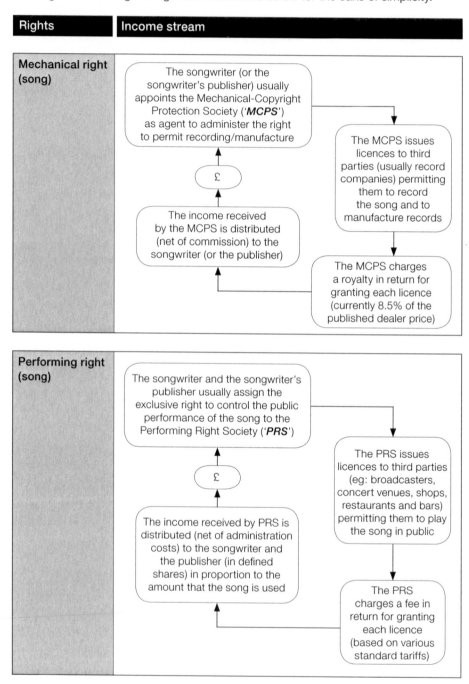

Rights	Income stream

Phonographic performance right (sound recording)

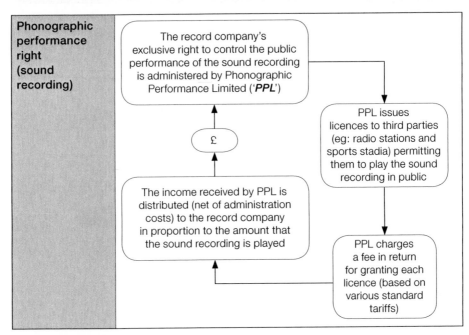

The record company's exclusive right to control the public performance of the sound recording is administered by Phonographic Performance Limited ('**PPL**')

£

PPL issues licences to third parties (eg: radio stations and sports stadia) permitting them to play the sound recording in public

The income received by PPL is distributed (net of administration costs) to the record company in proportion to the amount that the sound recording is played

PPL charges a fee in return for granting each licence (based on various standard tariffs)

Performer's statutory rights (performance)

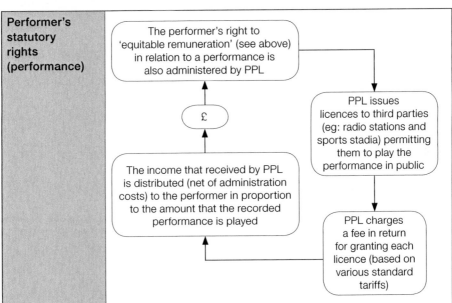

The performer's right to 'equitable remuneration' (see above) in relation to a performance is also administered by PPL

£

PPL issues licences to third parties (eg: radio stations and sports stadia) permitting them to play the performance in public

The income that received by PPL is distributed (net of administration costs) to the performer in proportion to the amount that the recorded performance is played

PPL charges a fee in return for granting each licence (based on various standard tariffs)

Performer's contractual rights (performance)

➤ The performer should have a recording contract (or session musician agreement) setting out the performer's consent to the recording and exploitation of the performance by the record company.

◆ This gives rise to a contractual right for remuneration from the record company, either as a flat fee (for a session musician) or a per-unit royalty or share of net receipts (for a featured artist signed to the company) – see Section C of this Chapter.

➤ The chart below outlines the flows of rights in the music industry for a song embodied in a sound recording (with revenues flowing in the reverse direction in each case).

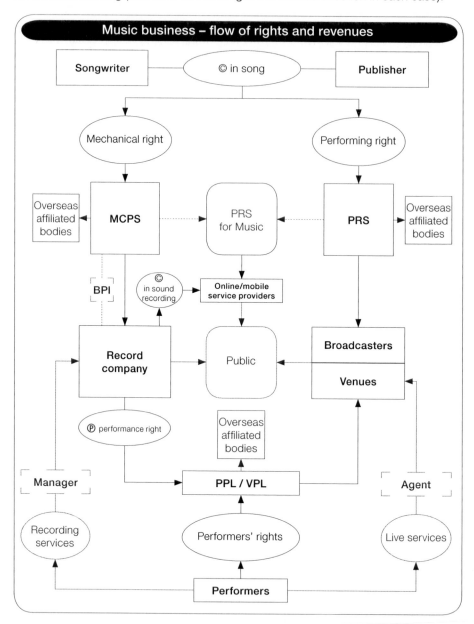

➤ NB: while the songwriter and performers are separated for clarity, recording artists often write their own material, in which case they participate in both sources of income.

◆ The chart also shows the role of the artist's manager and booking agent, who (among other things) negotiate the artist's recording and live contracts respectively.

◆ The chart does not show grants of synchronisation licences or the administration of 'production/library music', which are considered in Section C of Chapter 4.

◆ Nor does it show the full position for **digital** licensing of songs – see below.

➤ People that are new to the music industry are often confused by the overlapping layers of rights (and the corresponding entitlements to remuneration). It can help to look at a worked example.

Worked example

➤ Take a CD with a retail price of £13.75. The proceeds of sale might be split as follows:

Amount	£	Participant
Retail price (inc VAT)	13.75	
VAT (17.5%)	(2.05)	to HM Revenue & Customs
Retail price (ex VAT)	11.70	
Retail margin (30%)	(2.70)	to retail outlet
Dealer price ('PPD')	9.00	
Packaging deduction	(2.25)	to record company
Royalty base	6.75	
Producer royalty (3%)	(0.20)	to record producer
Artist royalty (net 15%)	(1.01)	to artist
Balance	5.54	
Mechanical royalty	(0.77)	to MCPS (for publisher/writer(s))
Proceeds after royalties	4.77	to cover costs of production, manufacture, marketing and distribution and label's margin

➤ The division of the retail price can be represented graphically as follows:

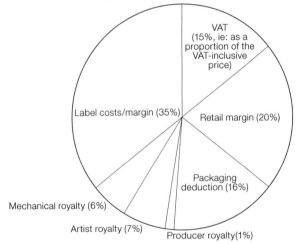

➤ This is not an entirely realistic example, but it is not far off the current commercial practice and clearly illustrates the ratio of reward as between record company and artist, which is commonly around 4:1 (or 5:1) in the record company's favour.

◆ NB: this example ignores factors that would otherwise complicate this example (eg: discounts, free goods, royalty deductions and recoupment of advances). Those concepts are explored in Section C of this Chapter.

➤ Other forms of commercial exploitation give rise to separate revenue streams. For instance, if the record is played on radio in the UK, each radio station concerned must pay licence fees (as a proportionate fraction of an annual 'blanket' licence fee):

a) *for performance of the recorded song* – to the PRS, which will (after commission) pay 50% to the music publisher and 50% to the writer(s) of the song, *and*

b) *for performance of the sound recording* – to PPL, which will (after commission) pay 50% to the record company and 50% to the artist (and/or any backing vocalists/musicians performing on the record).

II   Music industry organisations

➤ As seen above, the collecting societies play an indispensable role in the music industry.

◆ Individual artists, songwriters and publishers could not effectively license or monitor the wide variety of users of music in the UK, so a number of societies have been established to conclude collective bargaining agreements on behalf of their members and to grant and administer music licences.

◆ Users of music also prefer to deal with a central organisation, such as a collecting society, rather than having to contact each copyright owner individually.

➤ The roles of the collecting societies and the other main organisations in the UK music industry are outlined below.

1   PRS for Music

➤ This is an operational alliance (originally named 'The MCPS-PRS Alliance') between the MCPS (see 2 below) and the PRS (see 3 below). It was formed in 1997 to create shared back-office and administrative functions and was re-named as 'PRS for Music' in 2009.

◆ PRS for Music collects and pays royalties to the members of the MCPS and PRS respectively when their songs are:

a) recorded (eg: when physical CDs are manufactured) or reproduced when made available via electronic services (eg: online or via mobile networks) ('*made available*') (MCPS), or

b) performed, broadcast or disseminated when made available (eg: streamed), whether performed live or pre-recorded (PRS).

➤ While there is an overlap of membership (ie: songwriters may be and publishers will be members of both societies), MCPS and PRS remain separate societies in terms of their constitution, rights controlled and income streams.

◆ Both organisations are non-profit-making and deduct a small administration fee to cover their operating costs.

2   Mechanical-Copyright Protection Society (MCPS)

➤ The MCPS is usually appointed as agent on behalf of copyright owners to administer the exploitation of their 'mechanical rights' and to ensure that the copyright owners are commercially rewarded whenever their songs are recorded and otherwise reproduced (eg: via CDs, DVDs and online).

◆ Unlike in the case of the PRS and PPL, no copyright is assigned.

• Some large publishing companies choose to administer the mechanical rights themselves rather than appointing MCPS as agent.

➤ The MCPS' traditional function is to grant licences of songs to third parties (eg: record companies) permitting them to manufacture physical records.

◆ The MCPS collects a royalty – currently 8.5% of the 'published price to dealer' (or 'PPD') of each record (eg: in CD or 12" vinyl format) – based on the amount of records that are manufactured (or, in the case of major record companies, shipped) for sale.

➤ The MCPS has certain other functions:

◆ If (and to the extent) authorised by a member, the MCPS administers the member's 'synchronisation' rights (ie: allowing the member's songs/ compositions to be used in timed relation to audiovisual productions).

• NB: publishers often reserve the right to grant synchronisation rights directly to the producer – see Section C of Chapter 4.

◆ The MCPS issues 'blanket' licences to broadcasters (ie: granting mechanical and some synchronisation rights across MCPS repertoire).

◆ The MCPS operates a scheme for use of music in DVDs.

◆ Licences to exploit 'making available' rights are considered below.

➤ After deducting its commission, the MCPS distributes the income that it receives to the relevant copyright owners.

➤ There are similar organisations to the MCPS in other countries (eg: Harry Fox Agency in the USA). The MCPS has reciprocal agreements with such organisations enabling it to collect money from the overseas exploitation of its members' works.

3 **Performing Right Society (PRS)**

➤ UK publishers and songwriters assign the performing right in their songs to the PRS for the duration of their membership.

◆ In return, the PRS:

• licenses performance, broadcast and 'making available' rights to users (eg: under blanket licences to broadcasters and internet service providers and under annual or one-off licences to venues, clubs, restaurants and bars), applying a variety of negotiated rates and set tariffs, *and*

• collects income arising from the exploitation of those rights, *and*

• pays income to its members in varying proportions depending on how much a work has been performed, broadcast or made available (eg: at concerts, via TV or radio broadcasts or online), as assessed through a mixture of actual reporting and representative samples.

➤ There are similar organisations to the PRS abroad (eg: BMI and ASCAP in the USA, GEMA in Germany and SACEM in France). The PRS has reciprocal agreements with such organisations enabling it to collect money from the overseas exploitation of its members' works.

➤ NB: both mechanical and performing rights are involved in making music available digitally, and digital platforms are fast becoming the main distribution platforms for music.

♦ Historically, all music-publishing collective licensing took place on a country-by-country basis.

- With the emergence of digital music platforms (eg: online and via mobile telephones), it has become impractical for digital music stores and mobile content providers to obtain a licence in each territory.

♦ On 16 July 2008 the European Commission issued a decision ruling that certain concerted practices between the collecting societies in the European Economic Area were anti-competitive, and requiring the societies to bring to an end (*Case COMP/C2/38.698 – CISAC*):

- for online, satellite and cable exploitation, the current co-ordination between the societies leading to territorial limitations, *and*

- restrictions on movement between members of societies, *and*

- any exclusive rights to administer repertoire under reciprocal contracts.

  ▪ Certain societies had already been working with music publishers to try to create multi-territorial licences (see below), so the European Commission did not impose any fines on the societies, recognising their previous efforts to find market-led solutions.

♦ The Dutch society, BUMA/STEMRA, relying on this decision, purported to grant a pan-European online licence to a digital music provider, beatport.com.

- In August 2008, however, the PRS successfully obtained an interim injunction from a Dutch court preventing BUMA/STEMRA from administering PRS repertoire.

  ▪ The Dutch court noted that the European Commission had found the actual co-ordination between the societies to contravene *EC Treaty Art 81* (now the *Treaty on the Functioning of the European Union* ('**EU Treaty**') *Art 101*), but had not found the societies' reciprocal agreements to be inherently anti-competitive.

♦ At the time of writing, the societies are still in the process of responding to the European Commission's decision. Music users have called for a pan-European 'one-stop shop', but this has yet to emerge. For Anglo-American repertoire, all 4 of the major music publishers have withdrawn their **digital** mechanical rights from PRS for Music (and EMI its digital performing rights as well) and have set up their own, individual 'one-stop shops' for pan-European digital/mobile exploitation of such repertoire.

- The first was EMI, which in January 2007 launched a joint venture with PRS for Music and GEMA named CELAS.

- From January 2008 Warner-Chappell launched a non-exclusive Pan-European Digital Licensing ('PEDL') initiative with each of PRS for Music, SACEM and Sweden's society, STIM.

- In January 2008 Universal set up an exclusive scheme (now named Direct European Administration and Licensing or 'DEAL') with SACEM.

- From July 2008 Sony ATV launched an exclusive scheme called PAECOL with GEMA.

➤ For **non-withdrawn** digital rights in the UK, the PRS has joined with the MCPS in creating a licensing scheme. The current scheme is as follows:

PRS for Music licences for UK digital music services

➤ PRS for Music operates various types of online licence permitting users to make music available to the UK public via most types of online and mobile music services (subject to the repertoire exclusions noted above).

- ◆ Each of these licences covers performing and mechanical rights, but not:
  - moral, graphic, adaptation or synchronisation rights, which would need to be licensed direct from the relevant publisher, *or*
  - the right to use any sound recordings, which would need to be licensed direct from the relevant record company (as things stand, as PPL has a very limited digital mandate), *or*
  - advertising, sponsorship, audio-visual, ringtone, podcasting or simulcasting rights, which would need to be licensed direct from the relevant publisher and record company respectively.
- ◆ Each licence runs until 30 June 2012.
- ◆ PRS for Music collects from each licensee certain percentages of gross revenue' (including end-user payments, plus advertising and sponsorship revenue) derived from the exploitation concerned, eg:
  - *for music downloads* – 8% (or, if greater, defined minimum amounts on a per-download basis), *and/or*
  - *for on-demand streaming and limited/tethered download services (**not** funded by subscription)* – 10.5% (or, if greater, 0.085p per track streamed), *and/or*
  - *for on-demand streaming and limited/tethered download services (funded by subscription)* – 8% (or, if greater, defined minimum amounts per subscriber on a monthly basis).
    - There are similar licences (and similar types of licence fees) for webcasting services, with distinctions drawn between interactive/non-interactive, subscription/non-subscription and single-artist/multiple-artist services.

➤ PRS for Music also operates a limited online exploitation licence ('**LOEL**'), permitting music to be made available to the UK public via a range of digital music services by small-scale or non-commercial businesses (ie: whose gross revenue from the music service is less than £12,500 per year).

- ◆ The licence covers performing and mechanical rights, but is subject to similar exclusions to those in the larger-scale online licences.
- ◆ Annual licence fees are payable, based on defined types of service and bands of usage linked to total downloads/streams per annum.

4   **Phonographic Performance Limited (PPL)**

➤   PPL is a not-for-profit company, whose members consist of:

- ◆ record companies, *and*

- ◆ performers on sound recordings.

➤   PPL issues blanket and one-off UK public performance licences in respect of sound recordings to:

- ◆ venues (eg: pubs, clubs, shops, restaurants and bars) that play sound recordings in public, *and*

- ◆ traditional TV and radio broadcasters who use sound recordings in their transmissions, *and*

- ◆ online and mobile TV/radio broadcasters (unless the relevant record company has reserved the right to grant these rights direct).

  - • NB: at the time of writing, PPL has not established a digital licensing scheme for all of its record-company members' repertoire, but digital licensing is a fast-evolving area and this may change.

➤   PPL collects and distributes royalties arising in proportion to use of individual sound recordings (which is assessed in a similar way to the PRS system).

- ◆ 50% of the income is distributed to record-company members and 50% to performer members, except where performers are not entitled to equitable remuneration (eg: 'dubbing', ie: the mechanical reproduction of a master), in which case all monies are paid to the relevant record company.

➤   PPL has reciprocal arrangements with similar bodies overseas enabling PPL to collect money from the overseas exploitation of its members' works.

➤   PPL has a sister company, Video Performance Limited ('**VPL**').

- ◆ PPL and VPL share centralised management, in much the same way as PRS for Music brings together the PRS and the MCPS.

- ◆ VPL is the collecting society set up by record companies in 1984 to license the public performance by broadcasters, programme producers and suppliers of video jukeboxes of 'short-form music videos' (ie: promotional videos produced to support the release of a single).

- ◆ Its members consist of owners of the UK copyright in those music videos (largely the UK major and independent record labels).

- ◆ VPL (which is, at the time of writing, to be re-branded as 'PPL Video') issues blanket licences to music channels (eg: MTV).

  - • The licence fees that VPL collects from end users are paid out to VPL members in proportion to individual videos' use (after deduction of VPL's administration costs).

5   **Musicians' Union (MU)**

➤   The MU is the only UK trade union that consists solely of musicians.

➤   The MU negotiates on behalf of musicians with all the major employers of musicians in the UK (eg: the BBC).

◆   The MU lays down minimum session rates that musicians not contracted to record companies should accept and provides several standard contracts of engagement (eg: for studio sessions or live engagements). These rates are contained in an agreement between the MU and the BPI (see below).

➤   The MU publishes leaflets relating to management, recording and publishing agreements, as well as sample documents with commentary.

◆   It also provides a free contract advisory service to its members and runs regular seminars and workshops on the music business.

6   **British Phonographic Industry (BPI)**

➤   The BPI is the UK record industry's trade association.

◆   It is a non-profit-making organisation, whose members consist of the major record companies, associate members (eg: manufacturers and distributors) and independent labels.

➤   Its 3 main roles are:

a)   protecting its members' ability to exploit the copyright in sound recordings by:

i)   combating bootleg and counterfeit recordings via its anti-piracy unit (both offline and online), *and*

ii)   bringing criminal and civil litigation on its members' behalf, *and*

iii)   running public education programmes), *and*

b)   promoting British music in the UK and abroad (eg: organising the Brit Awards and overseeing the official British music charts), *and*

c)   representing its members by:

i)   lobbying the Government, *and*

ii)   negotiating terms with third parties (eg: the rates of royalties payable for mechanical and other licences granted by the MCPS and the session rates payable to MU members).

7   **Association of Independent Music (AIM)**

➤   AIM is a non-profit-making trade organisation for UK independent record companies and independent distributors. It lobbies on behalf of its members and provides support services to its members.

8   **Music Publishers Association (MPA)**

➤ The MPA is a non-profit-making trade association representing the interests of music publishers that are based or working in the UK.

◆ On behalf of its member publishers, the MPA:

- negotiates agreements with music users (eg: the BBC), *and*

- lobbies on behalf of publishers at UK and European level, *and*

- leads applications to the Copyright Tribunal.

  ▪ It also runs seminars, courses and social events.

9   **British Academy of Songwriters, Composers and Authors (BASCA)**

➤ BASCA is an organisation representing the interests of UK songwriters, composers and lyricists.

◆ It provides support services to its members, lobbies on their behalf and promotes recognition of composing and songwriting talent (eg: by presenting the Ivor Novello Awards).

10   **Music Managers Forum (MMF)**

➤ The MMF was set up in 1992 by the managers of Simply Red and Dire Straits as a forum for discussion and action among managers of artists and record producers.

◆ It lobbies on behalf of managers and their artists at UK and European level, and provides support services to its members (eg: workshops on different aspects of the music industry).

11   **Featured Artists Coalition (FAC)**

➤ The FAC was founded in October 2008 by dozens of UK featured artists, including Radiohead as prominent spokespersons.

◆ The FAC encourages featured artists to sign its charter and campaigns on behalf of artists for changes in law and commercial practice.

12   **UK Music**

➤ UK Music was launched in October 2008 as a new umbrella organisation representing the collective interests of the UK music industry.

◆ Its members include AIM, BACS, the BPI, PRS for Music, the MMF, the MPA, the MU and PPL.

◆ Its purpose is to promote awareness and understanding of the interests of the UK music industry at all levels, and its activities include:

- policy development on issues of relevance to its membership at UK, EU and international levels, *and*

- music education, skills development and awareness initiatives.

III   Enforceability of music contracts – introduction

➤   The 1960s and 1970s saw some notoriously unfair contracts between artists and their managers, record companies and publishing companies.

◆   A series of artists successfully challenged the enforceability of these one-sided contracts in the courts from that time through to the 1990s.

➤   The artists relied on 3 long-established contractual principles (often in combination):

a)   restraint of trade, *and*

b)   undue influence, *and*

c)   minors' capacity to contract.

◆   These 3 principles are examined below.

IV   Restraint of trade

➤   It used to be common for an artist to sign an extremely long-term exclusive contract, often with little obligation in return from the other party.

◆   Such contracts have been successfully challenged invoking the long-standing doctrine of restraint of trade (eg: in the leading music industry case on restraint of trade, *Schroeder Music Publishing v Macaulay* [1974] 1 WLR 1308).

➤   If a contract is in restraint of trade at common law, it is voidable (ie: capable of being set aside) at the instance of the claimant from the date of judgment.

◆   The contract is enforceable (and the defendant retains the benefit of the contract) until it is set aside (*Petrofina (Great Britain) v Martin* [1966] Ch 146).

●   The non-artist party may seek a declaration that the contract is valid, but it is far more common for the artist to be the claimant (as is assumed below).

▪   The court may instead 'sever' (ie: strike out) the offending part(s) as long as the remaining part is not affected.

▪   The court will not, however, substitute a reasonable restriction for an unreasonable one (*Silvertone Records v Mountfield* [1993] EMLR 152, the 'Stone Roses' case).

➤   At the heart of the doctrine is a tension between the public interest in freedom of contract and freedom of trade (*Herbert Morris v Saxelby* [1916] 1 AC 688).

◆   This is not dissimilar to the tension in competition law between business interests and consumer protection in the context of anti-competitive restrictive practices.

➤ The prohibitions of anti-competitive agreements and abuse of a dominant position under the *EU Treaty Arts 101* and *102* and *Competition Act 1998 Ch I* and *II* can apply to music industry contracts. A claim was brought on *Art 101* (then *Art 81*) grounds in *Panayiotou v Sony Music Entertainment (UK)* [1994] EMLR 229 (the 'George Michael' case), but without success (albeit with little evidence put before the court).

◆ It seems likely that the common-law doctrine will continue to be of more immediate relevance to music industry contracts, so the detailed rules of competition law are beyond the scope of this Section.

➤ A 2-stage test is applied to determine whether contractual restrictions are in restraint of trade at common law (*Panayiotou*, confirming principles established in the leading case, *Esso Petroleum v Harper's Garage (Stourport)* [1967] 2 WLR 871):

Steps	
1	Does the contract attract the doctrine of restraint of trade at all?
2	If so, are the restrictions contained in the contract justified?

Step 1 | Does the contract attract the doctrine of restraint of trade at all?

➤ The restrictions under the contract must be in restraint of trade in 'ordinary parlance'.

◆ A person should (in the absence of justified restrictions) be free to carry on his trade as he sees fit, so any restraint on this freedom is potentially in restraint of trade.

● There are several recognised types of provisions that are *prima facie* in restraint of trade, including non-compete obligations and post-termination restrictions.

➤ The court must then consider whether, in all the circumstances, sufficient grounds exist for excluding the contract from the application of the doctrine.

◆ Eg: there is a public interest in upholding a compromise agreement, so the doctrine does not apply at all in that context (*Panayiotou*, as above).

● It is not possible to determine what constitutes 'sufficient grounds' for this purpose by reference to a formula that applies in all cases. Whether the contract involves a restraint of trade is a question of fact to be applied to the facts of the case 'with a broad and flexible rule of reason' (*Esso Petroleum*, as above).

➤ The doctrine does not apply to the extent that the contract simply regulates and promotes trade during the term of the contract (*Esso Petroleum*, as above).

◆ Music contracts, however, tend to involve restraints of trade that apply during the term of the contract, which (where excessive) are invalid as they are unnecessary or capable of enforcement in an oppressive manner, especially where they are unduly restrictive because of an inequality of bargaining power (*Schroeder Music Publishing v Macaulay* [1974] 1 WLR 1308).

● Management, recording and publishing contracts routinely give one party exclusive rights in respect of the services of the other for a fixed duration, so the doctrine of restraint of trade should always be borne in mind.

Step 2	If so, are the restrictions contained in the contract justified?

➤ If the restrictions attract the doctrine of restraint of trade, it is necessary to consider whether they are:

a) reasonable as between the parties, *and*

b) reasonable so far as the public interest is concerned.

- ◆ These are the 2 limbs of the 'Nordenfelt' test, which is derived from *Nordenfelt v Maxim Nordenfelt Guns and Ammunition* ([1894] AC 535).

a) Reasonableness between the parties

- ◆ It is for the defendant to prove that the restrictions are reasonable as between the contracting parties. There is a balance to be struck between:

  a) adequate protection of the defendant's legitimate interests, *and*

  b) the artist's freedom to further the artist's career.

- ◆ The defendant must first prove that the restrictions are 'reasonably necessary' for the protection of the party's 'legitimate interests' (*Schroeder Music Publishing v Macaulay* [1974] 1 WLR 1308).

  - ● Managers, record labels and publishing companies need to impose some restrictive clauses, especially as an artist is never a truly 'overnight' success.

    - ■ They have a legitimate interest in trading effectively and making a return. The restrictions (eg: guaranteeing the artist's exclusive provision of services over a defined term) help them to make a better product (in terms of the artist's output), to plan more efficiently and to generate larger profit margins than they would in the absence of any restrictions.

    - ■ They also have a legitimate interest in protecting their investment of time and/or money in the artist, which they would not recover if the artist were completely free to work with third parties.

- ◆ Whether the restrictions go beyond what is adequate to protect the defendant's legitimate interests is a question of fact which varies from case to case. The restrictions must be weighed up against the artist's contractual rights.

  - ■ What may be held to be restrictive in one case may not be in another.

- ◆ In the context of music industry agreements, the following factors are relevant:

  a) the duration of the contract (including any option periods), *and*

  b) obligations on the defendant to further the artist's career, eg: to what extent:

    i) the manager must secure a recording contract within a defined period, *or*

    ii) the record company must release each album delivered under the contract within defined periods, *or*

    iii) the publishing company is obliged to exploit a songwriter's songs, *and*

  c) the artist's remuneration (ie: the consideration for the restrictions), *and*

d) ownership of the artist's copyright works and other rights (together with the duration and assignability of such rights), *and*

e) any right on the defendant's part to reject the artist's copyright works, *and*

f) termination rights (eg: whether both parties have the right to terminate), *and*

g) any missing terms that should have been included in the contract, *and*

h) the extent to which the contract is negotiable, and the parties' relative bargaining positions, age and experience (*Panayiotou v Sony Music Entertainment (UK)* [1994] EMLR 229).

- The court looks at the cumulative effect of the restrictions (*Zang Tumb Tuum Records v Johnson* [1993] EMLR 61, the 'Frankie Goes To Hollywood' case).

  - Where the validity of the whole contract is challenged, the question is whether the contract is fair 'taken as a whole' (*Schroeder Music Publishing v Macaulay* [1974] 1 WLR 1308).

  - The validity of the contract is determined at the date of signature, so the motives of the claimant in challenging the contract at the time of the claim are irrelevant.

- The court does not apply a principle of proportionality as such.

  - Many of the leading cases have involved contracts that are unfair due to a lack of reciprocity (eg: the contract is exclusive and there is no corresponding obligation on the part of the defendant to exploit the products of the artist's services).

    - This could lead to a 'sterilisation', rather than 'absorption', of the artist's services – words used by Hodson LJ in *Esso Petroleum v Harper's Garage (Stourport)* ([1967] 2 WLR 871) and quoted in the music cases.

    - This can be contrasted with a case in which the restrictions are 'commensurate' with the artist's rights under the contract (*obiter* comment in *Panayiotou*, as above).

b) **Public interest**

- If the restrictions are reasonable as between the parties, they must also satisfy a public-policy requirement, ie: that the artist should be free to earn a living and to give the 'fruits of his particular abilities' to the public.

  - The burden of proof shifts: it is for the claimant (ie: artist) to show that the restrictions are contrary to the public interest (*Herbert Morris v Saxelby* [1916] 1 AC 688).

    - NB: if the restrictions have been held to be reasonable between the parties, they are extremely unlikely to be held to be contrary to the public interest.

    - It can be difficult to distinguish between the two limbs of the *Nordenfelt* test, as it is hard to conceive how a reasonable restriction on the artist could offend against the public interest in the artist's freedom to earn a living.

➤ Given the mainly successful challenges brought by artists in the past, it is in the interest of a manager or music company to try avoid the application of the doctrine:

Restraint of trade in practice

➤ Most standard-form music contracts have been amended in light of the decided cases in an effort to maximise the benefits to managers and music companies, while not offending against the doctrine of restraint of trade.

◆ This is not a precise science, given that each case turns on its facts.

● The practical constraints on managers and music companies arising from the doctrine are examined in Sections B to D of this Chapter.

➤ In addition to ensuring that the contract is sufficiently fair, the manager or music company should ensure that the artist has taken expert professional advice from a specialist entertainment lawyer.

◆ This does not, of itself, make unreasonable restrictions fair, but it is a relevant consideration for the court in weighing up factors such as unequal bargaining power and an unconscionable bargain.

V Undue influence

➤ An inexperienced, impressionable artist may be swayed into concluding an unfair contract with an unscrupulous manager or music company (eg: by placing trust in a misleading explanation of the terms of the contract).

➤ 'Undue influence' arises in a relationship between 2 parties where there is (*Royal Bank of Scotland plc v Etridge (No 2)* [2002] 2 AC 773 – the leading case on undue influence):

a) 'trust and confidence, reliance, dependence or vulnerability on the one hand, *and*

b) ascendancy, domination or control on the other'.

➤ Undue influence is an equitable doctrine which, if successfully pleaded, releases a party from contractual obligations. The contract is set aside as an unfair bargain.

◆ NB: a contract is enforceable until it is set aside, and the court may grant other equitable remedies (eg: an account of profits unfairly obtained).

➤ There are 4 steps to consider in relation to a claim of undue influence:

Steps	
1	Did the defendant exert actual undue influence?
2	Is the defendant presumed to have exerted undue influence?
3	Was the contract not explicable by ordinary motives?
4	Are there any defences?

Step 1 — Did the defendant exert actual undue influence?

➤ In the absence of a presumption (see below), the claimant must prove that the defendant **actually** exerted undue influence to induce the claimant to enter into the contract (*Barclays Bank Ltd v O'Brien* [1994] 1 AC 180).

  ◆ It is, however, rare that a defendant will have actively induced (eg: pressurised) an artist into signing an unfair contract in bad faith.

    ● In many of the leading cases, the defendant provided a contract to the artist that was on standard industry terms at the time (even if unfair in hindsight).

Step 2 — Is the defendant presumed to have exerted undue influence?

➤ Alternatively, undue influence is presumed (so need not be proved by the claimant) by virtue of the relationship between the contracting parties in 2 situations (*Royal Bank of Scotland plc v Etridge (No 2)* [2002] 2 AC 773):

  a) where there is a fiduciary relationship between the parties by operation of law (eg: between solicitor and client or employer and employee), *or*

  b) where the relationship between the parties is such that a presumption of undue influence should be made since, in fact, the claimant generally placed trust and confidence in the defendant and/or the defendant exercised substantial control over the claimant's financial affairs.

➤ The relationship between artist and manager is likely to give rise to a presumption of undue influence under the second category, as is the relationship between an artist and the individual representative(s) of a record label or publishing company (*John v James* [1991] FSR 397).

  ◆ Whether a presumption arises is, nonetheless, a question of fact. The precise circumstances will be relevant (eg: the degree of control exerted by the defendant over the artist's career and the artist's age and experience).

  ◆ The second category of presumed undue influence is rebuttable (*Etridge*, as above). The best way to rebut it is to show that the artist gave informed consent to entering into the contract in the first place:

Rebutting a presumption of undue influence

➤ The defendant should ensure that the artist has taken independent professional advice from a specialist entertainment lawyer and has fully understood the terms of the contract before signing it.

  ◆ In all of the leading cases, the artist received either no legal advice at all or inadequate advice (eg: due to a conflict of interest or due to insufficient contact with the artist's legal adviser).

➤ This does not prove that the artist acted with a free will, but is persuasive.

Step 3	Was the contract not explicable by ordinary motives?

➤ If there is actual or presumed undue influence, the claimant must generally prove that the transaction 'cannot be explained by ordinary motives' (*Royal Bank of Scotland plc v Etridge (No 2)* [2002] 2 AC 773).

◆ This need not be shown if undue influence can be proved in other ways, but the defendant bears the burden of disproving undue influence if the claimant can show:

a) a relationship of actual or presumed influence, *and*

b) that, in all the circumstances of the transaction, a reasonable person would (in the absence of explanation by ordinary motives) infer that the transaction represented the beneficiary's taking advantage of the position of influence (*Etridge*, as above).

● NB: following *Etridge*, there is no need to prove (as was previously thought) that the transaction was 'manifestly disadvantageous' to the claimant.

■ Whether a transaction can be readily explained depends on the nature of the transaction and the parties' relationship: the greater the disadvantage to the claimant, the more cogent the explanation must be to disprove a finding of undue influence.

➤ In practice, a record label, music publisher or manager should try to ensure that a contract is reasonably advantageous to the artist:

Concluding a fair and reasonable contract

➤ The contract should, from the outset:

◆ not be unduly one-sided, eg: has a fair duration of commission (*Armatrading v Stone* (1984), unreported, 17 September 1984), *and*

◆ be on arm's-length terms, especially where is it is with a company affiliated to one with which the artist already has a relationship (*O'Sullivan v Management Agency and Music* [1984] 3 WLR 448).

Step 4	Are there any defences?

➤ Since undue influence is an equitable doctrine, the usual bars to the exercise of the court's equitable jurisdiction can be raised as defences by the defendant, eg:

◆ *acquiescence* – ie: the artist has intentionally and unequivocally induced the defendant to believe that the artist would not challenge the contract, *or*

◆ *'laches'* – ie: once the artist becomes aware of having entered into an unfair contract, the artist delays too long before bringing an action against the defendant.

VI   Contracts with minors

➤ Since artists are often young people or children, the rules relating to 'minors' can be of particular relevance to music contracts.

◆ A 'minor' is, for the purposes of contract law, a person under the age of 18 (*Family Law Reform Act 1969 s 1*).

➤ Under contract law, the general rule is that a contract with a minor is voidable at the option of the minor during his minority or within a reasonable time thereafter (*Proform Sports Management Ltd v Proactive Sports Management Ltd* [2006] EWHC 2903, the 'Wayne Rooney' case).

◆ A contract is therefore potentially unenforceable against the minor, although it is binding on the other contracting party (where that party is not a minor).

● A minor wishing to 'repudiate' a contract (ie: declare that it is void) must do so before the minor's 18th birthday or within a 'reasonable' time thereafter.

▪ What amounts to a 'reasonable' time varies from case to case.

▪ The minor may not be able to repudiate the contract if the minor has taken active steps to affirm the contract (eg: continued to perform the contract).

➤ There are, however, important exceptions to that rule, and there is a 2-stage test for the enforceability of a contract with a minor (*Proform Sports*, as above):

Steps	
1	Is the contract for 'necessaries'?
2	Is the contract for the minor's benefit?

Step 1	Is the contract for 'necessaries'?

➤ If it is a contract for 'necessaries', it will be enforceable, subject to step 2.

Contract for 'necessaries'

➤ Aside from a contract to supply necessary goods (eg: food) and/or services (eg: medical services), a contract for 'necessaries' is one that is (or is analogous to) a contract of service, apprenticeship or education (*Roberts v Gray* [1913] 1 KB 525).

◆ A management contract has been held analogous to a contract of service (and so enforceable) where the manager was obliged to organise matters essential to the business of the artist (*Denmark Productions Ltd v Boscobel Productions Ltd* [1968] 3 WLR 841, the 'Kinks' case).

➤ In contrast, a contract with an agent was held unnecessary to permit a player to earn a living, unlike the employment contract with his football club (*Proform Sports*, as above).

Step 2	Is the contract for the minor's benefit?

➤ Even if a contract is for 'necessaries' (so otherwise binding by its nature), it is unenforceable if its terms are prejudicial to the minor's interests.

◆ If the contract contains both prejudicial and beneficial terms, the question is whether the contract was, taken as a whole, for the minor's benefit as at the date of signature (*De Francesco v Barnum* [1890] 45 ChD 430).

➤ Whether a contract is beneficial is a question of fact in each case, so a label, publisher or manager should pre-empt any dispute that a minor might bring.

Contracts with minors in practice

➤ The other party should ensure that:

◆ the contract is not unduly one-sided, provides for practical assistance to the minor in furthering the minor's music career (eg: commitments to provide studio facilities) and contains fair remuneration provisions, *and*

◆ the minor has taken independent professional advice from a specialist entertainment lawyer before signing the contract.

➤ There is no legal rule that prevents the other party from entering into a contract with an adult (eg: the minor's parent or guardian) under which the adult:

a) approves the contract with the minor (as an inducement for the other party to enter into the contract), *and*

b) guarantees that the minor will honour his contractual obligations, *and*

c) indemnifies the other party (ie: agrees to reimburse the other party on a debt basis) for any losses arising from:

i) failure by the minor to perform his contractual obligations, *or*

ii) any attempt by the minor (or the adult) to repudiate his contract.

◆ This type of guarantee is enforceable (*Minors' Contracts Act 1987 s 2*).

● The adult is likely, on commercial grounds, to resist giving a guarantee (and should at least try to ensure that it ceases to have effect when the minor reaches the age of 18).

● It is not uncommon for an adult simply to confirm that the adult and minor have received expert legal advice on the minor's contract and are satisfied that it is clearly for the minor's benefit.

➤ Nothing under the *CDPA* prevents a minor from being the author or owner of a copyright work. A minor can also effectively assign the copyright in a work under a written contract, and the setting aside of a voidable contract does not effect a re-assignment to the minor (*Chaplin v Leslie Frewin (Publishers) Ltd* [1966] Ch 71).

➤ NB: the engagement of child performers under the compulsory school age (ie: put simply, of 16 years of age or younger) is also governed by legislation.

◆ For certain performances by a child, the producer of the performance must obtain a licence from the relevant local education authority.

● See the *Children and Young Persons Act 1963*, the *Children (Performances) Regulations 1968*, related statutory instruments and local-authority guidance, which are all beyond the scope of this Section.

B Management contracts

	A manager's role
II	Management agreement

I A manager's role

➤ Few artists have the expertise – or (when successful) the time – to run their business effectively, and any business will fail without proper management.

   ◆ It is also extremely difficult, on a personal level, for artists to 'sell' themselves effectively to a commercial partner (eg: a record label or publishing company).

      ● For these reasons, most artists appoint a manager to act for them.

         ■ Choosing a manager is an important career decision. A bad artist with a good manager often does better than a good artist with a bad manager.

➤ At the early stages of a manager's career, the manager's functions tend to be varied.

   ◆ A manager starting out with a new artist will organise gigs and studio sessions, negotiate deals, collect the money, handle publicity and even drive the van.

➤ As the artist develops and becomes more successful, the artist will be able to employ specialists (eg: booking agents, producers, lawyers, accountants, press officers and road crew). The manager's main role is then to oversee the artist's career and to negotiate deals to further each aspect of that career.

   ◆ The manager is often described as a 'personal manager' – as distinct from a 'business manager', ie: the artist's financial adviser (usually an accountant).

➤ A manager rarely commits in writing to investing in an artist (eg: paying for 'demos' or rehearsal studios or, on a larger scale, funding the recording of an album).

   ◆ In return for any investment, a new artist may be expected to sign a development deal with the manager (granting recording or publishing rights to the manager).

➤ For an artist, therefore, there are 3 main reasons to appoint a manager:

   a) the manager's knowledge of – and, critically, contacts in – the industry (eg: a new artist will look to a manager to secure recording and publishing deals), *and*

   b) organisational support, allowing the artist to focus on creative matters, *and*

   c) ideally, a genuine bond of friendship and creative rapport, which can count for a great deal in a business where mutual trust and confidence in artistic direction are (perhaps surprisingly on the face of it) often in short supply.

➤ The artist may pick a respected manager with 'clout' and extensive contacts.

   ◆ Equally, many long-term management relationships have come about where an artist and a manager start out as unknowns and 'grow' together.

➤ In legal terms, when acting on the artist's behalf in negotiating deals with third parties, the manager acts as an 'agent' for the artist (who is the 'principal' at common law).

◆ NB: the *Commercial Agents (Council Directive) Regulations 1993* do not apply, as they apply only in the context of the sale or purchase of **goods** (*r 2(1)*).

➤ The agency relationship at common law has several legal implications:

Agency relationship at common law
➤ Where the manager has actual or apparent authority, the manager can bind the artist to contractual obligations to third parties. ◆ Since it is the artist that is liable under those contractual obligations (and not the manager), the artist should try to ensure that: ● the limits of the manager's authority are carefully defined, *and* ● the artist fully understands (and takes professional advice on) the consequences of each contract entered into by the artist. ➤ Several obligations are implied by law. The manager must: ◆ act in person (ie: must not delegate), unless otherwise agreed, *and* ◆ act with due care and skill (eg: try to obtain the best contractual terms when negotiating a deal on the artist's behalf), *and* ◆ act in good faith towards the artist, so must: ● avoid conflicts of interest and disclose any that arise, *and* ● account to the artist for all monies received by the manager on the artist's behalf (and maintain separate accounts), *and* ● not make a secret profit (eg: accept a bribe), *and* ● not, during or after the agency, disclose/misuse the artist's confidential or private information (*Ash v McKennitt* [2006] EWCA Civ 1714). ➤ Certain compensation arrangements will apply unless the contract specifies or implies otherwise: ◆ The manager does **not** have an implied right: a) to receive any remuneration in return for providing services, *or* b) after the manager has ceased to act as agent, to continue to receive remuneration (eg: commission) based on income arising from activities conducted by the artist during the agency period. ● The manager will want to include such rights in the contract. ◆ The manager does, however, have an implied right to be reimbursed for expenses incurred when acting on the artist's behalf. ● The artist will want to impose contractual limits on this right.

➤ Because the manager acts as an agent and usually has authority to book professional engagements for the artist (eg: gigs or personal appearances), the manager arguably has statutory duties under the *Conduct of Employment Agencies and Employment Businesses Regulations 2003* ('**CEAEBR 2003**').

Statutory duties of 'employment agencies'

➤ The extent to which the *CEAEBR 2003* apply is uncertain. The *CEAEBR 2003* are aimed at booking agencies, but managers are potentially caught by the wide definitions of 'agency' (which includes an individual) and 'employment' (which extends to contracts for services).

◆ Managers should err on the safe side by complying with the requirements imposed on agencies under the *CEAEBR 2003*.

➤ The detailed provisions of the *CEAEBR 2003* are beyond the scope of this Section, but the agency's obligations include requirements:

◆ to provide the 'work-seeker' (ie: the potential provider of services to a third-party 'hirer') with **written** terms of business, which must include specified details (eg: the services to be provided by the agency, the agency's authority (if any) to act on the work-seeker's behalf, the method of calculation of any fee payable by the work-seeker to the agency, termination arrangements and sub-contracting restrictions) (*r 16*), *and*

◆ to ensure an engagement is suitable for the work-seeker (*r 17*), *and*

◆ to obtain details from the hirer in advance about any engagement before the introduction of any work-seeker (*r 18*), *and*

◆ not to introduce a work-seeker unless the agency has obtained confirmation that the work-seeker has the experience, training and qualifications that the hirer considers necessary (*r 19*), *and*

◆ to operate a client account on behalf of a work-seeker (*r 25*).

➤ Civil liability attaches to failure to comply with the *CEAEBR 2003* (*r 20*).

Practical implications of agencies' statutory duties

➤ In practice, a reputable, well-organised manager operating under a written management contract will largely (if not entirely) satisfy the requirements of the *CEAEBR 2003*, which in many ways codify best practice.

➤ For even modestly successful acts, managers will rely on professional booking agents, who will assume the statutory duties.

➤ In practical terms, by representing an artist, the manager acts as a buffer between the artist and each person doing business with the artist (eg: a record label or publishing company), allowing the artist to concentrate on artistic development.

II   Management agreement

➤   A manager will often insist on having a written contract setting out the terms of the relationship. The contract is known as a 'management agreement'.

◆   In particular, the manager will want comfort about:

a)   how long the relationship will last, *and*

b)   the level (and duration) of remuneration for services provided to the artist.

● Ultimately the relationship between artist and manager is based on trust. If this is lacking, it is unlikely to succeed.

■ For this reason, some of the best-known managers in the business have operated on a 'handshake', with nothing reduced to writing.

■ The norm is, however, to agree terms in writing – perhaps after a trial period of 6 months. Should a dispute arise, a written contract provides clear evidence as to the terms originally agreed.

➤   In essence, a management agreement is simply a contract for the supply of services by the manager to the artist. The contract therefore falls into 2 main parts:

a)   the nature, scope, duration and area of the manager's appointment, *and*

b)   the manager's remuneration for providing the services.

◆   It is usually supplemented with standard 'boilerplate' clauses.

➤   As a contract for **personal** services, it cannot be specifically enforced by the artist against the manager (ie: the artist cannot force the manager to act for the artist).

➤   Conversely, a management agreement, like any other contract, can be subject to the doctrines of restraint of trade and undue influence – see Section A of this Chapter.

Enforceability of the management agreement

➤   It is important for a manager to ensure that the artist receives independent advice (preferably from a specialist entertainment lawyer) and fully understands the terms of the contract before signing.

◆   Otherwise, there is a risk that the contract could be found unenforceable – or even set aside altogether – by a court.

➤   For this reason, it is common practice (especially with a new artist) for a manager to pay a contribution towards the artist's legal fees to ensure that the artist has been properly advised on the terms of the contract.

◆   Even though the artist's lawyer is likely to negotiate better terms for the artist, it is ultimately in the manager's interest to be able to rely on the contract, especially should a dispute arise.

➤ Although the terms of the contract are always a matter for negotiation between the parties, a fairly consistent commercial practice has emerged and the following provisions are generally (if not always) included:

Clause	Terms
Parties	➤ The parties may simply be an individual artist (eg: a singer-songwriter) and an individual manager.
	◆ The remainder of this Section assumes, for the sake of simplicity that this is the case (except as noted below).
	➤ On both sides, however, the parties need to consider the appropriate business medium through which to contract.
	◆ It may be appropriate for either party to set up a special vehicle (eg: a private limited company or a limited liability partnership) to isolate risk in the venture.
	◆ It may also be more tax-efficient (in particular, for international performers) to set up trading vehicles for different territories.
	• From a UK perspective, the tax advantages of this sort of structure under previous legislation have generally been withdrawn, so it is less common now for artists to set up complex tax-driven business structures.
	➤ A solo artist is generally likely to set up vehicles for particular ventures (eg: tours) rather than for the purpose of entering into a management agreement (under which there is no direct commercial risk).
	➤ Most groups constitute a partnership for statutory purposes, as they carry on a business in common with the intention of making a profit (*Partnership Act 1890 s 1*).
	◆ The group members will sign in their individual capacity unless they set up a special vehicle, as a partnership at law does not have a legal identity separate to its partners.
	• A group may, however, decide to formalise their partnership by setting up a special entity (or series of entities) providing their services. In such cases, each individual group member should enter into an 'inducement letter' with the manager, promising to perform the contract personally if necessary.
	➤ For any group structure, a written 'band agreement' can be advisable, in order to set out the position on contentious issues such as:
	a) how the band's income is split, *and*
	b) how copyright in jointly written songs is split, *and*
	c) if the band splits, how capital is withdrawn and who remains entitled to use the band's name.
	◆ In practice, band agreements are often not signed, as the issues are so divisive that a band cannot agree on them or (in extreme cases) they even catalyse a band split.
	• A new group may well not have the financial resources to take professional advice on complex arrangements.
	■ Complex structures are also expensive to maintain (in terms of corporate and accounting compliance costs) – as well as to unwind.

Clause	Terms
Appointment	➤ The artist usually appoints the manager as the artist's sole and exclusive manager. ◆ This means that the artist cannot appoint another manager, but the manager is free to represent other artists. ● Both parties should think carefully about this before entering into the contract. There is no point in an artist appointing a manager, or the manager agreeing to act, where the manager will not be able to devote sufficient time or operational resource to managing the artist due to other commitments.
Scope of representation	➤ The contract should define the area of representation to which the appointment relates. ◆ The manager will want a widely drafted clause that appoints the manager for 'all branches of the entertainment industry'. ● Given the increasing convergence of the entertainment industry, a manager will want to ensure that the scope covers not just the music industry, but also wider activities, such as movie roles, appearances in stage musicals, modelling, literary activities other than lyric-writing (eg: writing a novel or autobiography), product endorsement and sponsorship. ◆ The artist may want to limit the scope to the 'music industry', and should consider whether certain activities should be excluded. ● The artist may have already appointed (or wish to appoint) a specialist agent for certain activities (eg: remixing and production, modelling or acting), in which case it should be made clear that those activities are excluded. ■ Included activities will be 'commissionable' (ie: activities for which the manager receives a commission), so the artist should not suffer a double deduction of commission (ie: the manager's and the agent's share). ■ In any event, the manager may not be skilled in all the areas of representation that the artist requires.
Term	➤ The duration of the appointment (known as the 'term') should be clearly defined and is a matter of commercial negotiation. ◆ Any contract that attempts to 'tie in' the artist for lengthy periods could subsequently be challenged by the artist for being in restraint of trade. It should not run for longer than 5 years. ➤ There is usually an initial period, which is commonly a fixed period of 3 years (or, at the most, up to 5 years). ◆ Alternatively, the initial period is linked to the duration of the recording and promotion of album(s) (eg: 1-3 'album cycles'). The artist should insist on a long-stop date (eg: 3-5 years), as each album cycle can easily take 2-3 years. ● The term is often extended automatically thereafter, subject to termination on written notice by either party. ■ The manager may alternatively try to secure an option to extend (eg: for 1-2 years). The artist should resist this, unless the option can only be exercised if the manager has achieved specified income levels for the artist.

Clause	Terms

Early termination	➤ The artist should try to include a right to terminate the term early if the manager fails to achieve a specified goal within a period of 9-18 months.
	
	  ◆ A period of 12 months is a common compromise.
	
	    ● The goal may be signing a recording contract with a major record label (or a label approved by the artist) or achieving a minimum amount of earnings.
	
	➤ The artist has a right to terminate at common law for:
	
	  a) breach of a fundamental term of the contract, *and/or*
	
	  b) breach of a 'fiduciary' duty (ie: duty to act in good faith) imposed by the agency relationship (see above, as well as the Kinks case, *Denmark Productions Ltd v Boscobel Productions Ltd* [1968] 3 WLR 841).
	
	➤ The artist should, however, insist on including an express right to terminate the term of the manager's appointment if the manager:
	
	  ◆ is in material breach of the contract (this is usually subject to a 'cure' period, eg: 30 days), *or*
	
	  ◆ becomes bankrupt or insolvent, *or*
	
	  ◆ is convicted of any criminal offence involving dishonesty, *or*
	
	  ◆ is incapacitated (subject to allowance for reasonable periods of holiday and illness).
	
	    ● The manager may want reciprocal rights of termination, although, in practice, the manager is far less likely to want to terminate the term.
	
	➤ Termination is usually without prejudice to the manager's right to receive post-term commission (see below), irrespective of the nature of the breach, although the artist may try to argue (probably unsuccessfully) that certain types of breach (eg: the manager's insolvency) should bring that entitlement to an end.

Keyman clause	➤ If the manager is part of a management company, the artist will want a provision specifically naming the person within the company who will undertake the manager's services. This is known as a 'keyman' clause. ➤ The artist should have the right to terminate the term if the company fails to provide the services of the 'key man' for a specified consecutive period (eg: 3-4 months) or for a specified aggregate period (eg: 6 months) within a specified period (eg: 12 months).

Territory	➤ The manager usually insists on representing the artist throughout the world.
	
	  ◆ The artist should consider whether:
	
	    ● any territories should be excluded altogether (especially North America, Japan or any other major territory where the manager may not have suitable experience or contacts, nor sufficient presence or operational resource) to allow the artist to appoint an different manager there, *or*
	
	    ● a suitably experienced and well-connected consultant or 'sub-manager' should be appointed in any such territories.

Clause	Terms
Manager's obligations	➤ There should a widely drafted definition of the manager's obligations in general (eg: to render 'all services customarily rendered by a personal manager in the entertainment industry').
	◆ The manager cannot guarantee success, so should not make any firm commitments about attainment of goals or levels of success (other than in the context of reasonable conditions attached to the duration of the term of the manager's appointment).
	➤ There should also be a clause setting out specific obligations, eg:
	a) to advise the artist on the artist's career, *and*
	b) to use 'best endeavours' (or at least 'all reasonable endeavours') to promote the artist's activities, *and*
	c) to negotiate, in consultation with the artist and the artist's lawyer, all necessary contracts on the artist's behalf, *and*
	d) to oversee projects relating to the artist's activities (eg: the choice of producers for recording sessions, preparation of artwork, production of 'promo videos' and touring), *and*
	e) to ensure that the manager's other activities (eg: managing other acts) do not prejudice the manager's ability to perform the manager's obligations under the contract.
	➤ The case of *Martin-Smith v Williams* [1998] EMLR 334 confirmed that, in the case of a group, the manager's duties are to the group as a whole, rather than to any individual member.
Authority of the manager	➤ The manager is often expressly authorised to make certain types of agreements (eg: for one-off appearances) on the artist's behalf.
	◆ The artist should ensure that these are subject to the artist's prior approval in principle.
	➤ Major contracts should be subject to the artist's final approval and should actually be signed by the artist, not least because they concern the artist's own commitments and level of remuneration.
Artist's obligations and warranties	➤ The artist is commonly obliged:
	◆ to undertake to perform the artist's activities to the best of the artist's ability, *and*
	◆ to warrant that the artist:
	• is 18 years old or older (ie: has the legal capacity to enter into the agreement – see Section A of this Chapter – failing which a parent or legal guardian will need to approve the contract), *and*
	• has taken legal advice on the contract from a lawyer with expertise in the entertainment industry (ie: to counter allegations that the contract is invalid on grounds of restraint of trade or undue influence – see above), *and*
	• has not entered into any other agreements that conflict with the agreement with the manager (eg: does not have an existing management agreement and has not agreed to pay a former manager commission for activities conducted during the current manager's term).

Clause	Terms
Commission	➤ In return for providing services, the manager is almost invariably paid a 'commission', ie: a percentage of the artist's income arising in the agreed territory from the commissionable activities undertaken by the artist during the term of the manager's appointment.

➤ In return for providing services, the manager is almost invariably paid a 'commission', ie: a percentage of the artist's income arising in the agreed territory from the commissionable activities undertaken by the artist during the term of the manager's appointment.

♦ In the UK, the percentage is generally 20% – perhaps 15% (or even 10%) for very successful acts (or if based on true 'gross' income). 25% might be justified if the manager makes a substantial cash investment in the artist, but this is very rare.

● 'Escalations' (ie: increases of the rate based on a rise in income) or decreases based on a rise in income are rare.

■ Occasionally, an established artist may pay the manager an agreed fee or salary, but this is not the norm.

➤ The sources of income generally include all music activities, eg:

♦ recordings (whether audio or audiovisual), *and*

♦ live appearances (in concert, broadcast or webcast), *and*

♦ songwriting and other composing (eg: for TV), *and*

♦ merchandise and product endorsement.

● The sources will also include any other entertainment fields in which the manager represents the artist.

■ Activities excluded from the scope of representation (see above) will not attract a commission.

➤ For each source of income, the artist is likely to receive an 'advance' against the artist's share of income. Each advance will be non-returnable, but 'recoupable' (ie: recoverable) by the company paying the advance.

♦ Advances can be substantial (especially in the case of recording and publishing contracts) – in fact, the artist may never receive any 'back-end' payments from these deals.

● The manager will insist on taking a commission from all advances.

■ This is fair, but the manager should not be entitled to commission on sums received on the artist's behalf but used by the relevant company to recoup the advance – otherwise the manager would effectively receive double commission (which is known as 'double-dipping').

➤ The artist should try to ensure that commission is only payable on sums **actually received** by the artist or, where applicable, by an entity on the artist's behalf (eg: a touring vehicle) – otherwise, the artist will have no money from which to pay the commission.

♦ Following the case of *Martin-Smith v Williams* ([1998] EMLR 334), the contract should, however, clarify whether the manager can take commission from income that the artist is entitled to receive where the artist has chosen to waive or release that entitlement.

● Eg: a record label may purchase equipment for the artist and agree to debit the artist's account by an amount equal to the cost – in effect, reducing the sums to be paid out to the artist, and in turn the sums commissionable by the manager.

■ The manager will argue (and usually succeed in arguing) for a right to take commission from that amount. The phrase 'monies received by **or credited to** the artist' is often used to address this issue.

Clause	Terms
Exclusions and deductions	➤ It is very rare – at least in the UK – for the commission to be calculated on the artist's true 'gross' income.

➤ It is very rare – at least in the UK – for the commission to be calculated on the artist's true 'gross' income.

◆ The artist does not want to be a position where expenditure on an activity (eg: a tour) exceeds the income derived from it, but the artist still has to pay commission.

➤ The basis of calculation is usually an effective 'net' – even if not generally defined as such (as the net element varies from activity to activity). This is achieved by:

◆ excluding certain monies from the gross income, eg:

• VAT or similar sales taxes, *and*

• 'tour support' (ie: sums paid by the artist's record company to make good a shortfall on a loss-making gig or tour), *and*

◆ deducting specified costs from certain sources of income, eg:

• recording and video production costs that are paid by the artist (or paid by the record company as a recoupable advance against the artist's share of income under the recording contract), eg: sums paid to third-party producers, mixers, engineers and session musicians or to the artist to acquire studio equipment, *and*

• all costs of a gig or a tour that are paid by the artist (eg: each agent's fee (typically 10% or 15% of gross income for the relevant territory), session-musician and road-crew wages, sound and lights, travel and accommodation), *and*

• costs of sale of merchandise that are paid by the artist, *and*

• where the artist has a literary, acting or similar agent, the agent's commission (although the manager may insist on approving the rate of commission or the deduction may be capped at 10% of gross income from such source).

➤ Even where the basis of calculation is more like a true 'gross', income from gigs and tours is commonly calculated on the basis of net profits, although the rates and net elements vary considerably as this can be a contentious aspect of the contract.

◆ The MMF, which promotes the interests of managers, recommends a mixed approach: 10-15% of gross income (less sales taxes) or 20-30% of net profits, whichever is greater.

◆ UK artists often succeed in arguing for a net-profits basis. A manager, unlike a booking agent, earns from other sources, so does not have a strong argument for a gross basis.

• Whatever the basis agreed in the contract, the parties often take a pragmatic approach on a tour-by-tour basis.

  ▪ One approach is to treat a fee for the manager's overheads as an expense in the tour budget.

➤ Where deductions are agreed, the manager will insist on having a right of approval over recording, video and touring budgets (which are by far the most significant outgoings for an artist).

◆ This is to try to ensure that the costs will be kept under control, and that the activities will ultimately be profitable (and, in practical terms, commissionable).

• For each right of approval, the artist should try to ensure that it is 'not to be unreasonably withheld or delayed'.

Clause	Terms
Post-term commission	➤ At the end of the term, the artist would preferably be free to appoint a new manager and to pay commission on the artist's activities conducted after the term without suffering a double deduction of commission (ie: to both the outgoing and incoming manager). ◆ Under the common-law agency rules (see above), the manager is not entitled to further commission (regardless of the source), unless agreed otherwise. ➤ Under the contract, the manager usually continues to receive commission – after the manager's term of appointment has ended – on income derived from the commissionable activities conducted by the artist during the term (eg: songs written and albums recorded during the term, which may sell well for years after the term). ◆ The manager usually argues for (and often succeeds in getting) the right, in addition, to receive commission on activities conducted during a short period immediately following the term (eg: 4 or 6 months), where conducted under a contract entered into (or substantially negotiated) during the term. ➤ The duration of the entitlement to post-term commission used, in the 1960s and 1970s, to be 'in perpetuity', but that is no longer standard practice (except sometimes in the USA). The duration should therefore be limited to a fixed period (known as the 'sunset period'). ◆ The 'sunset period' mechanism is a matter of commercial negotiation and can be the most contentious clause of the contract. ◆ It commonly takes the form of an initial period (eg: 5 years) during which the manager continues to commission at full rate, followed by a period (often of equal length to the initial period) during which the manager commissions at half rate. ● In any event, the right to receive commission ceases altogether at the end of the last period. ◆ Managers often argue for (but rarely get) a much longer sunset period and extra steps, eg: 20 years in all, split into 5 years at full rate, 5 years at 15%, 5 years at 10% and 5 years at 5%. ● Managing an artist is a risky investment of time and resource, so managers feel that there should be a suitable 'upside'. ◆ At the other end of the spectrum, many artists succeed in getting much shorter sunset periods, eg: 6 or 8 years in all, split into 3 or 4 years at full rate, plus 3 or 4 years at half rate. ● That success derives from 2 main arguments: a) future income largely derives from the artist's efforts (eg: via touring) to promote the back catalogue, *and* b) a new manager will want to commission (even if at a reduced rate) monies arising from exploitation of the back catalogue. ◆ The duration can, in practice, be a moot point, as the income may tail off dramatically in the later years of the sunset period if the back catalogue is not exploited. ● One problem for a successful artist is where, years later, an older album is repackaged (eg: as a box set). The artist will want to incentivise the then-current manager by allowing the manager a right to commission on the re-issued album.

Clause	Terms
Remuneration of consultant or sub-manager	➤ Where a consultant or sub-manager is appointed (see 'Territory' above), the manager should bear the cost of remunerating the consultant or sub-manager from the manager's share of income arising in the relevant territory (eg: the manager may pay 50% of the manager's share to the consultant/sub-manager and retain the balance). ◆ The artist would usually be responsible for reimbursing the consultant's/sub-manager's expenses.

Accounting	➤ The artist is usually entitled to collect all income, as a matter of principle (ie: since it largely represents the artist's money).
	
	◆ The artist is, however, often required under the contract to appoint an accountant (whose identity is to be approved by the manager) to collect income on the artist's behalf and to administer commission payments to the manager.
	
	   • A new artist will want to keep professional costs to a minimum and may ask for the right in the short term (eg: until the signing of a record deal) to set up a bank account in the artist's name into which all income is paid.
	
	     ■ The manager will want, during that period, to be entitled to receive bank statements.
	
	➤ Accounting is often quarterly, although a manager will want to ensure that significant sums (eg: 'advances' paid on account of future income under the artist's recording contract) are commissionable within a fixed period (eg: 30 days) after receipt by the artist.
	
	➤ Where an accountant is in place, the manager will want to have the right to examine the books maintained by the accountant to verify that the manager is receiving all sums due.
	
	◆ Such 'audit rights' are similar to those described in Sections C and D of this Chapter on recording and publishing contracts, except that they are exercisable **against** the artist, rather than **by** the artist (it being the record label or publishing company, not the artist, that collects income under those contracts).

Expenses	➤ Under the contract, the manager can usually reclaim business expenses that the manager has – as it is often put – 'directly and identifiably' incurred in the course of providing management services to the artist (eg: mobile phone calls, travel and accommodation).
	
	◆ The artist will usually insist on limiting the recovery of expenses incurred without the artist's approval by imposing a cap:
	
	   • on individual items of expenditure (eg: £500), *and*
	
	   • on aggregate expenses in a period (eg: £1,000 per month).
	
	◆ The artist will also want to ensure that:
	
	   • the manager's general overhead costs are excluded, *and*
	
	   • where the manager represents other artists, expenses are apportioned fairly between each artist.
	
	➤ Expenses are often reclaimed on a monthly or quarterly basis.
	
	◆ A new artist may have no income from which to reimburse the manager, so the contract may provide for expenses to be carried forward to subsequent accounting periods.

Clause	Terms

| **Group provisions** | ➤ Where the artist is a group, the group members are usually jointly and severally liable for the artist's obligations under the contract (ie: each member is liable for the acts and omissions of the others).

 ➤ The manager will also want (and usually succeed in arguing for):

 ◆ the artist to ensure that any new member(s) of the group will become parties to the management agreement, *and*

 ◆ any members who leave the group to remain bound by the management agreement whether they continue as solo artists, work together as a smaller group or join another group. |

| **Intellectual property** | ➤ The contract should contain a clause which makes it clear that the manager does not actually own any of the artist's:

 ◆ copyright or performance rights, *or*

 ◆ rights to exploit the artist's name and likeness (eg: by way of merchandising, sponsorship or endorsement deals). |

| **Confidentiality** | ➤ The artist will want an express confidentiality clause preventing the manager from disclosing the artist's private affairs without prior authorisation from the artist. |

| **Assignability and sub-contracting** | ➤ The artist should ensure that the manager cannot assign the benefit of the contract (or sub-contract the manager's obligations) to a third party.

 ◆ The artist will generally only agree to enter into a management agreement on the strength of the artist's personal relationship with the manager and the manager's industry contacts, so will not want a third party to represent the artist without the artist's consent.

 ➤ The manager may want the flexibility to transfer the contract to a company controlled by the manager (eg: a 'loan-out company' set up to provide the services of the manager).

 ◆ The artist will usually agree to this, but should insist:

 a) on a 'keyman' clause preserving the manager's personal involvement (see above), *and*

 b) that the manager remain personally liable under the contract until the management company enters into a direct agreement with the artist to perform the manager's obligations under the contract. |

C Recording contracts

*References in this Section are to the Copyright, Designs and Patents Act 1988 ('**CDPA**'), unless otherwise stated.*

I	Generally
II	Legal basis of a recording contract
III	Recording agreement

I Generally

➤ A recording contract is often the main source of revenue for an artist.

◆ This is less true than it used to be, as sales of recorded music (especially albums) have declined significantly since 2000. Nonetheless, an artist remains unlikely to achieve widespread international success without releasing records and having the marketing support of a record label.

● The decline in record sales is having a seismic effect on the record industry, and is forcing record labels to re-consider their traditional business models.

■ It may well be that legal/commercial practice in the record industry will be affected radically over the next few years. This Section gives a snapshot of current practice, without attempting to predict how that will change.

➤ A traditional 'major' record company has a variety of functions, including:

a) scouting for 'talent' and signing artists through its 'A&R' (ie: artist and repertoire) department, *and*

b) selecting material to be recorded and financing recordings by its artists, *and*

c) manufacturing, promoting and distributing records.

◆ An 'independent' record company often focuses on artist development and relies (either largely or wholly) on one of the major record labels or their subsidiaries for finance and distribution (especially international distribution).

➤ A record company distributes each recording by various means, including:

◆ selling records in various physical formats (eg: CDs), *and*

◆ increasingly, digital distribution (eg: downloads/streaming via the internet), *and*

◆ licensing the rights in the recording to third parties (eg: 'synchronisation' licences permitting third parties to use a sound recording in a film or TV soundtrack), *and*

◆ public performance of the recording (eg: on radio).

● In return, the artist is usually paid a sum for each record sold (a 'royalty') and a lump-sum 'advance' (ie: a fixed prepayment of royalties) for each album recorded under the contract.

■ In a 'production agreement' (eg: with a small independent label), the artist usually receives a share of 'net receipts' rather than a royalty – see below.

➤ The decline in recorded-music sales has affected the balance of power between well-known artists and labels. Some artists are acting as their own labels (eg: Radiohead) or entering into recording joint ventures with sponsors (eg: Groove Armada).

◆ Labels of all sizes are branching out into wider music activities (eg: live music).

II   Legal basis of a recording contract

➤ In legal terms, a recording contract serves 2 main functions. The record company:

a) engages the exclusive recording services of musical performer(s), *and*

b) takes a grant of rights from the performer(s) to produce and exploit audio-only and audio-visual recordings of their performances.

◆ Even where there is a group of performers, the contract commonly describes the group as the 'artist'.

● For the sake of simplicity, this Section assumes a solo artist, except where a distinction is drawn.

➤ To record an artist's performances, the record company must deal effectively with the artist's rights in the performances.

Performers' economic rights

➤ The artist has 'economic rights' in each performance under *ss 180-205B*:

a) transferable '**property rights**', including the performer's consents to:

◆ copying recordings, *and*

◆ issuing copies to the public, *and*

◆ renting or lending copies to the public, *and*

b) non-transferable '**non-property rights**', including the performer's consent to recording a live performance.

➤ The record company should obtain:

a) an 'assignment' (ie: acquire ownership) of the property rights, *and*

b) consents in relation to the non-property rights.

◆ NB: even if the artist transfers the 'rental right' to the record company, the artist retains a right to receive 'equitable remuneration', which cannot be transferred except to a collecting society (*s 191(b)*).

● The relevant UK collecting society is PPL, which:

▪ collects amounts representing equitable remuneration from record companies, *and*

▪ pays its performer members – see Section A of this Chapter.

Performers' moral rights

➤ The artist also has 'moral rights' in each performance under *ss 205C-212*:

   a) to be identified as a performer (known as the 'paternity right'), *and*

   b) to object to any modification of a performance that is 'derogatory' (ie: prejudicial to the artist's reputation) (known as the 'integrity right').

    ◆ Moral rights cannot be transferred, but can be waived by the artist.

➤ The record company should therefore secure a waiver of such moral rights from the artist, as it will not always be possible to credit the artist and the record company will need flexibility to edit and remix each performance for release in different formats.

    ◆ If the artist has written any of the **songs** that have been recorded, the record company should also obtain a waiver from the artist of, and agreement not to assert, the artist's moral rights under *ss 77-89* (and any equivalent laws in overseas jurisdictions) as an 'author' of the musical compositions and lyrics.

➤ A record company usually acquires the **exclusive** right to make recordings of an artist's performances with a view to exploiting them commercially.

   ◆ By doing so, the record company acquires certain statutory rights as party to an 'exclusive recording contract':

Statutory rights under an exclusive recording contract

➤ The record company (or any person to whom it transfers the benefit of the contract) is entitled to bring a legal action directly against a person who:

    ◆ makes illicit recordings of an artist's performances (*s 186*), *or*

    ◆ imports or commercially exploits illicit recordings (*ss 187-188*).

➤ To release a record of a performance, the record company must own or control the copyright in the **recording** of the performance:

Copyright in 'sound recordings'

➤ Only sound is recorded during most studio sessions.

    ◆ Regardless of the medium on which the recording is made, it is a 'sound recording' for the purposes of the *CDPA* (*s 5A*).

➤ A record company usually undertakes all arrangements (including providing funding) necessary for the making of a sound recording, so it is the 'producer' (in legal, rather than creative, terms) of the sound recording (*s 178*).

    ◆ Assuming the record company is the legal 'producer', it is the first owner of the copyright in the sound recording (*s 9(2)(aa)*).

Assignment of copyright in 'sound recordings'

➤ In case the record company is not the first owner of copyright, it should anyhow take an 'assignment' (ie: full transfer) of any rights that an artist may have in the sound recording – especially where the artist has or will have 'produced' any recordings that are the subject of the contract (ie: in the sense of paying the studio bills).

◆ The record company will also want to be the full owner of the recording so that it can receive the money collected by PPL and VPL on behalf of record companies in relation to the public performance of recordings.

● This should be distinguished from the equitable remuneration collected by PPL and VPL on behalf of performers – see above.

➤ The record company must equally deal with the copyright in the songs recorded by the artist:

Copyright in songs

➤ There is an entirely separate copyright in the song (ie: music and lyrics) embodied in a sound recording.

◆ The relevant songwriter(s) are the first owner(s) of the copyright in the musical compositions and literary works comprised by a song.

● They may have entered into a separate music publishing contract in relation to the rights in the song – see Section D of this Chapter.

➤ In order to reproduce a song in the form of records, a record company has to pay 'mechanical' royalties to the relevant copyright owner.

◆ The copyright owner is usually the music publisher of the songwriter(s) or, where the publisher has appointed a collecting society as agent, the relevant collecting society (ie: the MCPS in the UK).

● The society then pays the publisher, which pays the songwriter(s) after deducting its share – see Section D of this Chapter.

◆ The record company does **not** have to pay public performance fees, which are payable by each person that plays the song in public (eg: on the radio or at a gig) to the relevant collecting society (ie: the PRS in the UK).

● The society then pays a share (usually 50%) to the publisher and the balance direct to the songwriter(s) – see Section D of this Chapter.

➤ So an artist who writes and performs songs will receive income from:

a) each of the **songs** – under the artist's publishing contract (as well as via the relevant collecting societies, eg: the MCPS and the PRS), *and*

b) each **performance** of the songs – under the artist's recording contract (as well as via the relevant collecting societies, eg: PPL and VPL).

➤ To promote a record by making a promotional video (eg: to be shown on MTV), the record company must own or control the copyright in the 'film' comprised by the video.

Copyright in 'films'

➤ A video is a 'film' for the purposes of the CDPA (s 5B).

- ◆ A record company should take an assignment of the copyright in the film from the film's 'producer' (if not the record company itself) and 'principal director', who are the first owners of copyright in the film (s 9(2)(ab)).

  - • Since an artist is unlikely to produce or direct a video, the artist is unlikely to own any of the copyright in the video.

    - ▪ Nonetheless, the record company should, for good measure, acquire any rights that the artist may have in the video and in any copyright works incorporated in the video (eg: the screenplay).

III Recording agreement

➤ A recording contract with a major record company is usually referred to as a *'recording agreement'*.

- ◆ A recording contract may be referred to as a *'production agreement'* where an artist signs to:

  - • a small independent label that has no distribution capacity and relies on concluding a deal with a larger record company in order to release records, *or*

  - • entrepeneur(s) (eg: independent record producers) that are prepared to fund an artist to make recordings with a view to securing a record deal with a record company or an independent distributor.

- ◆ NB: a production agreement is unrelated to a contract for the services of a record producer (a *'producer agreement'*), which sets out the terms of engagement and the producer's remuneration for record production services. The terms of a producer agreement are beyond the scope of this Chapter.

Production agreement

➤ A production agreement is extremely similar to a full recording agreement (even if more concise), because the entity signing the artist has to secure all the rights that it would need to license the artist's recordings to a larger record company or to a distributor.

- ◆ The main difference is that a production agreement is likely to have a simpler, 'net receipts' remuneration structure – see below.

> ### Commercial implications of a production agreement

> ➤ In a production agreement, the entity signing the artist effectively acts as a 'middle man' and takes a cut.

> ◆ Artists usually prefer to sign direct to a major, but an independent entity may:

> a) be prepared to invest in the artist before a major is willing to become involved, *and/or*

> b) provide an 'A&R' (ie: artist and repertoire) function that a major cannot replicate (eg: for breaking 'underground' music) – even if the artist's recordings are then licensed to a major.

> • The A&R role includes liaison with artists on creative direction (including the selection of songs and producers).

> • The remainder of this Section applies equally to a recording agreement or a production agreement, except where a distinction is drawn.

➤ The commercial terms of recording contracts differ greatly, depending on:

a) the artist involved (ie: whether new or established), *and*

b) the record company (ie: independent or major).

◆ As with all commercial contracts, the main terms (eg: royalties and advances) are a matter of negotiation.

• Supply considerably exceeds demand when it comes to bands and solo acts trying to 'make it' in the music business, so the record company (even an independent label or an entity with money to invest) often has the upper hand in the negotiation.

▪ A record company must, however, balance this position of strength with the 3 general considerations of enforceability of contracts considered in Section A of this Chapter, ie:

a) restraint of trade, *and*

b) undue influence, *and*

c) the contractual capacity of minors.

◆ Where the artist has appointed a manager, the manager usually leads the negotiation, with assistance from the artist's lawyer.

• The manager should not act for the artist if the manager has a financial interest (eg: owns shares) in the record company.

▪ It is not uncommon for a manager to propose to sign a new artist under a production agreement to an entity owned by the manager. In such a case, the manager should not be entitled to commission on the artist's recording income – see Section B of this Chapter.

➤ The structure of the agreement will, however, be similar, whatever the status of the artist, and the following points should always be considered:

Clause	Terms
Engagement	➤ There should be a clause setting out the engagement of the artist's recording services by the record company.

Clause	Terms

Exclusivity	➤ The record company usually demands that the artist is exclusively contracted to it as a performer throughout the entire period in which the artist is to provide recording services (the '**recording term**').
	
	 ◆ The record company will not want:
	
	    a) a third party to capitalise on an artist's success when it has not contributed to the cost of marketing the artist, *or*
	
	    b) competing products in the marketplace.
	
	       ■ Classical and jazz deals are often non-exclusive, since the labels rarely invest heavily in any artist and collaboration with other artists is the norm.
	
	 ➤ The artist is usually required to obtain the record company's consent before:
	
	 ◆ recording for any other record company, *or*
	
	 ◆ having a live performance recorded for television, video, film or webcast.
	
	 ➤ The artist is normally allowed to 'guest' (ie: make a non-featured appearance) on another artist's record, as long as the record company is credited on the record sleeve.
	
	 ◆ The usual form of credit is 'X appears courtesy of ABC Records'.
	
	    ● The artist cannot generally be a **featured** artist on another artist's record without the record company's consent.
	
	 ➤ The artist should be free to work as a record producer, remixer, engineer and/or session musician for third parties.
	
	 ◆ This can be a critical source of extra income for the artist, as advances rarely amount to a satisfactory wage for artists (especially groups).

Clause	Terms

Re-recording restriction	➤ There is usually a 're-recording restriction' preventing the artist from re-recording material previously recorded for the record company.
	
	 ◆ This often lasts for 5 years after the recording term (see below) has expired.
	
	    ● The purpose of the restriction is to protect the record company's exclusivity.
	
	       ■ The restriction does not prevent the artist from performing the material live, but does prevent the artist from making a live recording of the material.
	
	 ◆ The artist should try to ensure that the restriction only applies to material **released** by the record company during the recording term or within a short period (eg: 12 or 24 months) after the end of the recording term.

Clause	Terms

Duration	➤ The recording term usually lasts for:
	
	a) a fixed initial period, *plus*
	
	b) at the record company's option, a number of 'option periods'.
	
	    ◆ The record company needs to have the flexibility, depending on the level of success of the artist's releases, to extend the term or to 'drop' the artist (ie: to release the artist from the contract by not exercising the next option).
	
	➤ The contract usually specifies a 'minimum commitment', ie: a minimum number of new recordings that the artist has to deliver during each contract period.
	
	    ◆ This will be expressed as an album or single(s) (or both) and must consist of material previously unrecorded by the artist.
	
	    ◆ An 'album' usually has a minimum playing time (eg: 40 minutes) and must consist of at least 10 or 12 different tracks, each of a minimum playing time (eg: 2½ minutes).
	
	        • In addition to the actual commitment, the artist will be required to deliver a few (eg: 3 or 4) 'B-sides' or 'bonus tracks', which the record company will need for marketing purposes.
	
	➤ Each contract period usually lasts for at least 12 or 18 months and continues (if later) for a specified period (eg: 6 months) after delivery of the minimum commitment.
	
	    ◆ This is to allow the record company time to release a record and to make an informed decision about whether to exercise its option for the next period (which it must usually do before the expiry of the current period).
	
	        • If the artist fails, for reasons within the artist's control, to deliver a minimum commitment within a specified period of time (eg: 18 months), the record company can often elect:
	
	            ■ to extend the contract period (eg: for 6 months), *or*
	
	            ■ to terminate the recording term.
	
	        • To protect against an inadvertent failure to exercise an option, the record company usually requires the artist to serve notice of such failure on the record company, following which the record company has a 'cure period' (eg: 15 working days) within which to exercise the option.
	
	➤ The record company should try to avoid problems with restraint of trade – see the case law referred to in Section A of this Chapter.
	
	    ◆ The total recording term must not result in the artist's being bound for too long. There are no hard and fast rules about what is an excessive duration, but on the basis of the case law:
	
	        • There should probably not be more than 6 contract periods.
	
	            ■ A major record company often demands 5-6 contract periods (especially for a new artist). An independent may settle for less (eg: between 1 and 4 contract periods).
	
	        • Each contract period should be capped at 2 or 3 years.
	
	    ◆ The 'minimum commitment' should be for a specified number of recordings that is attainable by the artist.
	
	    ◆ The record company should be obliged to release the artist's works – see below.

Clause	Terms
Recording procedure	➤ The contract should set out a recording procedure, including: ◆ the parties' rights (often mutual approval) in relation to creative decisions (eg: the choice of material and record producer), *and* ◆ the record company's obligation to provide monies and studio facilities in accordance with the agreed budget, *and* ◆ the artist's technical obligations in terms of delivery materials.

Acceptability of recordings	➤ The record company will reserve the right to refuse recordings if it considers that they are not of a satisfactory quality.
	
	◆ This is a controversial issue:
	
	    ● The record company does not want to be forced to release material that is not commercial.
	
	    ● The artist, on the other hand, is usually keen to retain creative independence and credibility, so will want to restrict the right of refusal to 'technical' considerations, as opposed to matters of 'artistic' taste or 'commercial' judgement.
	
	◆ One compromise is to link the acceptable artistic/commercial quality to that of recordings previously accepted by the record company – but there is an almost unavoidable problem of subjectivity in making this judgement.

Grant of exploitation rights	➤ The artist always grants the record company the right to exploit the products of the artist's recording services under the contract (the '**recordings**').
	
	◆ The way in which the recordings are defined varies from contract to contract, but will be defined widely to encompass:
	
	    a) the 'masters' (ie: the tapes or digital media from which records are made), including both audio and audio-visual recordings, *and*
	
	    b) all record formats and media of exploitation (whether now known or invented in the future), including both physical carriers (eg: CDs and DVDs) and their notional electronic equivalents (eg: downloads, streamed files and ringtones).
	
	        ● The record company must ensure that it can exploit the recordings freely, including via any new media that may be developed during the course of the contract.

Ownership of copyright	➤ The contract usually confirms that ownership of any recording produced under the contract vests in the record company for the life of copyright (including any reversions, renewals, revivals and extensions of copyright) and thereafter (to the fullest extent possible) in perpetuity. ◆ Subject to certain exceptions, UK copyright in a sound recording lasts for 50 years from first release (*s 13A(2)*). ● For good measure, the record company will take an assignment of all of the artist's rights in the recordings.

Clause	Terms
Alternative copyright arrangements	➤ A superstar artist may succeed in negotiating a reversion of copyright to the artist (eg: after 25 years). ◆ This is only likely to happen in the course of a renegotiation, and then as concession in return for a new benefit to the record company (eg: an additional option period). ➤ Very rarely (eg: in the case of an artist that has funded the artist's own recordings), ownership of the recordings vests in the artist from the start. ◆ The artist will then grant the record company a 'licence' (ie: permission) to exploit the recordings for a limited period of time (eg: 5, 7 or 10 years).

Territory	➤ The record company usually insists on 'the world' as the territory for the purposes of the rights granted by the artist.
	
	◆ A definition as wide as 'the universe' may be used to cover the possibility that copyright may be created in space by virtue of satellite distribution.
	
	➤ If the territory is not 'the world', the record company will require protections in relation to the excluded territories.
	
	◆ For example, the record company will want to ensure that:
	
	  • record companies in the excluded territories are not able to release any recordings at an earlier date (as this could lead to a threat from imports), *and*
	
	  • the excluded territories are not subject to more favourable terms than those agreed with the record company.

Performers' consents	➤ Recording contracts are based on exploiting rights in musicians' performances. To avoid infringing these rights, the record company must obtain consent to exploitation from all performers involved. ◆ From an artist's perspective, such consents would ideally apply only to record sales, and references to 'audiovisual rights' or to 'other uses' would be specifically negotiated. In practice, the record company routinely obtains consents for all media. ➤ If session musicians are involved in the recording, there is a special form negotiated by the BPI and MU that they should sign, which deals with the relevant consents and contains grants of rights to the record company.
Moral rights	➤ The artist normally waives the artist's moral rights, both: a) as a performer, *and* b) where also the songwriter, as author of the material recorded.
Name and likeness	➤ The artist will almost invariably grant the record company the right to use the artist's name and likeness for promotional purposes. ◆ The artist should ask for a right of approval over each likeness (eg: photograph) used. • The grant of rights should not normally extend to actual merchandising rights – see below.

Clause	Terms
Website rights	➤ The record company is usually granted ownership and control of the artist's official website. ➤ The artist should try to ensure that: ◆ the record company will maintain the site to a reasonable standard and bear the costs of maintaining the site (without recoupment from the artist's royalties), *and* ◆ the artist receives a share of income generated from sales via the site (eg: of CDs or, with the artist's consent, merchandise), *and* ◆ all rights in the site revert to the artist at the end of the recording term (even if the record company continues to have non-exclusive rights to maintain an unofficial site thereafter), *and* ◆ the artist has the right to operate a separate 'fan site' at all times (or at least to access the fanbase material and data during the recording term and to have these transferred to the artist at the end of the recording term).
Merchandising	➤ The artist usually retains full control of merchandising rights. If so, these should be specifically reserved by the artist in the contract. ◆ Merchandising rights may feature in a '360° deal' – see below. ➤ The artwork commissioned for records is typically owned by the record company, so the artist should try to secure a free licence from the record company to use the artwork on merchandise. ◆ The record company may insist, as a condition of granting the licence, on being reimbursed for 100% or (as a compromise) 50% of the artwork costs.
'Ancillary rights' and '360° deals'	➤ Record companies increasingly obtain what are referred to as 'ancillary rights' (eg: merchandising and live performance rights). ◆ If a label obtains **all** of an artist's ancillary rights, the deal is known as a '360° deal' – or a '270° deal' if it does not include certain rights (eg: publishing and management rights). ◆ Traditionally, artists would never agree to grant such rights, since they would exploit the rights themselves via third parties (eg: merchandisers, tour promoters, publishers and managers). ● But new artists (and even established artists – notably Robbie Williams and Madonna) have been agreeing to allow their record companies to collect income arising from the exploitation of defined ancillary rights and to retain a specified percentage of the net profits (eg: between 10% and 50%). ◆ The artists are agreeing to this because: ● as new artists, they have limited opportunities elsewhere, *or* ● as established artists, the record company is offering substantial up-front investment (eg: guaranteed advances on touring and/or merchandising). ➤ The commercial practice for these deals is not fully settled, but '360° elements' are now a feature of virtually every recording agreement. ◆ It is, in any event, largely a matter of bargaining power, and depends on what the record company is offering to make the deal attractive to the artist.

Clause	Terms

Controlled compositions	➤ An artist often writes or co-writes the songs recorded. For this reason, the contract will contain a 'controlled compositions' clause.
	
	  ◆ 'Controlled compositions' are songs that are written, owned and/or controlled by an artist (whether in whole or in part).
	
	    ● As stated above, the record company has to pay mechanical royalties to the relevant copyright owner (ie: in the case of controlled compositions, usually the artist's publisher, via the MCPS or equivalent collecting society or agent overseas).
	
	      ■ It is in the record company's interest to pay as low a mechanical rate as possible, since the record company always bears the cost of paying the mechanical royalty (without recoupment from any income source) and does not deduct it from the artist's royalty base (see below).
	
	      ■ Since the rate is fixed in the UK by agreement between the MCPS and the BPI, this is not an issue in the UK.
	
	➤ The clause dealing with controlled compositions is primarily designed to reduce the mechanical royalty rate that the record label (or each of its affiliates or licensees) has to pay to the copyright owner in respect of sales in **North America** of records containing controlled compositions.
	
	  ◆ Under US and Canadian law a record label can obtain a compulsory licence by paying a 'statutory rate' (in the USA) or an 'agreed industry rate' (in Canada), but can also negotiate direct with an artist's publisher.
	
	    ● The record label will prefer to obtain a licence direct from publishers (or, where the publishers have appointed a collection agent, the Harry Fox Agency in the USA or the Canadian Mechanical Rights Reproduction Agency), but will not be prepared to pay more than the going compulsory rate, which sets an upper limit for negotiation by the artist.
	
	  ◆ In practice, the artist is likely to be asked to grant (or to procure that the artist's publisher will grant) a licence in respect of controlled compositions at not more than 75% of the compulsory rate.
	
	    ● The applicable compulsory rate is fixed as at the date of the contract, the date of recording or (more favourably to the artist, as the rate generally rises over time) at the date of delivery of the recording or (more favourably still) at the date of manufacture or release of the record.
	
	    ● The record company usually insists on limiting the rate payable to a fixed number of tracks (eg: 10-12 per album or 2 per single) at the single-song compulsory rate, even if the record contains a greater number of tracks.
	
	  ◆ The record company will also require the artist to grant (or to procure the grant of) favourable terms for 'synchronisation licences' in relation to controlled compositions (eg: a free licence for promotional use).
	
	    ● In this context, a 'synchronisation licence' (or 'synch licence' for short) is a licence to incorporate a song in timed relation to an audio-visual medium (eg: a music video).

Clause	Terms

Remuneration	➤ The artist must receive remuneration for the artist's services. Otherwise, the contract is in restraint of trade and, on a practical level, the artist would have no incentive to enter into the deal.
	
	➤ If signed to a major label, the artist usually receives:
	
	  a) royalties from the record company, based on a percentage of earnings derived from sales of the artist's records, *and*
	
	  b) advances for each contract period that are 'recouped' (ie: recovered) from royalties otherwise due to the artist.
	
	    ◆ An artist will not receive any royalties until all recoupable sums (eg: advances, recording costs and certain video costs – see below) have been recouped by the record company.
	
	➤ If signed to a small independent label, the artist may receive advances, but the ultimate basis of remuneration may be different (see 'Alternative remuneration structures' below).

Royalty base for physical formats	➤ In a simple world, the artist would receive a royalty (expressed as a percentage of the wholesale price) for each record sold. The amount payable to the artist would simply be the royalty per unit multiplied by the number of units sold.
	
	  ◆ The reality is not, at a fundamental level, that different, but a complex practice has emerged as labels have devised ingenious ways to reduce the base on which royalties are calculated.
	
	➤ Royalties are not paid at all on records (known as 'free goods') that are given away for promotional purposes (ie: not sold).
	
	  ◆ Free goods often extend not only to 'actual' free goods (ie: those genuinely given away to DJs and journalists etc.), but also to a notional number of records (eg: 10% or 20%) that are treated as being given away rather than sold (which are known as 'automatic' free goods).
	
	    ● The artist should try to impose a cap on the number of records that the record company can treat as free goods.
	
	➤ Royalties are calculated on 'net sales' of records (ie: records sold and not returned).
	
	  ◆ In the UK (unlike the USA), records are rarely sold on a 'sale or return' basis, but dealers are entitled to return:
	
	    ● faulty products, *and*
	
	    ● commonly, up to 5% of records distributed to the dealer.
	
	  ◆ Historically, labels paid royalties on only 90% of net sales (justified by the fact that, in the days of '78s', 1 in 10 manufactured broke), and this practice continues in rare instances.
	
	➤ Royalties are not calculated on the actual price received on net sales, but on an artificially constructed 'royalty base price'.
	
	  ◆ In the UK the royalty rate is usually calculated on the 'dealer price' (ie: the wholesale price), which also known as 'PPD' (standing for 'published price to dealer'), for each unit sold and not returned, after deduction of:
	
	    a) all applicable duties and sales taxes (eg: VAT) and 'withholding taxes' (see the explanation of withholding tax below), *and*
	
	    b) an artificial 'packaging deduction'.

Clause	Terms

Royalty base for physical formats (continued)	◆ Historically, record companies argued that the artist should receive a royalty for the recorded music itself, not its container (eg: the 'jewel box' and inserted booklet for a CD).
	
	    ● The dubious practice of deducting a notional amount for 'packaging' has stuck.
	
	        ■ The amount deducted is expressed as a percentage of the dealer (or sometimes retail) price, net of taxes.
	
	        ■ The rate varies from format to format (eg: 20% for vinyl, 25% for CDs and 30% or 35% for DVDs).
	
	        ■ The artist should ensure that the 'headline' royalty rate (see below) factors in any packaging deduction.
	
	➤ In practice, the record company's distribution arm (or independent distributors) will offer retail outlets discounts on the published dealer price to encourage them to stock the artist's records.
	
	    ◆ The artist should check that these discounts are not deducted in calculating the royalty base.

Royalty base for new media	➤ There is diverging practice as to how royalties are calculated for music distributed and sold digitally:
	
	a) across the internet (eg: via downloads or streaming), *or*
	
	b) via other telecommunications systems (eg: mobile telephones or other wireless devices).
	
	    ◆ A notional wholesale price per track has been constructed by certain online music stores (eg: iTunes).
	
	        ● There remains, however, at the time of writing a wide variation in the pricing models for digital distribution outlets and there is no suitable dealer price on which to calculate royalties.
	
	➤ The trend to date has been for the record company to calculate royalties on the record company's **net receipts** from new media exploitation, ie: the gross receipts after deduction of:
	
	a) a packaging deduction (usually equal to the CD rate) – a practice widely criticised, given that there is no physical packaging for a digitally transmitted record, but reluctantly accepted, *and*
	
	b) the record company's costs of sale (eg: sales taxes, digital rights management (DRM) costs, internet service provider (ISP) deductions, discounts, rebates, referral fees, agency fees, affiliate fees and charges levied by credit-card companies), *and*
	
	c) where borne by the record company instead of the ISP, mechanical licence fees payable to music publishers.
	
	    ◆ The royalty rate for physical records (see below) is then applied to this base.
	
	        ● This is also widely criticised, given that the record company does not suffer the manufacture and distribution costs that it suffers in the case of physical carriers.
	
	            ■ At time of writing, this practice is nonetheless largely tolerated by artists, but this could well change as digital distribution accounts for an ever larger proportion of the recorded-music market.

Clause	Terms
Other net-receipts royalty bases	➤ Third parties will in some instances account to the record company on a flat-fee basis or by reference to set fee per unit sold (rather than by reference to a percentage of price). ◆ The record company will use its net receipts as a base, and will usually apply the royalty rate for records (see below). ➤ There should be a sweep-up clause providing for the artist to be remunerated for types of exploitation not covered elsewhere in the contract. ◆ Since these are unpredictable and/or specially negotiated (eg: licences for 'synchronisation' of the sound recordings in films, TV programmes or adverts, or revenues arising via the artist's official website), the royalty base is usually the record company's net receipts derived from such exploitation. ● The artist should try to ensure that the royalty rate applied to such base is 50% for the more predictable sources, although the record company may try to apply the royalty rate for records (see below), which is considerably lower.

Clause	Terms
Royalty rates	➤ The 'headline' royalty rate for an artist (ie: the UK album rate ignoring the reductions described below) varies widely and depends on: a) how successful the artist is (or is, in the record company's estimation, likely to be), *and* b) the record company involved (eg: an independent will offer a lower rate than a major, as it needs to make a profit margin on the rate that the independent receives from its distributor). ➤ Where the royalty rate is calculated on the dealer price, then (assuming a conventional packaging deduction – see above): ◆ A new artist can expect to receive a headline rate of between 13% and 18% of PPD. ◆ An established artist will receive, say, between 19% and 24% of PPD (or an even higher percentage if a superstar). ● Even the higher rates amount, on the face of it, to a small proportion of earnings. In fact, when the expenses borne by the label (eg: marketing costs) are taken into account, the profit ratio is more like 2:1 or 3:1 in the label's favour. ■ The label's justification for this is that it still has to pay its overheads and cover its losses on unsuccessful acts. ➤ Historically, contracts used to provide for royalties to be calculated on the 'retail price', as opposed to PPD, and some are still in force. ◆ For some time, those contracts have been based, not on the actual retail price (which varies widely from store to store), but on a notional retail price calculated by multiplying the dealer price by between 125% and 132% (depending on the format), in order to reflect the mark-up added by retailers. ● Applying the same 'uplift' percentage to a retail royalty rate gives an equivalent PPD royalty rate (since, to reflect the lower dealer base price, a proportionately higher percentage of PPD has to be applied to result in the same amount payable to the artist).

Clause	Terms

Escalations in royalty rate	➤ A new artist will receive a relatively low headline rate, so may wish to negotiate 'escalations' (ie: stepped increases) based on success.
	
	◆ This creates a sliding scale of remuneration.
	
	➤ One mechanism is for the applicable album/single rates in each territorial category to increase (eg: by 1 percentage point) from specified contract periods (eg: increases from albums 3 and 5).
	
	➤ An alternative (or additional) mechanism is to use 'gold' and 'platinum' record sales (as measured in different territories) as trigger-points for successive increases in the rate for a given album.
	
	◆ The record company will usually insist that the escalation, once achieved, applies only:
	
	   ● to sales in excess of the trigger level, *and*
	
	   ● on a prospective basis (usually from the accounting period after that in which the relevant triggers are attained), *and*
	
	   ● on a country-by-country basis (ie: only in each country in which the escalation is achieved, and not worldwide), *and*
	
	   ● on an album-by-album basis (ie: only to the hit album, and not also to all subsequent albums).

Reductions in royalty rate	➤ There is usually a reduced headline rate for singles (eg: a rate that is 2 or 3 percentage points less than the album rate).
	
	➤ For each of the album and single headline rates, the royalty rate is usually reduced (eg: to a rate that is 1 or 2 percentage points less than the UK rate) where a record is sold outside the UK in any of the major territories (eg: the USA, France, Japan, Germany and Spain).
	
	◆ The record company needs to allow for a margin to be retained by its overseas affiliates or licensees.
	
	   ● The rate is usually further reduced for minor overseas territories (eg: to a rate that is 1 or 2 percentage points less than the major-territory rate).
	
	      ■ Where a currency exchange rate is relevant, the record company should, when calculating royalties, apply the same rate at which the record company is paid.
	
	➤ The royalty rate is usually reduced for all formats where a record is not sold at full price.
	
	◆ Since the costs of production (eg: mechanical royalties, which are levied on all records manufactured) remain the same, the record company argues that it should receive a higher share of income from a reduced-priced record to cover those costs.
	
	   ● Royalty rates are accordingly reduced (eg: to 1/2 of the otherwise applicable rate) for:
	
	      ■ 'mid-price' and 'budget-price' records (but the mid-price rate should be a 75% or 2/3 rate, not a 1/2 rate), *and*
	
	      ■ mail-order records (eg: via 'record clubs'), *and*
	
	      ■ 'premiums' (ie: records licensed for distribution as promotions for a third party's products or services), *and*
	
	      ■ soundtrack albums and multi-artist compilation albums (as opposed to the artist's own 'greatest hits' albums).

Clause	Terms
Reductions in royalty rate (continued)	➤ The record company also reduces the royalty rate where a full-priced record results in a lower profit margin for the record company (eg: unconventional CD packaging with high production costs). ➤ The artist should seek: ◆ reasonable reductions (eg: to no more than 1/2 for mid-price records and no more than 2/3 for budget-price records), *and* ◆ restrictions on such uses without the artist's approval (eg: no budget sales for 1 or 2 years after first release of a record), *and* ◆ where negotiable, an obligation on the record company to pay the greater of (i) the reduced rate or (ii) 50% of the record company's net receipts from such exploitation (especially in relation to premiums and compilations, which may sometimes be quite profitable for the record company).
Reduction for new formats	➤ When a new physical carrier is devised, the record company's margin is reduced because the costs of production are initially high. ◆ The contract is likely to contain a clause whereby the otherwise applicable album/single rate is reduced for newly invented physical formats (eg: to 75% of that rate). • The artist should try to ensure that this is deleted, or that the reduction applies only until the format is no longer new. ▪ One approach is to have the reduced rate increase in steps (eg: of 5 or 10 percentage points) over a limited period (eg: 2 or 4 years) until the full rate applies. ▪ An alternative (or additional) mechanism is that the full rate applies once the new format accounts for a specified proportion of the recorded-music market (eg: 20%).
Reduction for TV advertising	➤ If the record company carries out TV advertising for a particular record, the artist's royalties in respect of that record are often reduced (eg: to 50% of the otherwise applicable rate) to reflect the record company's exceptional investment. ◆ If so, the artist should try to ensure that: • the reduction only applies to records sold: a) in each country where the advertising is received, *and* b) during a defined period, eg: i) starting with the 'sell-in' of the TV campaign, *and* ii) ending once the total 'royalty foregone' (ie: the money the artist would have received but for the reduction) equals 50% of the campaign costs, *and* • the artist has a right of approval over the budget (as this affects the duration of the reduction in the royalty rate). ◆ The record company may want the same principle to apply to radio (and even online) advertising. The artist should resist this. ➤ Alternatively, there is no reduction in the royalty rate, but a percentage of the cost (eg: 50%) is recoupable from the artist's royalty. ◆ If so, the artist should insist on a right of approval over the budget (as this affects the artist's ability to recoup).

Clause	Terms
Reduction for record producers	➤ Record producers usually demand an up-front fee – sizeable if a 'name' producer – plus a royalty (usually between 1%-5% of PPD, 3% being fairly standard). ◆ The fee is usually recoupable from the producer's royalty share. ➤ The producer's royalty is usually paid out of royalties due to the **artist** (ie: not out of the record company's share of revenue). ◆ So the artist's royalty rate is effectively reduced by the number of percentage points (known as 'points') paid to the producer. ◆ The artist should try to ensure that the producer accepts pro-rata reductions similar to those applying to the artist so that, where the artist earns less, the producer earns proportionately less.
Advances	➤ Advances are usually paid to the artist on signing the contract and at the start of each option period. ◆ This is an inducement to the artist to enter into the contract. ● In the case of a new artist, it effectively provides a wage that allows the artist to 'give up the day job' and to focus on recording. ➤ The artist is never liable to repay the money (which in effect represents risk capital invested in the artist by the record company), and advances are usually described as 'non-returnable'. ◆ For a new artist, this is a highly speculative venture for the record company. The vast majority of new artists do not 'make it', and the successful artists in effect bankroll the unsuccessful ones. ➤ The record company, however, has a 'first charge' (ie: security) over the artist's royalties, so any royalties earned by the artist under the contract will first be applied towards recoupment of the advance. ◆ This ensures that the record company recovers its up-front outlay in full before the artist receives any royalties under the contract. ➤ The record company will seek to recoup its advances from **any** royalties earned by the artist under the contract, not just from royalties earned from a particular single or album. ◆ This is called 'cross-recoupment' (or 'cross-collateralisation'). ● In this way, advances for unsuccessful records are recovered from earnings from the 'hit' records. ◆ Cross-recoupment between the contract periods is acceptable. ● The artist should – unless the record company offers unusually favourable deal terms in other areas – strongly resist any attempt by the record company to cross-recoup advances from income arising from: a) other contracts with the record company relating to previous recordings (eg: an established artist's 'back catalogue'), *or* b) other types of contract with the record company's affiliated companies (eg: its publishing arm), *or* c) other areas governed by the recording contract (eg: income from any specially negotiated 'ancillary rights', such as merchandising or live performance rights granted to the record company).

Clause	Terms
Size of advances	➤ The size of each advance paid by the record company is often negotiable, but is ultimately a commercial decision taken by the record company. ◆ Where the artist is established, the record company will have historical sales data on which to project income, from which it can calculate a suitable size of advance. ● The status of the artist is also a relevant factor. ◆ With a new artist, the record company has to estimate the likelihood that it will recoup, and relevant factors include: a) the commercial appeal of the artist's material, *and* b) earnings of similar artists, *and* c) competition to sign the artist. ➤ The artist should try to ensure that: a) the amounts payable increase for each option period, *and* b) advances are paid in full irrespective of whether previous advances have been recouped by the record company.
Recording costs	➤ The record company is usually obliged to pay all the artist's costs of recording. ◆ These include fees payable for studio time, tracklaying engineers, session players, equipment hire, mixing and mastering. ➤ In a recording agreement, recording costs are almost invariably recoupable from the artist's royalties. ◆ Generally, part of the artist's main advance represents an amount designated as a recording budget. ● Ideally, the artist will often prefer a costs-exclusive advance, as recording sessions typically go over budget, in which case the artist has less to live on. ■ Artists with their own studio facilities where they can make first-class recordings may be happy with an all-in deal (and might even make a margin on the budget set). ➤ In either case, it is in the artist's interest to ensure that the recording budget is not excessive – otherwise the artist will never recoup and will not receive any back-end remuneration. ◆ The artist should ensure that recoupable recording costs are restricted to direct costs of recording and exclude costs of packaging (eg: artwork) and promotion. ● Equally, the record company will want to keep costs down to reduce its risk and to make a profit. ■ The record company will often make the artist responsible for paying for any excess costs over the budget. ➤ In a production agreement, recording costs (along with packaging and promotional costs) are treated differently – see below.
Manufacturing and distribution costs	➤ The costs of manufacturing and distribution should be borne by the record company and should not be recoupable from the artist's royalties.

Clause	Terms
Remixing costs	➤ Remixing costs are usually recoupable, even though a remix arguably forms part of promoting a record. The artist should argue for: a) the costs of each remix to be recoupable only from royalties arising in relation to the remix, *and/or* b) a right of approval over the budget for each remix.
Promotional costs	➤ In practice, the record company normally carries out a certain amount of promotion on behalf of the artist, but it usually resists committing to specific obligations under the contract. The contract deals instead with the cost consequences of the promotion that the record company actually carries out. ➤ The costs of promotion should be borne by the record company and should **not** be recoupable from the artist's royalties (except as noted below in the case of promotional videos and TV advertising). ◆ If the artist wishes to use independent promoters (rather the record company's in-house team), the record company may insist that the costs of independent promotion are fully recoupable. ➤ The label should reimburse the artist for any expenses (eg: travel and hotel costs) incurred by the artist for promotional purposes.
Tour support	➤ The record company may agree to contribute funds towards a loss-making tour in order to enable the artist to promote a record. ◆ This is known as 'tour support' and can be a key area of investment, especially where the tour 'breaks' a band. ➤ Tour support is usually fully recoupable from the artist's royalties. ◆ If the amount of the shortfall is unknown, the record company usually caps the amount that it will contribute and specifies which touring costs can be deducted from touring income (for the purposes of calculating the shortfall). The deductible costs are unlikely to include commission payable to the artist's manager or booking agent.
Promotional videos	➤ The record company will insist on the right to call on the artist to make promotional videos ('promo videos'). ◆ It will initially pay the costs of producing promo videos that are made at the record company's request (up to a budgeted amount approved by the record company in advance). ● The artist should also try to obtain a right of approval over the budget (which affects the artist's ability to recoup), the creative treatment and the production details. ➤ The record company usually recovers its outlay as follows: a) 50% of the cost is recoupable from the artist's royalties in the same way as recording costs and advances, *and* b) the other 50% is recoupable from income arising from commercial exploitation of the video (eg: via DVD sales and TV broadcast). ➤ Subject to recoupment, the artist should receive: ◆ royalties on DVD sales (at a similar rate to CD sales), *and* ◆ a share (eg: 50%) of the record company's net receipts from exploitation via TV broadcast.

Clause	Terms
Alternative remuneration structures	➤ In a production agreement (see above), the artist is commonly paid a share of the record company's 'net receipts' (ie: the company's gross earnings less specified costs of production and promotion, such as recording costs).

◆ This approach has several advantages for the record company:

- It avoids any potential mismatch (and shortfall) between the royalty rates payable:

    a) by the record company's licensee(s) to the record company, *and*

    b) by the record company to the artist.

- Recording and marketing costs are usually deducted 'off the top' (ie: before the net receipts are split), so the record company does not have to pay the artist for loss-making records: contrast the position where (subject to recoupment) the company pays the artist a royalty per unit sold.

- The deal is simpler, so quicker (and therefore cheaper) to negotiate and conclude.

◆ The artist's share of net receipts should be no less than 50%, but 55% or 60% (or even 65% or 70%) is perhaps more typical for the initial contract period.

- The artist's share is commonly 'escalated' (ie: increased) for each successive contract period of the recording term (eg: by 5 percentage points).

- Where the artist's share is low, it may also be escalated if the artist achieves certain trigger-points, such as specified levels of sales or income (eg: 'gold'/'platinum' sales).

    ■ The escalation will apply for the remainder of the contract term or merely for the remainder of the contract period.

◆ The artist should ensure that the 'net' element of 'net receipts' is carefully defined and should try to secure rights of approval over allowable deductions.

- It is common for virtually all costs of production, manufacturing, distribution and promotion to be deductible (other than the record company's basic overhead costs).

◆ The artist should also try to ensure that as few deductions as possible are made from the artist's share of net receipts (as opposed to being made 'off the top', in which case the deductions are in effect borne by the record company in proportion to the record company's share of net receipts).

- Any advance(s) payable to the artist will be recoupable from the artist's share.

➤ Occasionally, the record company (eg: a specially established joint venture between a label and an artist) gives the artist an equity stake in the record company itself (eg: 50%) by issuing shares in the company to the artist.

◆ All (or part) of the artist's remuneration is then paid by way of dividend to the artist as a shareholder in the company.

- This can be an extremely complex arrangement and will always be specially negotiated.

Clause	Terms

Accounting and audit rights	➤ Whatever the royalty structure, the record company should, at regular intervals, send the artist a financial statement showing all worldwide record sales and any royalties due (after recoupment).
	
	◆ The statement should be accompanied by payment.
	
	  ● The record company usually accounts to the artist twice a year within 90 days of the end of 30 June and 31 December.
	
	➤ The artist should ensure that it has 'audit rights' (ie: is entitled, at least once every 12 months, to have a suitably qualified accountant check that the record company is accounting properly for all royalties due). The accountant should have the right to take copies of the accounts and to inspect all relevant documents.
	
	◆ Record companies routinely try to restrict challenges to the accounting after 2 or 3 years from each accounts date.
	
	  ● The statutory limitation period is 6 years, so the artist should seek as long a period as possible.
	
	    ■ A common compromise is a 2/3-year period of objection, then a 12-month period within which to bring a claim.
	
	◆ The artist should try to recover the audit costs where an audit reveals an underpayment in excess of certain percentage.
	
	  ● 5% or 10% is not uncommon.
	
	    ■ The record company may insist on a 'de minimis' cap (ie: below which the audit costs are not recoverable), whereby the underpayment must exceed the **greater** of that percentage or a fixed sum (eg: £5,000).
	
	➤ The record company is always entitled to retain 'reserves' (ie: to hold back payment of royalties) against returns of records by retailers.
	
	◆ The artist should try to ensure that the reserves are capped (eg: at 25% or less of royalties otherwise due) and 'liquidated' (ie: paid out to the artist to the extent that records are not returned) over 1 accounting period or equally over 2 accounting periods.

Withholding tax (artist resident overseas)	➤ If the artist is resident overseas for tax purposes, sums actually payable to the artist under the contract as copyright royalties may be subject to a 20% deduction for 'withholding tax' in the UK. ➤ The UK, like most countries, collects a 'withholding tax' from non-resident entertainers (including recording artists) on most forms of income arising in the country (eg: royalties and advances). ◆ The record company is required (unless making a gross payment under relevant tax legislation) to make a deduction at source on the artist's behalf. The requisite proportion of the payment to the artist is 'withheld' by the record company at source, hence the expression 'withholding tax'. ➤ When UK withholding tax is due on income arising under the contract, a certificate confirming the amount of tax paid is available to the artist. The artist can generally use this certificate in connection with the artist's income tax return in the artist's country of residence. ◆ If so, the record company should be required to provide the artist with all relevant certificates received by the record company and other reasonable assistance, so that the artist can apply for a tax credit or rebate. ➤ The relevant tax legislation is beyond the scope of this Section.

Clause	Terms
Withholding tax (artist resident in the UK)	➤ If the artist is resident in the UK for tax purposes, the artist's overseas earnings may be subject to foreign withholding taxes for which the record company's overseas licensees are obliged to account. ◆ The record company is usually not obliged to gross up or indemnify the artist in respect of any amounts withheld on this basis. ● If the record company receives a tax credit (which it uses) or repayment in the UK in respect of foreign tax, the record company should, from the artist's perspective, be obliged under the contract to credit a pro-rata amount of the credit or repayment to the artist's royalty account. ■ Record companies often successfully resist this.
Release commitment	➤ Ideally, the artist will want the record company to commit to releasing the artist's minimum commitment in each contract period – even actively 'plugging' (ie: marketing) each record released. ◆ If the record company does not make any substantial release commitment, the contract is arguably in restraint of trade (*Silvertone Records Ltd v Mountfield* [1993] EMLR 152). ● The record company cannot, however, guarantee success (no matter how large the marketing spend or how much airtime a record receives on radio or cable channels). ■ The contract will therefore often contain a specific acknowledgement by the artist that the record business is highly speculative, and that the timing and manner of any release is a matter for the record company's commercial judgement. ➤ The main 'release commitment' accordingly takes the form of a right for the artist (as the artist's sole remedy) to terminate the recording term if the record company fails to release the minimum commitment in a defined major territory (eg: UK) within a defined period after delivery of the minimum commitment (eg: 6 months). ◆ At the end of that period the artist usually has a right to serve notice on the record company requiring it to release the minimum commitment within a 'cure period' (eg: 3 months). ● If the record company fails to do so, the artist can terminate the recording term and is free to sign with another label. ➤ The artist should try to negotiate a right to require that, on termination of the recording term, the copyright in the sound recordings be 're-assigned' (ie: transferred back) to the artist. ◆ If the record company agrees to this, it will probably insist on being reimbursed for its recording costs and having an 'over-ride' royalty on earnings from future releases by the artist's new record label or distributor. ➤ There is usually a further (weaker) commitment to release in defined foreign territories (eg: the other major territories). ◆ This is typically within a defined period (eg: 6 months) after release in the main territory and subject to a 'cure period'. ● The artist's remedy is usually the right to choose a distributor in the territory concerned to release the album in question.

Clause	Terms
Artist's warranties	➤ The record company will require certain warranties and undertakings from the artist, which usually include that the artist: a) has the right to enter into the contract and is not bound by (and will not enter into) any conflicting contracts with other record companies (ie: is free to provide the artist's exclusive recording services to the record company), *and* b) is not a minor – see Section A of this Chapter, *and* c) is entitled to grant and assign the rights purported to be granted and assigned to the record company, *and* d) will join, and remain a member of, a trade union (eg: the MU) and any similar organisation where necessary to enable the artist to comply with the artist's contractual obligations, *and* e) will attend recording sessions promptly and perform to the best of the artist's ability, *and* f) will not record material that is defamatory or obscene or infringes any third-party rights, *and* g) will, free of charge to the record company, attend interviews, public appearances etc. that have been arranged by the record company for promotional purposes, *and* h) will record under the artist's professional name (and only under a different name with the record company's prior approval).

Assignment of the contract	➤ The record company (especially a major) will usually insist on being free to 'assign' (ie: to transfer outright) its rights under the contract and to sub-contract its obligations under the contract to a third party of its choice.
	
	 ➤ The artist should try to ensure that the contract cannot be transferred in this way unless the assignee enters into a direct covenant with the artist to perform the record company's contractual obligations.
	
	 ◆ This provides an assurance to the artist that the new label will be obliged to process payments.
	
	    ● Under the rules of privity of contract, the original label remains liable for the record company's obligations under the contract in the absence of such a direct covenant.
	
	    ● The artist does not want to be in a position where, for instance, the original label becomes insolvent (and so unable to afford to pay royalties to the artist), but the solvent new label is not obliged to pay royalties to the artist.

Termination	➤ There is rarely a contractual right to terminate the contract itself. There are usually provisions specifying circumstances in which the recording **term** can be terminated. These are commonly: ◆ material breach by either party, subject to a 'cure period' (eg: 30 days, or longer for late delivery of recordings), *or* ◆ the winding-up of the record company, an agreement with its creditors in consequence of debt or a similar insolvency event. ➤ After termination, the record company will usually be entitled to exploit the recordings made during the recording term, but should be obliged to account to the artist for all royalties relating to such exploitation (as well as for all mechanical royalties payable).

Clause	Terms
Group provisions	➤ If the artist is a group, there will be provisions dealing with what happens if a member of the group leaves.
	◆ If one or more members leave, the leaving member(s) will be required to give notice to the record company.
	◆ The record company will remain obliged to account to the leaving member(s) for their share of income from existing albums.
	◆ The record company will usually have the option:
	● to terminate the recording term as regards the leaving member(s) or remaining member(s) (or altogether), *and/or*
	● to require the remaining member(s) to continue to perform the contract, *and/or*
	● to treat the leaving member(s) as a solo artist (or a separate group) as if signed to a continuing contract on the same terms (but, where appropriate, with the provisions changed as required to reflect the circumstances).
	◆ The group should try to ensure that:
	● a time limit (eg: 45 or 60 days from the date of the notice of the split) is imposed on the exercise of the option, failing which the leaving member(s) are automatically released from the contract, *and*
	● whatever decision is taken, separate accounts are maintained for the 2 camps, and there is no cross-recoupment:
	■ between each camp (ie: each camp is liable only to recoup a pro-rata share of any unrecouped balance on the group's royalty account at the date of split), *or*
	■ between new and old recordings (eg: the costs of future recordings by the remaining member(s) should not be recouped from the royalty entitlement of the departing member(s) in relation to the existing albums), *and*
	● if the advances for continuing member(s) are to be reduced pro rata, the reductions should be capped appropriately (eg: at 50%) for each member (or set of members) affected.
	◆ The record company will want to control whether the leaving or remaining member(s) can use the group name (such right to prevail over any partnership agreement between the members).
	➤ The group will also be obliged to try to ensure that a new member that joins the group is made a party to the contract for the remainder of the recording term.

D Publishing contracts

*References in this Section are to the Copyright, Designs and Patents Act 1988 ('**CDPA**'), unless otherwise stated.*

I	Music publishing
II	Types of publishing income
III	Benefits of a publishing contract
IV	Exclusive songwriter agreement

I Music publishing

➤ A writer of music or lyrics can earn substantial income from 'publishing'.

◆ In this context, 'publishing' means the commercial exploitation of musical compositions and lyrics themselves (rather than any records incorporating them).

● This source of income is increasingly becoming more significant for a musician than the musician's earnings from sales of recorded performances.

➤ To promote such commercial exploitation and to administer any income arising, a musician generally works with local collecting societies, as well as a specialist music publishing company ('**publisher**').

➤ Music publishing is based on 2 types of copyright:

a) the copyright in musical compositions (eg: melody and backing track), *and*

b) the copyright in any accompanying lyrics (eg: the words of a song).

Music and lyrics under copyright law

➤ For the purposes of the *CDPA (s 3(1))*:

a) a musical composition is a 'musical work', *and*

b) lyrics amount to a 'literary work'.

◆ Both types of work attract copyright protection (*s 1(1)(a)*).

➤ The copyright in a **sound recording** of the music/lyrics is entirely separate, as is the copyright in a **film** or **broadcast** incorporating them (*s 1(1)(b)*).

Recording and publishing

➤ The distinction between recording and publishing is crucial in the music industry, as copyright in audio and audiovisual recordings forms the basis of a separate revenue stream (ie: traditionally, under a recording contract) and, correspondingly, a different business model (ie: a record label).

◆ The distinction is currently becoming blurred as music companies (or the recording and publishing arms of the majors) increasingly attempt to acquire both revenue streams when signing an artist.

➤ This Section assumes, for the sake of simplicity, a single composer (**'writer'**) and focuses on writer agreements and on songs (being the most common form of commercially released music).

♦ In practice, several writers may collaborate, and instrumental music can also be important commercially (mainly in classical music and jazz).

● Most points noted below apply equally to songs and to instrumental pieces.

➤ Under a writer contract, a writer grants commercial exploitation rights in specific songs to a publisher, in return for which the publisher:

a) promotes the commercial exploitation of the songs by making an onward grant of rights to third parties for various types of use (eg: for release on CD or via download, or for use in a film or TV programme or in an advert), *and*

b) on the writer's behalf, collects income arising, *and*

c) pays that income to the writer after deducting a share of its receipts.

♦ The amount retained by the publisher is to cover its costs and profit margin.

➤ The conventional logic for an artist writer has been to wait until the artist has signed a record deal before signing a publishing deal.

♦ The prospect of an imminent record release – especially of an album – drives up the value of the publishing deal.

● That logic holds true, but publishing companies can provide the funding needed by an unsigned artist at a critical stage in launching a career.

➤ There are 5 main forms of publishing contract:

Publishing contracts	
1 **Exclusive songwriter agreement**	➤ This is commonly referred to as an **'ESA'** for short. ♦ Under an ESA, a publisher engages a writer's songwriting services for a period of time (known as the **'term'**). ● The agreement may also cover songs that the writer has written before the term, especially if the writer has not previously entered into a publishing agreement. ■ The usual contractual terms of an ESA are considered in section IV below.
2 **Single song assignment**	➤ This deals with a writer's (or another rights-owner's) 'assignment' (ie: outright transfer) of rights in an existing single song (rather than a catalogue).
3 **Catalogue agreement**	➤ Under this type of agreement, a publisher acquires an existing catalogue of songs outright from a writer (or, more commonly, from a previous publisher).
4 **Administration agreement**	➤ Here, a publisher is appointed to 'administer' an existing or future catalogue (ie: to handle registrations with collecting societies, to conclude licences and to collect income arising from exploitation of the catalogue).
5 **Sub-publishing agreement**	➤ Here, a secondary publisher is appointed to administer a catalogue in a particular overseas country (or countries).

II Types of publishing income

➤ An important source of income for a writer is the exploitation of 'mechanical rights' (ie: permitting third parties, usually record companies, to reproduce the song in a recording and to manufacture copies of it).

◆ Income from this source has reduced with the decline in sales of recorded music.

◆ Most publishers appoint the MCPS as their agent to administer collection of this income, although some larger publishing companies administer it themselves.

Legal basis of 'mechanical' rights

➤ Mechanical rights are based on 1 of the 6 exclusive rights that a copyright owner has in a copyright work, ie: the right to copy the work (s 17).

➤ The most valuable source of income for a writer is now generally the exploitation of 'public performance rights' – see below.

◆ The UK collecting society dealing with public performance rights is the PRS. The sources of income that the PRS collects include radio play, TV broadcast, live performance (on air and/or at venues) and digital exploitation.

Legal basis of 'public performance rights'

➤ Performance rights are based on 2 of the exclusive rights that a copyright owner has in relation to a copyright work, ie: the rights:

◆ to perform the work in public (s 19), and

◆ to 'communicate' it 'to the public' (s 20).

Communication to the public

➤ 'Communication to the public' is a technical legal term used in the CDPA (defined in s 20(2)).

◆ In legal terms, it encompasses both 'broadcasting' and 'making available to the public', which are deliberately defined in a techology-neutral way to try to ensure that the definitions are flexible enough to cover new technological developments in this fast-changing area.

◆ In current industry terms:

• 'broadcasting' means 'push' communications, ie: scheduled broadcast (whether via an analogue or digital aerial signal) and equivalent digital platforms (eg: podcasting and streaming), and

• 'making available to the public' means 'pull' communications, ie: on-demand digital services (eg: subscription access to tracks) and downloads.

◆ The PRS and MCPS each have standard-form contracts with their writer and publisher members and with their licensees, which are beyond the scope of this Section.

- See Section A of this Chapter for details of the societies' general arrangements and the PRS for Music website for full details.

➤ A publisher also administers 3 other main sources of income:

a) 'synchronisation rights' or 'synch rights' for short (ie: the right to incorporate music in films, TV and radio programmes and adverts), *and*

b) 'grand rights' (ie: the right to use music in a dramatic presentation, such as a musical or stage show), *and*

c) 'print rights' (ie: the right to print sheet music).

Legal basis of 'synch', 'grand' and 'print' rights
➤ These rights are also based on exclusive rights under copyright, ie: ◆ *synch rights* – to copy, show and communicate a copyright work (*ss 17, 19* and *20*), *and*   ◆ *grand rights* – to perform and adapt a work (*ss 19* and *21*), *and*   ◆ *print rights* – to copy, and to issue copies of, a work (*ss 17* and *18*).

➤ As a general rule, none of these 3 rights is administered by UK collecting societies.

◆ An important exception is the synchronisation of music with TV programmes, which is covered by 'blanket licence agreements' (ie: collective bargaining arrangements) between the MCPS, the PRS and the respective UK broadcasters.

➤ A publisher usually reserves the right to administer synch rights (for non-TV purposes) and grand rights, and negotiates with third parties on a case-by-case basis.

◆ The publisher's grant of rights usually takes the form of a 'licence' (ie: permission) to use the music, in return for paying the publisher:

- *synch rights* – a flat fee and/or a 'royalty' (ie: a contingent payment based on actual exploitation of the work in which the music is used), *or*

- *grand rights* – a share of the show's 'box office' (ie: ticket sales).

➤ Once a major source of income for writers, sheet music is now of limited commercial significance, except in special cases, eg:

◆ classical or jazz composers whose works are still in copyright, where copies are sold or hired for orchestral or home use, *and*

◆ songbooks of superstar artists (or compilation songbooks of hit songs).

- A publisher usually engages a specialist company to print and distribute sheet music, in return for a royalty based on sales (or a share of net receipts).

III   Benefits of a publishing contract

➤   There are 4 main reasons why a publishing contract can benefit a writer:

a) A reputable publisher will have systems in place for administering and collecting publishing income which the writer would not otherwise receive, and will be skilled in negotiating deals with third parties that want to use the writer's songs.

◆ The publisher should ensure that the songs are registered with:

● all relevant collecting societies worldwide, *and*

● the relevant authorities in countries whose laws require copyright works to be registered before attracting copyright protection (eg: the USA).

◆ In the case of rights not administered by collecting societies, the publisher should negotiate licences and enforce collection of the relevant income.

b) The publisher usually pays the writer an 'advance' on account of future royalties (or a series of advances in a contract including a number of options to extend). In the case of a successful writer, these advances can be substantial.

c) If the writer is an unsigned artist (eg: a singer-songwriter), the publisher can use its experience and contacts to help to secure a record deal.

◆ The publisher may provide studio time for the artist to record 'demos'.

● The publisher may provide financial support in the form of money for 'pluggers' (ie: independent promotion), poster campaigns and/or 'tour support' (ie: making up the shortfall on gigs) to help to 'break' the artist (eg: where the artist releases a 'white label' to attract the attention of 'taste-makers').

d) Whether a writer is an artist or not, the publisher should use its industry contacts:

◆ to arrange co-writing opportunities with established writers or artists, *and/or*

◆ to try to get a well-known recording artist to 'cover' (ie: to record versions of) the writer's songs (including co-written songs), *and/or*

◆ to 'place' the writer's songs in audio or audiovisual productions other than records or music videos (eg: film soundtracks, TV theme tunes and adverts).

Self-publishing for established writers

➤ An established writer might consider setting up a publishing company.

◆ The advantage is that the writer can retain ownership of copyright, allowing full control over exploitation and direct remuneration.

◆ The drawback is the amount of administrative work required, eg:

● dealing with collecting societies, *and*

● collecting royalties from companies granted rights that are not administered by collecting societies (eg: synch rights).

■ The writer can try to overcome this by entering into an administration agreement with an established publishing company which will, in return for a share (eg: 5%, 10% or 15%) of income arising, deal with all of the administrative work.

IV   Exclusive songwriter agreement

➤ The ESA is the most common – and most important – form of publishing agreement in the music publishing business.

◆ This is because the ongoing relationship largely suits both parties:

a) It allows the publisher to build up a 'catalogue' of songs by the writer.

● Often, however, the writer is engaged before the writer has had a proven track record. This presents both:

▪ an opportunity for a massive return on the publisher's investment where the songs are 'hits', *and*

▪ a risk, which the publisher usually spreads by engaging a number of writers and by selecting writers likely to be successful (eg: writers that have just signed a major recording deal).

b) The publisher usually pays the writer a series of advances on account of future income throughout the term.

● Because the writer grants rights in several songs, the publisher will pay a larger amount than for a single song. This may in effect provide a wage that allows the writer to stop 'flipping burgers' (as it is often put) and to devote time to songwriting and building a wider music career.

▪ Details of other types of publishing contract are beyond the scope of this Section, but have many features in common with an ESA – especially the publisher's essential obligations to collect income arising from the songs and to remit it to the rights-owner.

➤ In the case of an ESA, the writer signs to a publisher on an 'exclusive' basis (ie: throughout the term, the writer provides songwriting services only to the publisher, although the publisher is free to engage other writers at the same time).

Exclusivity and restraint of trade
➤ Note the possibility that the doctrine of restraint of trade could affect such an agreement.   ◆ If the publisher has no obligations of any kind to exploit the songs, the contract is voidable (ie: cancellable) as being in restraint of trade (*Schroeder v Macaulay* [1974] 3 All ER 616).   ➤ As a result of this doctrine: a) the duration of the term (including any extensions exercisable at the publisher's option) must be kept within reasonable limits, *and*   b) the publisher must at least use reasonable endeavours to exploit the songs.

➤ Although each ESA differs, certain provisions should always be included:

Clause	Terms
Parties	➤ The parties will be the publisher and the writer, but it is important for both sides to check that they are dealing with the right parties. ◆ The publisher will want to ensure, when dealing with a band or a writing team, that all relevant co-writers also sign the contract. ● This gives the publisher ownership of all contributions to each song and therefore full: a) collection rights (for the whole revenue stream), *and* b) control over licensing decisions – which can sometimes be problematic where different publishers represent joint owners' or co-owners' shares of a song. ◆ The writer will want to ensure that the publisher is a reputable company that has the relevant experience, contacts and resources to perform its side of the bargain. ● It is common for an independent publisher to rely heavily on a third-party administration company and/or series of connected companies overseas. This may reduce the writer's share of income in comparison with a major publisher that has a truly international operation and few (if any) 'middle men'. ➤ The writer may also have set up a 'loan-out' company for the writer's songwriting services. If so, the company enters into the contract. ◆ The writer then needs to sign an 'inducement letter' that assures the publisher that the services will be provided by the loan-out company, failing which the writer will provide the services direct to the publisher in the writer's personal capacity.
Term	➤ The publisher engages the writer to provide songwriting services exclusively to the publisher for a 'term'. ◆ The term usually consists of 1 initial period, plus a number of (eg: 2 or 3) additional 'option periods' (ie: separate, consecutive extensions exercisable at the publisher's option). ● If the publisher fails to exercise an option, the writer is often required, as part of an 'option warning mechanism', to notify the publisher that an option has not been exercised. The current contract period does not end unless the publisher fails to exercise the option within a further 'cure period' (eg: 10 working days from the date of the notice). ➤ At the end of the term, the writer is free to provide songwriting services to a third party, but the publisher usually continues to administer songs written during the term for a further period known as the *'retention period'*, which begins at the end of the term. ◆ The songwriting term should not be confused with the term of the contract itself. After the end of the songwriting term, the ESA will continue in full effect for the duration of the retention period (and, commonly, for a 'collection period' lasting 12, 18 or 24 months thereafter), while the publisher collects monies and the writer remains entitled to receive royalties. ➤ NB: in publishing contracts dealing with an existing catalogue, there is no songwriting 'term', but simply a defined rights period.

Clause	Terms
Minimum commitment	➤ The duration of each of the contract periods may be fixed (eg: 12, 24 or 36 months).
	➤ Alternatively, it will be linked to delivery by the writer of a minimum number of songs (which is known as the '*minimum commitment*'), a specified percentage of which must be written by the writer.
	◆ Fulfilment of the minimum commitment is often linked to the commercial release of the minimum commitment on a major record label in a major territory or specified major territories.
	• The relevant contract period will end within a specified period of time (eg: 90 or 180 days) after fulfilment of the minimum commitment.
	◆ Where the writer is an artist with a record deal, the commitment is in effect an album's worth of material (or at least a substantial part of an album, eg: 10 songs written as to 60%).
	• The aim is to ensure that the publisher is not obliged to pay any further advance until the songs are likely to have generated sufficient revenue to justify such an obligation.
	• The sanction for failure to fulfil the commitment is often:
	a) an automatic extension of the current contract period until the minimum commitment is fulfilled, *and/or*
	b) the non-payment (or proportionately reduced payment or delay in payment) of the advance payable in the next option period (if the option is exercised).
	• The writer should therefore try to ensure that:
	a) each contract period is capped at 2 or 3 years (so that the term does not run indefinitely), *and*
	b) the minimum commitment can alternatively be fulfilled if the advance payable for the contract period has, at the end of the previous period (taking into account so-called 'pipeline' income not yet received), been 100% recouped from the writer's share of income.
	▪ This is to prevent an unfair situation in which the writer has had a massive 'hit', but has not still not technically fulfilled the minimum commitment.
	▪ As a compromise, the publisher may ask for a higher recoupment percentage (eg: 125% or 150%).
Grant of rights	➤ Usually the writer 'assigns' (ie: transfers ownership of) the copyright in the writer's songs to the publisher.
	◆ In special cases (eg: where the writer is a 'star' singer-songwriter), the writer may instead grant a limited licence.
	• A licence is more typical in an administration agreement, and an ESA based on a licence may in many other respects resemble an administration agreement – see further below.
	➤ The publisher will prefer (and will usually insist on) an assignment because:
	a) a licence is terminable for breach of contract, *and*
	b) as an owner, the publisher has enhanced rights to protect the copyright in the songs (eg: to take legal action in its own name).

Clause	Terms

Songs covered by the grant of rights	➤ The songs in which copyright is being assigned (or licensed) should be clearly defined in the contract.
	
	◆ These generally include all songs written by the writer (and parts of songs co-written with other writers) during the term.
	
	   ● References below to 'songs' include parts of songs co-written by the writer (to the extent of those parts).
	
	◆ The publisher will, where possible, want to take an assignment (or licence) of songs written by the writer before the term.
	
	   ● This is standard practice where a writer is a new artist with no previous publishing deal – especially where the songs are 'demos' that have secured the artist a major record deal.
	
	      ■ It may not be possible for the writer to grant these rights, as the copyright in those songs may have already been assigned (or licensed) to a previous publisher.
	
	      ■ A publisher will be keen, however, to avoid any claim by the writer that a song was written before the term (and is therefore not controlled by the publisher), so a publisher often takes a grant of rights in pre-term songs to the extent not already granted to a third party.
	
	◆ The publisher will also want the grant of rights to cover songs:
	
	   a) written before the term, but completed during the term, *or*
	
	   b) begun during the term, but completed shortly afterwards (eg: within 4 months after the term).
	
	➤ The writer is usually required, as each new song is written, to execute a single-song assignment in the publisher's standard form confirming the grant of rights in the song in favour of the publisher.

Performance rights	➤ A fractional share (typically half) of the performance rights cannot be assigned to the publisher where the writer is a member of a performing right society.
	
	◆ This is because, in order to authorise the society to collect performance income, the writer has enter into a separate agreement with the society relating to performance rights.
	
	➤ For historical reasons, the UK performing right society, the PRS, calculates payments in fractions of 12, rather than as percentages.
	
	◆ PRS rules provide that a writer must receive, direct from the PRS, at least 6/12 of all performance income (which is known as the 'writer's share').
	
	➤ Technically, the writer can receive as much as 8/12 of such income, with the publisher receiving the remaining 4/12.
	
	◆ The publisher, however, typically includes a clause in the ESA requiring the writer to inform the PRS that the writer is only to receive 6/12 of all performance income.
	
	   ● The effect of this is that the PRS will pay the other 6/12 of the performance income (which is known as the 'publisher's share') direct to the publisher.
	
	      ■ The publisher can, therefore, share in this revenue stream and apply some of the writer's performance income towards recoupment of any advances paid to the writer.

Clause	Terms
Waiver of moral rights	➤ The publisher almost invariably insists that the writer waives the writer's moral rights as an author under *CDPA Pt I Ch IV*. ◆ The publisher needs to be free to authorise others to use the songs in circumstances where it is not possible to credit the writer as author and/or necessary to edit or adapt the songs (eg: to translate lyrics for overseas use or to make an arrangement of a song for the purposes of a cover version). • The writer should ensure that, in return, the publisher will: ▪ use reasonable endeavours to procure a credit in accordance with music industry practice, *and* ▪ afford the writer certain approvals of types of usage (eg: in relation to advertising - see further below).
Name and likeness rights	➤ The publisher should always take a grant of rights to exploit the writer's name, approved likeness and biographical material in connection with the promotion and exploitation of the songs.
Rights period	➤ The duration of the grant of rights should be clearly stated. ◆ The publisher's standard-form ESA may require an assignment (or, in special cases, a licence) for the songs' full copyright term (ie: the life of the writer plus 70 years) and thereafter, to the fullest extent possible, 'in perpetuity' (ie: forever). • The writer should strongly resist this – except in special circumstances (eg: music designed for inclusion in audiovisual productions, such as film music or 'library' music, where a complete buy-out of music rights is standard). ➤ In practice, the rights period is usually confined to the songwriting term plus the retention period. ➤ The usual range for the retention period is between 5 and 25 years. ◆ The writer will want to keep this shorter, the publisher longer. A retention period of 10 or 15 years is a fairly common compromise. The writer is unlikely to succeed in achieving a shorter period unless the writer is established or the publisher cannot afford a significant advance. • An alternative compromise is for the writer to concede a long retention period on the basis that advance(s) are payable during the retention period (eg: after the first 5 years of the retention period, the publisher pays the writer a sum based on a multiple (eg: 3 or 4) of the average royalties for the previous 6 accounting periods). ◆ The retention period is often automatically extended to the accounting date following its expiry. ➤ In the case of an assignment, the publisher should be obliged to re-assign all copyright and other rights in the songs to the writer at the end of the retention period. ➤ In the case of a licence, the retention period can vary greatly and is a matter for negotiation between the parties. It could be as short as 5 or 7 years in the case of an established writer or even just 12, 24 or 36 months (terminable thereafter on 3 months' notice) in the case of an administration-style agreement.

Clause	Terms
Territory	➤ The publisher usually insists on taking a grant of rights to administer the songs throughout the world. ◆ This raises the level of income to be collected and also spreads the risk that the publisher may fail to recoup advances. ● The geographical area in which the publisher can administer the songs is known as the 'territory'. ➤ Where the writer is in a very strong bargaining position, the writer may be able to exclude certain countries from the territory and to do a series of direct, territory-specific deals for those countries. ◆ The advantages of such direct deals for the writer are that: ● the income from the relevant country will not be used to recoup an advance paid in respect of another, *and* ● royalties arising in the relevant country may be paid through to the writer sooner than under a worldwide deal. ◆ Such deals, however, increase the writer's legal spend on negotiations and involve a greater amount of monitoring. ● For this reason, worldwide deals are the norm.
Approval rights	➤ The publisher may agree to make certain forms of exploitation subject to the writer's prior written approval (eg: grand rights, synch licences, use of titles/lyrics in commercials, merchandising use and material adaptations and translations). ◆ The publisher will want such approvals not to be unreasonably withheld or delayed.
Reserved rights	➤ Some writers succeed in reserving certain rights to themselves (eg: grand rights). ◆ This is extremely rare, and most likely to occur where the writer is a 'star' artist or a successful stand-alone writer.
Termination	➤ The writer should try to ensure that the songwriting term (and, ideally, the retention period) can be terminated in the event of the publisher's material breach, insolvency or cessation of business. ◆ The publisher is likely to resist early termination of the retention period (whatever the cause), but is likely to agree to early termination of the term (partly to avoid restraint of trade). ➤ Where copyright is assigned to the publisher, the writer would ideally want a right, in the event of early termination of the term or retention period, to require the publisher to re-assign the copyright. ◆ The publisher will resist this strongly. ● In any event, as a matter of public policy, a purported right to require re-assignment in the event of insolvency is contrary to the interests of the publisher's creditors and is generally thought to be 'void' (ie: of no legal effect from the outset).
Writer's obligations	➤ Aside from fulfilling the minimum commitment, the writer has minor obligations under the contract (eg: to provide the publisher with information about, and copies of, songs written under the contract).

Clause	Terms
Writer's warranties	➤ The writer usually warrants (among other things) that, at the time of the songs' creation: ◆ the songs are original to the writer, and the writer owns all rights in them and has not disposed of such rights, *and* ◆ the songs do not infringe the rights of any third party, eg: are not based on any 'samples' (ie: direct copies of sound recordings) from third-party recordings and do not contain any 'interpolations' (ie: replayed elements) from other songs, *and* ◆ the songs are not defamatory, *and* ◆ none of the songs has already been exploited, *and* ◆ the writer has not entered into a similar deal with a third party. 　• The warranties are commonly backed by an indemnity. 　　■ The writer should try to ensure that the writer is not liable for claims under the indemnity unless such claims are the subject of a settlement approved by the writer or of a final judgment of a court of competent jurisdiction.
Publisher's obligations	➤ The publisher should be obliged to secure the exploitation of the songs, either itself (eg: by selling sheet music) or via third parties. ◆ The publisher typically agrees to use 'reasonable endeavours' to exploit the songs, usually via the bona fide grant of mechanical, synch, broadcast and/or print rights. 　• Where copyright is assigned to the publisher, the writer commonly has a right to require the publisher to re-assign all rights in a song to the writer if the publisher fails to exploit the song within a given period of time (eg: the songwriting term plus 2 years). 　　■ The publisher may insist on a short 'cure period' (eg: 1 to 3 months) within which to exploit the song, so preventing the exercise of the re-assignment right. ◆ In practice, the main exploitation is carried out by record labels (via the manufacture and release of records), by broadcasters playing the songs on TV or radio or by the writer (or other artists) performing the songs at live concerts. ➤ The publisher should also commit to administering the songs properly, including taking all reasonable steps: ◆ to register the songs with appropriate collecting societies, *and* ◆ to collect all income arising from exploitation (including prompt and accurate recovery of income due from overseas licensees). ➤ The publisher's main obligation is therefore to collect income arising and to pay through specified amounts to the writer. ◆ Payments typically take the form of: 　• royalties calculated on the various types of income received by the publisher from the exploitation of the songs, *and* 　• 'advances' payable at the beginning of each contract period, which are non-returnable but 'recoupable' (ie: recoverable) from royalty payments subsequently due to the writer.

Clause	Terms
Advances	➤ The publisher usually pays the writer an advance against the writer's future income for each contract period.
	◆ Each advance is non-returnable, but recoupable by the publisher from the writer's share of royalties.
	➤ The amount of each advance (if any) is a matter of negotiation.
	◆ The sum payable for the initial period will reflect the publisher's educated guess as to what the writer might earn from the writer's songs in the initial period.
	• The estimate will be informed by:
	▪ the level of commercial interest in the writer (eg: whether the writer has a good manager and/or a record deal with an established label), *and*
	▪ where there is a 'race' between publishers to sign a writer, the deal terms offered by other publishers, *and*
	▪ where the writer has a record deal, the likely level of income from mechanical and performance rights, based on projections of records manufactured and airplay.
	◆ If the contract contains any option periods, the advance payable in each option period usually increases for each subsequent period.
	• The increases are often linked to the earnings of the previous period (eg: 2/3 of such earnings or, less generously, 50% of the writer's share of mechanical income in the previous 2 accounting periods), but then subject to a minimum level ('floor') and maximum level ('ceiling') in a so-called 'minimax' formula.
	▪ Usually, the minimum levels are not less than the advance for the initial period and step up in defined increments.
	▪ Each maximum level is often double the minimum level.
	▪ From the writer's perspective, the payment of each advance should not depend on whether the previous advance was recouped.
	• An alternative approach is to fix the increases in large increments, but to reduce them by the amount of any unrecouped balance as at the end of the previous period.
	➤ Each advance is usually payable in instalments, eg: as to:
	◆ 25% at the start of a contract period, *and*
	◆ 25% on commencement of recording the minimum-commitment album for that period, *and*
	◆ as to the balance on fulfilment of the minimum commitment.
	• The balance may be staggered between releases in major territories (eg: as to 25% on the UK release of a minimum-commitment album and as to 25% on its US release).
	➤ For an unsigned artist writer, the majority of the initial advance may be deferred until the writer has signed an approved recording contract.
	➤ Where a very high royalty is payable (eg: under an administration-style agreement), it is likely that no advance will be payable at all.

Clause	Terms
Royalty rates	➤ Royalty rates differ depending on the source of publishing income.

➤ Royalty rates differ depending on the source of publishing income.

    ◆ The level of each rate is a matter of negotiation, and should be higher if no (or low) advances are payable under the contract.

        ● The publisher will not actually pay any royalties to the writer (whatever the source of income) until it has recouped each advance from the writer's share of income.

➤ **Mechanical income** – Income from the exploitation of mechanical rights will be paid by a record company:

    ◆ to the MCPS, which will then pay it to the publisher after deducting a commission, *or*

    ◆ direct to the publisher.

        ● The writer should receive at least 70% of what the publisher receives, although this figure may be as high as 80% (or even up to 85% or 90% for very successful, established writers or in the context of administration agreements).

            ■ One exception is the rate for commissioned music or 'production/library music' written for inclusion in audiovisual productions, which is usually 50%.

➤ **Public performance income** – The writer should receive a percentage of the 'publisher's share' of performance income.

    ◆ This rate is usually 50% of the 'publisher's share' (especially where mechanical and other rates are 75%).

        ● The rate is lower because the writer also receives the 'writer's share' direct from the PRS. In this way, the writer has an effective 75% rate (ie: 50% direct, plus 25% from a half-share of the publisher's 50%).

➤ **Synch fees** – The publisher may generate income by granting synch licences to third parties.

    ◆ The rate should be the same as for mechanical royalties, although it is commonly reduced (by, say, 10 percentage points) for synchs that are 'procured' by the publisher.

    ◆ The writer should request a right of approval over synch usage.

➤ **Sheet music income** – The publisher may also sell sheet music.

    ◆ The writer usually receives between 10% and 15% of the retail selling price (or, if calculated on a receipts basis, the same rate as the mechanical rate).

➤ **Other income** – There should always be a sweep-up category for income not covered under the more predictable sources of revenue (eg: grand rights income, or income derived from licensing rights for new devices not yet covered by collecting society arrangements).

    ◆ The rate is usually the same as the mechanical rate.

➤ **'Black box' income** – Only extremely successful writers are likely to participate in this revenue stream.

    ◆ 'Black box' income is the income that collecting societies have collected under collective bargaining arrangements (eg: with broadcasters) but cannot attribute to any particular songs.

        ● It is usually distributed between publishers on a set formula and is, in effect, a windfall for publishers that is not usually passed on to writers.

Clause	Terms

Reduced royalty rates for 'covers'	➤ All royalty rates (except for the rate for performance income) are commonly reduced in the case of 'covers'.
	
	◆ In this context a 'cover' is a recording of a writer's song made by a third party.
	
	   ● Writers have argued – usually without success – that the publisher should not be given any extra reward simply for fulfilling its contractual obligation to exploit the songs.
	
	➤ Most royalty rates are reduced by 10 or 15 percentage points (eg: from 75% to 60%).
	
	◆ The reduction in the rate for performance income is, pro rata, 20 or 30 percentage points (eg: from 50% to 20%), to compensate for the fact that the 'writer's share' is fixed at 50%.
	
	➤ To justify the reduction, the publisher is often required to have 'procured' (ie: directly caused) the cover.
	
	◆ In practice, writers often procure covers themselves, so may be reluctant to have their share reduced when their efforts bring about the opportunity. Also, third parties may unilaterally decide to record a song, in which case the publisher cannot fairly take the credit.
	
	   ● The publisher should also not be allowed to make a reduction where a sub-publisher has procured the cover and already reduced the amount paid to the publisher.
	
	     ■ Covers deductions may not be appropriate for writers that purely write for third parties, especially where the writers are active in procuring their own covers.

Royalty escalations	➤ A writer that has not previously had a publishing contract may find it difficult to negotiate favourable royalty rates.
	
	◆ One way for the writer to overcome this problem is to negotiate 'escalations' (ie: successive increases in royalty rates) based on achieving specified levels of success, eg:
	
	   ● an increase by 5 percentage points if a minimum-commitment album achieves 'gold' sales in a specified major territory (eg: the US or the UK), *plus*
	
	   ● a further increase by 5 percentage points if the album achieves 'platinum' sales in that territory.
	
	     ■ The escalations may apply to all songs in the catalogue on a prospective basis or (less favourably for the writer) only to the songs written in the relevant contract period.
	
	◆ An alternative is that the rates escalate each time the publisher exercises an option to extend for an additional contract period (eg: in terms of the mechanical rate, 70% for period 1, 75% for periods 2 and 3 and then 80% for period 4).

'At source' calculations	➤ The writer should, where possible (eg: if the publisher is a major publisher), ensure that royalties are calculated on the publisher's gross earnings 'at source' (ie: as if paid direct on income arising in each territory), rather than on net sums actually received by the publisher in the UK (which is known as a 'receipts' basis). ◆ The royalty rates given above are at-source figures.

Clause	Terms
'Receipts' calculations	➤ 'Receipts' can be a much lower figure after deduction of the fees of the publisher's licensees (eg: sub-publishers and administrators) – especially if cumulative deductions are made as between a series of licensees around the world. ◆ Some publishers will offer an at-source deal for the major territories, but a receipts deal for minor territories. ➤ If the writer does receive royalties on a 'receipts' basis (which is standard in the case of an independent publisher), the writer will ultimately receive less and should therefore try to negotiate: ◆ a cap on the deductions that can be made in aggregate by overseas licensees, sub-publishers and administrators (eg: 25% worldwide, but 50% worldwide for 'synch' and 'cover' income, for which a higher level of retention is commonly made by licensees, reflecting the work involved in 'placing' the relevant songs), *and* ◆ a higher royalty percentage to compensate for the deductions (eg: an uplift of 5 or 10 percentage points in comparison with the at-source figures given above).
Royalty base	➤ The royalty 'base' (ie: the income on which royalties are calculated) is usually all gross earnings of the songs (whether calculated on an 'at source' or 'receipts' basis) after deduction of: ◆ VAT or similar taxes applicable in overseas countries, *and* ◆ standard commissions retained by bona fide collecting societies and/or collecting agencies, *and* ◆ reasonable fees paid to arrangers, adaptors and translators.
Withholding tax	➤ Sums payable to the writer will also be subject to deductions or withholdings for income or other taxes required to be deducted or withheld under the laws of overseas countries – see Section C of this Chapter for further consideration of 'withholding tax'. ◆ The writer should ensure that the publisher provides the writer with the necessary certificates (where available) so that the writer can seek a credit for any tax withheld.
Accounting and audit rights	➤ The publisher usually accounts to the writer twice a year, within 90 days after 30 June and 31 December. ◆ A writer should insist on accounting and audit rights equivalent to those granted under a recording contract – see Section C of this Chapter. ➤ The PRS accounts direct to each writer member for the 'writer's share' of performance income on a quarterly basis (but with 2 main distributions per year). ➤ Whether paid by the publisher or the PRS, foreign royalties will take a long time to come through the so-called 'pipeline' (eg: between 12 and 24 months). ◆ This is due to the chain of payments passing from overseas collecting societies and licensees to local sub-publishers, then to the publisher and finally to the writer, with quarterly or semi-annual accounting delays imposed at each payment stage.

Clause	Terms
Sub-publishing	➤ An ESA is likely to contain a clause on 'sub-publishing'. ◆ The publisher often needs the right to appoint 'sub-publishers' in other countries. ● This is because the publisher (eg: an independent) may not have affiliated companies or branch offices overseas. ■ Even a major publishing company is likely to rely on sub-publishers in minor territories. ● The sub-publisher is effectively a sub-contractor, and undertakes the publisher's activities in the overseas territory, ie: ■ registering and protecting copyrights, *and* ■ promoting local exploitation, *and* ■ collecting and administering income arising (other than income remitted by overseas collecting societies, which is remitted to affiliated UK societies direct). ● The contract between the publisher and sub-publisher will be similar to the ESA and will contain clauses equivalent to those considered in this Section, except that the publisher takes on the role of the person granting rights in the songs and the sub-publisher assumes that of the person being granted the rights. ➤ The writer should try to ensure that the publisher is paid an amount based on the sub-publisher's at-source receipts. ◆ The sub-publisher is usually entitled to deduct commission of: ● 10% or 15% (or as much as 20% or 25% if it has paid a large advance to the publisher) for non-covers income, *or* ● between 20% and 50% (often double the normal rate) for income from a cover originated by the sub-publisher. ◆ The sub-publisher's net income (ie: after deduction of its commission, plus expenses) will therefore be substantially lower than the sub-publisher's at-source receipts. ● Accordingly, the amount paid to the writer is reduced if based on the sub-publisher's net income. ➤ If the publisher (eg: a major) has a network of affiliated companies abroad, it should be allowed to appoint them as sub-publishers, provided that it is required to do so on arm's length terms. ◆ The publisher should not be allowed to appoint 2 sub-publishers in the same territory, as each one would be entitled to the income from exploitation of the works. ● The writer should try to ensure that the sub-publishers cannot appoint sub-sub-publishers (which would further reduce the amount ultimately paid to the writer).
Group provisions	➤ Where the writer is an artist and fellow group members are signed to the same ESA, there will be provisions dealing with the situation where group member(s) leave the group, new member(s) join or the group splits. ◆ These 'group provisions' will be extremely similar to those in a recording contract – see Section C of this Chapter.

Clause	Terms
Controlled compositions	➤ Where the writer is also a recording artist, the ESA should deal with 'controlled compositions'. ◆ 'Controlled compositions' are songs that are written, owned and controlled by an artist (whether in whole or in part). ➤ In an artist's record contract, the clause dealing with controlled compositions is designed to reduce the mechanical royalty rate that the label has to pay to the publisher to exploit recordings in the US and Canada – see Section C of this Chapter. ◆ A reduced rate will be set by reference to a percentage (eg: 75%) of the compulsory licence rate in North America. ● The recording contract often provides that the artist will reimburse the record label for any excess that the label has to pay over the reduced rate, or (more favourably to the artist) that the excess will be deducted from record royalties. ➤ To avoid this sanction under the recording contract, the writer should try to ensure that, under the terms of the ESA, the publisher agrees to grant a mechanical licence at the reduced rate to the writer's record label (or, where the writer is an unsigned artist, future label). ◆ The publisher's standard-form ESA is likely to require the opposite (ie: that the writer has not agreed, and will not agree, with a record label to reduce mechanical income to less than the statutory or agreed industry rate). ● The writer should try to negotiate the clause to reflect (or to anticipate) the actual (or likely) commitments to the writer's record label.
Synch licences for controlled compositions	➤ A recording contract may also require the artist to ensure that the record label is granted a synch licence in respect of controlled compositions that is: ◆ free for promotional videos, or ◆ at a lower than customary rate for DVDs released for sale. ● Where the writer is also a recording artist, the writer should try to ensure that the publisher will agree to grant synch licences on such terms.
Assignment of the contract	➤ The publisher will want to be free to assign its rights under the contract and/or to sub-contract its obligations under the contract to a third party of its choice (or perhaps to novate the contract fully). ➤ The writer should try to limit this freedom by: ◆ restricting the type of assignee to an affiliated company of the publisher (or to a person taking over the publisher, the publisher's group of companies or the publisher's business), and ◆ requiring the assignee to enter into a direct covenant with the writer to perform the publisher's obligations under the contract. ● In absence of such restrictions, the risk is that the writer may end up contracted to a new publisher that the writer did not choose, while the original publisher (which would, but for such a covenant, remain liable for the publisher's obligations) can no longer perform its payment obligations under the contract.

This Chapter examines:

A   Overview

*References in this Section are to the Copyright, Designs and Patents Act 1988 ('**CDPA**'), unless otherwise stated.*

I   Introduction

➤ This Chapter deals with the production of feature films and TV programmes.

  ◆ A feature film is usually produced for cinema, DVD/Blu-ray release and broadcast (via 'pay' and free TV) and, increasingly, for exploitation via digital distribution.

  ◆ TV programmes are usually made primarily for broadcast (whether on TV or via equivalent online media).

➤ In this Chapter, feature films and TV programmes are generally considered together as their production involves similar issues (both legal and practical).

TV as film

➤ A TV programme is treated as a 'film' for copyright purposes because it falls under the definition of a film given in s 5.

  ◆ A TV programme often involves fewer investors and a smaller production budget than a feature film, but otherwise involves most of the same operational issues.

  ● The advent of digital media is also bridging the divide between film and TV as traditional distribution platforms 'converge' with new forms of transmission.

  ◆ References in this Chapter to a '*film*' include a TV programme, unless a distinction is drawn.

➤ This Chapter concentrates on the perspective of an independent producer and the relationships that such a producer has to form in order to make a film.

  ◆ An in-house production team needs to deal with several of the issues considered in this Chapter (eg: rights acquisition), but not others (eg: external finance).

➤ A 'producer' is typically a production company (or another separate legal entity), so is referred to in this Chapter as 'it', to distinguish it from its individual personnel (eg: an individual producer responsible for day-to-day production activities).

II   Stages of production

➤ Production falls into the following stages:

- ◆ **Development** – The producer must develop the concept and script for the film and plan for production (eg: consider the budget and identify finance options).

  - The producer will need to finance the development steps. There are some external sources of development finance in the UK (eg: the UK Film Council), but this is a risky investment with limited chance of a return, so hard to obtain.

- ◆ **Rights clearance** – The producer must 'clear' (ie: obtain grants of) all third-party rights in the film (eg: copyright and related intellectual property rights) to ensure that the film can be exploited without infringement of such rights.

  - Rights must be cleared both in the film itself and in all 'underlying works' (eg: the script) that are incorporated in the film. The process begins during development and continues throughout production.

- ◆ **Finance** – The producer needs to raise finance for the production. This can be obtained from a variety of sources.

  - The ways of financing a production are examined in Section D of this Chapter.

    - ▪ The financier(s) of a feature film usually insist on an outright transfer of ownership ('assignment') of rights in the film in return for providing finance.

    - ▪ TV commissioning arrangements vary, but usually take the form of an exclusive 'licence' (ie: permission) granted by the producer to the commissioner, mainly to broadcast the programme for a defined period (eg: 5 years).

- ◆ **Production** – As part of the process of putting finance in place, the producer enters into a production agreement with the financier/commissioner and can then prepare for filming (eg: hiring the director, cast and crew and other personnel).

  - Once shooting begins, the producer still has to consider the issues of rights clearance and finance, which recur throughout the production of the film.

- ◆ **Distribution and exploitation** – On or before completion of a feature film, the producer or owner of rights in the film (eg: the financier) (**'rights-owner'**) usually enters into a distribution agreement with a major distributor (eg: a Hollywood studio) or a series of contracts with independent distributors.

  - At the core of these arrangements is a licence enabling distributor(s) to exploit the film. The licensed rights may be limited (eg: by territory and/or media).

    - ▪ A TV programme is broadcast by the commissioner, and then exploited via secondary media (eg: pay TV and/or digital platforms) by the commissioner and/or producer (depending on the agreed terms).

➤ These stages are considered in greater detail in Sections B to F of this Chapter.

➤ The producer will have to enter into several different contracts dealing with the respective stages of production, especially in the context of a feature film.

◆ Where a broadcaster commissions a TV programme or a non-media company commissions a promotional film, there is often one contract that governs all stages. Rights clearance is still a separate exercise to be conducted by the producer.

● For the sake of clarity, each stage is treated in Sections B to F of this Chapter as if it is a separate exercise.

III   UK film and TV production

➤ In the 1990s the UK domestic feature film industry expanded on 3 fronts:

a) the number of films produced increased, *and*

b) consumer demand for the cinema increased (largely due to the introduction of multiplex cinemas throughout the UK), *and*

c) domestic investment increased (eg: via distribution of National Lottery money).

➤ Since 2000, changes in tax relief have reduced the domestic sources of finance for film production (especially private investors), but the UK film industry has survived.

◆ In 2007 the 20 top-earning films produced/co-produced in the UK grossed around £244 million in the UK, around 29% of total receipts (source: UK Film Council).

● UK-originated hits in 2008 included *Slumdog Millionaire* and *Quantum of Solace*, which were both extremely successful around the world.

■ The tax credit system introduced by the *Finance Act 2006* has, in practice, allowed producers to obtain loans against the value of future tax credits.

➤ UK TV programme production is also significant internationally. Eg: the estimated total revenue from international sales of UK-produced TV programmes in 2007 was £663 million, representing a 23% increase from 2006 (source: PACT).

◆ The introduction of digital broadcasting, free-to-air digital services and new satellite and cable channels has provided a broader distribution platform.

● This has increased demand for new productions (eg: sport) and increased overseas licensing, despite fears that broadcasters would rely on 'repeats'.

◆ An Ofcom review published in January 2006 found that:

● the UK TV industry spent around £2.6 billion per year on original programming – one of the highest levels of domestically originated content in the world, *and*

● the sector comprised over 800 firms around the UK.

◆ Since then, however, TV advertising sales have declined dramatically (caused in part by the rise of internet advertising). This has caused UK commercial channels (notably ITV) to make significant cut-backs in production of new programmes.

● Certain programmes have managed buck the trend (eg: *The X Factor*).

IV   Financing film production

➤ Few independent producers can make a feature film without raising external finance.

➤ The financing of a film often involves several different sources of finance.

◆ Where there are several financiers, a special purpose vehicle ('**SPV**') is usually established to isolate risk in the venture.

● Production finance is provided to the SPV, which acquires all rights in the film in the first instance and then makes onward grants of rights as necessary to distributors and to any other entities exploiting the film.

▪ The scale of finance required, together with the tax incentives available in different countries around the world, means that most feature films are funded from a variety of international sources.

➤ The major Hollywood 'studios' are still the major international source of film finance.

◆ The 6 main Hollywood studios (and their respective major subsidiaries) are, in descending order of market share in 2008 (source: Box Office Mojo):

a) Warner Bros (Warner Bros, New Line, HBO and Castle Rock), *and*

b) Paramount (Paramount), *and*

c) Sony (Columbia, MGM and United Artists), *and*

d) Fox (20th Century Fox and Fox Searchlight), *and*

e) NBC Universal (Universal, Focus and Working Title), *and*

f) Walt Disney (Walt Disney, Touchstone and Miramax).

● The major studios are of roughly equal size and influence.

● Together, the major studios account for more than 85% of the North American market (source: Box Office Mojo) and around 68% of the UK film market (source: UK Film Council).

➤ In the UK, there is no such 'studio' system. There are 3 main sources of film finance:

1   Public funds

➤ The UK Film Council contributes finance to films through its 3 film funds – see section VII below.

2   Broadcasters

➤ The BBC and Channel 4 each have film arms that make feature films:

◆ BBC Films, which co-produces around 8 films a year, works with US and UK distributors (eg: *The Duchess* and *Revolutionary Road*), *and*

◆ Film4, which co-produces around 8 films a year for global and UK markets (eg: *Slumdog Millionaire* and *The Last King Of Scotland*).

3   **Independent sources of finance**

➤   There are several other sources of film finance. These include:

♦   national and regional funding and European subsidies, *and*

♦   'equity investors' (ie: individuals, companies or other entities providing cash before production begins), *and*

♦   distribution advances from the pre-sale of distribution rights, *and*

♦   sales agents' advances from the pre-sale of sales agency rights, *and*

♦   product-placement, merchandising and sponsorship deals, *and*

♦   tax relief schemes (eg: as introduced by the *Finance Act 2006*), *and*

♦   international co-producers.

V   TV production in the UK

➤   UK broadcasters provide the bulk of the finance for in-house and independent UK productions of TV programmes.

♦   A broadcaster provides funding in return for a grant of broadcasting rights and secondary exploitation rights.

➤   There are 3 categories of UK producers:

1   **Major broadcasters**

Major broadcasters

➤   The major broadcasters are the 4 traditional 'terrestrial' broadcasters, ie: the 'free-to-air' TV channels that are, at the time of writing, transmitted via analogue and digital aerial signals.

♦   All UK TV broadcasting is in the process of switching to a digital signal, region by region. The process is due to be complete in 2012.

➤   The 4 major UK broadcasters are as follows:

1   **British Broadcasting Corporation (BBC)**

♦   The BBC derives its revenue from:

●   the UK TV licence fee, *and*

●   licensing to overseas broadcasters, licensing 'repeats' to cable and satellite channels, DVD/Blu-ray sales and other secondary exploitation (eg: merchandising and book publishing).

♦   The BBC produces programmes in-house and commissions programmes from independent producers.

Major broadcasters (continued)

- ◆ When commissioning independent productions, the BBC generally meets all production costs (treating these as a fee in return for the grant of UK broadcast rights) and cash-flows production.

  - In some cases, the BBC's overseas distribution arm, BBC Worldwide, may agree to provide a proportion of the production budget by way of an 'advance' against income from overseas exploitation of the programme.

2 ITV

- ◆ The Independent Television (ITV) network comprises 15 regional Channel 3 licensees and a number of digital channels.

  - ITV plc holds 11 of the regional licences and sells advertising for all 15 licences. Of the other 4 licences, the 2 licences for Scotland are held by SMG, the Northern Ireland licence by UTV and the Channel Islands licence by Channel Television.

- ◆ The ITV channels (along with all of the other commercial broadcasters) derive their revenue from:

  - advertising and sponsorship, and

  - licensing to overseas broadcasters, licensing 'repeats' to cable and satellite channels, DVD/Blu-ray sales and other secondary exploitation.

- ◆ ITV's central Commissioning Team commissions programming across the whole ITV network.

  - When commissioning an independent production, it enters into a 3-way agreement with a selected regional licensee and the relevant producer.

- ◆ ITV has a Nations & Regions Production Fund, dedicated to commissions from producers based outside London.

3 Channel 4

- ◆ Channel 4 does not produce any TV programmes in-house, but relies wholly on independent production for its TV programmes, being established on a 'publisher-broadcaster' model.

4 Five

- ◆ Virtually all of Five's commissioned programmes are made by independent producers.

➤ As well as commissioning their own programming, the major broadcasters license in films and programmes from overseas rights-owners.

2   **Digital-only broadcasters**

> ### Digital-only broadcasters
>
> ➤ The digital-only (or 'non-terrestrial') broadcasters are the satellite, cable and/or online channels (eg: BSkyB and UKTV).
>
> ➤ They mainly:
>
> ◆ commission programmes from independent producers, *and*
>
> ◆ license in feature films and TV programmes from overseas rights-owners.
>
>   ● Some rely on a substantial proportion of 'user-generated content', also known as 'UGC' (eg: Current TV).
>
> ➤ The digital-only broadcasters have created a market for 'repeats' of feature films and TV programmes, and some channels are exclusively devoted to these (eg: UKTV Gold).
>
> ◆ Pay-per-view and subscription channels offer first runs of feature films before they are broadcast on free-to-air services.
>
> ➤ The digital-only broadcasters also provide channels exclusively devoted to specialist programming (eg: sport and music).

➤ The 'terrestrial' broadcasters are currently more involved in production than their 'non-terrestrial' counterparts.

3   **Independent producers**

➤ A large number of independent producers are involved in film and TV production in the UK.

◆ There are a few large companies (the 'super-indies', some being broadcasters that lost licences in previous franchise bids).

    ● The rest are smaller companies that rely on the major broadcasters and larger independents for production finance.

VI Production quotas

➤ UK film and television production is protected, and in effect promoted, by a broadcast quota system for 'original' productions.

◆ Independent producers are further supported by the broadcast quota system for independent productions, which is designed to promote a diversity of producers.

➤ Under both EU and domestic legislation, broadcasters must reserve fixed proportions of qualifying transmission time ('***quotas***') for 'original' productions.

Original production quotas under EU law

➤ *Directive 89/552/EC*, now known as the 'Audio-Visual Media Services Directive' ('**AVMS Directive**'), requires EU member states to ensure, 'where practicable and by appropriate means', that broadcasters reserve more than 50% of their transmission time (excluding the time appointed to news, sports events, games, advertising, teletext services and teleshopping) for 'European works' (*Art 4(1)*).

♦ The precise definition of 'European works' is beyond the scope of this Section (see *Art 1(n)* for full details). Essentially, most categories of European works must satisfy 2 criteria:

● *personnel* – the works must be mainly made with authors and workers residing in 1 or more of the 'European' states (ie: what one would, in ordinary-language terms, think of as European countries, ie: not limited to the EU member states), *and*

● *production*:

▪ the works must be produced by ... *or*

▪ production must be controlled by ... *or*

▪ for co-productions with third-nation producers, the majority of the funding of production costs must come from,

... 1 or more producers established in 1 or more of those European countries.

➤ The *AVMS Directive* was amended (and given its current name by) *Directive 2007/65/EC*. In the context of quotas, the amendments take into account the emergence of alternative delivery platforms by:

♦ extending the full quota requirements to providers of '**linear**' audiovisual media services (ie: **scheduled** services such as traditional television, webcasting, streaming and near-video-on-demand services on any delivery platform, including the internet and mobile telephones) (*Arts 1, 4* and *5*), *and*

♦ applying a 'light-touch' regulatory approach to '**non-linear**' (ie: **on-demand**) media service providers by requiring them simply to 'promote, where practicable and by appropriate means, production of and access to European works' (*Art 3i(1)*).

● The changes were implemented in the UK by the *Audiovisual Media Services Regulations 2009*, which came into force on 19 December 2009 and amended existing legislation.

➤ NB: the detailed provisions of the *AVMS Directive* and the *Audiovisual Media Services Regulations 2009* (eg: concerning product placement and protection of minors) are beyond the scope of this Section.

Original production quotas under UK law

➤ The *Communications Act 2003* ('*CA 2003*') *s 278* requires Ofcom to include conditions in the licences of all 'licensed public service channels' (ie: each of the Channel 3 licensees, Channel 4 and Five) to ensure that an appropriate proportion of total airtime (excluding advertisements) is allocated to the broadcasting of 'original productions' each year.

  ◆ The same rules apply to the BBC and to Sianel Pedwar Cymru (S4C) services (*CA 2003 ss 198* and *203* and *BBC Agreement cl 49*).

  ◆ 'Original productions' are defined under the *Broadcasting (Original Productions) Order 2004* as programmes commissioned with a view to their first being shown on TV in the UK on the relevant channel or service, as long as they are also 'European programmes' within the meaning of *Art 5* of *B(OP)O 2004* (ie: programmes which are a 'European works' for the purposes of the *AVMS Directive* – see above).

➤ The quotas vary from broadcaster to broadcaster, from channel to channel and between peak and off-peak transmission times, eg:

  ◆ The quotas agreed by Ofcom for original productions (first shows and repeats) for 2009/2010 for the BBC's first 3 channels are, respectively:

    • *BBC One* – 70% (90% at peak times, ie: 18:00 to 22:30), *and*

    • *BBC Two* – 70% (80% at peak times), *and*

    • *BBC Three* – 70% (70% at peak times).

  ◆ Five's equivalent quota for 2010 is 50% (40% at peak times).

➤ Under both EU and domestic legislation, broadcasters must also reserve quotas for 'independent' productions:

Independent production quotas under EU law

➤ At least 10% of broadcasters' transmission time (excluding the time appointed to news, sports events, games, advertising, teletext services and teleshopping) must be reserved for European works created by independent producers (*AVMS Directive Art 5*).

  ◆ Alternatively, member states may require broadcasters to allocate at least 10% of their programme budget to independent productions.

    ◆ An adequate proportion of independent productions should be recent (ie: less than 5 years old).

➤ NB: the *AVMS Directive* (as implemented in the UK by the *Audiovisual Media Services Regulations 2009*) has extended these quota requirements to all 'linear' (ie: scheduled) media service providers across all platforms – see above.

Independent production quotas under EU law (continued)

➤ Independent works are defined as European works that are created by 'producers who are independent of broadcasters' (*AVMS Directive Art 5*).

◆ The European Commission's *Suggested Guidelines* of 11 June 1999 (which are non-binding but persuasive) provide that:

● a broadcaster must not 'hold too large a share in the capital' of the production company, and vice versa, *and*

● ownership of the producer is only one issue to be taken into account among other considerations (eg: the amount of production supplied to the same broadcaster and the ownership of any secondary rights).

Independent production quotas under UK law

➤ All 'licensed public service channels' (ie: each of the Channel 3 licensees, Channel 4 and Five) must ensure that, each year, not less than 25% of all qualifying programming is allocated to a range and diversity of 'independent productions' (*Broadcasting Act 1990 s 16* and *CA 2003 s 277*).

◆ The same rules apply to the BBC and to S4C services (*CA 2003 ss 198 and 203* and *BBC Agreement cl 52*).

➤ *CA 2003 s 309* applies in a similar way to **digital terrestrial** TV programming not comprised in a licensed public service channel (eg: the 'freeview' channels other than the major broadcasters) – except that the quota is 10%.

◆ There is no quota under UK law for the digital-only non-terrestrial broadcasters (eg: satellite and cable channels).

➤ Under the *Broadcasting (Independent Productions) Order 1991*:

◆ 'Qualifying programmes' are, essentially, all programmes made or commissioned by the broadcaster, excluding adverts, 'repeats', news, Open University programmes and party political broadcasts (*para 2*).

◆ To be eligible for the independent quota, a producer must not (*para 3*):

a) be an employee of a broadcaster, *or*

b) own more than a 25% shareholding in a broadcaster (unless the producer is incorporated or based in the EEA and the broadcaster in question broadcasts exclusively outside the EEA), *or*

c) be a company owned by 1 UK broadcaster as to more than 25% (or by 2 or more UK broadcasters as to more than 50% in aggregate), *or*

d) be required under the commissioning agreement to use the broadcaster's production facilities, or not to use another broadcaster's production facilities.

> ## Independent production quotas in practice
>
> ➤ The BBC has set its own commitment, in addition to guaranteeing 50% of programming output for in-house hours and the 25% independent production quota, that the remaining 25% forms a 'window of creative competition' (ie: hours for which both in-house and external producers can compete).
>
> ➤ Ofcom conducted a review of the UK television production sector and consultation process in early 2006 and concluded that there was no need to recommend changes to the independent production quota system.

➤ Note: regional quotas for production outside the M25 area apply to the major broadcasters (*CA 2003 ss 286* and *288*), but are beyond the scope of this Section.

◆ See the websites of Ofcom and the major broadcasters for further information.

VII Industry organisations

➤ There are a large number of organisations serving the UK film and TV industry, eg:

◆ government departments and agencies, *and*

◆ national and regional screen agencies, *and*

◆ nationwide organisations, eg:

● the British Board of Film Classification (BBFC), *and*

● the British Film Institute (BFI), *and*

● the British Academy of Film and Television Arts (BAFTA), *and*

◆ the EU pre- and post-production support programme, MEDIA 2007, *and*

◆ training and educational organisations (eg: film schools), *and*

◆ representative guilds, unions, foundations and other organisations established to protect the interests of entities and professional personnel involved in film and TV production, eg:

● Producers Alliance for Cinema and Television (PACT), *and*

● Writers' Guild of Great Britain (WGGB), *and*

● Directors Guild of Great Britain (DGGB), *and*

● Equity, *and*

● Musicians' Union (MU), *and*

● Broadcasting, Entertainment, Cinematographic and Theatre Union (BECTU).

■ The representative bodies are examined in Section E of this Chapter, in the context of engagement of production personnel.

➤   Apart from the professional bodies, the main organisations are as follows:

Organisation	Role

Department for Culture, Media and Sport (DCMS)	➤ The DCMS is the government department responsible for policy on culture, media and sport generally.
	
	➤ Its general responsibilities include:
	
	◆ the framework for broadcasting in the UK, *and*
	
	◆ supporting the development of the UK's creative industries.
	
	➤ In particular, it:
	
	◆ negotiates co-production treaties with other countries, *and*
	
	◆ sets government policy on UK film industry issues, working with other departments (eg: HM Treasury on film tax relief), *and*
	
	◆ funds British film initiatives such as the UK Film Council, *and*
	
	◆ provides direct financial support for 'culturally British' films via:
	
	    ● 'grant-in-aid' funding (ie: direct from the DCMS budget) and National Lottery funding distributed through a number of organisations (eg: the UK Film Council), *and*
	
	    ● tax incentives, *and*
	
	◆ has ultimate responsibility (delegated to the UK Film Council) for issuing certificates confirming that a film qualifies for tax relief under the *Finance Act 2006*.
	
	    ● UK film tax relief is considered in Section D of this Chapter.

HM Treasury	➤ The Treasury is the UK ministry responsible for formulating and implementing the government's financial and economic policy. ◆ It works with the DCMS to set policy on film tax incentives.
HM Revenue & Customs (HMRC)	➤ HMRC is the government department responsible for collecting and administering direct taxes (eg: income tax, capital gains tax and corporation tax) and indirect taxes (eg: VAT and stamp duty). ◆ Each type of tax affects investors in films and producers. ◆ In particular, HMRC administers UK film tax relief and publishes detailed guidance on the system and how it works in practice.
UK Film Council	➤ The UK Film Council was set up in 2000 by the DCMS as a strategic agency for film in the UK. ◆ It follows DCMS-set policy and financial directions. ➤ The UK Film Council invests DCMS grant-in-aid funding and National Lottery money in the UK film production through 3 film funds: ◆ *Development Fund* – supporting screenplay development with an annual budget of £4 million (eg: *Brideshead Revisited*), *and* ◆ *Premiere Fund* – facilitating the production of mainstream films with an annual budget of £8 million (eg: *Becoming Jane* and *St Trinian's*), *and* ◆ *New Cinema Fund* – backing innovative film-making (especially short films), new talent and electronic production technologies with an annual budget of £5 million (eg: *This Is England*).

Organisation	Role

UK Film Council (continued)	➤ The UK Film Council also supports UK cinema:
	◆ *Print and Advertising Fund* – The UK Film Council supports distribution of a wider range of films to audiences across the UK with an annual budget of £4 million.
	◆ *Digital Screen Network* – The UK Film Council has equipped around 25% of UK cinemas with digital projection equipment.
	➤ The UK Film Council also distributes funding in support of:
	◆ the Regional Screen Agencies, *and*
	◆ the British Film Institute, *and*
	◆ an international development strategy, *and*
	◆ a personnel diversity strategy, *and*
	◆ training schemes, eg:
	• First Light, a scheme for young film-makers, *and*
	• Skillset, a training strategy for the UK film industry.

National Screen Agencies	➤ There are 3 self-governing screen agencies covering the 3 nations of Northern Ireland, Wales and Scotland, ie:
	◆ Northern Ireland Screen (established in 1997), *and*
	◆ Scottish Screen (established in 1997), *and*
	◆ Film Agency for Wales (established in 2006).
	➤ They are responsible for the strategic development and promotion of various media sectors at a national level.

Regional Screen Agencies	➤ In England, there are 9 Regional Screen Agencies ('*RSAs*').
	◆ They were set up during 2002-2003 as autonomous strategic development agencies to promote media at a regional level.
	• The RSAs are:
	▪ EM-Media, *and*
	▪ Film London, *and*
	▪ Northern Film and Media, *and*
	▪ North West Vision and Media, *and*
	▪ Screen East, *and*
	▪ Screen South, *and*
	▪ Screen West Midlands, *and*
	▪ Screen Yorkshire, *and*
	▪ South West Screen.
	➤ The RSAs are funded by the National Lottery (via the UK Film Council), the Regional Development Agencies for each English region, European Regional Development Funding and other partners.
	◆ The RSAs set up a partnership, Screen England, to co-ordinate and promote the RSAs' joint activities and strategies and to work in strategic partnership with the UK Film Council.

Organisation	Role

Office of Communications (Ofcom)

➤ Ofcom is the body established by the *Office of Communications Act 2002* as the regulator of the UK communications industries.

◆ Ofcom's general duty is to promote and protect the interests of consumers across TV, radio, telecommunications and wireless communications services (*CA 2003 s 3(1)*).

➤ Ofcom's particular duties include (*CA 2003 s 3(2)*):

◆ securing the availability throughout the UK of a wide range of:

• electronic communications services, including high-speed services (eg: broadband), *and*

• TV services of high quality and broad appeal, *and*

◆ maintaining a plurality of providers of different TV services, *and*

◆ applying standards that provide adequate protection for TV audiences against:

• offensive or harmful material, *and*

• unfair treatment of persons, *and*

• unwarranted infringement of privacy.

➤ Ofcom has revised the *Ofcom Broadcasting Code*, which came into effect on 16 December 2009 and is published on Ofcom's website.

◆ The *Code* applies to all UK broadcasters – but with certain exceptions in the case of the BBC, which has further obligations under its *Royal Charter* and the related *BBC Agreement*.

◆ The *Code* reflects objectives set out in the *Broadcasting Act 1996 s 107* (as amended) and *CA 2003 ss 319-327*, including:

• protection of persons under the age of 18, *and*

• due impartiality and accuracy of news reporting, *and*

• protection from offensive and harmful material, *and*

• prevention of:

■ misleading, harmful or offensive advertising, *and*

■ unsuitable sponsorship (eg: product placement), *and*

■ anti-competitive 'cross-promotions' (ie: promotions by one channel of another channel or broadcast service).

◆ The revised version of the *Code* gives effect to requirements relating to TV under the *AVMS Directive* – see above.

➤ Ofcom's remit includes:

◆ digital TV services (eg: Freeview, Sky and Virgin Media), *and*

◆ internet TV services (eg: Home Choice).

➤ Ofcom's remit does not extend to:

◆ content transmitted via the internet or mobile telephones (for which the relevant service provider is responsible), *or*

◆ premium-rate services, such as text services and ringtones (which are regulated by Phonepay Plus), *or*

◆ the content of TV adverts (which is regulated by the Advertising Standards Authority), *or*

◆ the accuracy of BBC programmes (for which the BBC is responsible).

B   Development

*References in this Section are to the Copyright, Designs and Patents Act 1988 ('**CDPA**'), unless otherwise stated. References in this Section to a '**film**' include a TV programme, unless a distinction is drawn.*

I	Concept development
II	Script development
III	Other development steps
IV	Development agreement

I   Concept development

➤ Whatever the genre of a film, it begins with the concept for the film.

  ◆ The producer should protect the concept from being copied by, or disclosed to, a rival producer while the concept is being developed.

  ● The risk is that the competitor may base a production on the same concept, which could ultimately force the producer to abandon production.

➤ The concept cannot be protected by copyright, because there is no copyright in an idea as such and, at the development stage, the concept is unlikely to have been recorded in a copyright work.

Status of a concept for copyright purposes
➤ Copyright in a literary or dramatic work (eg: a screenplay) only exists if the work is recorded, eg: in writing (*CDPA s 3(2)*). There is no copyright in an idea: ◆ only the **expression** of an idea attracts copyright protection (*Football League Ltd v Littlewoods Pools Ltd* [1959] Ch 637), *and*   ◆ identical ideas can be originated independently and still attract copyright protection (in a fixed form), as long as one is not copied from the other.

➤ A producer therefore needs to protect all communications about the concept (eg: creative briefs, outline treatments or format proposals) by having each relevant party enter into a written undertaking to keep the concept confidential.

Keeping a concept confidential
➤ A concept for a film is potentially protectable under the general law of confidence – even without a prior confidentiality agreement – if it is (*Fraser v Thames Television Ltd* [1983] 2 All ER 101):   ◆ clearly identifiable, *and*   ◆ potentially attractive in a commercial sense, *and*   ◆ realisable.   ➤ It is prudent, however, for the producer not to rely on implying a relationship of confidence, but to enter into an express confidentiality agreement.

➤ In the film and television industry, it is not unusual for separate producers to be developing extremely similar concepts independently and at the same time.

♦ Eg: Oliver Stone and Baz Luhrmann each started development on separate movies about Alexander the Great following a revival of 'sword and sandal' epics.

➤ A producer should therefore take the following steps to ensure that a potential competitor does not 'steal' the concept:

1 **Keep evidence of the date of the concept**

➤ The producer should keep careful records of the development of the concept, noting the dates of the creation of each element of the concept.

➤ To prevent against any dispute as to 'ownership' of the concept, the producer should send a copy of an outline treatment of the concept (**'treatment'**):

♦ by registered post to itself or, preferably, to an independent professional (eg: a lawyer or accountant) to retain unopened, *or*

♦ for registration with an industry organisation (eg: the WGGB-approved Script Vault or the US Copyright Office, which register works for a fee).

• This provides evidence of when a concept was developed into a recordable form and would assist in proving that it pre-dated a rival concept in a claim for breach of confidence (in relation to the idea) or infringement of copyright (in relation to the treatment).

2 **Clear contributors' rights**

➤ A concept often evolves from a meeting to 'bounce' ideas.

♦ The producer should 'clear' all rights from each contributor to the discussion (see Section C of this Chapter).

3 **Assert copyright ownership**

➤ A treatment is likely to amount to a copyright work (unlike the concept).

♦ For the purposes of US copyright law (and the copyright laws of other overseas jurisdictions), a copyright notice should be placed prominently on all communications attaching copies of the treatment.

• This takes the form of the copyright symbol ©, followed by the year in which the treatment was written and the name of the producer.

4 **Exercise caution in submissions**

➤ When submitting a concept to a financier (eg: a film studio or broadcaster) with a view to obtaining development finance, the producer should try to ensure that the terms of any submission agreement prepared by the financier do not effectively allow the financier to develop a similar concept.

♦ Eg: the producer should not waive its right to sue the financier for copyright infringement or breach of confidence.

5   Protect a concept for a format

➤   It is difficult to protect a concept for a TV format under English law.

Format rights

➤ The elements that make up the format may not amount to work(s) that can be protected in an action for copyright infringement, even if the name and key features of the show (eg: catchphrases and gimmicks) are copied (*Green v Broadcasting Corporation of New Zealand* [1989] 2 All ER 1056).

   ◆ Lawsuits to protect format rights have since 2001 found more favour in overseas jurisdictions (eg: Hungary and Brazil).

      • The Dutch producer of the reality TV show 'Big Brother', Endemol International, brought a successful action in May 2007 to prevent a Maltese company from broadcasting an unauthorised derivative series.

         ▪ It remains to be seen whether English courts will uphold format rights to the same extent.

➤   In practice, companies are routinely recognised as 'owning' format rights, and large sums are often paid in 'licence fees' to the 'owners'.

Protecting format rights

➤   The producer can register a format with the Format Recognition and Protection Association ('**FRAPA**'), an international format industry association established in 2000 to protect formats.

   ◆ For a fee, FRAPA registers any creative work that describes the format (eg: outlines and treatments) under a confidential, online filing system.

   ◆ This helps to establish precedence of a concept in a dispute.

➤   The producer should try to ensure that, before broadcast, the financier or commissioner undertakes to keep the format confidential.

➤   Once aired, the format becomes public knowledge (losing its confidential status), but the producer should try to support any potential copyright claim (or any claim in passing-off) by compiling:

   ◆ detailed evidence of each element of the format that attracts copyright protection (eg: treatments, scripts, logos, artwork and music), *and*

   ◆ 'bibles' of contracts entered into as part of the rights clearance process (see Section C of this Chapter).

II   Script development

➤   Before the producer seeks development finance, the concept needs to be developed into a treatment, first-draft script or first-draft screenplay (for short, a '**script**').

◆   The producer therefore needs to find and commission a scriptwriter.

●   The Writers' Guild of Great Britain ('**WGGB**') represents scriptwriters. WGGB and the Producers Alliance for Cinema and Television ('**PACT**') have negotiated a model form of contract as a reference point for negotiations.

◆   The scriptwriter is the first owner of the copyright in the script, unless employed by the producer (s 11). The producer must therefore 'clear' (ie: acquire grants of) all copyright and related rights in the script; otherwise, use of the script is an infringing act under the *CDPA* (see Section C of this Chapter).

◆   A scriptwriter's agreement should include the following terms:

> ### Scriptwriter's agreement
>
> ➤   The structure of the contract is that the producer commissions the scriptwriter to write the script in return for a specified fee.
>
> ➤   The contract should accordingly set out:
>
> ◆   the basic script fee and any subsequent use fees (including a schedule of payment instalments payable at each stage from commission through to delivery and acceptance of the script), *and*
>
> ◆   any share of net profits to be payable to the scriptwriter, *and*
>
> ◆   an 'assignment' (ie: a full transfer of ownership) of the entire copyright in the script (or at least the right to produce a film based on the script, with rights reserved to the scriptwriter defined), *and*
>
> ◆   a waiver of 'moral rights' (see Section C of this Chapter), *and*
>
> ◆   the scriptwriter's warranties as to full ownership of the rights granted (backed with an indemnity for breach of warranty), *and*
>
> ◆   delivery dates and response times for each draft of the script, *and*
>
> ◆   agreed screen credits (which may incorporate by reference the WGGB- and PACT-approved *Screenwriting Credits Agreement 1974*).

➤   The script may be based on an 'underlying work' (eg: an existing novel or play).

◆   The producer must acquire or 'clear' all copyright and other rights in the underlying work in order to allow the work to be adapted into a script (see Section C of this Chapter).

●   The right to adapt a work is one of the rights of a copyright owner (s 21).

- The producer must check carefully that the person purporting to own the copyright is in fact the rights-owner.

  - Copyright does not need to be registered in the UK (unlike in the USA), so there is no searchable register of copyright works.

- The acquisition often takes the form of an option to buy the film rights.

  - The reason for obtaining an option is to enable the producer to acquire rights in the film without being fully committed. The producer will pay a smaller fee for the option than for the full purchase price for the film rights.

- The option agreement should include the following terms:

Option agreement

➤ In return for paying the option fee, the producer should acquire:

a) on an exclusive basis, all rights that it requires to develop the film (eg: the right to base a script on the underlying work), *and*

b) the right to exercise the option to acquire the full film rights.

➤ The option is usually for a fixed initial term (eg: 1 or 2 years), which is extendable either unilaterally or with the agreement of both parties.

- The initial period needs to be reasonably long, as the development process often takes a number of years to complete before actual shooting for the film begins.

➤ The contract should also set out:

- the option fee (eg: 10% of the full purchase price), *and*

- any fees for extending the initial period, *and*

- the full purchase price, eg:

  - a specified lump sum, *or*

  - an amount equal to 2-5% of the production budget, capped at defined minimum and maximum limits, *and*

- any share of 'net profits' (ie: net profits derived from exploitation of the film) to be payable to the rights-owner, *and*

- the full film rights to be granted on exercise of the option, ie: usually:

  - an assignment of all rights required by the producer and its successors in title to produce and exploit the film, *and*

  - a waiver of 'moral rights' (see Section C of this Chapter), *and*

- the rights-owner's warranties as to full ownership of the rights granted (backed with an indemnity for breach of warranty).

III   Other development steps

➤   As part of the development process (in addition to developing – and commonly further developing – the concept and script), the producer commonly:

- ◆   prepares a budget, cashflow and production schedule, *and*

- ◆   considers finance options, *and*

- ◆   approaches possible co-producers, *and*

- ◆   identifies key cast and crew (and, where the budget allows, may take an option over their services), *and*

- ◆   identifies locations, *and*

- ◆   initiates the 'rights clearance' process (see Section C of this Chapter), *and*

- ◆   obtains any necessary legal and financial advice in relation to the development work, *and*

- ◆   where possible, enters into a development agreement.

IV   Development agreement

➤   The producer needs finance to carry out each of the development steps.

- ◆   Obtaining finance at the development stage is particularly difficult because the producer has little to offer the financier that is tangible: essentially, money is being invested in a concept, so the investment is highly speculative.

➤   A distributor, broadcaster or larger production company may be prepared to provide development finance.

- ◆   The amount made available varies considerably depending on the source of the finance (eg: for a significant development project, £20,000-£30,000 is not unusual in the UK, but a major Hollywood studio might provide £200,000-£300,000).

➤   When a financier can be found, the producer usually enters into a development agreement.

- ◆   The structure of the contract is the provision of production finance to the producer in return for:

  - ●   an assignment to the financier of copyright in specified work(s), *or*

  - ●   a grant to the financier of a first charge over such work(s).

- ◆   The financier may include in the agreement an option to finance the actual production if it is satisfied that all the preparatory steps have been completed satisfactorily.

  - ●   PACT provides a model form of contract to its members.

➤ The development agreement should include the following terms:

Clause	Terms
Nature of project	➤ The contract should set out the working title of the film and other specifications of the film (eg: its proposed duration and subject-matter).
Development work	➤ The scope of the development work needs to be defined so that it is clear what the producer has to deliver. ➤ This may include (depending on the nature of the project and the development steps already undertaken): ◆ acquiring rights in any underlying work (eg: under an option agreement – see above), *and* ◆ preparing a detailed treatment, *and* ◆ engaging a scriptwriter to prepare successive drafts of a script or screenplay (or to adapt an existing treatment or first-draft script), *and* ◆ preparing a budget, cashflow and production schedule. ➤ The contract should specify the deadline for completing the work.
Finance	➤ The contract should provide full details of the development finance to be made available, including the: ◆ amount, *and* ◆ method of payment (ie: lump sum or instalments), *and* ◆ frequency of payment (eg: monthly in arrears or in a number of tranches on specified dates). • For example, the monies may be paid in several instalments relating to stages of development of the project. • In addition, amounts may be allocated to specific tasks that need to be carried out. ➤ The financier will often insist on: ◆ paying the monies into a separate bank account (for the producer to apply for the purposes specified in the contract), *and* ◆ receiving bank statements and receipts to verify the producer's expenditure on the development work. ➤ Occasionally, if the producer has engaged an individual to carry out the development work, that individual may be paid a separate fee. ➤ The monies are usually made available by way of a loan, which is secured against an assignment of rights (see 'Rights' below) and becomes repayable in defined circumstances, eg: if: ◆ the financier commits to producing or co-producing the film (in which case the monies will usually be re-paid out of the production budget on or before shooting for the film begins), *or* ◆ the producer sells rights in the film to a third party (in which case the monies will usually be re-paid out of the proceeds of sale). ➤ The financier will expect, in addition to such repayment: ◆ a premium (eg: equal to 25% or 50% of the monies lent), *and/or* ◆ interest at a defined rate (eg: a rate over LIBOR), *and/or* ◆ a defined percentage of the film's net profits (eg: 1%).

Clause	Terms
Production services	➤ The producer will want the financier: ◆ to commit within a defined period (eg: 3, 6 or 12 months – the shorter, the better from the producer's perspective) whether or not to produce/co-produce the film (ie: by financing, or contributing to the financing of, the film), *and* ◆ if the financier makes such a commitment, to undertake to engage the producer to provide production services for the film, *and* ◆ to specify the producer's remuneration for those production services (eg: a fixed fee and a defined share of net profits). ● The financier will expect any such commitment to be subject to the parties' entering into a long-form production, finance and distribution agreement, which will confer on the financier wide-ranging rights of approval over key elements of the film (eg: the budget, cashflow, financing arrangements, script, principal cast, director and individual producer).

Clause	Terms
Rights	➤ The financier often insists on an assignment of 100% of the copyright in the development work produced during the development period (eg: the script). ◆ As stated above, the alternative is for the financier to take a first charge over all rights in the development. ➤ An assignment or charge provides the financier with a form of security for its investment in the project. ◆ The financier may prefer an assignment because it provides an actual ownership interest, but a charge may be appropriate in the context of a small-scale, private investment. ● An assignment may also assist in characterising the financier as the 'producer' of the film for the purposes of applying for a tax credit – see Section D of this Chapter. ➤ The producer should ensure that the remuneration it receives represents the value of the rights assigned or charged. ◆ The producer is often in a weak bargaining position (depending on its reputation).

Clause	Terms
Reserved rights	➤ The producer should carefully consider its options before agreeing to a full assignment. ◆ In some circumstances, it may be possible to negotiate an assignment of a lower percentage (eg: 50%) or an assignment of the script only (rather than all of the development work). ➤ In no circumstances should the producer agree to assign any rights in the **film** itself or any of the exploitation or 'ancillary' rights relating to the film (eg: merchandising rights). ◆ The producer should retain as many rights in the film as possible, in case it becomes necessary to conclude an agreement for the financing of actual production with a third party, which will require an assignment or licence of all rights in the film itself, including source material (eg: the script).

Clause	Terms
Buy-back ('turn-around')	➤ The producer should insist on a right to buy the rights back from the financier (ie: to have the rights re-assigned to the producer or to have any charge released) if the financier does not commit within a defined period to producing or co-producing the film. ◆ This is known as a 'turn-around clause'. ● The producer must be free to take the project to a third party if the development financier decides not to make the film. ● If the film is to be made by a third party, the producer will need to be able to assign the rights in the development work to the third party, so must buy the rights back from the development financier before it can do so. ■ In such circumstances the development financier might seek to receive a credit (eg: 'in association with'). ◆ The consideration payable for the buy-back is usually the same as the development finance, plus: ● a premium, *and/or* ● interest, *and/or* ● a percentage of net profits. ■ This is equivalent to the sums that are to be repaid to the financier out of the production budget if it commits to producing or co-producing the film. ■ The amount is usually payable on or before entering into a finance agreement with a third party.

C Rights clearance

*References in this Section are to the Copyright, Designs and Patents Act 1988 ('**CDPA**'), unless otherwise stated. References in this Section to a '**film**' include a TV programme, unless a distinction is drawn.*

I	Introduction
II	Copyright and related rights
III	Content clearance
IV	Exceptions
V	Insurance

I Introduction

➤ A producer must not infringe third-party rights in making and exploiting a film.

- ◆ In this Section, '**producer**' means the main production entity, as opposed to any individual engaged by that entity to provide production services.

➤ Each contributor to a film (eg: the scriptwriter, any individual producer and each member of the cast and crew) has legal rights in such contributor's contribution, eg:

- ◆ copyright in a work to be used in the film (eg: the script, artwork or music), *or*

- ◆ rights in a performance filmed and/or recorded for the film.

➤ The content of such contribution or of the completed film may also be subject to:

- ◆ other rights (eg: under the law of defamation – see Chapter 2 Section A), *and/or*

- ◆ other statutory or regulatory restrictions (eg: those governing offensive material – see Chapter 2 Section B).

➤ The relevant rights/content must accordingly be 'cleared' to ensure that the production and subsequent exploitation of the film will not infringe third-party rights.

Remedies for infringement
➤ The rights-owner's remedies for infringement of uncleared rights include: ◆ damages (or an account of profits), *and/or*   ◆ an injunction to prevent the distribution or broadcast of the film (potentially resulting in a substantial loss of revenue to the producer), *and/or*   ◆ delivery-up of all copies of the infringing film to the rights-owner.   ➤ The producer may also be liable for breach of warranty under contracts with the financier, distributor and/or broadcaster of the film.

➤ In special circumstances, the distributor or broadcaster may decide that the commercial benefit or public interest in exploiting the film without full clearance outweighs the potential consequences of legal action – but this analysis is not to be taken lightly.

➤ For intellectual property, the producer needs to establish suitable rights of ownership in each participant's contribution – or a clear 'chain of title', as it is commonly known.

  ◆ A financier will not finance the film without a satisfactory 'chain of title report'.

  ◆ The producer usually has to warrant to the financier and each distributor and broadcaster of the film that it has cleared all necessary rights.

➤ 'Rights clearance' (also known as 'rights acquisition') generally takes the form of:

  ◆ an 'assignment' (ie: an outright transfer of ownership) of the rights from the rights-owner to the producer, *or*

  ◆ a 'licence' (ie: grant of permission) from the rights-owner for the producer to use the rights for permitted purposes.

    • A full assignment is preferable to a licence, which may be non-exclusive, limited in time and by territory and subject to other restrictions in the scope of use.

Grants of rights in practice

➤ In practice, certain rights are usually acquired under licence (eg: 'library' music or archived film footage).

➤ There may be several owners of a work incorporated in a film (eg: copyright can be owned jointly or divided by term, territory or language).

  ◆ A grant of rights should be taken from each rights-owner.

➤ Whether the rights clearance takes the form of an assignment or licence, the producer should ensure (budget permitting) that each grant of rights is as wide as possible, ie:

  ◆ unconditional and irrevocable, *and*

  ◆ outright, ie: 'absolute' (in the case of an assignment) or 'exclusive' (in the case of a licence, where exclusivity is required), *and*

  ◆ for the longest period of time required for the exploitation of the film (eg: continuing for as long as the rights subsist and, as far as possible, 'in perpetuity'), *and*

  ◆ for the widest territory required for exploitation of the film (eg: the 'universe'), *and*

  ◆ for all media in which the film is to be exploited (eg: 'all media now known or discovered in the future'), *and*

  ◆ freely transferable to allow for full exploitation of the film, ie:

    • assignable and licensable (in the case of an assignment), *or*

    • sub-licensable (in the case of a licence).

➤ The producer should also ensure that the rights granted are not subject to reversion or revocation if the contract in which the grant of rights is contained (eg: a services agreement) is terminated for any reason.

- ◆ The rights-owner's rights should be specifically restricted to the right to sue the producer upon termination for compensation.

- ◆ Any right for the rights-owner to seek an injunction to prevent exploitation of the film (eg: distribution or broadcast) should be expressly excluded.

  - ● The producer must be entirely free to exploit the completed film.

➤ An assignment or licence is appropriate for property rights (eg: copyright and performers' property rights).

- ◆ The producer should secure an irrevocable and unconditional waiver of all 'moral rights' in writing from each contributor (s 87).

  - ● The waiver should always be backed with an agreement 'not to assert' moral rights, as moral rights cannot be waived in certain jurisdictions (eg: France).

  - ● The main moral rights to be cleared from contributing 'authors' for *CDPA* purposes and (to the extent described below) 'performers' are the:

    a) *Paternity right* – ie: the right to be identified (*ss 77* and *205C*).

    - ■ The producer needs flexibility in compiling the title credits, which may not (depending on the medium and/or distribution platform) allow for full acknowledgement of authors and performers.

    - ■ In return for granting such a waiver, a key contributor (eg: a scriptwriter, director or actor) may insist on a contractual obligation to receive a screen credit as author/performer in an agreed form (binding on the producer and subsequent owners and distributors/broadcasters of the film), both in the film and in any promotion for the film (eg: a trailer).

    b) *Integrity right* – ie: the right to object to 'derogatory treatment' of the work (*ss 80* and *205F*).

    - ■ The producer needs flexibility in relation to integrity rights when:

      i) incorporating the contribution in the film (eg: re-writing the script to meet production requirements), *and/or*

      ii) editing the film to remove or adapt a contribution (eg: to comply with product-placement rules or age-certificate requirements), *and/or*

      iii) creating foreign-language versions, *and/or*

      iv) cutting the film (eg: for different distribution platforms or allowing for broadcasts with advertising breaks).

- ◆ Other permissions and clearances of non-property rights (which cannot be assigned) take the form of simple consents or direct grants of rights, eg:

  - ● consents in relation to performers' non-property rights, *and*

  - ● a right for the producer to use the name, likeness and biography of the contributor in making, promoting and exploiting the film.

➤ The producer should carefully consider the scope of usage rights that need to be cleared.

  ◆ Eg: the film may be made primarily for broadcast, but it may also be suitable for theatrical release, DVD/Blu-ray distribution and/or digital distribution.

  ◆ So it may be useful to acquire 'ancillary' exploitation rights, eg:

    • to adapt the film for another medium (eg: radio or theatre, for which the scriptwriter may insist on a share of net receipts), *and/or*

    • to make a remake of, or sequel or prequel to, the film (which may trigger a payment to the scriptwriter of an additional fee, eg: 50% for a remake or 33% for a sequel), *and/or*

    • to publish the script in the form of a book of the film, *and/or*

    • to develop an electronic game based on the film, *and/or*

    • to release a soundtrack album, *and/or*

    • to use an actor's name and likeness in merchandise.

➤ Each rights-owner usually requires a fee in return for the grant of rights, so the producer should consider the scope of rights required and how much it is prepared to pay.

Remuneration for rights clearance

➤ Each contributor is usually paid a basic fee in return for granting rights.

  ◆ The fee often forms part of the overall remuneration for the contributor's services, in which case there is no separate fee for the rights.

    • So-called 'above-the-line talent' (ie: contributors engaged before shooting begins, such as a 'name' director or a 'star' actor) are usually paid an additional element of contingent compensation based on the net profits of the film, and perhaps even a separate bonus based on US box-office performance.

➤ Where the budget allows, the producer should acquire all necessary rights before the film is exploited, since:

  ◆ there is a risk that the contributor may refuse permission to use the contribution, in which case the contributor may take legal action against the producer (e.g. to prevent the exploitation of the film), *and*

  ◆ the contributor will command a larger fee if the film is a 'hit'.

➤ The budget for the film may not, however, cover the purchase of all rights at the outset of production, so it may become necessary:

  ◆ to purchase additional rights at a later stage, *or*

  ◆ to negotiate first-refusal rights over the rights (or restrictions on the contributor's right to exploit the rights for a defined period after initial exploitation of the film).

➤ It may also not be cost-effective for the producer, having decided which rights are required, to secure the widest possible grant of rights.

◆ The producer may choose to limit the grant of rights to certain uses or means of exploitation (eg: TV, film and DVD rights, but limited digital distribution rights).

● For films that are likely to have a limited:

■ lifespan, *and/or*

■ geographical application (eg: corporate films and advertisements),

… the commissioner of the film may allow the producer to limit the term and/or territory in order to keep acquisition costs down.

● Another way to keep costs down is to negotiate 'use fees' that are contingent on certain types of use of a contribution (e.g. overseas or in a DVD release).

➤ A full purchase of rights (a 'buy-out') is usually preferable (even if more expensive).

➤ Another factor in the remuneration that is payable to a contributor is 'equitable remuneration'.

'Equitable remuneration' and rental rights

➤ A copyright owner has the right to rent copies of the copyright work to the public (ss *16(1)(ba)* and *18A*).

◆ When an author (or prospective author) of a literary, dramatic, musical or artistic work concludes a contract with a film producer for inclusion of the work in a film, it is presumed (unless agreed otherwise) that the author transfers such rental right to the producer (s *93A*).

◆ The principal director will also transfer the rental right in practice.

➤ In return for transferring such rental right, such author/director has a right to receive 'equitable remuneration' from the producer or from the producer's licensee or assignee (eg: a distributor or broadcaster) (s *93B*).

◆ An equivalent presumption and right applies to performers (eg: actors) in relation to performances featured in a film (ss *191F* and *191G*).

● NB: rental remuneration should be carefully distinguished from the right to equitable remuneration that arises when a sound recording is performed in public (s *182D*).

➤ The right to equitable remuneration for transfer of the rental right cannot be:

◆ assigned, except (s *182D(2)*):

● to a collecting society, *or*

● by a person acquiring title under a will or by operation of law, *or*

◆ waived or otherwise excluded or restricted (s *182D(7)*).

> ## Rental remuneration in practice

> ➤ The *CDPA* does not define what amounts to 'equitable remuneration'.

>> ◆ The performer or payer may apply to the Copyright Tribunal to determine the sum payable, but this right is rarely exercised in practice.

>> ◆ At present, there is no collecting society that administers rental remuneration (in contrast to public performance remuneration relating to sound recordings, which is administered by PPL).

>> ◆ Nothing prevents the parties from agreeing a buy-out lump sum.

> ➤ To avoid paying re-use fees, a producer should therefore ensure that:

>> ◆ each contributor assigns his rental right to the producer, *and*

>> ◆ the agreed fee payable to the contributor includes (and is stated to include) equitable remuneration.

II   Copyright and related rights

➤ Rights clearance is an essential, ongoing part of the production process and should be dealt with in a systematic and structured way in relation to each contributor.

◆ The multiple creative layers (i.e. contributors and contributions) involved in a film makes rights clearance complex.

➤ Clearance takes the form of including appropriate grants of rights, consents and waivers in each contributor's contract of engagement.

➤ The main rights to be cleared are copyright and related rights.

◆ Some rights are usually cleared before production begins (eg: rights in the script and rights to film an actor's performance and to exploit the filmed performance).

• Others are obtained during production (eg: rights in the soundtrack).

➤ The 3 principal intellectual property rights to be considered are:

◆ copyright, *and*

◆ rights in performances, *and*

◆ moral rights.

• See Sections A, B and C respectively of Chapter 1 for each of these rights.

➤ For each right, there are 3 issues to consider:

a) ownership of, and/or entitlement to, the rights, *and*

b) whether or not uncleared use of the rights would amount to infringement, *and*

c) if yes to b) above, the solution.

➤ The table below sets out a checklist for approaching clearance of each contributor's copyright and related rights.

Contributor	Rights clearance

Author (script)	➤ **Copyright**
	
	◆ *Who owns it?* The author is usually the first owner of copyright in a work (*s 11*). An exception to this rule is where the author produces the work in the course of employment (*s 11(2)*).
	
	• The first owner may also have assigned or licensed the copyright to another person, in which case the current rights-owner should be approached.
	
	• Often, the scriptwriter is commissioned by the producer to write the script. Here, the scriptwriter is unlikely to be an employee and will therefore usually be the owner. The scriptwriter (as owner) has the exclusive right, for example, to copy (*s 17*) and to adapt (*s 21*) the work.
	
	◆ *Would use amount to infringement?* Yes. If the producer carries out the acts without permission, an infringement of the owner's copyright is likely.
	
	◆ *What is the solution?* The producer should obtain a licence or assignment of copyright. The financier is likely to require a full assignment throughout the universe in perpetuity in all media.
	
	• Clearing source material is fundamental to the whole film project, and clearance should be obtained during the development process.
	
	• Where appropriate, an assignment by way of present assignment of future copyright should be obtained before the script is written.
	
	• A well-known author may insist on assigning film and TV rights only, rather than the whole copyright.
	
	• It may be difficult for the producer to establish what fee should be paid.
	
	    ■ There is no 'going rate' for a script, in contrast to rates for 'above-the-line talent' (eg: principal cast and key crew), for whom recent fee rates become common knowledge among producers.
	
	    ■ An established writer may insist on a profit participation (eg: 2.5% of the net profits of the film).
	
	➤ **Moral rights**
	
	◆ *Who can exercise the rights?* The scriptwriter is, as an author of a literary work, entitled to moral rights.
	
	◆ *Would use amount to infringement?* Yes. Production may infringe either or both of the paternity and integrity rights.
	
	◆ *What is the solution?* The producer should obtain a suitable waiver of moral rights from the scriptwriter.
	
	• NB: any well-drafted waiver of moral rights should specifically include an 'agreement not to assert' the moral rights.
	
	    ■ This is to cover overseas jurisdictions (eg: France) in which moral rights cannot be waived.
	
	• The producer should not commit to a sole credit in return.
	
	    ■ It is occasionally necessary to bring in a new scriptwriter during production, in which case the producer will need to allocate screen credits as due.

Contributor	Rights clearance

Author (underlying work)	➤ Frequently, a scriptwriter bases the script on an existing literary work (eg: a novel or a play).
	
	  ◆ A literary work cannot be 'adapted' (eg: turned into a screenplay), nor can the adaptation be reproduced in the film or exploited without the copyright owner's permission (*s 21*).
	
	➤ The following rights in the underlying work should be cleared:
	
	  ◆ **Copyright** – The author is the first owner of copyright in it, although ownership may have been transferred to another rights-owner (eg: to a literary publisher or to the author's estate). Use of the work for the script can amount to copyright infringement. The producer should obtain an assignment or licence.
	
	  ◆ **Moral rights** – The author of the work has moral rights in it. Since use of the work in the script may amount to infringement, the producer should obtain a waiver as above.
	
	➤ Clearance should be obtained during the development process before the producer tries to obtain development finance.
	
	  ◆ It is common to take an exclusive 'option' over an underlying work for a defined period (eg: 2 or 3 years). This allows the producer to try to secure finance for the project (partly to pay the full fee for the clearance) and to undertake other pre-production steps (eg: identifying locations and engaging key cast and crew).
	
	    • The main points to be covered by the option agreement are:
	
	      ■ the duration of the option period, *and*
	
	      ■ any extensions to the option period, *and*
	
	      ■ the cost of the option (usually 10% of the full fee), the cost of any extensions and the full fee payable, *and*
	
	      ■ profit-share arrangements (if any), *and*
	
	      ■ the rights to be granted on exercise (including any exclusions of rights).
	
	    • Where relevant, the producer may wish to acquire a rolling option on titles in the series of books written by the underlying author (and even the right to create scripts based on the characters created by the author).
	
	➤ The producer may also incorporate copyright works other than the script in the film (eg: literary/dramatic works and artistic works).
	
	  ◆ The copyright and moral rights in such works should be cleared in the same way (whether they are used in whole or in part).
	
	  ◆ Music and extracts from films are considered separately below.

Film footage owner	➤ Many films incorporate existing footage from other films or programmes. ➤ The following rights in such footage should be cleared: ◆ **Copyright** – The first owners will have been the producer and director of the footage, but their rights will almost certainly have been assigned to the producer or commissioner (eg: original broadcaster) of the footage. Incorporating substantial clips in the new film will amount to copyright infringement. The producer should obtain an assignment or licence of the footage from the current rights-owner.

Contributor	Rights clearance
Film footage owner *(continued)*	◆ **Moral rights** – The original authors of the footage (the producer and director) have moral rights in it. Since incorporation of the footage in the new film may amount to infringement, the producer should obtain waivers as above or, at least, the benefit of the waivers granted to the current rights-owner. ➤ In the grant of rights, the current rights-owner should warrant that it obtained all necessary rights and waivers from the original producer and director of the footage and should indemnify the producer of the new film against breach of warranty. ◆ Without a right of recourse against the current rights-owner, the producer of the new film must obtain the relevant rights and waivers from the original director and producer.
Director	➤ **Copyright** ◆ *Who owns it?* The director is one of the first authors of the film, together with the producer (*s 9(2)(ab)*). Accordingly, the director is, at the time of creation of the film, a joint owner of the copyright in the film. ◆ *Would use amount to infringement?* Yes, eg: copying, issuing copies to the public, renting and lending are some of the rights exclusive to the copyright owner. These are likely to be infringed during exploitation of the film if not authorised. ◆ *What is the solution?* The producer should obtain a full assignment of rights from the director. ➤ **Moral rights** ◆ The director has moral rights in the film, which may be infringed if not waived. The producer should obtain an appropriate waiver.
Producer (individual)	➤ NB: a production entity and an individual producer (eg: an employee or contractor of that entity) are separate legal persons. ◆ Accordingly, in order to avoid any doubt in relation to ownership of rights in the film, the production entity should clear any rights to which the individual producer is entitled. ➤ **Copyright** ◆ *Who owns it?* For copyright purposes, a 'producer' of a film is the person 'by whom the arrangements necessary for the making of the ... film are undertaken' (*s 178*). ● The identity of such 'producer' is a question of fact, and it may arguably be the individual producer. ● If so, the individual producer is the joint author of the film together with the director (*s 9(2)(ab)*) and is, at the time of creation of the film, a joint owner of the copyright in the film. ◆ *Would use amount to infringement?* Yes, copying would. ◆ *What is the solution?* The production company should obtain a full assignment from the individual producer. ➤ **Moral rights** ◆ If the individual producer is first author, he has moral rights in the film, which may be infringed if not waived. The production entity should obtain an appropriate waiver of moral rights.

Contributor	Rights clearance

Actors and other performers	➤ **Copyright**
	
	  ◆ An actor or other performer does **not** have a copyright in a performance as such, but may contribute to the script (eg: by responding to questions in an interview or improvising lines).
	
	     ● The performer's spoken words are protected under copyright as a literary work, so should be cleared.
	
	➤ **Rights in performances**
	
	  ◆ *Who owns these rights?* Each performer has rights in his 'performance' under *CDPA Pt II*.
	
	     ● 'Performance' means (*s 180(2)*):
	
	       ■ a dramatic or musical performance, *or*
	
	       ■ reading or recitation of a literary work, *or*
	
	       ■ variety act or similar presentation.
	
	  ◆ *Would use amount to infringement?* Yes, filming and issuing copies of the performance would amount to infringement.
	
	  ◆ *What is the solution?* The producer must obtain the performer's consent to record and exploit the performance.
	
	     ● The actors' union, Equity, includes such consent in its standard-form terms of engagement.
	
	     ● It is prudent to clear all possible performances, even if exceptions may apply under the *CDPA* (see section IV below). The producer should:
	
	       ■ ask each 'extra' to sign a consent form granting all rights in his contribution to the producer, *and*
	
	       ■ when filming in a public area, put a prominent notice on the set stating that, by walking through the area, each member of the public grants consent to be filmed.
	
	     ● Where a performer has an exclusive recording contract with a record label, the label's consent should be obtained.
	
	➤ **Moral rights**
	
	  ◆ *Who can exercise the rights?* Since the amendments to the *CDPA* introduced by the *Performances (Moral Rights, etc.) Regulations 2006*, a qualifying performer has been entitled to moral rights in a performance – see Section C of Chapter 1.
	
	     ● NB: the rights do **not** apply to film productions, although they do apply to live broadcasts and sound recordings.
	
	     ● It is, nevertheless, best practice to clear all performers' moral rights (whether existing or future) in relation to a film in case moral rights relating to audio-visual productions are introduced in the future.
	
	       ■ In fact such rights have been cleared for several years due to the requirements on signatories to international treaties (including the UK) to introduce performers' moral rights.
	
	  ◆ *Would use amount to infringement?* No (except as noted above), but clearance is still advisable (and routinely accepted).
	
	  ◆ *What is the solution?* The producer should obtain a suitable waiver of moral rights in writing from each performer.

Contributor	Rights clearance

Composer and musicians	➤ Virtually all films have a musical soundtrack, which comprises compositions (and any accompanying lyrics) and sound recordings.
	◆ Clearing music is expensive (eg: £3,000 to use a 30-second clip of a commercial recording) and complex, so a producer often hires a 'music supervisor' to oversee the process.
	➤ The soundtrack for a film often comprises 3 musical elements:
	1 Musical score (musical composition)
	◆ **Copyright**
	• *Who owns it?* The composer as first author.
	• *Would use amount to infringement?* Yes.
	• *What is the solution?* Obtain a licence or (subject to the 'writer's share' of PRS income – see Chapter 3 Section D) an assignment from the copyright owner.
	▪ The composer may have an exclusive agreement with a music publisher. If so, the producer should obtain a suitable grant of rights from the publisher.
	▪ If the film is shown in US cinemas (where local societies do not collect public performance income), the producer can obtain a licence from the PRS. In practice, the PRS only issues such licences if requested by the composer, and the composer's fee is often inclusive of such US 'theatrical income'.
	◆ **Moral rights**
	• *Who can exercise the rights?* The composer.
	• *Would use amount to infringement?* If credited, unlikely, due to the implied licence afforded by the hiring of the composer, but an express waiver should be obtained from the composer.
	2 Featured songs (musical compositions and lyrics)
	◆ **Copyright**
	• *Who owns it?* The songwriter(s) are the first owner(s) of copyright in the musical compositions (as musical works) and lyrics (as literary works), but they may well have assigned the 'mechanical' (ie: reproduction) rights in the song to a music publisher.
	▪ NB: the copyright in the song is distinct from the copyright in the sound recording (see item 3 below).
	• *Would use amount to infringement?* Yes.
	• *What is the solution?* Obtain a licence or an assignment from the copyright owner.
	▪ In practice, the owner is likely to be a music publisher (which will probably have retained rights to 'synchronise' the song with the film).
	▪ The producer is only likely to obtain a limited licence to reproduce the song in timed relation with the film (known as a 'synchronisation licence' – or a 'synch licence' for short).

Contributor	Rights clearance
Composer and musicians *(continued)*	<ul><li>NB: collecting societies may also control certain rights in the musical compositions, lyrics and sound recordings (eg: MCPS, PRS, PPL and VPL). They can often help to identify the relevant rights-owner.</li><li>In some cases, the MCPS can to issue a 'synch licence' for use of musical compositions/lyrics.</li><li>Separate fees may become payable by distributors and broadcasters to such societies. See Section A of Chapter 3 for a description of the societies' roles.</li></ul>♦ **Moral rights** • *Who can exercise the rights?* The songwriter(s), who may have granted a waiver of moral rights in favour of their publisher and the publisher's licensees. • *Would use amount to infringement?* Unlikely. In most cases, the soundtrack simply reproduces the song unaltered (bar technical edits), although the producer should try to obtain a waiver (or the benefit of any waiver granted to the publisher). 3 **Sound recording (of musical score and featured tracks)** ♦ **Copyright** • *Who owns it?* The author of a sound recording is the person by whom the arrangements necessary for the making of the sound recording are undertaken (*s 178*).<ul><li>For the score, this is commonly the film producer.</li><li>For tracks, this is often the artist's record company, which usually restricts the artist's ability to record for third parties without the record company's consent.</li></ul>• *Would use amount to infringement?* Yes. • *What is the solution?*<ul><li>For the score, confirm in the composer's agreement that the film producer owns the copyright in the sound recording.</li><li>For songs, obtain an assignment or licence from the record company (or relevant copyright owner).</li><li>NB: a) A record company usually licenses, rather than assigns, a sound recording for use in a film (a 'master use licence' or 'synch licence' – not to be confused with the 'synch licence' to be obtained from a music publisher). b) A record company sometimes allows use on an accompanying CD and/or digital version of the soundtrack. c) The cost of the licence depends on its duration and the fame of the artist. d) The producer may have to settle for a fixed initial period, with agreed fees for continued use.</li></ul>

Contributor	Rights clearance

Composer and musicians
(continued)

◆ **Rights in performances**

- *Who has the rights?* Each musician and vocalist performing on the sound recording has rights in the recorded performance.

- *Would use amount to infringement?* Yes.

- *What is the solution?* Obtain consent from each performer to record and exploit the performance.

   - For a featured track, approach the record company. Check that the record company can grant this consent: it will typically have taken a grant of these rights from all performers, but perhaps subject to consent rights. If it cannot do so, each individual performer must give consent.

◆ **Moral rights**

- *Who can exercise the rights?* Each musical performer.

- *Would use amount to infringement?* Unlikely.

   - For the score, the composer is likely to direct the way in which any personal performance is recorded, but an express waiver should be obtained.

   - For a track, the soundtrack will, in most cases, simply reproduce the sound recording unaltered (bar technical edits), but the producer should still try to obtain a waiver (or at least the benefit of any waiver granted to the record company).

➤ NB: a composer's or musician's agreement will commonly contain a grant of all relevant rights in the composition, sound recording and performance, especially if there is no publisher or record label involved.

- ◆ The producer should take grants of ancillary rights required (eg: use in DVDs and, if appropriate, on a soundtrack album).

➤ 'Production' or 'library' music (also known as 'stock' music in the USA) is non-commissioned music produced specifically for use in audio-visual productions.

- ◆ A grant of rights should be taken from the production/library music company, which will have cleared all rights in the musical compositions, lyrics and sound recordings.

- ◆ The cost of library music (eg: £400 for a 30-second clip) is considerably less than the cost of using 'commercial' music (ie: music recorded for release in its own right).

Other creative crew

➤ Other crew members (eg: story editors, costume designers, set designers, props designers, special-effects personnel, choreographers and film editors) make contributions to a film that may be protected under copyright and related rights.

- ◆ It is standard practice to take a wide grant of rights from each crew member to cover any rights that he may have in his contribution (including copyright, rights in performances and moral rights).

   - This grant of rights is contained either in a long-form contract of engagement (for key crew members) or in a short consent form (for regular crew members or casual contributors).

III   Content clearance

➤ As well as clearing contributors' rights in each contribution, the producer must check that:

♦ the rights of third parties other than the contributors are not infringed, *and*

♦ requirements under legislation and regulatory regimes are not breached,

... in each case, in relation to:

• the script or screenplay on which the film is to be based, *and*

• the completed film itself.

➤ This checking process is commonly referred to as 'content clearance'.

♦ The checks need to be made, respectively, at the beginning and end of the production process.

Content clearance

➤ During pre-production, the producer should engage a lawyer or clearance agent:

♦ to prepare a script clearance report, *and*

♦ to conduct the clearance process.

➤ The commissioner of the film (eg: a broadcaster) may require the producer to complete a form in relation to the final edit of the film, detailing all clearances of third-party rights obtained.

➤ The aim at both stages is to minimise the risk of civil or criminal proceedings and/or regulatory sanctions in the following areas:

♦ copyright and related rights (as examined above), *and/or*

♦ defamation (see Chapter 2 Section A), *and/or*

♦ offensive material (see Chapter 2 Section B), *and/or*

♦ contempt of court (see Chapter 2 Section C) and official secrets, *and/or*

♦ breach of confidence (see Chapter 1 Section J), including:

• rights of 'privacy' or 'publicity', *and*

• 'image rights', which are more developed in foreign jurisdictions (notably, the USA), *and/or*

♦ trade marks (see Chapter 1 Sections L and M), *and/or*

♦ passing-off (see Chapter 1 Section N), *and/or*

♦ advertising and sponsorship (see Chapter 5) and any other regulatory regimes.

➤ Eg: the script may contain a phrase (eg: in the title of the film) that qualifies for trade-mark protection (eg: the name of a well-known character, such as Harry Potter).

- ◆ If so:

  - ● where possible, the phrase should be removed from the script, *or*

  - ● an assignment or licence should be obtained from the proprietor of the mark.

➤ Where a film is based on a real individual, particular care should be taken:

Real individuals

➤ There is a risk that a living individual may sue the producer for:

- ◆ defamation (NB: it is **not** possible to defame a deceased person), *or*

- ◆ misuse of private information, *or*

- ◆ passing-off.

  - ● Rights under the law of confidence (including in relation to privacy) and goodwill may in applicable circumstances pass to a deceased's estate, so it is possible an the estate might bring an action in misuse of private information or in passing-off.

➤ The producer can take some precautionary steps, eg:

- ◆ Avoid including allegations about the person that might be defamatory and/or false.

- ◆ Where the person is fictionalised, obtain a release from the person.

- ◆ Where required, obtain consent to filming in the person's home.

- ◆ Conduct checks on names, addresses and contact details used in the film to avoid unintentional references to living persons.

- ◆ Consider carefully whether use of private information might constitute misuse of the information.

  - ● Where feasible, try to obtain permission from the individual or from the estate to use the information.

- ◆ Avoid giving undue prominence to any association between the person and any product or service related to the film (eg: merchandise), in case the person brings a claim in passing-off.

  - ● Alternatively, try to obtain a licence of the marks protected under the law of passing-off.

➤ The producer should also clear copyright and moral rights in any source material for the film (eg: an interview) contributed by the individual.

IV Exceptions

➤ There is no need to clear material whose use will not infringe third-party rights.

◆ The law recognises that:

● some material should not be protected by intellectual property rights, *and*

● a contribution may not be significant enough to require clearance.

➤ There are 2 main instances in which clearance is not required:

1 Public-domain material

➤ The producer need not clear rights in material that is in the public domain. Material may be in the public domain for 2 reasons:

a) It may never have attracted copyright protection, eg:

i) It may comprise facts or information.

● Care needs to be taken over the use of a factual account (eg: a biography or history), as copyright may subsist in the account (*Harman Pictures NV v Osborne* [1967] 1 WLR 723), even if not in the facts.

ii) It may be so short that *de minimis* principles apply.

● Caution is required, however, as even a short phrase may be protected as a registered trade mark or in passing-off.

b) It may be out of copyright.

● The duration of copyright must be checked extremely carefully if the producer is to rely on this exception.

▪ Old works can be subject to renewals, reversions, revivals and extensions of copyright, and may be out of copyright in one country, but still in copyright in another country.

▪ An adaptation (eg: a musical arrangement) of a public-domain work may attract new copyright protection.

2 Defences to infringement (copyright and rights in performances)

➤ There are 2 important defences:

Defences to infringement
➤ **Fair dealing** ◆ A producer need not obtain an owner's permission to use extracts of a copyright work in a film where the work is used for the purposes of criticism, review or news reporting (*s 30*).

Defences to infringement (continued)

➤ **Fair dealing** (continued)

◆ A work used for criticism or review must be:

• a published work, *and*

• accompanied by a 'sufficient acknowledgement' of the source (citing the work's title/description and author).

◆ The source of a work featured in a filmed or broadcast news report of current events need not be acknowledged where an acknowledgement is not feasible.

• NB: the 'fair dealing' defence for news reporting does not apply to photographs, whose use must be cleared.

◆ The extent of copying allowed is not defined under the *CDPA*, but the extract must not be a 'substantial part' of the work.

• Copying should be limited not only in terms of quantity, but also quality (ie: the significance of the extract relative to the whole original work) – see Section A of Chapter 1.

• Various bodies (eg: the Society of Authors) provide guidelines on how much can be copied under the defence.

➤ **Incidental inclusion**

◆ Copyright in a work is not infringed by its 'incidental inclusion' in a film (*s 31*). What amounts to 'incidental inclusion' is not defined in the *CDPA*.

◆ A producer should only rely on the defence where the film contains a fleeting or partial glimpse of a copyright work (eg: an artwork shown briefly in the background of shot).

• Where possible, unauthorised third-party copyright works should be removed from the set or out of shot.

◆ The producer can include certain immoveable works (*s 62*), ie:

• buildings and sculptures, *and/or*

• models for buildings, *and/or*

• works of artistic craftsmanship,

... if permanently situated in a public place or in premises open to the public.

➤ **Rights in performances**

◆ The producer can rely on similar defences in relation to the use of performances (see *Sch 2 paras 2* and 3).

V   Insurance

➤   Even after a comprehensive clearance exercise, risks may remain.

 ◆   Eg: it is hard to protect against a claim – even if unfounded – of unauthorised use of an idea, such as a format or character.

➤   In addition to the risk that the rights-owner may bring a claim for infringement, the finance and distribution agreements (for a feature film) and the production agreement (for a TV programme) are likely to contain:

 ◆   a warranty that the producer has not infringed third-party rights or any applicable laws and regulations, *and*

 ◆   an indemnity for breach of warranty.

➤   The producer should therefore consider taking out an 'errors and omissions' (E&O) insurance policy to cover such risks, and may well be contractually obliged to do so.

'Errors and omissions' insurance

➤   An E&O policy typically provides cover against:

 ◆   defamation, *and*

 ◆   breach of confidence or infringement of privacy rights, *and*

 ◆   infringement of intellectual property rights (eg: copyright, moral rights, trade marks and rights in passing-off).

➤   The premium and excess set by the insurer depends on the degree of risk involved.

 ◆   The insurer will usually exclude its liability to cover certain claims.

➤   For a feature film, the financier usually requires the producer to maintain:

 ◆   minimum limits of E&O insurance (eg: $1 million per single claim and $3 million for all occurrences), *and*

 ◆   a minimum period of cover from the start of principal photography (eg: 3 years).

➤   For television programmes, the arrangements vary and depend on the commissioning channel.

 ◆   Eg: ITV has a blanket facility which allows a producer to acquire E&O cover at pre-set premiums.

D Finance

*References in this Section are to the Copyright, Designs and Patents Act 1988 ('**CDPA**'), unless otherwise stated. References in this Section to a '**film**' include a TV programme, unless a distinction is drawn.*

I   Introduction

➤ A producer cannot begin full-scale production of a film without obtaining finance to meet the costs and expenses of production (eg: the wages of cast and crew).

➤ In the context of a feature film, obtaining finance is often the main obstacle facing the producer.

- ◆ Financing a film is an extremely high-risk investment (even with 'bankable' stars and a large advertising spend), in contrast to the more predictable returns from investing in listed securities or real estate.

  - ● This fact limits the number of companies and individual investors that are prepared to risk capital in a film venture.

  - ● An investor usually needs to be convinced that a film will:

    - ▪ make a significant profit (eg: from lucrative sales overseas and via secondary formats such as DVDs), *and/or*

    - ▪ provide the investor with a tax-efficient investment opportunity (eg: giving rise to lawfully available tax losses, exemptions or deferrals).

- ◆ Some financiers are prepared to provide finance before production begins and/or during production.

  - ● Other financiers will only invest money once the film is complete.

    - ▪ In this case, the producer is presented with a cash-flow problem which can be resolved in part by 'discounting' the finance – see below.

➤ In the context of a TV programme, the whole budget required for the production (including any necessary cashflow) may be provided by a broadcaster or a large independent production company, in which case the finance issues considered in this Section have a straightforward solution.

- ◆ Nonetheless, the producer may only be able to raise part of the finance required from a single source, so may have to consider alternative funding arrangements (and perhaps a number of different sources) to make up the shortfall.

➤ Whatever the source of finance, the financier often requires:

- a grant of rights in the film, either as security for its investment (to be released on repayment) or as a long-term means of controlling the exploitation rights, *and*

- repayment of the investment (plus interest and expenses) in priority to other participants' remuneration from the film, *and*

- a return on the investment (eg: a share of the film's 'net profits').

Net profits

➤ 'Net profits' is a common definition in a finance agreement. It typically means all gross receipts derived from the licensing, distribution and other exploitation of the film, after deduction of:

- any repayment, interest and finance costs due to a bank, *and*

- advances recoverable by, and commission and expenses payable to, distributors, other licensees and agents (eg: sales and collection agents – see below), *and*

- the costs of manufacturing 'prints' of the film (ie: distribution copies) and advertising (known as 'P&A' costs), *and*

- any repayment, interest and finance costs due to other financiers in return for funding the budgeted costs of producing the film (eg: the completion guarantor and/or equity investors – see below), *and*

- any costs of production in excess of the budget.

  - In some cases, the gross-receipts base may be limited to defined distribution platforms or territories.

➤ The net profits of the film are commonly split between the financier(s) and the producer (eg: 50:50).

➤ Other key contributors (eg: the scriptwriter, director or a lead actor) may also be entitled to a share of 'net profits'. They will participate in either the net profits of the film or, less favourably, the producer's share of the net profits (known as the 'producer's net profits').

- A contributor may instead be owed a deferred fee (known as a 'deferment' or 'deferral'), ie: a fee agreed to be payable out of net profits (to the extent that net profits are sufficient to cover the fee).

  - If there are insufficient net profits to meet all deferments, the net profits available are commonly split between contributors 'pro rata' (ie: in proportion to the respective amounts due to them).

- The producer often has to obtain the financiers' consent to deferments as these commonly delay and reduce the share payable to them.

➤ Since there are several tiers of deductions and participations in many financing structures, a finance agreement commonly includes a 'recoupment schedule' that specifies how, and in what order of priority, the film's proceeds of sale are to be applied.

- ◆ The order of priority varies from film to film.

  - • If a bank is involved, it often has first priority and is often repaid before distributors and sales agents (see below) 'recoup' (ie: recover) their advances.

- ◆ Each participant should try to ensure that the 'net' element of sums recovered in priority to that participant's share does not contain unusual deductions.

II   Finance agreements

➤ A producer may need to enter into several contracts to conclude the finance arrangements. The number of contracts depends on the complexity of the arrangements.

- ◆ The simplest arrangement is where one entity finances the whole cost of production, without raising finance from other investors, in which case a single document can set out all of the arrangements.

➤ In the context of a feature film, a bank and various other investors are likely to be involved.

- ◆ The producer usually enters into a contract with the financiers known as an 'interparty agreement' or 'IPA'.

  - • An IPA sets out a framework for the production, finance and distribution of the film and controls any related or subsequent documents.

- ◆ A simpler finance agreement without a bank is often described as a 'production, finance and distribution agreement' or 'PFD agreement'.

➤ In TV production, the main document is often called the 'production agreement', 'commissioning agreement' or 'acquisition agreement'.

➤ The terms of each finance agreement are specific to the finance structure of the film.

- ◆ Various methods of raising finance are considered below, along with the main commercial terms relating to finance in each case.

  - • The terms for contracts dealing specifically with production and distribution are considered in Sections E and F of this Chapter.

III   Sources of finance

➤   Depending on the finance structure of a production, the entity raising finance may be a producer (ie: the entity actually making the film) or the ultimate rights-owner (eg: a studio or broadcaster).

◆   For the sake of simplicity, the entity raising finance is described below as the *'producer'*. Some sources of finance considered below are only available to the entity that owns the rights in the completed film (eg: the pre-sale of distribution rights).

➤   There are 6 common methods of raising finance:

1   Full commission with cash-flow

➤   This is the most convenient way to finance a film from the producer's viewpoint. All finance originates from one source, eg: a Hollywood film studio for a feature film or a terrestrial broadcaster for a TV programme.

◆   In return for making the large investment, the commissioner insists on:

●   a high level of control over the production (eg: approval of budget, cashflow, script, technical specification and cast and crew), *and*

●   the right to take over or abandon production in certain cases, *and*

●   a full transfer of ownership of copyright in the film ('assignment') so that the commissioner can freely exploit the completed film (or, at least, an exclusive grant of rights to use the film for defined media, territory and duration, ie: a 'licence').

➤   The producer is paid a production fee (eg: 10% or 15% of the production budget) and often a share (eg: 30%) of the film's net profits.

2   Equity investment

➤   A financier or group of financiers may invest 'equity' (ie: cash) in the film.

Equity investors

➤   Possible equity investors in the UK include:

◆   the BBC and Film Four, *and/or*

◆   national and regional funding bodies (eg: the UK Film Council, Film Agency for Wales, Scottish Screen, Northern Ireland Screen and Regional Screen Agencies), *and/or*

◆   venture capital and investment funds, *and/or*

◆   other production companies, *and/or*

◆   private investors (eg: high net-worth individuals).

410

➤ Equity investment takes 2 forms:

a) Investment in the producer

◆ The financier(s) may invest money in the producer:

• in return for being issued shares in the production entity, *or*

• by way of a loan.

◆ Whether the investment concerned takes the form of equity finance (ie: ownership of shares) or debt finance, it is described as an 'equity investment'.

• Direct investment in the producer usually takes place if the producer needs backing for several films. Investing in a 'portfolio' of films can spread risk for the investors if any investment failures are cancelled out (or exceeded) by investment successes.

• Where investors are to acquire shares in a producer of TV programmes, the parties should consider whether, for TV quota purposes, the producer will have 'independent' status and its output will be 'European' (see Section A of this Chapter).

b) Investment in the film

• Alternatively, financier(s) may simply lend money to the producer to provide cashflow for part of the budgeted cost of the film.

➤ In return, the equity investor(s) usually receive:

a) repayment of the amount invested (plus interest) from the first available receipts from exploitation of the film (eg: net amounts payable by a distributor on delivery of the completed film), *and*

b) a share of net profits.

◆ As security for their investment, the equity investor(s) usually take:

• an assignment of all rights in the film, *and*

• a charge over the film materials and assets of the producer,

... with a view to re-assigning the copyright to the producer and releasing the charge upon repayment of the amount invested (plus interest).

➤ If there is a group of financiers investing different amounts and entitled to different profit shares, the parties often set up a 'collection account'.

Collection account

➤ A collection agent is appointed to maintain and administer the account, into which the gross receipts of the film are paid.

➤ The agent may be a bank, a specialist collection agent or (in the case of a Hollywood feature film) the studio financing the film.

411

➤ The collection arrangements will be set out in a 'collection agreement':

Collection agreement

➤ The agent pays sums out of the account in a pre-agreed order.

◆ Commonly, each financier is repaid (to the extent that profits allow, in full) in a defined order of priority.

◆ Alternatively, as each tranche of net profits comes in, it is paid out to the financiers at the same time ('pari passu') and in proportion to the level of their respective contributions ('pro rata') until, to the extent profits allow, all are paid in full.

● Where there are insufficient profits, the amount recovered by each financier is effectively reduced pro rata.

◆ Other profit participants (eg: key cast and key crew) may also be party to the collection agreement.

---

3 Distribution advances

➤ Finance is sometimes raised (before or after the film has been completed) from a film distributor in return for a licence of rights in the completed film.

◆ The terms are set out in a 'distribution agreement' – see Section F of this Chapter.

➤ The distributor pays the producer a 'distribution advance' against future income from distribution (also known as a 'minimum guarantee') and acquires the right to exploit the film (eg: for a defined medium and territory).

◆ The advance is usually not payable until delivery of the completed film (along with related materials and the contributors' contracts).

● This can lead to cash-flow problems, unless the advance is 'discounted' by a bank or other lender – see below.

● Sometimes an instalment (eg: 10%) is payable on signature of the distribution agreement.

➤ The advance and any distribution expenses are recouped from the subsequent proceeds of sale by the distributor – often from the producer's share of those proceeds only (rather than all proceeds).

◆ The distributor pays any remaining proceeds ('overages') to the producer, after deduction of the distributor's commission.

➤ This form of finance arrangement is commonly described as a 'pre-sale' or 'negative pick-up' agreement.

◆ The process may be repeated for secondary media or further territories not covered by the main distribution deal.

➤ A specialist bank or lender may agree to 'discount' such an advance:

Discounting

➤ The bank/lender ('**bank**') pays the producer a 'discounted' (ie: reduced) amount against future receipts. The difference represents the bank's return on its risk in the early payment.

➤ A common discounting method is as follows:

a) A distributor provides a producer with a letter of credit, under which the distributor agrees to pay a distribution advance.

b) The producer assigns its right to receive the future advance to the bank, and notifies the distributor that it has done so.

c) Before the advance is due for payment, the bank pays a proportion (eg: 75%) to the producer. The percentage reflects the distributor's financial standing (eg: a Hollywood studio is more creditworthy than a small independent).

➤ To try to ensure that the distribution advance will ultimately be paid, the lender requires a guarantee from a specialist insurer that the film will be completed (if necessary, by such insurer) on budget, on time and in accordance with the distributor's specification.

◆ The person giving this guarantee (or 'bond') is known as the 'completion guarantor', and is paid a fee by the producer (eg: a sum equal to 5% of the budget).

● The bank insists on a guarantee as, even if it successfully sues the producer, the producer typically has insufficient assets to pay any damages awarded to the bank.

● The individual producer and director of the film enter into inducement letters entitling the guarantor to replace them if the film goes over budget or runs behind schedule.

➤ By way of further security, the bank usually:

◆ takes a charge over the producer's rights in the film (including underlying rights such as the script) and assets, *and*

◆ requires the producer to ensure that the laboratory processing the film will pledge to hold the film negative to the bank's order (while allowing distributors to order prints for distribution).

➤ On completion of the film, the bank receives the whole advance (plus a fee, interest and costs) – in priority to equity investors, so may be a party to the 'collection' arrangements – see above. On payment, the lender releases its security.

4   **Sales agent advance**

➤ A 'sales agent' is an agent appointed by a producer to secure distribution in territories where the producer has not appointed a distributor.

➤ The sales agent may provide an 'advance' against future income from sales to distributors appointed by the sales agent.

◆ The advance is paid during production or on completion of the film.

- If it is only payable on completion, the producer can approach a lender to discount the advance (in a similar way to a distribution advance).

◆ From the income generated by the distribution arrangements, the sales agent recoups the advance, deducts a percentage commission and then pays the balance to the producer.

- The sales agent's commission delays and reduces the profits available to any equity investors.

➤ The sales agent may instead simply provide a forecast of distribution advances likely to be secured by the sales agent.

◆ The producer can approach a specialist bank or lender to provide 'gap finance', ie: a loan against the proceeds of such predicted sales.

- The amount lent is between 1/2 and 1/3 of the forecast total.

5   **Product placement, merchandising and sponsorship**

➤ A producer may be able to raise part of the production finance through product placement, merchandising and sponsorship arrangements.

◆ A manufacturer of a product (eg: a car) may agree to invest equity in return for the prominent featuring of its product in the film.

◆ A merchandising agreement allows a merchandise company to exploit a particular feature of a film (eg: an actor's likeness) on merchandise.

- In return, the merchandise company pays royalties to the producer.

- The merchandise company often pays an 'advance' against royalties, either before production begins or on completion of the film.

◆ Sponsorship is a very common method of raising finance for a TV programme.

- The sponsor pays a fee (usually to a broadcaster) in return for showing the sponsor's name at the beginning and end of the programme and during any commercial breaks.

➤ A broadcaster must adhere to all applicable legal and regulatory restrictions placed on product placement, merchandising and sponsorship (eg: under the *Ofcom Broadcasting Code ss 9 and 10*).

6   **Bridging loan**

➤   Where there is still a shortfall in the funds raised and the producer needs to begin shooting the film, the producer may, as a last resort, approach a specialist lender to obtain a bridging loan.

➤   The lender will:

◆   charge a high rate of interest (reflecting the risk that the production may collapse before shooting begins), *and*

◆   insist on repayment from the first finance amounts paid to the producer (rather than the eventual proceeds of sale).

●   Bridging finance increases the film budget, so the producer will need to obtain consent from the other financiers before arranging it.

IV   Tax relief

*NB: UK film tax rules have changed substantially in the past few years and may be the subject of continuing clarification/modification by the Department for Culture, Media and Sport ('**DCMS**') and HM Treasury. In all cases, it is advisable to check the latest official guidance that has been published online.*

➤   Tax relief is often a significant factor in attracting investment in a feature film production.

◆   Many countries try to stimulate domestic film production by offering tax incentives (eg: deferrals, credits and rebates) for domestic productions or co-productions.

●   These incentives effectively subsidise domestic production.

▪   Overseas incentives are beyond the scope of this Section. Overseas government departments and industry bodies publish guidance online.

▪   UK film tax policy is set by the DCMS, working with HM Treasury.

●   UK tax breaks have in the past been available for:

▪   individual investors (as relief against income tax and capital gains tax), *and*

▪   the producer (as relief against corporation tax).

➤   In the March 2006 budget, significant reforms to the UK film tax relief system were announced.

◆   The reforms removed tax breaks that were previously available in relation to:

●   so-called 'sale and lease-back' tax-deferral structures, *and*

●   partnerships of individuals formed to invest in UK films.

▪   These artificial structures did encourage significant investment in film-making, but often resulted in unreleased films whose sole aim was to minimise tax.

◆   The aim of the reforms was to incentivise actual producers, rather than financiers.

415

➤ The March 2007 budget introduced further reforms by placing:

  ◆ further restrictions on so-called 'sideways loss relief', which previously allowed non-active partners in partnerships to offset film losses against ordinary (non-film) income and capital gains, *and*

  ◆ a new £2 million investment limit and 50-employee upper limit in relation to reliefs previously available to individuals acquiring shares in high-risk small companies via the Enterprise Investment Scheme (EIS), Corporate Venturing Scheme (CVS) or Venture Capital Trust (VCT) scheme.

    ● EIS and VCT had been regarded as useful schemes for the new regime.

➤ Under the UK film tax regime that was introduced by the *Finance Act 2006* (and which remains in place), the UK government provides financial support to makers of 'culturally British' films.

  ◆ A qualifying producer is entitled to a tax deduction which can be surrendered in return for payment of a tax credit – see below.

    ● The regime applies to any film where principal photography commences (or remains uncompleted) on or after 1 January 2007.

➤ The detailed rules and guidance are beyond the scope of this Section, but the main steps to be considered by a producer wishing to obtain the relief are as follows:

Steps	
1	The producer must be a 'film production company'.
2	The film must be intended for theatrical release.
3	The film must be 'culturally British' or a qualifying co-production.
4	At least 25% of production costs must be incurred in the UK.
5	The film must be certified as a qualifying film.
6	The producer must opt for loss relief or a tax credit.

Step 1   The producer must be a 'film production company'

➤ To be a qualifying 'film production company' (or '**FPC**'), the producer must be:

  ◆ within the charge to UK corporation tax (ie: partnerships and individuals cannot claim the relief), *and*

  ◆ actively responsible for the pre-production, principal photography, post-production and completion and delivery of the film.

    ● NB: the film rights need not be owned by the FPC once the film is completed.

➤ In a co-production structure, it is enough for the producer to make an effective creative, technical and artistic contribution to the film.

  ◆ A co-producer that only contributes funding cannot claim the relief.

➤ There can only be one FPC for a film. If a number of companies are involved in the production, the FPC is the company that is most directly involved in the process.

Step 2	The film must be intended for theatrical release

➤ The film must be a feature film that is genuinely intended:

◆ for 'theatrical release' (ie: to be shown commercially at cinemas), *and*

◆ to derive a significant proportion (ie: at least 5%) of its earnings from such theatrical release.

● The relief does not apply to films or programmes made solely for TV.

Step 3	The film must be 'culturally British' or a qualifying co-production

➤ **The 'cultural test'**

◆ The test for whether a film is 'culturally British' (known as the 'cultural test') is set out in the *Films Act 1985 Sch 1* (as revised following European Commission approval).

● The current test applies to each film whose principal photography commenced on or after 1 January 2007.

◆ The test is based on a point-scoring system. There are 31 possible points in all, and the 'pass mark' is 16.

● The test is split into four categories:

a) 'cultural content' (eg: UK setting, British lead characters, British subject-matter or underlying material, and/or dialogue in English or regional/minority language) – 16 points, *and*

b) 'cultural contribution' (eg: representative of or reflecting British culture, cultural heritage and/or cultural diversity) – 4 points), *and*

c) 'cultural hubs' (eg: shooting, visual effects, special effects, score recording and/or post-production taking place in the UK) – 3 points, *and*

d) 'cultural practitioners' (eg: director, scriptwriter, producer, composer, cast and/or crew being EU citizens or residents) – 8 points.

▪ There is a 'golden points' rule, under which a film scoring all 'cultural hub' and 'cultural practitioners' points and 4 points in the language part of the 'cultural content' category must also score:

i) 2 or more further points in the 'cultural content' category due to UK setting and/or British lead characters, *or*

ii) 4 points in the 'cultural content' category due to British subject-matter or underlying material.

▪ The test differs slightly for documentaries and animations.

➤ **Qualifying co-production**

- ◆ A 'co-production' is a film where creative control and responsibility for production is shared between British and international co-producer(s).

  - A co-production often qualifies for tax reliefs both in the UK and the country (or countries) of one or more of the overseas co-producers.

    - ▪ To do so, it must meet the:

      a) requirements of relevant international co-production agreement(s), *and*

      b) co-production certification procedures of each country.

    - ▪ In the UK, a co-producer must apply for a grant of co-production status to the DCMS (which is advised on this by the UK Film Council).

➤ A qualifying co-production for the purposes of UK tax relief is a film that is made in accordance with one of the international co-production agreements to which the UK is a signatory, ie:

a) the *European Convention on Cinematographic Co-production*, which contains a points-based test for a 'European' film and can be used to set up bilateral or multilateral European co-productions, *or*

b) a bilateral treaty between the UK and an overseas state.

- ◆ The UK currently has bilateral treaties with Australia, Canada, France, India, Jamaica, New Zealand and South Africa.

  - The terms of the *Convention* and those treaties are beyond the scope of this Section.

➤ If a film includes archive footage, no more than 10% of the film's playing time may include visual parts taken from other film(s), unless the parts:

a) were made by the same FPC, *and*

b) have not previously been certified as a culturally British film.

- ◆ The 10% limit may be waived in the case of a documentary.

Step 4	At least 25% of production costs must be incurred in the UK

➤ At least 25% of the 'core expenditure' incurred by the producer (or by the co-producers) must be 'UK expenditure'.

Expenditure criteria

➤ 'Core expenditure' is expenditure on production (plus pre- and post-production).

- ◆ It excludes development, distribution and marketing expenses. Eg: an option fee for underlying rights in a novel/play would be excluded, but the option exercise fee would qualify. Expenses incurred on acquiring more speculative rights (eg: character merchandising rights) would be excluded.

➤ 'UK expenditure' is expenditure on:

- ◆ services performed in the UK (eg: by the director, cast and crew to the extent that they perform services in the UK), irrespective of the nationality of the performers of the services, *and/or*

- ◆ goods/services that are used or consumed in the UK.

Step 5	The film must be certified as a qualifying film

➤ Before applying for the tax credit, the producer must obtain an appropriate certificate from the Certification Unit of the UK Film Council (as agent for the DCMS).

- ◆ The film must be certified as a 'British film', ie: culturally British or a qualifying co-production.

  - The producer may, at any point before or during production, apply for an **interim** certificate if it wishes to obtain tax relief during production – see below.

  - The producer must, in any event, apply after completion of the film for a **final** certificate in order to be able to make a final claim to HMRC.

Step 6	The producer must opt for loss relief or a tax credit

➤ For relief purposes, the relevant expenditure (**'relevant expenditure'**) is 100% of the core expenditure that is UK expenditure – but only up to 80% of the total core expenditure (UK and international).

➤ There are 2 types of relief available (*Corporation Tax Act 2009 ss 1200-1202*):

1 Loss relief

➤ The producer can set its losses from the film against its income from the film.
- ◆ All costs of production (including development costs) incurred by the producer are deductible.
- ◆ The producer can also deduct the following percentages of the relevant expenditure as an 'enhanced deduction':
  - *where the budget is more than £20 million* – 80%, *or*
  - *where the budget is £20 million or less* – 100%.

2 Tax credit

➤ Alternatively, the producer can surrender film losses up to a maximum amount equal to the relevant expenditure and apply to be paid a tax credit instead.
- ◆ The producer can still offset film losses that are not surrendered.

➤ To achieve the maximum tax credit, the producer (or UK co-producer) must incur 80% or more of the core expenditure in the UK. If so, the producer can apply for a cash payment equal to:
- ◆ *where the budget is £20 million or less* – 25% of losses surrendered, ie: worth 20% of total core UK expenditure (25% of 80% = 20% of 100%), *or*
- ◆ *where the budget is more than £20 million* – 20% of losses surrendered, ie: worth 16% of total core UK expenditure (20% of 80% = 16% of 100%).

➤ The tax credit can be claimed in instalments at the end of each accounting period, including during production of the film.
- ◆ This may help with the cash-flow for a film with a long production period.
- ◆ Alternatively, the producer may seek to discount the tax credit with a specialist lender in a similar way to a distribution advance – see section III above.
  - The lender will discount the finance in light of the risk that tax relief may not be granted (eg: because the final certificate is not granted, HMRC questions the producer's corporation tax return or the producer has not settled an outstanding liability to corporation tax).

➤ In practice, a producer usually opts for a tax credit. Discounting of tax credits has become standard practice and provided a valuable source of production finance.

V   Co-production agreement

➤ The tax advantages of a co-production between British and international partners have been outlined above.

➤ Irrespective of whether a co-production is ultimately tax-driven, the co-producers need to enter into a co-production agreement:

Co-production agreement

➤ The contract usually provides for:

- the contributions to be made by each co-producer, *and*

- the opening of production accounts in the relevant countries to administer the draw-down of production finance, *and*

- the sharing of accounting information, *and*

- mutual approval rights (but with a named co-producer having the final decision in the absence of agreement), *and*

- the production timetable, *and*

- a division of:

  a) ownership of copyright in the film and the film master (eg: in equal shares), *and*

  b) distribution rights (eg: in equal shares internationally, or by apportioning territories to respective co-producers), *and*

- the recoupment schedule, setting out amounts to be recovered from gross receipts in priority to the co-producers' participations, *and*

- the co-producers' participations in net profits (eg: in proportion to their respective contributions to the production budget), *and*

- a requirement for each party to provide each other co-producer with all necessary information and documents for the registration of the film with the competent certification authority in that co-producer's country.

E Production

*References in this Section are to the Copyright, Designs and Patents Act 1988 ('**CDPA**'), unless otherwise stated. References in this Section to a '**film**' include a TV programme, unless a distinction is drawn.*

I	**Production agreement**
II	**Pre-production**
III	**Personnel**

I   Production agreement

➤ Before full production can begin, a producer needs to conclude a production agreement with the financier of the production, eg:

◆ a film studio, *or*

◆ broadcaster.

➤ A production agreement sets out how a film is financed, made and delivered.

◆ It may include several different financiers, and it takes different forms depending upon the finance structure and who the parties are.

● Eg: the producer may itself be financing the production and engaging a provider of production services.

● For the sake of simplicity, in this Section:

▪ the party providing finance is referred to below as the '**financier**', *and*

▪ the party providing production services is referred to below as the '**producer**'.

➤ Where a production must begin as a matter of urgency (eg: due to an approaching deadline for broadcast), the financier may agree to enter into short-form 'heads of terms'.

◆ This is sometimes called a 'trust letter'.

● It will cover the scope and budget for the initial production work.

● It will be superseded in due course by a long-form production agreement.

➤ The production agreement should be subject to any controlling finance agreement (eg: an interparty agreement with a bank – see Section D of this Chapter).

◆ The controlling finance agreement should set out the circumstances in which the overall financier(s) can take over or abandon production of the film.

● The production agreement should also reflect any pre-sold distribution arrangements (see Section D of this Chapter).

▪ This will determine the technical specification of the film and the materials to be delivered.

➤ Whatever the financial structure of the production, the production agreement commonly includes the following terms:

Clause	Terms
Services	➤ The contract should specify the services that the producer is to provide during production and post-production.
Specification	➤ The financier will require a certain amount of control over the way in which the film is made.
	➤ The contract will therefore specify, or (where still to be confirmed) provide the financier with a right of approval over, the creative and technical specifications of the film (the 'specification'), eg:
	◆ the writer and content of the script, *and*
	◆ the director, *and*
	◆ key cast and crew, *and*
	◆ the duration of the film, *and*
	◆ film quality and other technical specifications, *and*
	◆ the shooting schedule.
	➤ The financier is usually entitled:
	a) to withhold payment of amounts due on delivery if the producer fails to comply with the specification, *and*
	b) to require the producer to bear the cost of any changes required as a result of such failure.
Delivery date	➤ The date for delivery of the completed film should be specified.
	◆ Time is usually 'of the essence' (ie: late delivery gives rise to a right for the financier to terminate the contract).
	➤ The financier should be required to confirm acceptance of the delivery materials within a defined period.
Finance	➤ The contract should state:
	◆ the approved final budget, *and*
	◆ the agreed cashflow schedule (if any), *and*
	◆ a method for managing the finance, including:
	• the opening and operation of a production bank account (over which the financier(s) may take a charge by way of security), *and*
	• weekly limits on draw-down (or rights for the completion guarantor (if any) to control draw-down), *and*
	• the maintaining of accurate accounts of production expenditure, *and*
	• reporting and auditing requirements, *and*
	◆ how to deal with responsibility for overspending (or 'overcost') (eg: the producer must apply the production fee to reduce the excess), *and*
	◆ how to deal with any underspending (eg: the producer shares any savings with the financier).

Clause	Terms
Producer remuneration	➤ The finance made available commonly includes a profit margin for the producer, but the contract should also specify: ◆ the production fee, *and* ◆ any back-end remuneration (eg: share of net profits).

Payment	➤ The contract should specify how and when the production finance is to be paid – usually in instalments, eg: ◆ on signature of the contract, *and* ◆ commencement of principal photography, *and* ◆ delivery of the film.

Insurance	➤ The producer is usually required to maintain insurance policies during production, including the following cover: ◆ principal cast and crew (including medical cover), *and* ◆ film negative and stock, *and* ◆ public liability, *and* ◆ employer's liability, *and* ◆ property damage (eg: props, sets, wardrobe and equipment), *and* ◆ errors and omissions (see Section C of this Chapter). ➤ The interests of the financier is usually 'noted' on the policies so that, in the event of a claim, the financier can recover its due share of monies paid out under the producer's policies.

Rights	➤ The producer usually assigns to the financier:
	
	◆ all rights in:
	
	  a) the film (including the entire copyright), *and*
	
	  b) all elements of it (eg: the script), *and*
	
	◆ the benefit of all waivers (eg: of moral rights) and consents (eg: in relation to performers' rights).
	
	➤ The way in which ownership is divided (eg: by term or territory) often depends on the respective financial contributions and the number of financiers.
	
	◆ In the context of a co-production, the parties will apportion among themselves:
	
	  • ownership of the copyright, *and*
	
	  • the exploitation rights (and the right to receive receipts).
	
	◆ An equity investor may take an assignment of rights to secure its investment.
	
	  • Such rights should be re-assigned on repayment of the sum invested.

Clause	Terms
Warranties	➤ The producer will have to warrant and undertake that: ◆ the film will be delivered in accordance with the specification, the approved budget, any cashflow and the shooting schedule, *and* ◆ unless otherwise approved, no amounts will be payable to third-party contributors after delivery, *and* ◆ the film will not contain defamatory or offensive material, *and* ◆ the film will not infringe any third-party rights (eg: copyright, moral rights or performers' consents), *and* ◆ the producer has not previously assigned, charged or otherwise disposed of the rights purported to be granted to the financier.
Indemnity	➤ The producer is usually required to indemnify the financier for breach of the producer's obligations or for breach of warranty.
Editing	➤ The financier will invariably reserve the right to approve the 'rough' and 'fine' edits of the film. ➤ Editing may be required: ◆ to comply with the law (eg: to remove any defamatory, obscene or otherwise offensive material – see Chapter 2), *and/or* ◆ to comply with the rules, regulations and guidelines of regulatory bodies such as Ofcom, *and/or* ◆ to make the film suitable for release through a particular distribution platform or in a particular distribution territory. ➤ Editing potentially infringes copyright and moral rights, so the producer must ensure that, for each contributor to the film, it has: ◆ acquired rights to the contributor's entire copyright, *and* ◆ obtained a suitable waiver of moral rights.
Credits	➤ The producer will have committed to accord screen credits to key contributors, both in the film and certain promotional materials (eg: trailers). ◆ Eg: key members of cast and crew may have insisted on the size of credit on screen, the minimum duration time and the order in which such credits appear. • The producer should ensure that the financier and ultimate licensees will honour those commitments (or at least rectify any inadvertent failure to do so in future exploitation).
Termination	➤ The financier will insist on the right to terminate the contract in appropriate circumstances, eg: if the producer: ◆ is in material breach of contract (usually if unremedied within a specified 'cure period'), *or* ◆ delivers the film late and/or over budget, *or* ◆ becomes insolvent. ➤ In such event, the financier will want the right (but not an obligation) to take over or abandon production.

II   Pre-production

➤ Once the production agreement and finance are in place, the producer carries out some preliminary steps before actual shooting ('principal photography') begins.

➤ The pre-production steps include:

1   Budget

➤ The producer is likely to have to revise the budget during production.

◆ It is necessary to control costs carefully to ensure that the producer does not run into problems of 'overcost' (and any requirements or sanctions that may apply under the production agreement in relation to these).

● The risk is that the producer makes no margin (or even a loss).

2   Production schedule

➤ The producer will also have to revise the timetable throughout production.

◆ Time is likely to be 'of the essence' for key delivery dates.

● The financier can usually terminate the production agreement for late delivery and take over or abandon production.

3   Personnel

➤ The producer needs to engage the cast and crew.

◆ The personnel involved and their terms of engagement are examined in section III below.

4   Film studios

➤ The producer needs to plan well in advance:

a) the dates on which studios will be required, *and*

b) the duration of filming.

➤ The producer must enter into a studio hire agreement.

> **Film studios**
>
> ➤ There are many established film studios in the UK.
>
> ◆ Pinewood Studios are the most famous (and largest) studios – traditionally home to the Bond movies. There are also many well-known, medium-sized studios (eg: Ealing Studios and Elstree Studios).

5   Filming on location

➤ If filming on location, the producer should contact the landlord to obtain permission to use the property (a 'location agreement').

◆ For certain locations (eg: public places), the producer should contact any relevant authority and notify the police of proposed filming times.

III Personnel

➤ The actual making of a film requires the services of several types of creative and technical personnel.

◆ Separate terms of engagement are not usually required where such personnel are employees of:

● the producer, *or*

● the ultimate owner of the film (eg: a commissioning broadcaster).

➤ Most independent personnel (eg: self-employed contractors, known as 'freelancers') belong to representative bodies.

◆ The terms of engagement for the majority of such personnel will be in the standard form negotiated on a collective-bargaining basis between the relevant representative body and various production organisations (eg: between the Producers Alliance for Cinema and Television and the various broadcasters).

◆ The collective-bargaining agreements often contain sets of tariffs or scales for the initial production stage and, in some cases, set fees for re-use contributions.

● NB: overseas representative bodies (eg: the Writers Guild of America, the Directors Guild of America and the Screen Actors Guild in the USA) are beyond the scope of this Section.

■ They are relevant to the production where the film features or involves overseas personnel (especially in the context of a co-production).

➤ Special terms will be agreed with key personnel (eg: the scriptwriter, director and leading actors).

◆ They may receive a share of the film's (or the producer's) net profits.

◆ The producer may enter into an option agreement with such personnel.

● The producer pays a percentage of the hiring fee on entering into such an option agreement.

■ This is usually deductible from the total fee if the option is exercised.

➤ All personnel agreements should set out:

◆ the duties of the personnel, *and*

◆ their terms of payment, *and*

◆ a grant to the producer (see Section C of this Chapter) of all necessary:

● rights (eg: copyright and performers' property rights), *and*

● consents (eg: in relation to performers' non-property rights), *and*

● waivers (eg: of moral rights).

➤ The following table summarises the respective roles of the personnel, the relevant UK representative bodies and the standard terms of engagement.

Personnel	Terms of engagement

Production services company	NB: where the producer is financing a production, the producer may engage a production company to provide production services.
	
	➤ *Role* – Carrying out rights clearance, engaging the cast and crew and ensuring that the film is produced in accordance with the terms agreed with the producer (eg: in terms of the specification, the approved budget, any cashflow and the production schedule).
	
	➤ *Representative body* – Producers Alliance for Cinema and Television ('**PACT**').
	
	  ◆ PACT represents independent film and TV production companies (but not individual producers).
	
	  ◆ PACT negotiates standard minimum terms with the WGGB, Equity, the MU and BECTU – see below.
	
	  ◆ PACT supplies model contracts for use by its members (eg: development, production and director agreements).
	
	➤ *Terms of engagement* – The terms of engagement will be as set out in section I above (the producer assuming the role of the financier).

Individual producers	➤ *Role* – The producer (ie: production entity) is likely to appoint several individuals to provide production services including:
	
	a) an executive producer, responsible for sourcing production finance, *and*
	
	b) an individual producer, with day-to-day responsibility for the actual shooting and for ensuring that the film is completed within budget and by the delivery date, *and*
	
	c) a line producer, to work with the filming crew and location staff.
	
	➤ *Representative bodies* – The Production Guild of Great Britain ('**PG**') and the Production Managers Association ('**PMA**').
	
	  ◆ Both are advisory/lobbying bodies.
	
	    • PACT provides production companies with a model agreement for use with individual producers.
	
	➤ *Terms of engagement* – For an employee, the terms will be set out in the individual's employment contract with the production entity.
	
	  ◆ For an independent contractor, the terms (other than the duties) will be broadly similar to a director's agreement (see below).

Personnel	Terms of engagement
Scriptwriter	➤ *Role* – Writing the script or screenplay for the film (eg: adapting a novel or writing on a specified theme stipulated by the producer). ➤ *Representative body* – Writers' Guild of Great Britain ('***WGGB***'). ◆ The WGGB represents writers in film, TV and other media. ➤ *Terms of engagement* – For scripts commissioned by producers, WGGB negotiates minimum terms with BBC, ITV and PACT and has several agreements in place for different types of production. ◆ The contract terms include minimum basic fees and repeat fees, as well as grants of rights in the script to the producer. ◆ NB: the WGGB/PACT model agreement for feature films has not been revised since 1992, so does not usually form the basis for negotiations. • The WGGB recommends a 35% uplift on the 1992 rates. ◆ See Section B of this Chapter for: • the terms of engagement of the scriptwriter, *and* • the terms to be agreed with the author of the work on which the script is based (eg: a novel which is adapted by the scriptwriter).
Director	➤ *Role* – Creative direction of the overall production, directing the cast of the film and co-ordinating production. ➤ *Representative body* – Directors Guild of Great Britain ('***DGGB***'). ◆ DGGB is mainly advisory, providing information on a range of issues, such as contracts and relevant legislation. ➤ *Terms of engagement* – Unlike other representative bodies, DGGB does not negotiate standard minimum terms on its members' behalf, although DGGB provides its members with a rate card and legal advisory service. PACT provides PACT members with a model contract. ◆ The director may be an employee of the producer, in which case the contract terms will be set out in the employment contract. ◆ For an independent director, the contract terms should include: • the period of engagement (including working hours), *and* • the director's duties (eg: liaising with the scriptwriter, working with the producer on the production schedule and locations, and directing and editing the film), *and* • the fee (including the payment schedule and any back-end remuneration), *and* • a grant of all necessary rights, waivers and consents, *and* • the director's screen credit, *and* • any promotional obligations during exploitation of the film.

Personnel	Terms of engagement

Actors and other performers	➤ *Role* – Acting and performing.
	
	➤ *Representative body* – Equity (which is its full name).
	
	◆ Equity is the trade union for:
	
	    ● performers (eg: actors, singers, dancers, variety and circus artists, television and radio presenters, extras and stunt performers – but not musicians), *and*
	
	    ● related professionals (ie: choreographers, stage managers, theatre directors and designers, stunt directors and theatre fight directors).
	
	➤ *Terms of engagement* – Equity negotiates standard minimum terms on its members' behalf with the BBC, ITV, PACT and other production organisations.
	
	◆ There are separate agreements for cinema and television production, as well as for secondary media (eg: video games).
	
	    ● The provisions of these standard-form contracts differ depending on the type of performer.
	
	    ● On a feature film, an Equity actor is paid:
	
	        ■ a minimum rate (at the currently published rate) per day or per week (such rates being inclusive of a pre-purchase payment for all subsequent usage rights), *and*
	
	        ■ daily holiday-pay contributions and overtime rates, *and*
	
	        ■ a royalty (shared among performers on a points system) based, at the producer's option, on a percentage of:
	
	          a) the film's net profits (ie: once the initial investment in the film has been recouped), *or*
	
	          b) gross receipts from sales to TV broadcasters and from sales of home videos.
	
	◆ For actors, the contract terms should include:
	
	    ● the period of engagement (including working hours), *and*
	
	    ● level of commitment to the project (eg: on a 'first-call basis', ie: taking precedence over other work), *and*
	
	    ● the actor's duties, *and*
	
	    ● the fee (including the payment schedule and any separate pre-purchase payments and/or back-end remuneration), *and*
	
	    ● a grant of all necessary rights, waivers and consents, *and*
	
	    ● the mechanics of production (eg: transport, accommodation, rehearsals and wardrobe), *and*
	
	    ● the actor's screen credit, *and*
	
	    ● any promotional obligations during exploitation of the film.

Personnel	Terms of engagement
Composer and musicians	➤ *Role* – Composing, performing and recording music to accompany the film.

➤ *Representative bodies* – For composers, the British Academy of Songwriters, Composers and Authors ('**BASCA**') and for musicians, the Musicians' Union ('**MU**').

➤ *Terms of engagement* – The MU negotiates minimum terms for engagement of musicians with PACT and the broadcasters.

◆ NB: BASCA does not negotiate minimum terms for composers, so a producer is free to negotiate with a composer.

● The commercial practice is extremely varied, and depends in each case on the standing of the composer.

◆ A producer often engages a composer to deal with all of the music for the film. The 'composer agreement' acts as a framework services agreement and should include the following terms:

● the composer's duties, which are likely to include:

■ composing and arranging the score, *and*

■ conducting, performing, producing and recording the score, *and*

■ engaging and paying (out of the composer's fee) session musicians to perform the score, *and*

● the delivery date for the score, parts and masters, *and*

● a grant of all necessary rights, waivers and consents (including the right to 'synchronise' the compositions and any sound recordings produced by the composer in timed relation with the film – see Section C of this Chapter), *and*

● the fee, including:

a) an up-front sum and staged payments (to provide adequate cashflow during production), *and*

b) any back-end remuneration (eg: 2.5% of the film's net profits, although for a TV programme, the up-front fee is usually a full 'buy-out' of all rights), *and*

c) if all rights in the compositions and masters are assigned to the producer (subject, in the case of the compositions, to the 'writer's share' of PRS income – see Section D of Chapter 3):

■ a share (eg: 50%) of the producer's music publishing income, *and*

■ (where relevant) a percentage of the producer's net receipts from a soundtrack album (eg: 25%-50%).

◆ The composer may previously have entered into exclusive services agreements with a record label and/or a music publishing company. If so, the producer needs to obtain:

● a release of exclusivity from the record label, *and*

● a grant of rights (including a 'synchronisation' licence) from the music publisher.

Personnel	Terms of engagement
Technical staff	➤ *Role* – Providing behind-the-camera technical support for the production via a range of functions (eg: casting, lighting, set and costume design, filming, special effects and production accounting). ◆ Such crew members are commonly referred to as 'below-the-line' personnel (in contrast to the 'above-the-line' cast and creative crew). ➤ *Representative body* – Broadcasting, Entertainment, Cinematograph and Theatre Union (**'BECTU'**). ➤ *Terms of engagement* – BECTU negotiates standard minimum terms for its members with the broadcasters and PACT. ◆ The agreement is flexible and covers the requirements of all relevant personnel. ◆ The terms allow for the buy-out of any rights that the technical staff may have (eg: copyright in designs).

F   Distribution and exploitation

*References in this Section are to the Copyright, Designs and Patents Act 1988 ('**CDPA**'), unless otherwise stated. References in this Section to a '**film**' include a TV programme, unless a distinction is drawn.*

I	Introduction
II	Stages of exploitation – feature film
III	Stages of exploitation – TV programme
IV	Secondary exploitation
V	Distribution agreement

I   Introduction

➤ Under the terms of the production and finance agreement for a film, the ultimate owner or assignee of the copyright and other rights in the film is typically the entity providing the main part of the production finance.

   ◆ For the sake of simplicity, that entity is referred to below as the '**owner**'.

➤ Once the film is complete, it is in the owner's interest to generate maximum revenue by distributing the finished product to the widest possible audience.

   ◆ The owner of a feature film will not (unless it is a Hollywood studio) have the specialist knowledge or financial resources to market and distribute the film.

      ● For this reason, the owner (eg: an independent producer) often enters into:

         ▪ a single distribution agreement with a Hollywood studio, *or*

         ▪ several agreements with independent distributors across the world.

      ● The distributor(s), in turn, enter into agreements with cinema operators and with sub-distributors (eg: manufacturers/shippers of DVDs and merchandisers).

   ◆ Where a broadcaster has fully financed a TV programme, that broadcaster is likely to be the primary broadcaster and to undertake secondary exploitation.

      ● The relevant programme commissioning agreement will also contain provisions relating to distribution (eg: via broadcast and secondary exploitation).

➤ The screen industry is moving from analogue transmission to digital transmission.

> ### Digital transmission
>
> ➤ To facilitate 'D-cinema', the UK Film Council has invested in the installation of digital projectors that transmit digital copies of a film stored on a hard drive (or perhaps in the future to be delivered via a digital network).
>
> ➤ Many households already have digital TV receivers, and all UK analogue TV signals will switched off on a region-by-region basis by 2012.
>
> ➤ Films are increasingly being transmitted via online and mobile services.

II Stages of exploitation – feature film

➤ Traditionally, a film is first released only in cinemas (known as a 'theatrical release').

♦ In this way, the owner aims to maximise revenues before releasing the film via other media by avoiding competition between different distribution platforms.

♦ The same principle is applied to a succession of further release 'windows'.

● The intervals between exclusive windows have shortened considerably in recent years (if not , in certain cases, been made simultaneous), partly to preserve revenues by keeping pace with the rapid distribution of 'pirate' copies of films.

● In practice, there are often 'dark' months in which the film is not exploited in order to differentiate between each stage of exploitation.

➤ The advent of new media (eg: internet-based TV or '*IPTV*') provides challenges to this conventional logic, as well as providing new opportunities via new revenue streams.

♦ Some independent films are released using a different window strategy (eg: *The Road to Guantanamo*, which was released in 2006 in cinemas, on DVD and online on the day after it was broadcast on Channel 4). A 'day and date' or 'simultaneous' release allows a smaller marketing budget and also makes the offering more attractive to consumers, allowing them to watch a film in a medium that is convenient to the consumer and at a time when the film is still 'fresh'.

● Even for 'blockbusters' post-theatrical windows now converge in some cases.

♦ Despite repeated (and continuing) predictions that cinemas will not survive the emergence of new distribution platforms, cinemas are still thriving.

● This appears to be because most home entertainment systems cannot replicate the experience of going out and seeing a film on the big screen.

■ The major US studios remain committed to the strategy and spend a vast amount (nearly as much as the production budget) on marketing films for theatrical release (ie: on 'prints and advertising' or '*P&A*' costs).

➤ The exploitation of a feature film therefore still broadly follows the conventional release cycle and falls into 6 main stages (or, where, simultaneous, types):

Stage	
1	Theatrical release
2	Non-theatrical release
3	DVD/download rental and retail
4	PPV/VoD
5	Pay TV
6	Free TV

➤ The following chart gives a rough timeline for these stages in the UK.

◆ NB: the timeline varies from film to film and from territory to territory, and will also change (perhaps beyond recognition) as new platforms emerge and/or prevail.

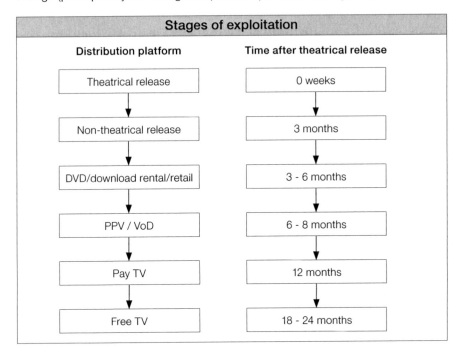

Stages of exploitation	
Distribution platform	**Time after theatrical release**
Theatrical release	0 weeks
Non-theatrical release	3 months
DVD/download rental/retail	3 - 6 months
PPV / VoD	6 - 8 months
Pay TV	12 months
Free TV	18 - 24 months

➤ The net effect of the various distribution deals entered into by the owner throughout the stages (or types) of exploitation is that the distributors make the greatest profit margin.

◆ An independent producer that is low down in the value chain suffers:

• a series of deductions by 'middle men' for each mode of exploitation (eg: agents' and distributors' fees), *and*

• further deductions in the form of financing costs.

Stage 1	Theatrical release

➤ Many 'blockbuster' films are now released on the same date around the world to prevent the adverse impact of illegally distributed 'pirate' copies on theatrical revenues.

➤ In the UK, a cinema must have a licence to show films to the public.

◆ Exhibiting a film is a form of 'regulated entertainment' whose provision is a 'licensable activity' governed by the *Licensing Act 2003* ('**LA 2003**') (*s 1(1)* and *Sch 1 para 2*).

• The cinema owner must obtain a 'premises licence' under that Act from the relevant 'licensing authority', ie: the local authority for the area in which the cinema operates (eg: a London borough council) (*LA 2003 s 2(1)*).

➤ The licence must include a condition requiring the admission of minors (ie: persons aged under 18) to be restricted in accordance with any recommendation made by the local authority or, where the local council specifies, by the British Board of Film Classification ('**BBFC**') (*LA 2003 s 20*).

◆ In practice, the local authority will, even where retaining its own discretion, have regard to the BBFC classification in making any such recommendation.

➤ It is critical commercially for a film to fall within the appropriate age-group category, so as to maximise the potential audience (and potential revenues). A distributor usually seeks authorisation from the owner to edit the film to meet local classification requirements.

◆ In the UK, the owner or distributor submits the film for classification. The BBFC charges a fee on a set tariff scale.

BBFC film classification

➤ The BBFC's current categories are as follows:

◆ U or Uc (Universal) – suitable for all ('Uc' for pre-school children), and should not upset those aged 4 years or older.

◆ PG (Parental Guidance) – general viewing, but some scenes may be unsuitable for young children (ie: under around 8).

◆ 12A – a child under 12 must be accompanied by an adult.

◆ 12 – suitable for persons aged 12 years or older.

◆ 15 – suitable only for persons aged 15 years or older.

◆ 18 – suitable only for persons aged 18 years or older.

◆ R18 (Restricted 18) – '18' rated and only to be shown in specially licensed cinemas or supplied in licensed sex shops.

➤ Deal terms between an owner and a theatrical distributor vary:

Theatrical distribution deal

➤ The most common form of deal is a 'net deal', where:

◆ the cinema operator retains a share of gross receipts (around 65% to 70% in the UK, 45 to 55% in the US, and 55% to 65% elsewhere), *and*

◆ the distributor, before paying any monies to the owner:

• charges a distribution fee of between 30% and 50% of the net receipts remitted to the distributor by the cinema operator, *and*

• from the balance, 'recoups' (ie: recovers):

  ▪ expenditure on 'P&A' costs, *and*

  ▪ any advance previously paid to the owner (plus interest).

➤ Despite the large retention taken by a cinema operator, it makes its largest profit margin on selling screen advertising and selling drinks and food to customers.

Stage 2	Non-theatrical release

➤ A feature film may also be released for public exhibition outside mainstream cinemas in return for a licence fee, eg:

◆ as in-flight entertainment on aeroplanes, *and/or*

◆ to passengers on ships, *and/or*

◆ for viewing on hotel or motel TV channels on a pay-per-view basis.

  • This form of release usually precedes release for home entertainment and generates a very small proportion of the film's total revenues.

Stage 3	DVD/download rental and retail

➤ A theatrical distributor is likely to acquire video distribution rights.

◆ In 2007 revenues from the video home entertainment market (including video retail and rental and video-on-demand) (about 55% of the UK market) far exceeded revenues from theatrical release (about 20%) or TV exploitation (about 25%) (source: UK Film Council).

  • As a result, independent producers that have to wait to participate in any net profits until 'upstream' investors have been paid in full are unlikely to participate in the net profits of a film until the video release stage.

➤ Until recently, DVDs and videos were offered for rental before being offered for retail.

◆ In the UK the rental and retail releases are now simultaneous.

◆ The market share for retail or 'sell-though' (about 44% of the UK market in 2007) far exceeds the market share for rental (about 7%) (source: UK Film Council).

➤ VHS-format videos have almost entirely been replaced by DVDs, and Blu-rays are gaining market share.

◆ It is questionable whether any physical format will survive as compression technology advances and broadband speed and market penetration continues to increase around the world, making new media counterparts more commercially viable.

  • Music downloads demonstrate the appeal of digital distribution to end users.

➤ Downloads are made available via digital stores (eg: iTunes), either for retail or rental. Download releases are often simultaneous with physical video releases.

➤ The supply of videos is regulated by the *Video Recordings Act 1984* ('**VRA**').

◆ The *Video Recordings (Labelling) Regulations 1985* ('**VR(L)R**') (made under *VRA s 8*) require classification certificates to be clearly labelled on videos.

  • The *VRA* sets out the basis for the BBFC classification categories (as above).

◆ The *VRA* created criminal offences, including supplying (or offering to supply) an unclassified film (*s 9*) and/or a video not complying with the *VR(L)R* (*s 13*).

- A video is exempted from regulation under the *VRA* (**'exempt'**) if is:

  - designed to inform, educate or instruct, *or*

  - concerned with sport, religion or music, *or*

  - a video game (*s 2(1)*).

    - Such a video is not exempt, however, if it depicts or is likely to a significant extent to encourage human sexual activity or gross violence (*s 2(2)*) or criminal activity (*s 2(3)*).

    - The BBFC does not decide whether or not a work is exempt. Unofficially, a distributor will label exempt videos with an 'E' symbol to show that the distributor believes the video to be exempt from classification.

- Certain types of supply are exempt. These include supplies:

  - made neither for a reward nor in the course of business, *or*

  - designed to provide a record of an event or occasion (eg: a wedding) for those taking part (or connected with those who took part) in it, *or*

  - solely for broadcast or in connection with a broadcast, *or*

  - as a submission to the BBFC for classification (*s 3*).

- In May 2008 the BBFC launched 'BBFC.online', a platform-neutral, self-regulatory scheme for classification and labelling of all forms of digital content delivery.

➤ The usual deal terms for wholesale of physical videos are as follows:

Physical video distribution deal

➤ The agreement between the owner and a video distributor usually takes the form of a licence.

➤ The distributor usually pays the owner an 'advance' against royalties (or 'minimum guarantee'), plus:

- a royalty (eg: 35% - 45%) based on the rental price, *and*

- a royalty (eg: 12.5% - 20%) based on the retail price.

  - Retail royalties are lower, as profit margins are higher for rentals.

➤ If a video distributor has not acquired TV rights, it will usually insist on a 'hold-back' (ie: defined period of delay) during which the owner will not broadcast (or authorise the broadcast) of the film.

- TV transmission – in particular, free-to-air broadcast – will reduce rental and retail income, especially given the widespread take-up of high-quality DVD and hard-disk recorders.

➤ Wholesale deals for digital downloads of films are, at the time of writing, still developing, and various digital stores are competing for market share.

- The terms of such deals are beyond the scope of this Section.

438

Stage 4	PPV / VoD

➤ Soon after a video release (or more or less simultaneously), the film is likely to be exploited by the most limited form of broadcast/cybercast, ie:

- ◆ 'pay-per-view' television ('**PPV**') via cable or satellite, where a consumer chooses to view a film at start times fixed by the broadcaster in return for paying a fee on top of any basic subscription package, *and/or*

- ◆ 'video-on-demand' ('**VoD**'), where a consumer pays to see films on a title-by-title basis over a distribution network such as cable, ethernet or DSL.

  - • 'True' VoD is streamed in response to the consumer's request in real time.

    - ■ 'Near' VoD ('**NVoD**') is a simpler offering used because of limitations in server or network performance, where the consumer has a more limited choice of films and start times are fixed (eg: every 15 minutes).

➤ The technical distinctions between these distribution platforms are being eroded with developments in technology.

- ◆ They may all be subsumed in pay-per-view forms of online delivery (often referred to under the banner of '**IPTV**').

  - • This mode of exploitation is widely seen as a potential legitimate solution to the problems posed by illicit peer-to-peer file-sharing and other forms of 'piracy'.

  - • It is also widely predicted that IPTV (in whichever form) will ultimately replace DVD exploitation as the most significant source of revenue for owners.

➤ Deal terms between an owner and a PPV distributor vary.

PPV distribution deal

➤ The most common form of deal is a 'net deal', where:

- ◆ the PPV TV service retains around 40% to 50% of gross receipts, *and then*

- ◆ the distributor:

  - • retains commission of around 25% to 35% of the net receipts remitted to the distributor by the PPV TV service, *and then*

  - • remits any remaining receipts to the owner.

➤ The terms of IPTV deals are developing as technology changes and are beyond the scope of this Section.

Stage 5	Pay TV

➤ 'Pay TV' refers to cable/satellite TV channels that are only available to subscribers.

   ◆ The film is shown on a channel that forms part of the basic package for which the consumer has paid a subscription fee.

      ● A new-media alternative to Pay TV is 'subscription video-on-demand' (known as 'SVoD'), where a consumer pays to see a large (or unlimited) number of films in return for paying a regular fee (typically monthly).

➤ Deal terms between an owner and a Pay TV distributor vary widely:

Pay TV distribution deal

➤ Usually:

   ◆ the Pay TV operator pays the distributor a fixed fee (which varies widely depending on the film's box-office performance and may increase to reflect the number of subscribers to the film), *and*

   ◆ the distributor, before remitting any receipts to the owner, retains commission of around 25% to 35% of the fixed fee.

Stage 6	Free TV

➤ The last mode of exploitation of a feature film is via freely receivable broadcast.

   ◆ The Free TV channels include:

      ● 'free-to-air' terrestrial stations with a non-encrypted, aerially transmitted analogue and/or digital signal that can be received free of charge (ie: BBC 1 and 2, ITV, Channel 4/S4C and Channel 5), *and*

      ● internet transmissions of such output (sometimes referred to as 'simulcast' or, where available on a limited delayed basis, 'catch-up services'), *and*

      ● 'freeview' digital channels transmitted via cable and/or satellite, *and*

      ● 'network' or 'syndication' free TV markets overseas.

➤ Deal terms between the owner and the Free TV distributor vary widely:

Free TV distribution deal

➤ Usually:

   ◆ the Free TV channel pays the distributor a licence fee which varies widely depending on the film's box-office performance, *and*

   ◆ the distributor, before remitting any receipts to the owner, charges a fee based on a percentage of the licence fee (eg: between 25% and 50% in the US and 20% and 40% outside the US).

III   Stages of exploitation – TV programmes

➤   A programme made specifically for TV is usually exploited by means of a system of rights windows that are designed to maximise revenue for similar reasons to the feature-film system.

◆   The windows are typically as follows:

●   a primary broadcast window, maximising ratings (and so potential advertising revenue for commercial channels), *and*

●   phased secondary modes of exploitation, eg: in rough chronological order:

▪   online streaming/temporary downloads, *then*

▪   VoD/PPV, *then*

▪   retail permanent download, *then*

▪   secondary TV transmission on other channels (eg: UKTV Gold).

➤   The secondary modes of exploitation are of particular significance to an independent producer to the extent that they revert to the producer (or the producer participates in net profits derived from them).

Secondary rights
➤   The *Communications Act 2003* ('**CA 2003**') effectively 'unbundled' secondary rights that were previously sold to commissioning broadcasters alongside primary broadcast rights.   ◆   Each 'public service' broadcaster (ie: each terrestrial channel) is required to draw up an Ofcom-approved code of practice for commissioning independent productions (*CA 2003 s 285(1)*).   ●   Among the conditions that Ofcom is empowered is impose is 'sufficient clarity ... about the different categories of rights ... that are being disposed of' (*CA 2003 s 285(3)(b)*).   ➤   Ofcom guidance on *s 285* states that producers should retain rights in their programmes unless these are explicitly sold to broadcasters and other parties.   ◆   This underlines independent producers' rights to capitalise on secondary rights – whether exploited by the producers themselves or sold to a terrestrial broadcaster separately to the primary broadcast rights.   ●   Other broadcasters (eg: BSkyB and other cable and satellite channels) are not required to negotiate new media terms with independents.

➤ This principle is reflected in the terms of trade agreed between PACT and the respective terrestrial channels. The detailed provisions of those terms of trade vary from broadcaster to broadcaster and are beyond the scope of this Section, but there are some common themes:

Terms of trade for independent producers

➤ The producer retains ownership of all rights in the programme, but grants the commissioning broadcaster a licence:

- to broadcast the programme …

- via any form of TV services …

- a set number of times during a defined licence period (eg: 5 years in the case of the BBC and ITV).

➤ After TV transmission, the broadcaster has an exclusive window in which to make the programme available via new media, eg:

- a 7-day streaming/non-permanent download period in the case of the BBC (as part of a 'catch-up' service for viewers that missed the original transmission), *or*

- a 30-day VoD/PPV option period in the case of ITV and Channel 4, subject to any extension negotiated.

  - During the exclusive period, the broadcaster pays the producer a share of VoD/PPV revenue, eg: 50% (in the case of ITV and Channel 4) or 75% (in the case of the BBC, if it acquires VoD rights).

➤ At the end of the TV licence period, all rights revert to the producer, although the broadcaster receives a share (eg: 15%) of net profits from all exploitation of the programme by the producer (including via new media).

- After a 'hold-back' period during which the producer's rights are suspended (eg: 30 days for single programmes or six months for a series), the producer is free to sell the programme(s) direct to consumers for permanent download ('download to own').

  - There is a separate 'hold-back' period for secondary exploitation on other channels (eg: UKTV Gold), eg: in the case of ITV:

    - 30 months after broadcast for a returning series, *or*

    - 18 months for a non-returning series.

IV   Secondary exploitation

➤ In addition to the mainstream system of rights windows, there are secondary modes of exploitation, eg:

- ◆ *merchandising* – based on the characters or content of the film, *and*

- ◆ *soundtrack album* – generating revenue via record sales and music publishing income, *and*

- ◆ *secondary new media rights* – such as electronic games for use on games consoles or PCs, and clips and ringtones downloaded for use on mobile telephones, iPods or other portable devices.

➤ Although secondary to the primary film, these can generate massive revenues, especially from merchandising derived from a film that appeals to a younger audience (eg: the Star Wars 'franchise' or CBBC hits such as Teletubbies).

➤ The owner is likely to enter into a series of agreements with different specialist companies to maximise secondary exploitation revenues:

Secondary exploitation agreements

➤ Most secondary exploitation agreements take the form of a licence of rights in return for payment of a licence fee.

- ◆ As with any licence, the scope, territory and duration of rights granted should be carefully defined.

- ◆ The owner should insist on approval rights over the material to be supplied to end users, as its quality can damage exploitation of the primary product.

V   Distribution agreement

➤ The various distribution platforms have been considered above. 1 or more of these is commonly covered by a single agreement between an owner and a distributor.

- ◆ The agreement may:

  - ◆ be a stand-alone 'distribution agreement', *or*

  - ◆ form part of a more comprehensive agreement (eg: a 'production, finance and distribution' or 'PFD' agreement).

- ◆ The contract terms for TV programmes have been outlined in section II above.

➤ For a feature film, the main contract terms are as follows:

Clause	Terms
Rights	➤ The rights clause is the fundamental part of the contract. ◆ The owner has the exclusive right under copyright to issue copies of the film to the public, so the distributor must obtain the right (usually a licence from the owner) to distribute the film. • The rights are usually licensed on an exclusive basis. • The owner retains ownership of the film. ➤ The rights granted may be for the whole world and for all media (eg: in a distribution deal with a Hollywood studio). ➤ Alternatively, the rights granted may be limited (eg: as part of a series of deals with different independent distributors) by: ◆ **Geographical area ('*territory*')** • The distribution rights may only be for a specific territory. ▪ Eg: there may be 3 distributors appointed: the first with the exclusive right to distribute in Europe, the second with rights in North America and Latin America and the third with rights for the rest of the world. ◆ **Type of media** • The rights may be divided into different types of media, eg: ▪ theatrical release, *and/or* ▪ non-theatrical release, *and/or* ▪ DVD/download, *and/or* ▪ PPV/VoD, *and/or* ▪ Pay TV, *and/or* ▪ Free TV, *and/or* ▪ secondary modes of exploitation (eg: merchandising, soundtrack album, games and mobile telephony). • Where rights are granted for all or several media, the owner will usually insist on 'hold-backs' to allow for the staged windows of exploitation considered in section II above. • The owner may well require the distributor to employ 'Digital Rights Management' ('**DRM**') technology to protect against copying of the film when it is digitally distributed. ▪ Downloads of music and music videos are now generally DRM-free. It remains to be seen whether consumer pressure will lead to DRM-free movie downloads.
Licence period	➤ The duration of the licence should be defined (eg: 15 or 20 years). ➤ The owner should be entitled to terminate the licence period if the distributor fails to perform, eg: ◆ fails to pay sums due to the owner, or commits any other material breach of the agreement, *or* ◆ becomes insolvent, *or* ◆ fails to achieve a specified revenue target. • Termination allows the owner to appoint a new distributor.

Clause	Terms
Remuneration	➤ The distributor receives gross receipts from the sale of the film in the agreed territories and media.
	◆ Before accounting to the owner, the distributor retains a fee or commission, which varies depending on the distributor's track record and the territory, medium and film's performance.
	● See section II above for the different percentage rates.
	◆ In addition, the distributor can deduct any reasonable, direct costs incurred by it in promoting and exploiting the film.
	● Since the 2 parties may have very different concepts of what is reasonable, it is usual to include a list of what can be deducted and such amounts may also be capped.
	● Deductible costs usually include the costs incurred by the distributor in exercising ancillary rights granted to it in order to facilitate the distribution of the film, eg:
	■ creating masters, additional prints and trailers, *and*
	■ shipping and customs clearance, *and*
	■ storage and insurance of the film materials, *and*
	■ editing to comply with legal requirements of the territory (eg: censorship or broadcasting codes), *and*
	■ editing to make the film more marketable (eg: to facilitate commercial breaks on TV), *and*
	■ 'dubbing' (ie: recording) foreign-language voice-overs or adding translated sub-titles, *and*
	■ classification fees, *and*
	■ copyright registration (where applicable), *and*
	■ promotion, advertising and marketing, *and*
	■ taxes imposed on the distributor in respect of exploiting the film (eg: withholding taxes), *and*
	■ manufacture of DVDs (plus packaging and freight), *and*
	■ taking legal action in the owner's name (if requested by the owner) in the event of local infringement of the owner's rights in the film (eg: piracy).
	● The owner will want the distributor to bear any sub-distribution costs without passing them on to the owner.
	◆ If the distributor has paid an advance, this is recouped next (plus interest) and the balance will be remitted to the owner.
Distribution advance	➤ The distribution advance is usually payable in instalments, eg:
	◆ on signature, *and*
	◆ on delivery of specified delivery materials, *and*
	◆ on acceptance of the delivery materials.
	● The distributor may agree to increase the advance if the film earns specified levels of box-office receipts.
	■ The owner often requests a bank or lender to 'discount' the advance – see Section D of this Chapter.

Clause	Terms
Accounting	➤ The distributor should maintain a separate account for the film.
	➤ The distributor should account to the owner regularly (eg: monthly for 6 to 12 months, then quarterly for 2 to 3 years and then yearly after that).
	◆ The owner should insist on the right to audit the distributor's financial books and records regularly (eg: every 6 or 12 months) to check that the accounting is accurate, and to be paid:
	● the costs of such audit in the event of a specified level of underpayment, *and*
	● in any event, the amount of any such underpayment.
Distributor's obligations	➤ The owner should ensure that the distributor is doing all that it can to promote the film.
	➤ The distributor should:
	◆ advertise the film and spend a minimum amount on 'P&A', *and*
	◆ organise staggered release dates for the different media and ensure that releases are achieved by the respective dates, *and*
	◆ clear the film with the appropriate regulatory bodies and organise any necessary censorship or classification to comply with their requirements, *and*
	◆ accord on-screen credits in accordance with the owner's agreement with each contributor, *and*
	◆ pay any re-use or residual fees that become payable as a result of the exploitation of the film, *and*
	◆ establish the necessary accounting and financial control mechanisms (including a joint bank account into which gross receipts are paid and held on trust for the owner, subject to permitted deductions), *and*
	◆ audit any approved sub-distributors and sub-licensees to ensure that they are making the necessary payments on time, *and*
	◆ achieve a specified performance standard (eg: use best endeavours to achieve the highest commercial receipts), *and*
	◆ obtain the owner's written consent before selling films below an agreed price in certain territories.
Delivery materials	➤ The owner will be required to deliver specified delivery materials at its expense, time being 'of the essence' (ie: non-delivery or late delivery will entitle the distributor to terminate the contract).
	➤ The contract will usually set out:
	◆ a detailed list of the delivery materials in a schedule to the contract, *and*
	◆ a period for acceptance of the delivery materials by the distributor, *and*
	◆ valid reasons for rejection (usually technical only), *and*
	◆ a mechanism for deemed acceptance if the distributor fails to notify the owner that it has accepted the delivery materials.

5 Marketing

This Chapter examines:

A   Advertising

References in this Section are to rules of the relevant Code, unless otherwise stated.

I	Advertising and the media
II	Regulatory framework
III	Self-regulation
IV	Clearance of adverts

I   Advertising and the media

➤ Advertising provides the main source of revenue for many different kinds of media.

- ◆ The terrestrial commercial broadcasters are almost entirely dependent on advertising revenue.

  - Eg: the ITV broadcasting companies generated more than £1 billion in revenue from advertising sales in the first half of 2008 (source: Reuters).

- ◆ Satellite broadcasters, such as Sky, derive some income from subscription fees, but still largely depend on income from advertisers.

- ◆ Advertising is increasingly significant in digital media (eg: on websites and mobile telephones), and forms a core part of the business model for many new media ventures.

➤ The most prominent type of advertising is 'above the line' advertising, ie: marketing targeted at the general public via television, radio, print media and digital media.

- ◆ Historically, an advertising agency would distinguish between (and invoice a client separately for):

  a) advertising in the media 'above the line' (ie: a line on the invoice), *and*

  b) creative and strategic advice 'below the line'.

- ◆ 'Below the line' advertising involves marketing that is directly targeted at individuals (or a particular group of individuals) or an audience.

  - Examples of 'below the line' advertising include:

    - sponsorship, which is considered in Section B of this Chapter, *and*

    - mailshots, for which data protection is an important issue (see Section K of Chapter 1).

  - The regulation of other forms of 'below the line' advertising (eg: advertorials and product placement) are beyond the scope of this Chapter.

➤ For the sake of brevity, the term 'product' is used in this Section to mean a product and/or service, unless a distinction is drawn.

➤ Since adverts for a product are targeted largely at individual end users, a need for consumer protection arises – especially in the context of impressionable consumers (eg: children).

◆ This has led to a complex network of legal and regulatory constraints on advertising. These are enforced by a variety of sanctions, including:

- adverse publicity for the non-compliant advertiser, *and/or*

- action taken by one of the self-regulatory bodies, such as the Advertising Standards Authority ('**ASA**'), *and/or*

- sanctions imposed by the Office of Fair Trading ('**OFT**'), *and/or*

- complaints and legal recourse taken by competitors, *and/or*

- in serious cases, significant fines and criminal sanctions.

◆ It is therefore of vital importance to media companies (eg: broadcasters and publishers), as well as to the advertisers themselves, that an advert does not breach either the law or regulations that govern them.

➤ It is often advisable to obtain specific advice (known as 'copy clearance') for an advert.

◆ Compliance with some key principles will help to prevent a claim:

Protecting against a claim

➤ Avoid making misleading pricing claims.

➤ Avoid making false or misleading claims about the product.

➤ Fit the advertising to the product and not *vice versa*.

➤ Avoid unfair comparisons – compare like with like.

➤ Do not unduly criticise or make unfair comparisons with a competitor.

➤ Think carefully before making any use of another person's intellectual property rights (eg: using another person's brand).

➤ Keep within accepted standards of decency.

II   Regulatory framework

➤   The regulatory framework for advertising consists of:

◆   the *Consumer Protection from Unfair Trading Regulations 2008* (‘**CPUTR**’), which relate to false and misleading advertising targeted at consumers, *and*

◆   the *Business Protection from Misleading Marketing Regulations 2008* (‘**BPMMR**’), which relate to misleading advertising targeted at businesses, *and*

●   The *CPUTR* and *BPMMR* repealed and replaced many legal rules on advertising that were formerly contained in several different statutes and regulations.

◆   the 3 self-regulatory codes regulated by the ASA, *and*

◆   intellectual property laws, such as the *Trade Marks Act 1994, and*

◆   media laws, such as privacy, defamation and obscenity, *and*

◆   industry-specific legislation (depending on the type of product advertised).

III   Self-regulation

➤   The ASA is the main body responsible for regulation of advertising in the UK.

◆   Details of what and how the ASA regulates are considered below.

➤   The advertising industry regulates ‘above the line’ advertising through a form of regulation known as ‘self-regulation’.

◆   This means that the rules governing such advertising are drawn up by bodies that are financed by the advertising industry.

➤   Regulation of media advertising is divided according to media type:

◆   **Broadcast media**

●   Ofcom is the regulatory body for all TV and radio advertising, but has outsourced advertising regulation to the ASA.

◆   **Non-broadcast media**

●   For print-media and online advertising (eg: for ‘banner ads’, ‘pop-ups’ and sponsored entries in search-engine results), the regulatory bodies are:

■   the ASA, *and*

■   the Committee of Advertising Practice (‘**CAP**’).

●   Other regulatory bodies include:

■   the Mobile Marketing Association, which regulates mobile advertising, *and*

■   PhonepayPlus, which regulates phone-paid premium-rate services.

➤ The basic principles for the self-regulation of broadcast and non-broadcast advertising are considered below.

Media type	Self-regulation
Broadcast media	➤ *Relevant Codes* – The TV Advertising Standards Code ('***TV Code***') and the Radio Advertising Standards Code ('***Radio Code***'). ➤ *Governing body* – ASA (outsourced from Ofcom). ◆ The ASA is made up of 12 independent council members who determine whether adverts comply with the *Codes*. ◆ The ASA is financed by the industry through a levy on adverts. • The Broadcast Advertising Standards Board of Finance ('***BASBOF***') collects money from broadcast advertisers (a voluntary 0.1% levy on broadcast advertising costs). ➤ *'Pre-vetting'* – An advertiser can (and should) seek advance comfort (while not a guarantee) that an advert complies with the relevant *Code* from: ◆ Clearcast, in the case of TV advertising, *or* ◆ the Radio Advertising Clearance Centre ('***RACC***'). ➤ *Method of regulation* – The ASA's main methods of regulation are: ◆ investigating complaints made by members of the general public, competitors or other persons, *and* • The majority of complaints are made using the ASA's online complaints form. • About 12,000 complaints are made each year, of which about a fifth are upheld. • The ASA's approach is to consider the general impact on a particular audience. • The number of complaints is irrelevant: it may uphold a complaint by 1 person if the advert is in breach of a *Code*. ◆ conducting regular surveys of adverts, *and* ◆ monitoring areas of concern (eg: health and slimming products, cigarette promotion, alcohol promotion and 'greenwashing', ie: making eco-friendly claims in relation to a product). ➤ *Powers and remedies* – The ASA cannot levy fines and cannot (unlike a court) enforce legislation. It can, however: ◆ ask the advertiser to withdraw or amend the advert, *and/or* ◆ ask media owners not to run the advert, *and/or* ◆ issue a public reprimand on the ASA's website (which is located at www.asa.org.uk), *and/or* • The ASA publishes weekly reports of its adjudications online, leading to adverse publicity for the advertiser. The media will report on newsworthy breaches of the *Codes*. ◆ request that the revocation or temporary withdrawal of the advertiser's trading privileges, financial discounts and other incentives available through membership of advertising trade bodies, *and/or* ◆ impose mandatory 'pre-vetting' (see above), *and/or* ◆ refer persistent breaches to the OFT (which can seek an injunction restraining further breach – the 'legal backstop'), *and/or* ◆ refer persistent breaches to Ofcom.

Media type	Self-regulation

Non-broadcast media	➤ *Relevant Code* – The British Code of Advertising, Sales Promotion and Direct Marketing (*'CAP Code'*).
	
	➤ *Governing body 1* – ASA (outsourced from Ofcom).
	
	  ◆ *Finance* – The Advertising Standards Board of Finance (*'ASBOF'*) collects money from non-broadcast advertisers (a voluntary 0.1% levy on non-broadcast display advertising).
	
	  ◆ *'Pre-vetting'* – An advertiser can (and should) seek advance comfort (while not a guarantee) that an advert complies with the *Cap Code* from the CAP Copy Advice team.
	
	  ◆ *ASA's methods of regulation* – As described above for broadcast media.
	
	  ◆ *ASA's powers and remedies* – As described above for broadcast media, except that the ASA cannot make a referral to Ofcom.
	
	➤ *Governing body 2* – CAP (with delegated authority from the ASA).
	
	  ◆ CAP is responsible for reviewing, amending and enforcing the *CAP Code*.
	
	  ◆ The ASA and CAP work alongside and complement each other.
	
	  ◆ CAP operates a website at www.cap.org.uk.
	
	    • The website provides an online version of the *CAP Code*, together with guidance and a news update section featuring the latest developments.

➤ A decision made by the ASA is subject to court challenge:

Judicial review of an ASA decision

➤ An ASA decision is subject to judicial review (*R v Advertising Standards Authority, ex parte DSG Retail Ltd*, 4 December 1996, unreported).

◆ The court's role is supervisory only.

◆ The court will intervene where the ASA has acted illegally, irrationally or has not followed the correct procedure.

  • Eg: the High Court dismissed an application for judicial review of the ASA's adjudication on the advertising for SmithKline Beecham's 'Ribena Toothkind'.

  • The ASA had found that adverts for the soft drink, which stated that it did not encourage tooth decay and actively benefited oral health, were misleading (*R (on the application of SmithKline Beecham plc) v Advertising Standards Authority* [2001] EWHC Admin 6).

IV   Clearance of adverts

➤ There are 4 steps to be followed when clearing an advert for broadcast or publication:

Steps	
1	Compliance with the relevant *Code*
2	Compliance with the general law
3	Compliance with industry-specific legislation
4	Non-infringement of third-party rights

Step 1	Compliance with the relevant *Code*

➤ See section III above to decide which *Code* applies.

◆ Check, where applicable, for compliance with the other media-specific codes, which are beyond the scope of this Section.

➤ The 3 main *Codes* are lengthy, detailed and complex.

◆ The *CAP Code* is summarised below to illustrate the general approach of the *Codes*, whose provisions are in many respects similar.

● For this reason, only brief overviews of the *TV Code* and the *Radio Code* are given – see the full text of the Codes at http://www.asa.org.uk/asa/codes/ for further details.

● Useful links to other rules and guidance are accessible on the same page.

➤ The main rules of the *CAP Code* are as follows:

Cap Code – regulation of non-broadcast advertising	
Scope of application	➤ The *Cap Code* applies to adverts in (r 1.1): ◆ print media (eg: newspapers and magazines), *and* ◆ electronic material (eg: emails, text messages and faxes), *and* ◆ media in public places (eg: posters, cinema and video), *and* ◆ online adverts (eg: 'banner ads' and 'pop-up ads'), *and* ◆ marketing databases containing personal information.
General principles	➤ An advert should (rr 2.1-2.5): ◆ be legal, decent, honest and truthful, *and* ◆ be prepared with a sense of responsibility to the public, *and* ◆ respect the principles of fair competition, *and* ◆ not bring advertising into disrepute, *and* ◆ conform with the *Code*. ➤ The primary obligation rests with the advertiser, although agencies, publishers and service suppliers must also abide by the *Code* (r 2.5). ◆ NB: the *Code* is applied in the spirit as well as in the letter (r 2.8).

Cap Code – regulation of non-broadcast advertising (continued)

Substantiation	➤ An advertiser must (r 3.1): ◆ hold documentary evidence to prove all substantiable claims **before** submitting the advert for publication, *and* ◆ send such evidence to the ASA if requested without delay.
Legality	➤ Adverts must be legal (r 4.1) and may only relate to a product that can be legally sold (r 4.2).
Decency	➤ An advert should not contain anything that is likely to cause serious or widespread offence (in particular, on grounds of race, religion, sex, sexual orientation or disability) (r 5.1). ➤ An advert may be distasteful without necessarily breaching r 5.1, and an advertiser should consider public sensitivities (r 5.2).
Honesty	➤ An advertiser should not exploit the credulity, lack of knowledge or inexperience of consumers (r 6.1).
Truthfulness	➤ An advert should not mislead by inaccuracy, ambiguity, exaggeration, omission or otherwise (r 7.1).
Matters of opinion	➤ An advertiser may state an opinion about a product, as long as it is clear that it is an opinion and not a fact (r 8.1). ◆ NB: a purely subjective opinion need not be substantiated.
Fear and distress	➤ An advert should not (r 9.1): ◆ cause fear or distress without good reason, *or* ◆ use shocking claims or images merely to attract attention.
Safety	➤ An advert should not: ◆ condone or encourage unsafe practices (particularly an advert addressed to or depicting children) (r 10.1), *or* ◆ encourage consumers to drink and drive, or suggest that the effects of drinking and driving can be masked (r 10.2).
Violence	➤ An advert should not condone, or be likely to provoke, violence or anti-social behaviour (r 11.1).
Political advertising	➤ An advert aimed at influencing voters in an election or referendum is exempt from the *Code* (r 12.1), whereas a central-government or local-government advert is subject to the *Code* (r 12.2).
Privacy	➤ An advert should not portray or refer to an individual in an adverse or offensive way. An advertiser should obtain written permission before portraying or referring to an individual. An advert should not claim personal approval where none exists (r 13.1). ➤ Any reference to a deceased person should handled with particular care to avoid causing offence or distress (r 13.3). ➤ References to the Royal Family are not normally permitted (r 13.4).
Testimonials and endorsements	➤ An advertiser should hold signed and dated proof for any 'testimonial' (eg: endorsement) used (r 14.1). ➤ A testimonial or endorsement should only be used: ◆ with the source's written permission (unless it is a genuine opinion from a published source) (r 14.1), *and* ◆ supported, where necessary, with independent evidence of accuracy of any opinion expressed (r 14.3).

Cap Code – regulation of non-broadcast advertising (continued)

Prices	➤ Any stated price should: ◆ be clear and relate to the product advertised (*r 15.1*), *and* ◆ include any VAT payable (unless addressed only to businesses able to recover VAT) (*r 15.2*). ➤ NB: CAP publishes *Help Notes* on lowest price claims, price promises and retailers' price comparisons.
Product availability	➤ A product must not be advertised as ready for purchase unless the advertiser reasonably believes that it can satisfy demand (*r 16.4*).
Guarantees	➤ An advertiser should be cautious about using the word 'guarantee', as it may be legally binding on the advertiser. Any substantial limitations on the guarantee should be spelled out in the advert. Before commitment, consumers should be able to obtain the full terms of the guarantee from the advertiser (*r 17.1*).
Comparative advertising	➤ Comparative claims are permitted in the interests of vigorous competition and public information (*r 18.1*). Comparisons should not mislead consumers by creating confusion between competitors or between their respective products or trade marks (*r 18.6*). ➤ Other comparisons (eg: those with the advertiser's own products or with products of non-competitors) should be clear and fair, and should neither mislead nor be likely to mislead. The elements of the comparison should not be selected in a way that gives the advertiser an artificial advantage (*r 19.1*). ➤ A comparison should not mislead consumers by creating confusion with any product or trade mark of a competitor (*r 19.2*). ➤ A comparative advert should not discredit or denigrate the products, trade marks, activities or circumstances of a competitor (*r 20.1*).
Denigration	➤ An advert (whether comparative or not) should not unfairly attack or discredit other businesses or their products (*r 20.1*).
Unfair advantage	➤ An advertiser should not take unfair advantage of the reputation of another organisation's trade marks or of the designation of origin of competing products (*r 20.2*).
Imitation	➤ An advert must not so closely resemble another that it misleads, is likely to mislead or causes confusion (*r 21.1*).
Identifying advertisers	➤ An advert should be presented in such a way that it is clear that it is an advert (*r 22.1*).
Free offers	➤ An offer should be described as 'free' only if consumers pay no more than the fair cost of: a) the response to the promotion (eg: by post, telephone, email or text message), *and* b) delivery (excluding packing, handling or administration), *and* c) any travel involved if consumers collect the offer (*r 32.5*).
Specific rules	➤ There are detailed specific rules on various types of advertising, eg: • prize promotions (*rr 33-35*) • charities (*r 37*) • distance selling (*r 42*) • database practice (*r 43*) • children under 16 (*r 47*) • motoring (*r 48*) • environmental claims (*r 49 – see below*) • health/beauty products (*r 50*) • weight control (*r 51*) • employment (*r 52*) • financial products (*r 53*) • tobacco products, rolling papers and filters (*r 55 – see below*) • alcoholic drinks (*r 56*) • gambling (*r 57*)

Cap Code – regulation of non-broadcast advertising (continued)	
Specific rules (cont.)	➤ Advertising of 'environmentally friendly' products (known as 'green-washing') falls under close scrutiny. Eg: environmental claims should not be used without qualification unless the advertiser has convincing evidence that the product will cause no environmental damage when taking into account the full life cycle of the product (*r 49.2*). ➤ NB: tobacco advertising is banned (other than at the point of sale) under the *Tobacco Advertising and Promotion Act 2002*.

➤ The main rules of the *TV Code* and the *Radio Code* are as follows (in overview):

TV Code – regulation of TV advertising	
Scope of application	➤ The *TV Code* applies to TV advertising (including terrestrial, satellite and cable channels) (*Introduction*).
Rules	➤ Most sections of the *TV Code* start with an explanation of the rule under the heading 'Background', followed by the rule itself. ◆ The rules are framed to ensure that adverts are legal, decent, honest and truthful and do not mislead or cause harm or serious or widespread offence (*Foreword*). ➤ The rules cover: ◆ general compliance with the law (*s 1*), *and* ◆ detailed, specific restrictions in areas such as: ● the distinction between TV programmes and advertising, and the editorial independence of TV programmes (*s 2*), *and* ● unacceptable products and services (eg: tobacco products and pornography) (*s 3*), *and* ● political and controversial Issues (*s 4*), *and* ● misleading advertising (*s 5*), *and* ● harm and offence (*s 6*), *and* ● advertising targeted at children under 16 (*s 7*), *and* ● medicines, treatments, health and nutrition (*s 8*), *and* ● finance and investments (*s 9*), *and* ● religion, faith and systems of belief (*s 10*), *and* ● 'other categories' (ie: premium-rate telephone services, distance selling, charities, homeworking schemes, instructional courses, the National Lottery, introduction and dating services, alcoholic drinks, driving standards and gambling) (*s 11*). ➤ The *TV Code* is accessible online at: http://www.asa.org.uk/asa/codes/tv_code/tv_codes/

Radio Code – regulation of radio advertising	
Scope of application	➤ The *Radio Code* applies to all adverts on all radio stations licensed by Ofcom (*Foreword*).
Rules	➤ The rules for radio are, by and large, extremely similar to the rules set out in the *CAP Code* and the *TV Code*, although the *Radio Code* does not follow the structure of either *Code* closely. ➤ The *Radio Code* is accessible online at: http://www.asa.org.uk/asa/codes/radio_code/

Step 2	Compliance with the general law

➤ An advertiser should comply with 3 aspects of the general law:

1 Consumer protection law

➤ In addition to applicable *Codes*, an advert is subject to consumer protection law. These rules are largely set out in the *CPUTR*.

Compliance with the *CPUTR*

➤ Each *Code* has been amended to take the *CPUTR* into account, so compliance with the *Codes* should minimise the likelihood of breach of the *CPUTR*. The *CPUTR*, however, represent secondary legislation and impose different sanctions to the *Codes* (including, in some cases, criminal sanctions) and ought, therefore, to be considered separately.

➤ 'Unfair' commercial practices are prohibited in general (*r 3(1)*).

- ◆ Any commercial practice is 'unfair' if (*r 3(3)*):
  - it contravenes the requirements of professional diligence, *and*
  - materially distorts the economic behaviour of the average consumer in relation to a product (or is likely to do so).
    - Eg: it would be unfair to make a misleading claim about what a product does in order to persuade a consumer to buy it.

➤ An advert is unfair (among other *CPUTR* reasons) if it misleads by (*r 5(2)*):

- ◆ giving false information, or (even if the information is factually correct) deceiving (or being likely to deceive), the average consumer as to:
  - the existence or nature of the product, *and/or*
  - the main characteristics of the product, *and/or*
  - the extent of the advertiser's commitments, *and/or*
  - the motives for the advert, *and/or*
  - the nature of the sales process, *and/or*
  - any statement or symbol used for sponsorship or approval of the advertiser or of the product, *and/or*
  - the price (including how the price is set), *and/or*
  - the existence of a specific price advantage, *and/or*
  - the need for a service, part, replacement or repair, *and/or*
  - the advertiser's nature, attributes and rights, *and/or*
  - the consumer's rights or risks, *and*
- ◆ causing, or being likely to cause, the consumer to take a transactional decision that the consumer would not otherwise have taken.

➤ Subject to certain conditions (which are beyond the scope of this Section), it is a criminal offence to make such a misleading statement (see *r 9*).

➤ 31 practices are always considered to be unfair, eg: falsely claiming to be a signatory to a code of conduct (*Sch 1*).

➤ The *CPUTR* are enforced by (*Pt IV*):

- ◆ trading standards authorities, *and*
- ◆ the OFT, *and*
- ◆ for TV and radio advertising, Ofcom.

➤ The other main consumer protection rules affecting advertising are as follows:

◆ **Price**

- The *Price Marking Order 2004* imposes additional rules on pricing in a retail context. Those rules are beyond the scope of this Section.

◆ **Comparative advertising**

- Comparative advertising is also regulated under the *BPMMR* – see step 4 below, as this relates to the non-infringement of third-party rights.

2 **Content clearance**

➤ The content of an advert needs to be cleared in the same way as a newspaper article or a film, so the following issues need to be considered:

◆ confidential and private information – see Section J of Chapter 1, *and*

◆ defamation and malicious falsehood – see Section A of Chapter 2, *and*

◆ offensive material – see Section B of Chapter 2.

3 **Laws relating to physical advertising methods**

➤ Other laws and regulations may be relevant depending on the physical method of advertising.

◆ Eg:

- The use of posters and billboards is potentially subject to:
  - local authority planning permission, *and*
  - the law of trespass.
- The use of aircraft to tow banners is subject to:
  - the *Civil Aviation Act 1982, and*
  - the *Civil Aviation (Aerial Advertising) Regulations 1995*.

Step 3	Compliance with industry-specific legislation

➤ In addition to the rules under the *Codes* and under the general law, many products, services and activities are subject to industry-specific regulation under primary and/or secondary legislation. These rules are too numerous to list exhaustively, but the ones more commonly encountered are as follows:

Regulated products	
Food products	➤ Food products are subject to the *Food Act 1984*, the *Food Labelling Regulations 1996* and the *Food Safety Act 1990*. ➤ General food and nutrition labelling are covered respectively by *Directive 2000/13/EC* and *Directive 90/496/EC*. ◆ NB: the European Parliament is considering *Proposal 2008/0028* for a new *Regulation* to merge and amend those *Directives*. ➤ *Regulation 1924/2006/EC* (on health and nutritional claims) imposes restrictions on claims that can be made in relation to food products and sets out mandatory labelling requirements. ➤ The Food Standards Agency provides non-binding guidance on food-advert claims (eg: on using the words 'fresh', 'pure' and 'natural').
Diet products	➤ Slimming claims about diet products are subject to the *Food Labelling Regulations 1996* (see *Sch 6*).
Alcoholic drinks	➤ Advertising is a significant tool for marketing brands of beers, wines and spirits. There is no specific legislation, but the *Codes* contain detailed restrictions and are strictly enforced by the ASA. ◆ Eg: under the *CAP Code*, an advert for an alcoholic drink should: • be socially responsible and neither encourage excessive drinking nor suggest that drinking can overcome boredom, loneliness or other problems (*r 56.4*), *and* • not be directed at people under 18 through the media, content or context in which the advert appears (*r 56.5*), *and* • not show people that look under 25 drinking, playing a significant role or behaving in an adolescent/juvenile way (*r 56.6*), *and* • not suggest that the drink has therapeutic qualities or can change moods or enhance confidence, mental or physical capabilities or performance, popularity or sporting achievements (*r 56.8*). ➤ An advertiser of alcoholic drinks should also comply with the voluntary Portman Group *Code of Practice* – see www.portmangroup.org.uk. ◆ When an advert for a product is found to contravene this *Code*, the Portman Group's Independent Complaints Panel asks retailers not to stock the product, unless the advert is suitably amended.
Tobacco products	➤ Following the introduction of *Directive 98/43/EC* (the '*Tobacco Directive*'), the UK (along with other EU member states) introduced a ban on nearly all forms of advertising and promotion of tobacco-related products. See step 1 above for the self-regulatory rules relating to the limited exceptions to the ban.
Pharmaceutical products	➤ Pharmaceutical products (eg: medicines) are regulated by the: ◆ *Medicines Act 1968, and* ◆ *Medicine (Labelling and Advertising to the Public) Regulations 1978.* ➤ Advertising of over-the-counter pharmaceutical products is regulated under a code administered by The Proprietary Association of Great Britain, which also provides a 'pre-vetting' service for such adverts.

Regulated services	
Financial services	➤ Advertising of financial services is largely subject to regulation by the Financial Services Authority, which enforces, and issues guidance on, financial services legislation.
	➤ Consumer credit advertising is regulated by the OFT.
Gambling	➤ An advertiser should ensure that an advert (eg: a prize promotion) is not an unlawful lottery for the purposes of the *Gambling Act 2005*.
	➤ The rules on unlawful lotteries are beyond the scope of this Section. The Gambling Commission issues useful guidance on these on its website at www.gamblingcommission.gov.uk.

Regulated activities	
Political advertising	➤ Political advertising on TV and radio is banned by the *Communications Act 2003 s 321(2)*.
	◆ This ban was unsuccessfully challenged as being contrary to freedom of expression under the *European Convention on Human Rights Art 10 (R (on the application of Animal Defenders International) v Secretary of State for Culture, Media and Sport* [2008] UKHL 15).

Step 4	Non-infringement of third-party rights

➤ An advert may contain a number of different intellectual property rights.

◆ Before the advert is broadcast or published, it is important to make sure that an appropriate rights clearance procedure has been followed.

◆ This may involve taking grants (eg: licences) of third-party rights.

◆ It may not, however, always be necessary (or desirable) to try to obtain grants of rights from a third party, especially from a competitor in the context of comparative advertising.

Comparative advertising

➤ Comparative advertising takes place where an advertiser uses a rival's product/service to emphasise the benefits of its own product/service.

◆ Since the advert often displays the rival's marks and designs, rights clearance issues frequently arise – see below.

➤ In clearing a TV or radio advert (which will involve making a film or sound recording), the same rights clearance issues need to be considered as for clearing rights for use in a film or TV programme – see Section C of Chapter 4.

◆ Eg: it is necessary to clear the rights of all contributors to the making of the advert (eg: the scriptwriter, producer, director, actors, composer and musicians).

➤ In print media, similar issues arise, such as clearance of copyright (eg: in any third-party literary or artistic works or typographical editions reproduced).

➤ In terms of the content of the advert, an advertiser should, before making use of (or making comparisons with) a rival's products or services, consider 3 sources of third-party rights.

1 Registered trade marks

➤ Use of a registered mark without the consent of the owner may amount to infringement under the *Trade Marks Act 1994* – see Section L of Chapter 1.

➤ At the time of writing, it is unclear how the regime under the *TMA 1994* applies to comparative advertising.

♦ An advertiser generally has a defence to trade-mark infringement if the use of a rival mark is in accordance with the honest practices of the trade and neither takes advantage of, nor is detrimental to, the reputation of the rival's mark (*TMA 1994 s 10(6)*).

• The courts have in the past held that, broadly speaking, honest comparisons in adverts should be allowed (eg: *Barclays v RBS*, The Times, 8 February 1996).

➤ Comparative advertising is, however, specifically covered by Directive 2006/114/EC (the '**Comparative Advertising Directive**'), which was implemented into UK law by the *BPMMR* – see below.

♦ An advertiser's freedom to make appropriate comparisons was upheld in *O2 Holdings Ltd v Hutchison 3G UK Ltd* ([2006] EWHC 534).

♦ When the case was referred to the European Court of Justice ('**ECJ**') on 31 January 2008, Advocate-General Mengozzi advised that use of a rival's trade mark in comparative advertising falls to be considered solely under the terms of the Comparative Advertising Directive, and not under the provisions of *Directive 89/104/EC* (ie: relating to trade marks).

♦ The ECJ looked at the point from the rival's perspective instead, ruling that a rival's right to bring an action for trade-mark infringement in a comparative advertising case is limited to cases where the rival can show that there is a likelihood of confusion (*O2 Holdings Ltd v Hutchison 3G UK Ltd*, Case C-533/06, 12 June 2008).

2 Passing-off

➤ An action in passing-off will succeed if the rival can show that:

a) it has goodwill in the mark used in the advert, *and*

b) the advert has resulted in confusion to its customers, *and*

c) as a result, it has suffered damage.

➤ A passing-off action is rarely successful, however, because the purpose of the advert is usually to contrast the advertiser's mark with the rival, rather than to derive any benefit to the advertiser from the goodwill in the mark.

3   **Regulation of comparative advertising**

➤ Comparative advertising must comply with *BPMMR r 4*. Comparative advertising is allowed under *r 4* where it:

a) is not 'misleading', ie:

 i) does not deceive (nor is likely to deceive) the traders to whom it is addressed or whom it reaches, nor is likely, by reason of its deceptive nature, to affect their economic behaviour, *and*

 ii) does not, for those reasons, injure (nor is likely to injure) a rival, *or*

b) is neither a misleading action under *CPUTR r 5* nor a misleading omission under *CPUTR r 6*, *or*

c) compares products meeting the same needs or intended for the same purpose, *or*

d) objectively compares 1 or more material, relevant, verifiable and representative features of those products (eg: price), *or*

e) does not create confusion among traders:

 i) between the advertiser and a competitor, *or*

 ii) between the advertiser's trade marks or products and those of a competitor, *or*

f) does not discredit or denigrate the trade marks, products, activities or circumstances of a competitor, *or*

g) for products with designation of origin, relates in each case to products with the same designation, *or*

h) does not take unfair advantage of the reputation of a competitor's trade mark or of a competing product's designation of origin, *or*

i) does not present products as imitations or replicas of products bearing a protected trade mark.

➤ It is a criminal offence to produce misleading advertising (whether comparative or otherwise) (*r 6*).

➤ NB: the *Codes* specifically address comparative advertising.

 ◆ Broadly speaking, the *TV Code*, *Radio Code* and *CAP Code* each allow comparative advertising, as long as the comparison between the products is fair (eg: a non-broadcast advert must comply with the requirements of the *CAP Code rr 18-20*).

 ◆ The ASA adjudicates on comparative-advertising complaints.

 • Eg: it found an advert misleading where a 12-month Virgin Media TV package for Setanta Sports was compared with a monthly package offered by BT Vision and Sky (adjudication, 14 May 2008).

B Sponsorship

I Introduction

➤ The simplest and most direct way for a company to market a brand is to advertise its products or services – either to the public at large ('above the line' advertising) or through communications targeted at individuals ('below the line' advertising).

➤ One possibility is to sponsor a third-party event or activity that already has a captive and enthusiastic audience. This positive association has a number of benefits:

- ◆ it boosts the company's profile, image and reputation, *and*

- ◆ it enhances brand awareness and encourages customer loyalty, *and*

- ◆ it indirectly promotes the company's products, services and commercial interests generally.

  - ● For instance, the London 2012 Olympic Games and Paralympic Games will be one of the largest sporting events ever held, watched on TV by billions of people worldwide. The marketing value for a business of being associated with such an event is enormous. For this reason, several major companies (eg: Adidas, BP, British Airways, BT, EDF and Lloyds TSB) – some with little or no connection with sport – have each invested millions of pounds to sponsor the event.

    - ■ Sponsorship is not just a marketing tool for multinational companies; it is also a valuable form of promotion for smaller firms.

➤ Sponsorship is also a valuable source of finance for events or activities.

- ◆ Eg: the company organising the London 2012 Games has raised a significant proportion of its budget for staging the Games through sponsorship. This is a useful supplement to other sources of finance, such as ticket sales and TV revenue.

➤ Companies often sponsor media productions, especially TV and radio programmes.

- ◆ There is, as in the case of advertising, a need to protect viewers and listeners, so special rules have been put in place to regulate the influence of sponsors.

➤ This Section examines:

- ◆ the main types of sponsorship, *and*

- ◆ the elements of an event sponsorship agreement, *and*

- ◆ the UK regulatory regime for sponsorship of media productions.

II   Types of sponsorship

➤ Although in principle anything can be sponsored, to be worthwhile for the sponsor, the sponsorship vehicle must attract an audience and portray a positive popular image.

- For this reason, sponsors tend to focus on sponsorship of sporting and cultural events, persons appearing at those events and TV and radio programmes.

  - It is becoming increasingly common for companies to sponsor media productions that are disseminated via the internet or mobile telephones (eg: specially produced short films or podcasts).

➤ There are 8 main types of sponsorship:

1   Sporting events and series

- *Example* – The energy company EDF is a 'Tier 1' sponsor of the London 2012 Olympic Games and Paralympic Games.

- *Form of association* – EDF has exclusive marketing rights in the utility services sector, including use of the official London 2012 logo and the right to describe itself as the London 2012 sustainability partner.

  - Eg: EDF can print the London 2012 logo on utility bills sent to its customers, and its status as a sustainability partner underlines its 'green' credentials.

2   Cultural events and festivals

- *Example* – The oil company BP sponsored the British Museum's 2008 exhibition on the Roman emperor Hadrian.

- *Form of association* – The exhibition was sub-titled as 'The BP Special Exhibition', and the BP logo was printed on all promotional materials for the exhibition.

  - The association reinforced the link between the sponsor and the positive features of the event, and the cultural connotations 'softened' the company's potentially industrial image.

3   Individuals

- *Example* – The sprinter Usain Bolt is sponsored by Puma.

- *Form of association* – Usain Bolt agrees to run in shoes made by Puma.

4   Teams

- *Example* – The British Olympic and Paralympic team, 'Team GB', is sponsored by Adidas.

- *Form of association* – 'Adidas' is printed on the team's sports kit.

  - In a football or rugby context, this form of sponsorship is known as 'shirt sponsorship'.

5   **Squads**

◆ *Example* – A squad, rather than the whole team, is sponsored (eg: the financial products group Skandia sponsors the GB Sailing Team).

◆ *Form of association* – The squad is named 'Skandia Team GBR'.

6   **Venues and stadia**

◆ *Example* – Emirates Airlines sponsors Arsenal FC's football ground at Ashburton Grove.

◆ *Form of association* – The venue is named the 'Emirates Stadium'.

7   **Supply of services or products**

◆ *Example* – A company provides technical services to the organiser (eg: the watch manufacturer Omega sponsors time-keeping at the Olympic Games).

◆ *Form of association* – Omega can describe itself as the 'Official Timekeeper for the Olympic Games' and use the official Olympic logo in certain promotions.

8   **Media productions**

◆ *Example* – The furniture retailer Harveys sponsors ITV's long-running soap opera, Coronation Street.

◆ *Form of association* – The sponsorship forms part of an integrated marketing campaign over several different media platforms (known as a '360° campaign'):

● conventional TV, via 'TV idents' (ie: screen trailers and 'bumper ads' around the TV broadcast of the programme and during advertising breaks), *and*

● the interactive TV service supporting the programme (including branding on the 'red-button service' and a sponsor-specific area), *and*

● the ITV mobile interactive service (including bumper ads and branding on the Coronation Street pages), *and*

● direct marketing (through special offers and promotions to customers listed on ITV's database via the ITV-owned website Friends Reunited).

◆ NB: TV and radio sponsorship should be distinguished from the situation where a programme features an event that has been separately sponsored.

● Eg: a sports programme may feature footage from the FA Premier League (currently sponsored by Barclays), but the programme itself could have a separate sponsor.

➤ Each form of association provides the basis for an agreement, which needs to be translated more fully into contractual rights and obligations.

◆ These agreements vary between different types of sponsored events or activities, although there are similar considerations common to all types of sponsorship agreement (eg: rights granted, commercial return and brand protection).

● Those considerations are examined in the following section.

III   Event sponsorship agreement

➤ One of the most common forms of sponsorship is event sponsorship. The clauses commonly found in an event sponsorship agreement are considered below:

Clause	Terms
Status of sponsor	➤ The organiser often divides rights of association with the event into hierarchical 'tiers' of sponsorship. ➤ Each tier confers a different status, for example (in descending order of priority) as: ◆ the 'main' or 'title' sponsor of the event (eg: Barclays in relation to the FA Premier League), *or* ◆ a 'secondary sponsor', which is typically a 'category sponsor' (ie: conferring rights of association within a specified industrial sector), *or* ◆ an 'associate sponsor', typically a third grade of sponsor with limited recognition rights, such as: • an official supplier, ie: the provider of specific products or services to the event (eg: beverages), *or* • a sponsor of a specific part of the event (eg: a particular race or an award), *or* • a media partner (a status that is sometimes split between the media, eg: between broadcasting and print media). ▪ There may also be underlying 'founding sponsors', with continuing rights of recognition. ➤ In a smaller-scale event with only one sponsor, the agreement should still carefully define the scope of rights granted.
Exclusivity	➤ An important concept running throughout the scope of rights granted is exclusivity. A right is far more valuable if the sponsor is the only person allowed to associate itself with the event in a particular way.
Grant of rights	➤ The main rights that are granted include the following: **a) Inclusion of the sponsor's name in the event title** ◆ *Explanation* – The right is extremely valuable, as each reference to the event involves publicity for the sponsor. ◆ *Exclusivity* – It would be highly unusual for the title to include 2 sponsors' names, so this right is usually exclusive. ◆ *Example* – Barclays sponsors the FA Premier League and has obtained the right for the event to be called the Barclays Premier League. The word Barclays is therefore used where it is written (eg: in a newspaper or on the TV screen or official website) or spoken (eg: on radio or TV). • NB: for certain types of event, the BBC may refuse to use the sponsor's name when referring to the event, in line with the BBC's editorial guidelines on undue prominence. The Premier League is an exception to this rule.

Clause	Terms
Grant of rights (continued)	**b) Inclusion of the sponsor's logo in the event logo**

♦ *Explanation* – The sponsor may want to incorporate its own logo into a special logo for the event. A combined logo will increase the sponsor's association with the event.

♦ *Exclusivity* – It would be unusual for the event logo to include 2 sponsors' logos, so this right is usually exclusive.

♦ *Example* – During the Beijing 2008 Olympic Games, the organiser permitted Coca-Cola to create a new composite logo that combined both parties' logos in a frame of 2 flags.

  • NB: where a combined logo has already been designed, the approved version should be reproduced in a schedule to the agreement.

    ▪ The agreement should also specify who owns the logo (and/or its component parts).

c) Sponsor's designation

♦ *Explanation* – In addition to, or instead of, using the sponsor's name in the event logo, the sponsor may wish to associate itself with the event through using a special designation (eg: 'Official Timekeeper for the Olympic Games').

  • The sponsor will want to be able to use the designation on all its products or services, and also for all marketing and merchandising purposes.

    ▪ The sponsor should also ensure that the organiser will use the designation in promoting the event.

♦ *Exclusivity* – Although only a single sponsor will usually be included in the name of the event, there can, in principle, be any number of official sponsors.

  • The organiser may well seek to maximise revenue by allowing the greatest possible number of sponsors to be associated with the event.

    ▪ In reality, if too many sponsors are appointed, the effectiveness of sponsorship is diluted and the value of the right is reduced correspondingly.

  • The organiser will usually agree to give each sponsor the exclusive right to associate itself with the event for a particular product or service group.

    ▪ If, however, there are to be several sponsors, these should be limited to non-competing product or service groups.

    ▪ Eg: it would usually be unacceptable for Coca-Cola and Pepsi – or for McDonald's and Burger King – to sponsor the same event.

♦ *Example* – There are many types of designation, such as:

  • In association with …

  • Sponsored by …

  • In conjunction with …

  • Brought to you by …

  • Official supplier to the … |

Clause	Terms

Grant of rights (continued)	**d) Use of the event title and/or logo in sponsor marketing**
	
	◆ *Explanation* – Since the event title and logo belong to the organiser, the sponsor needs permission to use them for its own marketing purposes (eg: to apply them to its products or services to promote its association with the event).
	
	◆ *Exclusivity* – The organiser will typically need to use the event title and logo itself and to allow others to use them, so this right is usually non-exclusive. It is, however, often agreed that the sponsor is the only company that can use the event title and logo within its category of products or services (eg: the sponsor is the only drinks sponsor of the event).
	
	    ● Where the sponsor's own name and logo are to be used in connection with the event (eg: as part of a combined logo), the sponsor should insist on the right to approve the use of its own name and logo by other sponsors.
	
	    ● Where the sponsor makes several products of different types (or supplies various types of services), the agreement should state whether the sponsor can associate itself with just one or all of such types.
	
	◆ *Example* – During the Beijing 2008 Olympic Games, the organiser permitted Coca-Cola to reproduce the composite logo on its drinks bottles.
	
	    ● NB: the organiser should restrict the sponsor from sub-licensing use of the event title and logo.
	
	e) Peripheral rights
	
	◆ *Explanation* – The agreement may also include a number of peripheral rights for the sponsor, often in the form of perks for the sponsor.
	
	◆ *Exclusivity* – Other sponsors may well have similar rights.
	
	◆ *Example* – The perks might include:
	
	    ● a quota of free tickets to the event, *and/or*
	
	    ● access to hospitality facilities such as marquees and restaurant and bar facilities, *and/or*
	
	    ● opportunities to meet and/or interview players or performers after the event.

Territory	➤ The organiser may also divide rights of association by territory, especially in the case of an event that is televised globally (eg: the Olympic Games) or where the organiser is the governing body of an international sport (eg: the International Olympic Committee). ◆ The agreement should contain suitable territorial restrictions.
Duration	➤ The sponsor will want the agreement to start before the event so that it can market its products or services with the event name and logo. It may also want to exploit the rights after the event has finished. ➤ The organiser may want to restrict the agreement to a single event so that it is free to appoint a different sponsor (or to open up competitive bidding) for subsequent events. ◆ The duration is usually for a fixed period.

Clause	Terms

Option to renew	➤ Either party may want to include an option to renew the agreement.
	
	◆ The option may be:
	
	    ● exercisable by either or both parties, *and/or*
	
	    ● conditional on:
	
	        ■ the relevant party's fulfilling its obligations under the agreement, *and/or*
	
	        ■ the achievement of certain targets (eg: a minimum number of tickets sold or minimum TV viewing figures).
	
	➤ The option should be certain in its terms. Otherwise, there is a danger that the agreement will be void for uncertainty.
	
	◆ Eg: there should be a mechanism for calculating the future remuneration to be paid under the agreement.

Sponsor's obligations	➤ The principal obligation is usually to pay a sponsorship fee. ◆ Payment may be made in a lump sum or by instalments. ● Instalments reduce the risk to the sponsor if the event does not take place. They can also provide an incentive for the organiser, as the payment schedule may be tied to the achievement of certain organisational steps. ➤ In addition to, or instead of, a sponsorship fee, the sponsor may be expected to provide certain products and/or services free of charge to the organiser (known as providing 'value in kind' or 'VIK'). ➤ Additional obligations include requirements: ◆ to comply with applicable laws and regulations (eg: where the event is broadcast, broadcasting regulations), *and* ◆ only to use the event title and logo for the permitted purposes.
Organiser's obligations	➤ The principal obligation is to ensure that the event is staged, eg: ◆ ensuring that certain teams (or groups) or specific players (or performers) participate, *and* ◆ hiring a suitable venue (eg: a stadium), *and* ◆ organising the sale and distribution of tickets, *and* ◆ providing staff to manage the event. ➤ Additional obligations may include requirements: ◆ to take out insurance cover against the risk of postponement or cancellation of the event, *and* ◆ to comply with any applicable laws and regulations (including any applicable governing-body requirements), *and* ◆ to obtain broadcast rights (if controlled by a third party), *and* ◆ to secure broadcast of the event via a third-party broadcaster. ➤ NB: certain obligations (eg: the participation of named persons or broadcast of the event) may be beyond the organiser's control, and this exposes the organiser to a risk of breach of contract. ◆ To get round this, the organiser might, where practical, agree to use 'best' or (as a lesser obligation) 'reasonable' endeavours to secure the agreement of the relevant third parties.

Clause	Terms
Force majeure	➤ The event may need to be postponed or cancelled due to reasons beyond the control of either party (known as circumstances of 'force majeure'). ◆ If such a circumstance occurs, either party should be entitled: • to suspend performance of the contract, *or* • if the circumstance continues for a specified period, to treat the contract as being terminated, in each case without liability to the other party. ▪ The triggering events depend on the form of sponsorship (eg: bad weather may be a triggering event in the case of a football match, but probably not for an open-air concert).
Brand protection	➤ Event sponsorship involves the sponsor's use of the organiser's (and/or a separate event owner's) name and/or logo. ◆ Event sponsorship may also involve the organiser's use of the sponsor's name and/or logo. • The sponsor's name and logo are likely to be protected by intellectual property rights: ▪ the name, as a registered trade mark and/or in passing-off, *and* ▪ the logo, *both* as a registered trade mark and/or in passing-off *and* under copyright. ◆ Brand protection is vital for the organiser, as: • the ability to raise money for an association with the brand depends entirely on the organiser's ability to control that association, *and* • this is ultimately achieved through the ownership and/or control and enforcement of intellectual property rights. ▪ A combined logo is likely to be controlled by one party, with each of the parties retaining ownership of the respective component parts. ◆ Consequently, the sponsorship agreement should cover: • which rights exist in a particular logo or name, *and* • which party owns the rights, *and* • which licences (in either party's favour) need to be included. ▪ If rights exist in a logo or name, the relevant owner will need to grant the appropriate licence to the user for the duration of the agreement. ▪ There may need to be reciprocal licences.
Miscellaneous	➤ The agreement should include the standard 'boilerplate' clauses that might be included in any other type of commercial contract (eg: provisions relating to confidentiality, termination, notices, assignability, governing law and jurisdiction).

IV Sponsorship of media productions

➤ The sponsor of a media production (eg: a TV or radio programme or a digital short) usually obtains credits that appear:

◆ within title/end sequences (known as 'integrated credits'), *and*

◆ going into and out of any commercial breaks (known as 'bumper credits').

➤ The contractual terms should cover the same areas as other sponsorship contracts.

◆ In a TV context, the parties to the agreement will usually be a large company and one of the commercial broadcasters (terrestrial or non-terrestrial).

➤ An additional and essential part of TV and radio sponsorship is the *Ofcom Broadcasting Code* (the '***Code***'), which regulates TV and radio programmes.

◆ References below are to sections and rules of the *Code*.

● The section on sponsorship does not apply to BBC services funded by the TV licence fee or 'grant-in-aid' (to which sponsorship is not relevant in practice).

■ 'Grant-in-aid' is the Parliamentary funding for the BBC World Service.

● NB: Ofcom publishes useful *Guidance Notes* on the Ofcom website.

➤ The key regulations are as follows:

Regulation of TV and radio sponsorship	
Legislative background	➤ Statute requires the prevention of 'unsuitable sponsorship', and news on TV/radio services must be (*Communications Act 2003, s 319(2)*): a) presented with due impartiality, *and* b) reported with due accuracy. ➤ The *Code* also mirrors several provisions of the *Audio-Visual Media Services Directive* (as amended – see *Directive 2007/65/EC*).
Principle	➤ Under the *Code*, the basic principle is also to prevent the 'unsuitable sponsorship' of programmes and to ensure 3 objectives in particular: a) transparency – ie: of sponsorship arrangements, *and* b) separation – ie: that sponsorship messages are kept separate from programmes and distinct from advertising, *and* c) editorial independence – ie: that the broadcaster maintains editorial control over sponsored content, and that programmes are not distorted for commercial purposes.
Scope of application	➤ The above principle applies in relation to: ◆ a *sponsor*, ie: a public or private undertaking (other than the broadcaster or programme producer), *that is sponsoring ...* ◆ a *sponsored programme*, ie: a TV or radio programme whose costs are met (in whole or part) by a sponsor with a view to promoting its own or another's name, trade mark, image, activities, services, products or any other direct or indirect interest, *on ...* ◆ a *sponsored channel*, ie: a TV or radio service whose production or broadcast costs are met (in whole or part) by a sponsor for such promotional purpose.

Regulation of TV and radio sponsorship (continued)

Content that may not be sponsored	➤ The following programmes may not be sponsored (*r 9.1*):
	
	◆ news bulletins and news desk presentations on radio, *and*
	
	◆ news and current affairs programmes on TV.
	
	    ● A 'current affairs programme' is defined as a programme containing explanation and analysis of current events and issues, including material dealing with political or industrial controversy or current public policy.
	
	        ■ NB: short specialist reports following a TV news programme (eg: sport, travel and weather reports) may be sponsored.

Prohibited and restricted sponsors	➤ No channel or programme may be sponsored by a sponsor that is not allowed to advertise on the relevant medium (*r 9.2*). ◆ Eg: current restricted/prohibited advertising on both TV and radio includes tobacco products, guns, pornography, bodies with political objectives, and prescription-only medicines. ➤ Sponsorship on radio and TV must comply with both the advertising content and scheduling rules that apply to that medium (*r 9.3*). ◆ Details of the prohibitions and restrictions can be found in the relevant advertising *Codes*. ● Eg: sponsorship by gambling companies must comply with the scheduling and content rules introduced to reflect the *Gambling Act 2005*.
Content of sponsored output	➤ A sponsor must not influence the content and/or scheduling of a channel or programme so as to impair the broadcaster's responsibility and editorial independence (*r 9.4*). ➤ There must be no promotional references (unless editorially justified and incidental) (*r 9.5*): ◆ to the sponsor, its name, trade mark, image, activities, services or products, or to any of its other direct or indirect interests, *or* ◆ that are generic references. ● 'Promotional references' include those that encourage the purchase or rental of a product or service.

Sponsorship credits	➤ **TV and radio**
	
	◆ Sponsorship must be clearly identified as such by reference to the sponsor's name and/or logo, and credits must be broadcast at the beginning and/or end of the programme (*r 9.6*).
	
	◆ The relationship between the sponsor and the channel or programme must be transparent (*r 9.7*).
	
	➤ **Radio**
	
	◆ During longer sponsored output, credits must be broadcast to create the degree of transparency required (*r 9.8*).
	
	◆ Credits must be:
	
	    ● short branding statements, but may contain legitimate advertising messages (*r 9.9*), *and*
	
	    ● cleared for broadcast in the same way as adverts (*r 9.10*).
	
	◆ Programme trails are also subject to the same sponsorship rules as programmes (*r 9.11*).

Regulation of TV and radio sponsorship (continued)

Sponsorship credits (continued)	➤ **TV**
	◆ Credits must be clearly separated from:
	a) programmes (by temporal or spatial means) (*r 9.12*), *and*
	b) advertising (eg: must not encourage the purchase or rental of products or services) (*r 9.13*).
	● The European Commission has stated that references to the sponsor's products or services are allowed if they are not given undue prominence.
	● It is also accepted by Ofcom that credits may include basic contact details (without inviting contact) and brief descriptions of the sponsor's business.
	■ The principal emphasis of the credit must be on the sponsorship arrangement.
	● Mandatory price information (eg: the cost of premium rate services) is acceptable if it is not part of an advertising message.
	◆ Where a programme trail contains a reference to the sponsor, the reference must remain brief and secondary (*r 9.14*).
Channel sponsorship	➤ Sponsorship of entire TV channels or radio stations as a whole is not prohibited by the *Code*.
	◆ In practice, however, the sponsorship of a whole channel (especially a news channel) may be unacceptable as a result of the programme-related restrictions under:
	● *r 9.1* (relating to news and current affairs), *and*
	● *r 9.3* (relating to content that cannot be sponsored due to medium-specific content and scheduling rules).
	◆ It may be acceptable to sponsor a channel that broadcasts some news or some other content that cannot be sponsored.
	● The channel must take great care to satisfy the basic requirements of transparency and separation
	■ Eg: channel sponsor credits should be placed in natural breaks in the schedule.

Index

Subject	Page	Subject	Page

Subject	Page

F

Subject	Page

Subject	Page

Subject	Page

Subject	Page